The Future of Indian Universities

'This book provides an extraordinarily important and timely discussion of the status and future direction of Indian universities. The challenges, ideas and priorities it addresses are critical for the future of Indian society as it strives to provide high quality university education for millions of its citizens and to deliver the social benefits and economic growth that can bring. They are also of global significance given the importance of developments in India, the world's largest democracy, during the twenty-first century. Professor Kumar and his colleagues consider the grand vision for higher education in India as well as addressing topics such as funding, regulation, curriculum design, inter-disciplinarity, science policy, knowledge creation, social responsibility, international comparisons, the role of the humanities and proposals for the way forward. This is required reading for anyone interested in global developments in higher education.'

Ian Jacobs
President and Vice-Chancellor,
University of New South Wales, Australia

'This book is a needed and valuable contribution in a public policy field of huge importance to India and its place in the world. Editor Professor C. Raj Kumar has assembled an impressive array of expert thinkers who identify with authority the contemporary, historical and future challenges and opportunities facing India's higher education sector. The book brings a laudable focus to the aspirations and expectations that motivate university leaders in India, including the priorities for stronger research performance and increasing international and interdisciplinary connections. *The Future of Indian Universities: Comparative and International Perspectives* should have a significant impact, helping build the national consensus in favour of a world class higher education sector.'

Glyn Davis
Vice-Chancellor,
University of Melbourne, Australia

'With sharp clarity of language, *The Future of Indian Universities* engages not only with the challenges confronting higher education in our country, but also the enormous promise and potential our institutions of learning hold, making this a must-read for scholars, policy makers, as well as all others who seek to help shape India's future by shaping well formed, intellectually enlightened minds.'

Shashi Tharoor
Member of Parliament &
Former Minister for Human Resource Development,
Government of India

'The first of its kind, this book not only provides a comprehensive assessment of higher education in India, but it represents a clarion call for investment in centres of academic excellence. The seeds of such efforts, the reader will learn, have already been planted in India, by none other than the book's editor, Professor C. Raj Kumar, at O.P. Jindal Global University. However, the central admonition of the book extends beyond one school or program. Rather, the book points forward by looking backward to India's history as a world leader in education and scholarship. By drawing attention to India's historic position atop the world's leading institutions of higher learning, it argues for the kinds of policies and investments necessary for it to return to that peak.'

Nathaniel Persily
James B. McClatchy Professor of Law,
Stanford University, USA

'How can India develop the world-class system of higher education necessary to support its people in achieving sustainable social justice and economic prosperity and the country in achieving its global aspirations as the world's largest democracy? This book, edited by Professor C. Raj Kumar, one of India's most passionate voices for higher education excellence, aims to answer that question through contributions from the best minds that explore the traditions on which Indian higher education can build and the barriers that it needs to overcome. The book is a foundational contribution to a growing national conversation about the necessity of reforming a critical part of national infrastructure.'

Lauren Kay Robel
Executive Vice President & Provost
and Val Nolan Professor of Law,
Indiana University, USA

'India is rapidly reemerging as one of the most important countries in the world. It needs world-class universities to ensure that it continues on this path. Vice-Chancellor C. Raj Kumar has assembled a world class collection of authors to address the critical issues administrators, faculty, and government policymakers need to address to ensure that India achieves this goal. It should be required reading for all those who care about India's future.'

David B. Wilkins
Professor & Vice Dean, Global Initiatives on the Legal Profession & Faculty Director, Center on the Legal Profession, Harvard Law School, Harvard University, USA

'This challenging book amounts to a wake-up call for Indian public officials and college-level educators. Professor C. Raj Kumar, the editor of this far-seeing volume and founder and Vice-Chancellor of the innovative Jindal Global University, knows whereof he writes about the current challenges of India's higher education system. The authoritative group of expert contributors lay out an urgent case for fundamental changes in the organization, curricula, funding streams, research programs, pedagogical techniques, diversification, internationalization, and assessment of the nation's post-secondary education systems. This detailed road map for reforms should inspire the future of Indian universities.'

Peter H. Schuck
Simeon E. Baldwin Professor of Law Emeritus,
Yale University, USA

The Future of Indian Universities

Comparative and International Perspectives

edited by

C. RAJ KUMAR

OXFORD
UNIVERSITY PRESS

OXFORD
UNIVERSITY PRESS

Oxford University Press is a department of the University of Oxford.
It furthers the University's objective of excellence in research, scholarship,
and education by publishing worldwide. Oxford is a registered trademark of
Oxford University Press in the UK and in certain other countries.

Published in India by
Oxford University Press
2/11 Ground Floor, Ansari Road, Daryaganj, New Delhi 110002, India

First Edition published in 2017

ISBN-13: 978-0-19-948065-4
ISBN-10: 0-19-948065-6

Typeset in Arno Pro 10.5/13
by Tranistics Data Technologies, Kolkata 700 091
Printed in India at Thomson Press (India) Ltd.

This book is dedicated to
Shri Pranab Mukherjee
Honourable President of India
*In profound appreciation of his outstanding contribution to the cause of
higher education and institution-building that has earned him
the recognition of being 'The Education President'*

Contents

Tables and Figures

TABLES

FIGURES

Foreword

As this year marks India's 70 years of Independence, it gives us cause to reflect on the state of the country's higher education institutions (HEIs) and the extent to which they have been able to complement the aspirations of its people. By the end of this decade, over half of the estimated population is expected to be under the age of 25. In a more optimal state of development, this 'demographic dividend' would be considered as one of the biggest opportunities for India at a time when youth populations are expected to decline in many other parts of the world, particularly in developed economies.

A young, aspiring population in a growing economy enables greater investments in areas including education, healthcare, technology, and innovation, aiding in the reversal of declining indicators such as poverty and unemployment. Sustainable education provisions, particularly in tertiary education, play a vital role here. The achievement of educational milestones will have dramatic implications for achieving sustainable development not only by spurring improvements in the socio-economic, political, technological, and environmental spheres, but also strengthening the country's democratic attributes and well-being of the society.

India's higher education system will be indispensable for creating a positive growth story for the country over the next decade. However, the higher education system in India is more complex than anywhere else in the world. At the time of Independence of India, there were only 20 universities, 500 colleges and about two hundred thousand students. This situation needed to change and now with about 760 universities and 38,000 colleges with an enrolment of over 3.4 crores students in higher education, the expansion of higher education has been truly spectacular. However, it is now a matter of concern, and continuous debate, as to whether this expansion has come at a cost of inevitable compromise with the quality of higher education.

Although the need for consistent and rapid improvement of quality in higher education was recognized as far back as the post-Independence decade when reforms in the sector were first discussed and initiated, India remains in need of crucial transformations in many aspects of its higher education system. Since the beginning of the last decade, with increasing demand for higher education, universities around the world, but more so in developing countries like India, have come under immense pressure for change. Globalization and rapid advances in information and communication technologies are driving this change. Institutions of higher education are expected to carry out research, provide skilled manpower for the industry and also contribute to social and cultural well-being of the society. Universities on their part have shown remarkable flexibility in trying to adjust to the new demands, but have to continuously deal with challenges such as broad liberal education versus highly specific skills-oriented education, a balance between research and teaching, enhanced global competition for students and faculty, internationalization of education, etc. How can a developing economy like India with its innumerable complexities across political, economic, and societal spaces contend with global forces of changes, while addressing issues that are central to India's development— access, equity, good governance and accountability? This question takes on added significance given the highly complex, heterogeneous nature of India's higher education system.

The relatively recent phenomenon of international university rankings by several agencies outside the university system has brought in yet another level of pressure on HEIs. Top global universities compete annually to be ranked in these league tables on the basis of performance criteria that include teaching, research, citations, international outlook, and industry income. These rankings are increasingly seen as a predominant measure of quality of HEIs. Indian institutions have fared poorly in these rankings. The best of our institutions, such as the Indian Institute of Science, Bangalore, have only been featured in peripheral rankings exercises such as the Times Higher Education BRICS and Emerging Economies rankings. Other pressing measures of performance and quality include governance, innovative practices in pedagogy, educational administration, and public accountability. While these global movements certainly call for a sense of urgency to continue to re-evaluate the state of our HEIs, the disdain that is often expressed by academics, administrators and other higher education stakeholders towards the performance of and challenges facing our higher learning institutions may call for some restraint and introspection.

The unique complexities, peculiarities, and characteristics of India's higher education ecosystem may be unparalleled. The policy and regulatory bodies of higher education in India have been mindful of this and the need for constant action and reform. The National Institutional Ranking Framework (NIRF) designed by the Ministry of Human Resource Development is one example. The University Grants Commission and the National Assessment and Accreditation Council are also currently exploring and consulting HEIs on reforms to existing mechanisms of regulation, compliance, and assessment.

The call for a prospective approach and spurred action is reflective in the publication of the book *The Future of Indian Universities: Comparative and International Perspectives*. India's best educational institutions were built through formal and informal collaborations and partnerships with leading global institutions, and it is imperative that we continue to reflect and share experiences across countries and systems. The study of international practices and systems of higher education can act as a valuable guide to expectations, trends, challenges, and needs in other societies and economies. This book published by Oxford University Press will also provide invaluable insights into reimagining the role of humanities and liberal arts in higher education—disciplines that India is yet to advance within its universities. Interdisciplinarity is another aspect of higher education curricula that India needs to develop; the book provides many insights into comparative perspectives in relation to institution building.

I would like to congratulate the editor, Professor (Dr.) C. Raj Kumar, the Founding Vice-Chancellor of O.P. Jindal Global University for his leadership and initiative, and all the authors of this book for the outstanding contributions they have made through their essays. The diversity of authors and perspectives is in itself a contribution to academic study and research on higher education in India.

The book is being published at a critical time when restrained introspection, sincere debate, and serious reflection will prove key to pushing beyond the immediate need to conform to current conventions and trends.

16 May 2017
Virander S. Chauhan
Acting Chairman
University Grants Commission, Government of India

Preface

Higher education systems across the world are in transition. The intensification of globalization, technological changes, shifts in demographic profiles, and concomitant changes in social attitudes have made it imperative that we rethink the role of universities and higher education to align them with the trends of our time. Rethinking the role of higher education and more specifically the role of universities requires us to ask a series of questions. Most important among them is the question of access, particularly in the contexts of developing societies. That we put in place resources and capacities that allow our growing young women and men opportunities is crucial but not sufficient. Higher education, if it has to serve social and economic purposes, should focus on developing institutional processes, pedagogical resources, and social bases that make educational processes meaningful, enriching, and economically viable for students. This would mean focusing as much on the quality of our institutional processes, quality of student experiences, and the social impact of our outcomes. This demands holistic, inclusive, and value-based approaches that prepare our young people to face the demanding challenges of a global world. These goals have to be attained by institutions of higher education in complex social, political, economic, regulatory, and institutional contexts particularly in developing societies.

Addressing the complex challenges of higher educational processes requires that we understand the underlying causes, anticipate long term trends, and collaborate with a range of national and international stakeholders. It also commends to us to appreciate the complex interplay of governance, resources, and knowledge systems. All of these at times may look simple but in practice are extremely complicated. My own experience of being the founding Vice-Chancellor of a private university in India has apprised me to both the enormity of the challenges and equally, the possibilities of the future.

One such future possibility is the opportunity to build institutional capacities to provide high quality education to our students. The word 'quality' means many things. But in the context of higher educational outcomes, it means paying attention to the student experience and graduate outcomes that are sensitive to the aspirations of our students, expectations of our societies, and the economic needs of our times. Ensuring that our students attain the economic and social goals they aspire to is neither easy nor impossible. This requires that we pay increasing attention to processes and build institutional mechanisms and organizational cultures that reflect our visions and expectations. Continuous and mindful attention to the needs of our student community; building institutional competencies and a robust human resource base; and pedagogical practices that are attuned to the contemporary and emerging social, economic, political, and technological trends of our time is imperative.

The need to design pedagogies that are relevant, develop classroom practices, and integration of technologies in delivery is increasingly gaining attention. As some of the authors point out in this book, there is a growing concern that our pedagogical practices have not evolved to match developments in educational theory and advances in other social and human sciences. It is also widely recognized that the complexities of our world place huge demands on our young people to acquire practical, conceptual, and cultural skills. While we may be doing reasonably well in delivering styled traditional educational contents, the dominant pedagogical practices are increasingly seen as inadequate for practical coping in everyday life and in professional practice. They are also seen as falling short in terms of developing good global citizenship, social responsibility, creativity, and ethical conduct. Our collective future will depend on our ability to cultivate attitudes of respect, empathy, responsibility, and service. Our pedagogical designs should reflect, embody, and express these objectives.

The other challenge we face in our times is the challenge of increasing global interconnectedness in the absence of educational opportunities to match it. While global economic and technological interactions are intensifying, this is not adequately reflected in the demographic and cultural profiles of educational institutions across the world. While more and more young people are gaining opportunities to work together in multinational spaces, the opportunities to immerse in cross-cultural educational spaces appears to be minimal. This is particularly acute in developing societies given the shortage of resources, historical experience, fragile policy, and institutional capacities. There is a need to diversify our student and faculty demographics to adequately reflect the demands of both the marketplace and socio-cultural trends in most societies.

The challenge of interdisciplinarity is a concern that has received inadequate public policy attention. In a world of complexity, the practical problems relating to social, political, legal, scientific, cultural, and security issues cannot be addressed from any one disciplinary base. The issues facing human societies and professional practices arise out of complex interactions between the above forces, demanding that we face them from multiple perspectives and using plural methodologies. Universities seeking to serve their respective societies will have to emerge as spaces that promote useful research that generate new forms of knowledge, innovative ideas, and socially relevant technological developments. This is only possible if we fully recognize the immense interdisciplinary potentialities inherent in the advances in natural and social sciences. Institutional practices should develop adequate sophistication, capacities, and focus to facilitate often difficult but necessary dialogues among faculties, societal stakeholders, and students. My own experience suggests that promoting high quality interdisciplinary research is not easy but I am increasingly convinced about the need to continually invest, enable, and realize its potentialities. Like many of the authors in this book, I believe it to be necessary, urgent, and doable, if we focus our attention and persist with our vision to serve the larger good.

In the emerging world, student, teacher, and societal creativity will be enhanced by increasing the diversity profile of our universities. Bringing together students and faculties drawn from a range of disciplines, educational backgrounds, demographic profiles, and political and ideological orientations is a basic building block for developing educated minds and innovative ideas for the future. Cross-cultural educational experiences have become necessary for preparing our young generation for future work and life. Educational institutions have an opportunity to emerge as microcosms of the real worlds that our graduates will inhabit. To the extent that the lived experience in the University represents that reality, our students will be adequately prepared for the complex nature of cultural and creative life that we expect them to participate in following their university education. The opportunities for diversification of our educational processes are huge. The interest in participating in educational processes outside of home universities is growing and we are in the midst of dramatic changes in our educational landscapes. This trend will only intensify in the coming years. Our success as educational leaders will be measured to the extent that we realize the inherent potentialities for making our institutions places where culture, experiences, and ideas come together to create novel ideas and innovations.

The chapters in this volume in one way or the other interrogate, surface, and debate these key concerns and more. Written by some of the best minds in the field of educational practice and theory, they represent the diversity of visions, strategies, and complex images that provide us well-rounded perspectives on the key challenges we face today in global educational spaces. The transformation of our educational systems will require us to be prepared for the challenges of the future.

This volume is an effort to critically examine the future of Indian universities in comparative and international perspectives, and the contributors have brought together academic writings, scholarship, and institutional experiences. I hope that readers will find in it ideas, tools, and practical suggestions for forwarding a progressive educational agenda.

Acknowledgements

This volume was inspired by an international conference on 'The Future of Indian Universities: Comparative Perspectives on Higher Education Reforms for a Knowledge Society' that was held on the campus of the O.P. Jindal Global University (JGU) in 2013. The conference was inaugurated by the Honourable President of India, Shri Pranab Mukherjee, to whom we owe gratitude for supporting JGU's efforts to build a world-class university in India. His vision and farsightedness in relation to institution building and excellence in Indian higher education, while promoting a progressive agenda for nation building has been a source of encouragement and inspiration for JGU. I would like to express my deepest appreciation to President Mukherjee for this.

I would like to appreciate the encouragement and support that we have received from the Office of the President over the years. Senior members of the President's Secretariat led by Ms. Omita Paul, Secretary to the President of India, Mr. Abhijeet Rai, Private Secretary to the President, and Mr. Shakil Alam, OSD to the President were exemplary in their help and assistance in engaging with me and our university over the years on many initiatives relating to higher education.

My profound thanks and appreciation are due to JGU's Founding Chancellor, Mr. Naveen Jindal. Chancellor Jindal's vision and his generous philanthropic initiative led to the creation of JGU in which he has ensured academic freedom, functional autonomy, and operational independence, which are the most fundamental values in any higher education institution.

I would like to thank the publishers of the book, Oxford University Press, and in particular their outstanding editors for their passionate commitment and dedication to this project and their institutional support for this publication. This volume would not have been possible without the efforts of the 18 exceptional contributors who believed in this project. I am grateful to each of them for participating and contributing to this volume.

I would like to thank the faculty members and other colleagues at JGU who have supported the work of the International Institute for Higher Education Research & Capacity Building (IIHEd) and this book project. I would like to thank Ms. Princy George, Assistant Director, Strategy and Institutional Research, and Fellow, IIHEd, for her help and support to this book project.

I would like to express my heartfelt gratitude to my parents, Professor K. Chockalingam and Dr. Vijayalakshmi Chockalingam, for helping me to believe in the cause of higher education and empowering me by supporting my higher education aspirations.

This book is seeing the light of the day because of my wife, Mrs. Pratibha Jain, Partner & Head of the New Delhi office of Nishith Desai Associates, who motivated me all along and encouraged and supported me in every respect to complete this work. I am grateful to her for inspiring me to do this as she took upon herself the responsibility of taking care of our home, while herself pursuing a responsible legal career.

Introduction

C. Raj Kumar

The Indian higher education system commanded awe and respect in the ancient world. Important seats of learning like Nalanda and Takshashila attracted the best students and academics from across the globe. Unfortunately, over a period of time, our higher education system lost its global competitiveness. This is exemplified by the fact that not many Indian higher education institutions feature in the annual world university rankings like the Times Higher Education World University Rankings or the QS World University Rankings. Several factors can be identified for India's weak performance in these rankings.

The first reason is the lack of incentives for research that is hampering progress. The amount of funding that is currently available for research in Indian universities is meagre by global standards. Apart from increasing the quantum of funds—and promoting specific research on the state of the Indian higher education system itself—there is a need for significant reform in the overall policy and management framework of disbursing research grants. For example, the existing framework to disburse grants is multilayered and complex, leading to inordinate delays, frustration, and loss of research focus among faculty members who are trying to secure these grants. A proactive regulatory mechanism set up by ministries like the Ministry of Human Resource Development (MHRD) of the Government of India can help mitigate these concerns.

Further, there is a need to attract and retain faculty with good research skills. This will require a review of the current system of faculty recruitment, appraisal, assessment, promotions, and rewards based on performance as measured through research contributions and publications.

Second, we do not have world class training programmes for academic administrators. High quality education administration is one of the seriously ignored aspects of the Indian higher education system. As providers of relevant educational support services, academic administrators form the backbone of any educational institution, especially one that aspires to constantly improve the academic experience of its students and teachers. Indeed, a world-class university requires world-class faculty supported by a world-class administration. Unfortunately, there are no comprehensive training programmes for academic administrators in India who deal with different nuances of our higher education system.

Specifically, the lack of managerial training programmes for higher authorities in education administration has compromised the evolution of generic best practices in the sector. Institution-building has suffered and creativity has been stifled as the Indian higher education system continues to be driven by individual persona and the charm of education administrators instead of adherence to sustainable and institution-driven quality assurance mechanisms and innovative processes.

Third, we need a more outward-looking approach. One of the strongest critiques of Indian higher education institutions is that they tend to get complacent with little success. Unique socio-political contexts cannot be used to justify the lack of sustained global competitiveness. There is a need for a renaissance in our attitude toward higher education. There is also a need to understand and contextualize global best practices for Indian conditions, for instance, in course design and pedagogy.

Indeed, international collaborations in the form of student exchanges, faculty exchanges, joint teaching, joint research, joint conferences, joint publications, joint executive education programmes, summer and winter schools, and study-abroad programmes are ways to promote the global engagement of Indian higher education institutions.

India's aspirations to establish world-class universities have never been greater. It has been time and again lamented that not a single Indian university has been among the top 200 in the world. However, the recently acquired distinction of two of India's reputed higher education institutions (Indian Institute of Science, Bangalore, and IIT, Delhi) being ranked among the top 200 in the world in one of the international rankings has given new hope and expectations for the Indian higher education system. The extraordinary contribution of the President of India, while serving as the Visitor to 114 higher education institutions, in exhorting the need for taking international rankings seriously with a view to promoting institutional excellence, acted as a catalyst. This has recently prompted Mr. Phil Baty, editor of the *Times Higher Education World University Rankings* to observe in relation to India:

'... *that a country with such a rich intellectual history and with such huge economic potential not only deserved but desperately needed universities that could compete at the highest level on the world stage ... it seems that we could be entering a new era, with India's leading universities and institutions playing a much greater role in shaping the future of global higher education.*'

A NEW IMAGINATION FOR INDIAN UNIVERSITIES

The release of the Times Higher Education BRICS & Emerging Economies Rankings 2016 demonstrated the need for stronger and sharper attention to issues of quality and excellence. The 2016 Rankings gave new insights into the performance and contribution of universities among the BRICS and emerging economies.

The results of the rankings showed that out of the top ten universities there were five universities from China, an improvement since the previous year when there were three universities; one from Taiwan; one from Russia; and two from South Africa. There was not a single Indian university in the top 10 universities among the BRICS and emerging economies with the Indian Institute of Science, Bangalore ranked as 16, an improvement from the previous year when it was ranked 25 in the list. The 2016 rankings once again demonstrated the extraordinary progress achieved by Chinese universities. The 2015 ranking of leading research universities in emerging economies had 27 Chinese universities in the top 100 and China maintained this in 2016 as well. The leading universities of China—Peking University and

Tsinghua University—took the first and second place with China having 5 of the top 10 positions and 13 of the top 50 positions.

While India had 9 universities in the top 100 in 2016, it declined from 11 universities in the top 100 in the previous year. This does not mean that these universities particularly performed poorly that year. It essentially means that universities from other countries performed much better. Indian universities need a transformational change for them to become relevant in the context of global rankings of universities. The last two decades have witnessed extraordinary changes in university systems around the world. India needs to take into account these developments and how they are affecting and impacting the nature of higher education around the world. The higher education system in India, including university governance systems, needs to consider the following reforms and policy initiatives:

1. Differentiated System of Recognizing Universities

There is an urgent need to recognize that not all universities in India need to be engaged in the same manner on different aspects of institution building. They need to be treated differently depending upon the kind of contribution they are making. Indian universities should not be differentiated because of them being public or private, but the differentiation should be based upon quality, performance and contribution with more resources made available for universities that are performing exceedingly well. It also needs to be recognized that not all universities in India need to be research focused universities, but they need to excel in other areas and should be measured for their quality and excellence on those focal areas of university development.

2. Significant Financial Support to Selected 50 Universities

Taking inspiration from the Project 5-100 initiative of the Russian Federation, India may consider nurturing 50 of its top universities with a view to empowering them in every possible manner to seek global excellence. There should be a clear mandate with funding and resources given to them to augment their capacities and position themselves for being better prepared for participating in the global rankings. While choosing the 50 universities, the policymakers should take into account institutional diversity and their potential for achieving global excellence as the main criterion for their selection. I would propose that these universities should be: central universities = 10; state universities = 10; private universities = 10; deemed universities = 10; and institutions of national importance = 10. This diversity in the selection process of the 50 higher education institutions will enable India to build strong capacity for establishing a few model institutions of excellence that can compete globally.

3. Overhaul of the Regulatory Framework

The issue of regulatory reform has been at the heart of policy reforms in higher education in India. There is an urgent need to seek complete overhaul of the regulatory framework for promoting fundamental reforms in higher education and university governance. Universities in India need to be made more autonomous in every sense of the word. Autonomy and independence of the universities from the government and the regulatory bodies will be the most important reform that is needed for seeking excellence. The agenda of the universities needs to be established by the faculty and students keeping in mind the needs and aspirations of all the stakeholders of the society.

4. Funding for Research and Incentives for Publications

There is no doubt that world-class universities are built and nurtured through a strong focus on research. There is a need to substantially increase the funding that is currently available for research in Indian universities. This aspect of policy seeks significant reform, both in terms of increasing the quantum of funding for research, but also the policy and management framework of disbursing research grants. There is also a need to significantly incentivize research and publications among faculty members. The current system of faculty recruitment, appraisal, assessment, promotion, and rewards is not necessarily based upon the performance as measured through research contributions and publications. If Indian universities need to become competitive and to be able to promote global excellence and seek its presence in the global rankings, they need to focus on research and create an environment that fosters a culture of research.

5. Internationalization of Faculty Members and Students

It is important that we need to focus on internationalization of faculty members and students within Indian universities. This is one of the major challenges facing Indian universities. The majority of Indian universities have faculty members who are only Indian nationals, unlike most parts of the developed world and increasingly, the countries in the emerging economies, which are hiring faculty members from around the world.

Indian universities have to create an enabling environment that will create favourable conditions for the recruitment of faculty and students from around the world. In a world that is globalized, knowledge creation and sharing of knowledge cannot be limited by nationality and place of origin. World-class universities have always attracted faculty and students from around the world. Indian universities need to learn from the experiences of other countries in the BRICS and emerging economies.

There has to be a new imagination of Indian universities. It has to draw its inspiration from the past, but will also have to look to the future. Transformational change needs to take place at every level of policymaking, regulation and governance in higher education, if Indian universities are serious about seeking global excellence and through that achieve higher rankings.

This book is a culmination of a range of ideas and perspectives that will shape India's aspirations of building world-class universities through comparative and international dimensions. It is a recognition that the future of Indian universities and their ability to seek global excellence will depend on three critical paradigms: first, the need for creating a vision for higher education that will focus on research and knowledge creation, institutional excellence and global benchmarking as the indicators for standard-setting; second, the need for pursuing substantial reforms relating to policy, regulation and governance of higher education; and third, the need for investigating a paradigmatic shift for promoting interdisciplinarity in higher education with a stronger and deeper focus on the pedagogy of teaching and learning in different fields of inquiry. These three strings of thought processes form the three sections of the book.

The book is divided into three sections. **Section I**: 'Indian Universities: Imaginations, Aspirations, and Expectations' has six chapters discussing different and interconnected themes: **Chapter 1**, 'The Future of Higher Education in India' by C. Raj Kumar, discusses the global rankings and current status of Indian universities. It points out the challenges faced by Indian higher education and lays out a vision to build world-class universities in India. **Chapter 2**, 'An Invitation to a Thought Experiment: Quality, Diversity, and the Epistemics of University' by Shiv Visvanathan, looks at the question of quality within a wider vision of diversity and democracy. It is an effort to show how epistemological approaches to knowledge and democracy help to determine the quality of knowledge, life, and well-being in a society. **Chapter 3**, 'The Future of Indian Universities: Voices from within Beckoning for the Future' by Indira J. Parikh, brings out the debate on the nature of education and provides an educational perspective of the future. The chapter prescribes that higher education institutions and universities need to accept students as a total human being and acknowledge her physical, social, spiritual, emotional and psychological self, and her multiple roles in numerous systems. **Chapter 4**, 'The Indian University in a Comparative Perspective' by N.R. Madhava Menon, explores universities as organizations in distress and proposes policy changes and highlights initiatives that are underway. Further, this chapter asks why India cannot follow foreign models in higher education. It argues that it is neither possible nor practical to abandon or subordinate the demands of access and equity for the sake of quality. **Chapter 5**, 'Strategic Management of Expansion of Higher Education in India: Key Policy Interventions for Change' by Pawan Agarwal, introduces system approaches in higher education by focusing on various subsystems, their dimensions and linkages. This chapter outlines widespread systemic changes needed to affect a paradigm shift in the cultural, policy, strategic, and operational environment of higher education in the country. **Chapter 6**, 'Building New Institutions of Excellence in India: Three Case Studies of Innovation' by Pramath Raj Sinha, discusses the experiences of building three different institutions and programmes—the Indian School of Business (ISB), Ashoka University, and the Young India Fellowship (part of Ashoka University) in India. The chapter points out that the educational institutions should address some unmet demand to stand out and requires context-specific educational reforms and innovation in governance and leadership.

Section II: 'Indian Higher Education in a Comparative Perspective: Policy, Regulation, and Management'. It has seven chapters that discuss different aspects of governance of higher education institutions: **Chapter 7**, 'Future of Indian Universities: Need for a Liberalized Legal Regime' by A. Francis Julian, analyses the legal regime governing the establishment of different types of universities such as central universities, state universities, deemed to be universities, state public universities, and state private universities. The chapter points out that the current legal regime applicable to universities in India is highly restrictive and Indian universities require a liberalized legal regime if the universities have to compete globally and achieve higher world ranking. **Chapter 8**, 'Global Competitiveness, Privatization, Dignified Spaces, and Curricular Reform in Indian Higher Education' by Kanti Bajpai, essays some answers to why, given that at the time of Indian independence, it could fairly be said that at least a dozen Indian universities were leaders in Asia and were of international repute, today Indian universities are in an egregious condition. The chapter points out that Indian higher education should move from 'alienation to engagement with the world', from public to more private universities, from 'spatial indifference to spatial sensitivity' and requires curriculum reform. **Chapter 9**, 'Challenges of Knowledge Creation for Indian Universities' by Stephen P. Marks, reflects on the basic purpose of knowledge creation in the university and then examines responsibilities of the university for promoting knowledge creation in a range of fields of investigation and levels of learning, as well as the ethical standards that apply. **Chapter 10**, 'Science-Policy Interfaces in an Era of Global Commodification' by Barbara Harriss-White, explores the proposition that the opposition between the expert knowledge of the academy and the practical knowledge of the policymaker is being realigned, in part by being de-politicized but in part by being commodified. **Chapter 11**, 'Creating Educational Excellence: The Role of Culture at the Indian Institute of Management, Ahmedabad' by Shailendra Raj Mehta, looks at the process of creation of culture at the Indian Institute of Management, Ahmedabad, India's leading business school, and one of the highest ranked business schools in the Asia-Pacific region and in the world. **Chapter 12**, 'Challenges of Creating a World-Class Global Private University in India: Perspective of an Administrator' by Y.S.R. Murthy, lay out the vision and mission of O.P. Jindal Global University and the impediments of creating a world-class global university in India. **Chapter 13**, 'Deconstructing the Discourse on University Social Responsibility' by Anamika Srivastava, argues that the raison d'être of a university is to be linked to the society and thereby it would be meaningful for the Indian universities of the future to embed social goals in its core activities of teaching and research rather than relying on a few of its departments to reach out to the community.

Section III: 'Pedagogy of Interdisciplinarity: Law, Humanities, and Global Studies in India'. It has six chapters that analyse specific disciplinary aspects of higher education within the framework of interdisciplinary pedagogy. **Chapter 14**, 'The Phoenix of Interdisciplinarity in Higher Education' by Yugank Goyal, aims to reclaim the position of interdisciplinarity in the context of higher education, with particular reference to India. This essay discusses how the disciplines emerged and what kinds of forces fossilized the hierarchical structures of pedagogical classifications. **Chapter 15**, 'The Role of Humanities in a University Education' by Alice Prochaska, reflects on some of the ways in which an education in the humanities can provide a framework for both understanding and action. The chapter shows that the humanities also provide a profound foundation for the sense of personal and national identity which in turn supports the international sensibilities that are vital to a true commonwealth of learning. **Chapter 16**, 'The Liberal Arts in the American Context: What India Can Learn from Western Liberal Education' by Carol M. Bresnahan, points out that there is a need to meld India's needs with a liberal arts education as practiced in Western colleges and universities, particularly in American ones, and tying this melding to the conviction that a liberal education is invaluable. **Chapter 17**, 'Public Policy as a Practice: Reflections Inspired by Alasdair MacIntyre's *After Virtue*' by R. Sudarshan, attempts to relate the pedagogy of public policy to the concept of practice articulated by Alasdair MacIntyre. The chapter discusses the challenges of establishing public policy as a discipline in India, examines the role of virtues, and limitations of economics, a dominant discipline in public policy schools and brings out the importance of public policy practitioners and teachers connecting with the public. **Chapter 18**, 'Global Studies in Indian Universities: Past Imperfect, Future Circumspect' by Sreeram Chaulia, gives answers to how Indian universities can make versatile international affairs professionals, who can be useful to government as well as in the international non-profit and for-profit sectors. **Chapter 19**, 'Clinical Legal Education and Democracy in India' by Sital Kalantry, through the experience of the author who co-taught a clinical programme at the Jindal Global Law School at O.P. Jindal Global University, India, brings out the connection between democracy in India and clinical legal education.

THE WAY FORWARD

As we move forward, we need to build collective consciousness and intellectual consensus on the need for building world-class universities. We should not shy away from pursuing excellence and also to draw upon inspiration from institutions of global excellence around the world. But we need to be grounded in our own vision and imagination of institutional excellence for us to develop world-class universities in India.

The Prime Minister of India and the Human Resource Development Minister are well suited to convene a brainstorming session for promoting the idea of special education zones (SEZs) in higher education with all stakeholders including educationists, parliamentarians, policymakers, philanthropists, institutions, and corporations. This could be the basis for creating the Prime Minister's task force on building world-class universities in India. This task force will be mandated to recommend all steps that involve the development of a vision, strategic plan, legal and regulatory processes, institutional mechanisms, policies, and guidelines that will enable the creation of SEZs in higher education. The time has come for us to recognize that we owe to the posterity for creating higher education opportunities that will enable the future generations of students to pursue world-class education in world-class universities in India.

Indian Universities

Imaginations, Aspirations, and Expectations

1 The Future of Higher Education in India

C. Raj Kumar

The higher education system in India is undoubtedly going through an important transition. There are huge challenges relating to the university system, which has unfortunately not been able to promote excellence in higher education. This has led to steady deterioration of academic standards and research prowess in many higher education institutions. While much of this problem is related to lack of vision, inadequate number of qualified faculty members available to teach and pursue research, poor governance models, and archaic regulatory structures, there is a lack of global consciousness among various stakeholders in higher education, which is worthy of serious examination. Undoubtedly, Indian higher education still suffers from the issues of access and equity. However, with the rise of global knowledge society, the establishment of educational institutions of global excellence has also become a priority for developing countries like India.

GLOBAL RANKINGS AND INDIAN UNIVERSITIES

While quality in higher education cannot be contained in a definition, global rankings of universities have emerged as a dominant way of measuring their performance. There is today a serious debate on the need for Indian universities to be in the top 200 universities of the world and the urgency of seeking reforms that will pave way for promoting excellence in higher education and research. It is important that Indian universities embrace the international rankings framework as well as international accreditation processes which will benchmark Indian universities with the world-class universities in many countries. Today, the Times Higher Education World Universities Rankings, QS World University Rankings, and the Shanghai Jiatong Rankings have become part of the institutional aspirations for many universities and higher education institutions in India.

The Times Higher Education BRICS and Emerging Economies Rankings 2016, which gives new insights into the performance and contribution of universities in BRICS and emerging economies, demonstrates a stronger and sharper attention to issues of quality and excellence to be paid by India.[1] The results of the rankings have shown that out of the top 10 universities, there are five universities from China, an improvement since last year when there were three universities, one each from Taiwan and Russia, and two from South Africa. There is not a single Indian university in the top 10 among the BRICS and emerging economies with the Indian Institute of Science, Bangalore ranked 16, an improvement from the previous year when it was ranked 25 in the list.

The 2016 rankings have once again demonstrated the extraordinary progress achieved by Chinese universities. The previous year's ranking of leading research universities in emerging economies had 27 Chinese universities in the top 100 and China has continued to maintain it. The leading universities of China—Peking University and Tsinghua University—have the first and second place, with China having five of the top 10 positions and 13 of the top 50 positions.

---

[1] *Times Higher Education* BRICS & Emerging Economies Rankings 2016, available at https://www.timeshighereducation.com/world-university-rankings/2016/brics-and-emerging-economies-0#!/page/0/length/25/sort_by/rank/sort_order/asc/cols/stats, accessed on 28 May 2015.

Table 1.1 exhibits India's disappointing story in the world university rankings. It shows three different types of ranking methodologies adopted by three institutions, which rate universities around the world, on an internationally benchmarked scale to quantitatively assess the quality of higher education in all major universities of the world. We picked up the top 200 universities of the world as ranked by the three methodologies, and estimated the total number of Asian universities in that list, as of October 2015. Amongst the countries, which are exhibited in that list, we have China, Japan, South Korea, Malaysia, Taiwan, and even tiny city-states like Hong Kong and Singapore. We do not, however, find a single Indian university in that list until 2015. It is only in 2015–16, when QS World University Rankings published its rankings, it had 2 Indian universities in the top 200 of the world.

While the poor performance of Indian universities in the global rankings is a matter of grave concern, it is worth noting the criterion based upon which these ranking agencies rank universities.

The Times Higher Education World University Rankings has underscored the importance of research and publications for rankings.[2] The rankings assess the universities on the basis of the following criteria: teaching (30 per cent); research (30 per cent); citations (30 per cent); international outlook (7.5 per cent); and industry income (2.5 per cent).[3] The QS World University Rankings methodology has further reinforced the importance of research and publications for universities to be globally recognized as institutions of excellence.[4] The weightage for the six indicators used for these rankings are as follows: academic reputation: 40 per cent; citation per faculty: 20 per cent; faculty–student ratio: 20 per cent; employer reputation: 10 per cent; international faculty ratio: 5 per cent; and international student ratio: 5 per cent.[5]

---

[2] *Times Higher Education World University Rankings 2014–2015 Methodology*, available at https://www.timeshighereducation.co.uk/world-university-rankings/2014-15/world-ranking/methodology, accessed on 28 May 2015.

[3] Same as above.

[4] *QS World University Rankings: Methodology*, available at http://www.topuniversities.com/university-rankings-articles/world-university-rankings/qs-world-university-rankings-methodology, accessed on 28 May, 2015.

[5] *QS World University Rankings: Methodology*, available at http://www.topuniversities.com/university-rankings-articles/world-university-rankings/qs-world-university-rankings-methodology, accessed on 28 May 2015.

Table 1.1 BRICS Universities in World University Rankings (Top 200) since 2011 to 2015

Year	QS World University Rankings					Times Higher Education World University Rankings					Shanghai Jiao Tong University's the Academic Ranking of World Universities (ARWU)				
	2015–16	2014–15	2013–14	2012–13	2011–12	2015–16	2014–15	2013–14	2012–13	2011–12	2015	2014	2013	2012	2011
Brazil	2	1	1	1	1	0	1	1	1	1	1	1	1	1	1
Russia	1	1	1	1	1	1	0	0	0	0	1	1	1	1	1
India	2	0	0	0	0	0	0	0	0	0	0	0	0	0	0
China	7	7	7	7	7	2	2	2	3	3	7	6	5	4	1
South Africa	1	1	1	1	1	1	1	1	1	1	0	0	0	0	0
Hong Kong	5	5	5	5	5	3	4	3	4	4	1	2	1	4	1
Japan	8	10	9	9	11	2	5	5	5	5	7	8	9	9	9
Singapore	2	2	2	2	2	2	2	2	2	2	2	2	1	1	1
Malaysia	1	1	1	1	1	0	0	0	0	0	0	0	0	0	0

Source: Compiled with data obtained from QS World University Rankings, https://www.topuniversities.com/qs-world-university-rankings, accessed on 18 May 2017; Times Higher Education World University Rankings, https://www.timeshighereducation.com/world-university-rankings/2017/world-ranking#!/page/0/length/25/sort_by/rank/sort_order/asc/cols/stats, accessed on 18 May 2017; and ShanghaiRanking's Academic Ranking of World Universities, http://www.shanghairanking.com/, accessed on 18 May 2017.

Academic reputation, the most significant indicator, is based on the views and perspectives of fellow academics around the world, which are producing the best research in their field of expertise.[6] This essentially means that 60 per cent of the weightage for these rankings are based on research contribution of universities.

The issue of deterioration in the academic standards in most Indian universities is indeed a matter of concern.[7] These rankings have demonstrated the fact that our higher education system needs to be overhauled for India to compete in the world of university education where academic innovation, intellectual freedom, and research excellence are constantly promoted. The challenges related to higher education in India deserve urgent attention and require determined responses.

CHALLENGES FACED BY INDIAN HIGHER EDUCATION

The state of our universities requires careful examination and critical reflection, as there has been a steady deterioration in the ability of our universities to serve as centres of knowledge. There are five major challenges that Indian universities must overcome to become truly global universities. These challenges are:

Cramped Institutional Vision

Indian universities have not yet fully absorbed the contemporary global realities of knowledge creation and their relevance for social transformation. With over 50 per cent of its population being below the age of 25, it is critical for the country to acquire a vision that is transformative for its youth. To face the global challenges of knowledge creation, problem solving and employment generation, India's youth need not just education, they also need empowerment. It is time that the Indian universities placed an emphasis on interdisciplinary education,

---

[6] *QS World University Rankings: Methodology*, available at http://www.topuni-versities.com/university-rankings-articles/world-university-rankings/qs-world-university-rankings-methodology, accessed on 28 May, 2015.

[7] Kumar, C. Raj. 'Building World-Class Universities in India.' *Seminar*, January 2014, p. 98.

recognizing the symbiotic relationship between the natural sciences, medicine, and other disciplines.

Lack of Innovation

While a large quantitative leap has resulted in the establishment of 650 degree-awarding institutions in India, quality and excellence seems to have suffered greatly in the process. Mediocrity has been institutionalized, leading to a complete lack of creativity and innovation. The mere celebration of a few islands of excellence, mostly specialized single-discipline institutions is not going to address larger problems. The quality of Indian universities has to be significantly enhanced and the best global practices need to be contextualized for an Indian audience. We need to understand and appreciate the remarkable transformation in higher education that has taken place in other Asian countries such as Japan, Singapore, and China. Like them, we must also transform our curriculum, courses, teaching pedagogy, faculty recruitment and student admission processes.

Indifference to Research

Research in any and every discipline can have a profound impact on our society. Because of their indifference to research, universities have been unable to provide solutions to social, economic and political problems that affect India. Indian universities ought to become fertile ground for the generation of ideas. Research produces knowledge that offers clarity and a more informed understanding of the subject at hand. Scholarships and publications help create a platform for scholars to reflect upon issues in a critical and coherent manner. Only by giving credit to the history of ideas, will we be able to challenge existing patterns of thought.

One-size-fits-all Funding

The question of funding for Indian universities is inevitably connected to the role of State and regulatory bodies. Major reforms ought to address the acute shortage of funds and availability of resources. The Indian university landscape has a range of actors: state government-funded public universities, central government-funded public universities; state private universities, deemed universities and many other colleges in the form of degree awarding institutions. The current system of a one-size-fits-all policy for funding and resource allocation needs examination. Every aspect of funding and resource allocation—tuition fee, scholarships, infrastructure, faculty salaries, research funding, endowments, etc.—needs to be thoroughly analysed.

Myopic Leadership

Leadership is central not only for providing an institutional vision, but also to reflect upon the larger role of the Indian universities that connect it to professions, the government, intergovernmental organizations, think tanks and NGOs. Leadership is about taking responsibility and being accountable for one's decisions. Unfortunately, leadership of an Indian university continues to be seen as a natural career progression for senior academics who regard a leadership role as their pinnacle of success, when they have but a few years left and very little to give. This practice needs a conscious review.

Conflicting Regulatory Mechanisms

The higher education regulatory environment in India is not only complex but also multilayered with different forms of ambiguity, uncertainty, and contradiction in the rules and regulations. While the state and central governments are involved in different aspects of regulating higher education, there are also a number of statutory bodies and institutional mechanisms which are regulating certain aspects of higher education. In addition, there have been a plethora of judgments of the Supreme Court of India and the various High Courts which have interpreted various aspects of laws, rules, and regulations of higher education. There are very few areas, if at all in higher education in India, which are not regulated. This has created a conundrum in which the higher education institutions have little opportunity to be imaginative and innovative in their approaches to institution building. One of the most effective ways of addressing conflicting regulatory mechanisms is by promoting, over a sustained period of time, institutional leadership. While the University Grants Commission could play the role of an institution that provides leadership in higher education policy, there is a greater need for ensuring legitimacy and credibility of our regulators for them to make an effective contribution to this aspect.

The most important purpose of the regulatory framework for higher education is to promote excellence. Promoting excellence in higher education is possible through a process of institutional mentoring facilitated by the regulators. The current approach of the regulators becoming inspectors and using monitoring, shaming, and impositions of sanctions against the institutions is not helping the aspiration of Indian higher education sector to achieve excellence. The vast numbers of higher education institutions in India have diverse challenges due to their institutional trajectories. The higher education regulator should be able to see the difference among institutions and should adopt unique forms of institutional mentoring that build capacity and contribute to achieving excellence.

There is an urgent need to revamp higher education in India so that Indian universities can compete with the universities of the world. Quality higher education is required not only for economic development but also for social transformation. In the next section, a vision to build world-class universities in India is presented.

BUILDING WORLD-CLASS UNIVERSITIES IN INDIA: A VISION

World-class universities are built on the basis of a strong foundation that has an inspiring vision and a mission to fulfill the vision. The vision should reflect the ideals and aspirations of the university.[8] Universities should be created with a strong vision that is built around the needs of a society. But these needs ought to be broad based and should reflect the collective imagination of a community. Universities are inherently pluralistic in nature, where there is diversity of disciplines and perspectives. The vision of a university should reflect that pluralism, while recognizing that there is no one model of a university.

Indian universities need to reexamine their founding vision on the basis of which they were established. It helps to articulate a vision of the university even after many years of its establishment, as the vision will help in galvanizing the academic consciousness among faculty, students and staff towards fulfilling a set of goals and objectives. The vision of the university should incorporate a farsighted approach towards learning and imagination among faculty and students, but be fully conscious of the reality of the university's existing challenges.[9]

---

[8] Kumar, C. Raj. 'Building World-Class Universities in India.' *Seminar*, January 2014, p. 98.

[9] Kumar, C. Raj. 'Building World-Class Universities in India.' *Seminar*, January 2014, p. 98.

Universities do not become world-class institutions as soon as they are created, but evolve to become world-class through long years of work pursued by the commitment and dedication of students, faculty, and staff. Even then, promoting excellence is an evolving project and that is why the vision of the university helps shape its present and future.[10]

Funding and Resources

World-class universities around the world are established and developed through a great deal of commitment of resources. The question of funding of Indian universities is inevitably connected to the role of state and regulatory bodies.[11]

The existing hierarchies of classifications for funding and resources have not been able to identify properly the true potentiality of Indian universities to become quality institutions. Every aspect of funding and resource allocation, ranging from tuition fee, scholarships for students, infrastructure in universities, faculty salaries, library development, research funding, including research infrastructure, endowments and philanthropy and many other issues for which substantial resources are required, needs a thorough re-examination.[12]

There is not enough understanding and realization that the resources that are required to build world-class universities are significant. Arguably, the precious resources that need to be available for universities may not, and indeed, cannot come from the state. It is in this context that there is a need for promoting private universities in India.[13] Deterioration in the academic standards of public universities in India is due to a number of factors, including, but not limited to poor infrastructure at our university campuses, lack of motivation among faculty to perform, inability of

---

[10] Kumar, C. Raj. 'Building World-Class Universities in India.' *Seminar*, January 2014, p. 99.

[11] Kumar, C. Raj. 'Building World-Class Universities in India.' *Seminar*, January 2014, p. 99.

[12] Kumar, C. Raj. 'Building World-Class Universities in India.' *Seminar*, January 2014, p. 99.

[13] Kumar, C. Raj. 'Building World-Class Universities in India.' *Seminar*, January 2014, p. 99.

universities to create a research environment for faculty publications, absence of interdisciplinary programmes for the students, lack of innovation in curriculum and course design, inadequate compensation for faculty and faculty development initiatives, and a bureaucratic and hierarchical governance structure that does not motivate faculty members to perform.[14]

Role of Government

The role of the government in higher education and university governance deserves a serious examination. At present, the role of the government in the case of state universities is significant and the higher education department of the state government is deeply involved in every aspect from the creation of the university to granting of approvals and permissions that need to be obtained for administering the university. This poses serious problems for university governance. The existing framework for the establishment of a university (public and private) in India requires legislation passed in the state legislative assembly or the national Parliament or through a decision of the University Grants Commission (UGC) and the Ministry of Human Resource Development, Government of India.[15]

There are elaborate procedures in place led by the higher education departments within the state government that are involved in every aspect of institution-building even before the creation of the university.[16] While this is desirable, there is a need to recognize that once the university is established, the role of the government departments and agencies will have to undergo a significant change. They ought to become facilitators and ensure autonomy and independence of the universities, so that the institutions are able to grow on their own. The need for seeking approvals and permissions from government departments for starting new academic programmes or new disciplines should be dispensed with so that the internal governance mechanisms of the university are activated to work effectively.

A serious concern for the higher education policy makers and educationists is the need to maintain high academic standards. There

---

[14] Kumar, C. Raj. 'Building World-Class Universities in India.' *Seminar*, January 2014, p. 99.

[15] Yash Pal et al., *2009 Report of the Committee to Advise on Renovation and Rejuvenation of Higher Education*, p. 52.

[16] Kumar, *Building World-Class Universities in India*, 99.

is a fear that in the absence of external checks and balances, universities will exercise powers in an arbitrary manner and offer courses and programmes, which are devoid of academic content.[17] This argument is problematic at different levels: first, it distrusts the university as an academic institution which is expected to act with a sense of responsibility; second, it creates an atmosphere of suspicion and animosity where faculty members of a university, who are expected to take critical decisions relating to the academic programmes, are not in a position to drive the academic agenda; and third, it creates opportunities for vested interests and corruption at the level of government departments exercising such powers.[18]

A better way to deal with this problem is to make the process of establishing a university more rigorous and transparent. The necessary conditions that need to be fulfilled to create a university should reflect the highest academic standards, availability of qualified faculty members, and the necessary resources and objective measures to assess the *bonafide* intentions of the promoters of private universities.[19] After the decision to establish a university is taken the government's role should be one of a facilitator and not that of a regulator. There is a need to empower departments, faculties and internal governance mechanisms within Indian universities so that they are able to take responsibility and are duly accountable for their decisions. Steadily, the role of government departments in the decision-making of the university should be negligible, if at all.[20]

World-class universities are not developed through government departments exercising powers over institutions; they are nurtured only when faculty members, students, staff and other stakeholders of the university are able to take decisions about the university in an independent and transparent manner.

Other Regulatory Reforms

One of the significant challenges of Indian universities is the role and responsibilities of regulatory bodies such as the University Grants Commission (UGC), Bar Council of India (BCI), Medical Council of India

---

[17] Kumar, *Building World-Class Universities in India*, p. 100.
[18] Kumar, *Building World-Class Universities in India*, p. 100.
[19] Kumar, *Building World-Class Universities in India*, p. 100.
[20] Kumar, *Building World-Class Universities in India*, p. 100.

(MCI), All Indian Council for Technical Education (AICTE), and other such bodies.[21] On the one hand, there is a need to ensure quality in universities and higher education institutions for which some degree of regulatory assessment and external accountability is essential. On the other, if we do not achieve the right balance, there is a serious risk of regulatory capture where higher education policies will not be driven by innovation and creativity in institution building, but by bureaucratic timidity, archaic rules and regulations and callous indifference of the regulatory bodies, besides nepotism and outright corruption.[22]

The current approach stifles innovation and creativity in the Indian university system where the regulatory bodies play a significant role in many aspects of university governance. Besides the more pivotal role that the regulatory bodies play in the inspection of universities to determine their suitability and worthiness for state funding, these bodies are also constantly involved in formulating policies that have a direct impact on the governance of universities. Given the fact that there are over 650 universities in India, there is little scope for any consultation whatsoever before any set of rules or regulations are drafted by the regulatory bodies and made uniformly applicable to all institutions.[23]

As a result, a good amount of time of the vice-chancellors and registrars of Indian universities is devoted to ensuring that they are in compliance with these rules and regulations. Indian regulatory bodies tend to exercise enormous powers, often in an arbitrary manner. Arbitrariness in the exercise of regulatory powers of higher education regulators has adversely affected the public image and reputation of these bodies.[24] Their role and responsibilities have been challenged, primarily because of the lack of trust in the ability of regulatory bodies to perform the tasks of a facilitator.

There is no doubt that there are serious instances of malpractice prevailing in the higher education sector. There are unscrupulous higher education providers who are engaged in illegal and unethical practices, which affect the interests of the students. But when regulatory bodies

---

[21] Kumar, *Building World-Class Universities in India*, p. 100; see also Yash Pal et al., p. 52.

[22] Kumar, *Building World-Class Universities in India*, p. 100; see also Yash Pal et al., p. 51.

[23] Kumar, *Building World-Class Universities in India*, p. 100.

[24] Kumar, *Building World-Class Universities in India*, p. 100.

paint the general institutional culture of all universities and colleges in the same manner as they would of dysfunctional institutions, there is a problem. It not only affects the morale of good institutional endeavours, but also creates a cynical environment where innovation cannot occur. World-class universities need a free, liberal and facilitative environment.

Outstanding Faculty Members

Of all the significant inputs that go into the making of a world-class university, it is necessary to recognize that the faculty is the most important and indeed the most significant.[25] Outstanding faculty members who can make great substantive contributions to teaching and research create world-class universities. It is only by hiring and retaining inspiring teachers and rigorous researchers that we can hope to establish world-class universities in India. At best, most Indian universities are largely teaching institutions. The focus of the academic agenda is to be engaged in teaching and the faculty members tend to teach a disproportionately higher number of hours in a week. This has undermined any possibility for the faculty members to be engaged in research and publication.[26]

Indian aspirations to build world-class universities ought to centre on the hiring of faculty from India and overseas. Globalization has created new opportunities for Indian academics to be able to move around the world and India is not their only option to pursue serious academic careers. In fact, many graduates from universities in India seek higher education opportunities around the world and even if some of them choose to come into academia, they rarely decide to work in India. There are a number of reasons why Indian universities are not in a position to attract very bright graduates across disciplines to come into academia in India, but this situation is changing with new opportunities.[27]

Inculcating culture of research and knowledge creation

Generally, the Indian universities do not provide sufficient opportunities, both in terms of time and space for pursuing research; there is also a serious lack of funds and other forms of resources to pursue research and

---

[25] Kumar, *Building World-Class Universities in India*, p. 100.

[26] Kumar, *Building World-Class Universities in India*, p. 101.

[27] Kumar, *Building World-Class Universities in India*, p. 100.

writing.[28] This has to change. So long as we do not provide for research to be the central focus of higher education, at least in some of our premier universities, we will not be able to build world-class universities. Universities are expected to be knowledge creating institutions. Knowledge cannot be created in the absence of scholars who are prepared to read, think, reflect and write. The essence of a great university is its ability to influence change through research and the process of the discovery of truth leading to a rigorous analysis that creates knowledge and promotes innovation. This is true in the case of hard sciences, social sciences and humanities. Indian universities need to recognize this aspect of university education for them to develop higher standards in their pursuit of excellence.[29]

Make Universities Accountable

Students are at the heart of a university community. Great institutions have attained a world-class status because of their alumni achieving distinction in various walks of life. Indian universities too have produced great alumni who have made outstanding contributions in India and around the world. Nevertheless, in recent times, questions have been raised as to what role Indian universities play to shape the education and learning process of the students. Access to the premier universities in India continues to be a luxury of the privileged few who have probably received sound quality education in their high school and are better equipped to do well in their examinations and standard tests which qualify them to be admitted into these universities.[30] However, one fundamental aspect that needs to be carefully examined about Indian universities and students is the learning outcomes.

The existing framework of accountability of the university to the students needs to be revisited. Most Indian universities do not even have a rudimentary form for students to be able to provide a feedback on the teaching of the faculty.[31] There are hardly any faculty development programmes with a view to enhancing the teaching abilities of the faculty. Students need to be given a holistic learning experience that will not only help them acquire substantive knowledge, but also develop their critical thinking and writing skills and their abilities to articulate effectively.

---

[28] Kumar, *Building World-Class Universities in India*, p. 100.
[29] Kumar, *Building World-Class Universities in India*, p. 100.
[30] Kumar, *Building World-Class Universities in India*, p. 100.
[31] Kumar, *Building World-Class Universities in India*, p. 100.

The current paradigm of a significant number of students largely engaged in learning on their own without value additions from outstanding teachers has to change.[32] Note that over the years, the students' own institutional expectations from most Indian universities have substantially reduced.

Teaching and research constitutes the centrality of pedagogy of learning and primacy of knowledge in a university. Almost all rankings use both of these as benchmarks for assessing the quality of universities.[33] The weightage given to research tends to be more in the rankings of universities recognizing the importance of research. Indian universities face the twin challenges of both teaching and research in their efforts to build institutions of excellence, as there has been a serious shortage of faculty members, including in the most prestigious institutions.

Furthermore, our research capacities in general tend to be mediocre, primarily because the faculty expertise in most Indian universities lacks academic rigor. The debate over teaching versus research is old and insipid. Indian universities must ensure that teaching and research go hand in hand and there is a lot that they need to do to strike a balance between these equally important objectives.[34]

A larger question that Indian universities need to address is about the importance of research and scholarship that can generate ideas for change. Research in every discipline, in the arts, humanities, sciences and social sciences, can have a profound impact on our society and beyond. Indifference and complacency to research has led to the inability of universities in India to produce knowledge that can impact policy, produce innovation, or provide solutions to social, economic and political problems that affect India as a nation.[35] Indian universities ought to become fertile avenues for generation of ideas through research and publications. Rigorous research in all fields is critical to India, as it will be expected to respond to new problems for which old solutions and perspectives may not be helpful. Research produces knowledge that gives clarity on the basis of an informed and deeper understanding of the issues involved.

---

[32] Kumar, *Building World-Class Universities in India*, p. 100.

[33] Kumar, *Building World-Class Universities in India*, p. 100.

[34] Kumar, *Building World-Class Universities in India*, p. 100.

[35] Kumar, *Building World-Class Universities in India*, p. 100.

International Collaborations, Global Consciousness, and Transnational Education

Indian universities have to carefully consider their policies for establishing global collaborations and activities that promote global interaction and provide for a global student experience.[36] It is not useful to sign numerous memoranda of understanding that do not translate into concrete forms of collaboration among universities leading to implementation of programmes for students and scholars. Universities, as a part of their internal governance mechanisms, need to evolve policies that will guide them in establishing collaborations with other institutions.

We need to innovate on programmes that enable direct interaction between foreign teachers and Indian students, and a true collaboration that provides for a rich student experience as opposed to collaborations that remain only on paper. One important area in which global collaboration can revolutionize student experience relates to teaching and learning. Today's technologically advanced world provides scope for innovation in terms of promoting e-learning and virtual global classrooms based on meaningful international collaborations. Such methods can provide students the benefit of interacting with academics and experts from around the world and gain from their knowledge and pedagogical methodology.[37]

If India is to create world-class universities, our focus needs to be on providing an experience of transnational education to the students. This will expose them to new and emerging frontiers of knowledge and perspectives. It will also introduce them to new cultures and people and help them to appreciate diversity in an increasingly cosmopolitan and interdependent world. Transnational education is no longer the luxury of a few, but a necessary aspect of educational and learning experiences around the world.

Break the Dichotomy between Public and Private Institutions

India should overcome its biases and prejudices based on merely whether the universities are private or public institutions. There is a need to assess universities on the basis of objective and determinable standards relating

---

[36] Kumar, *Building World-Class Universities in India*, p. 102.
[37] Kumar, *Building World-Class Universities in India*, p. 102.

to the quality of teaching, faculty, research and capacity building, rather than on the basis of it being public or private.[38] It needs to be noted that some of the top universities in the world are private: Harvard, Yale, Stanford and MIT, just as some of the oldest and most reputed ones continue to be public universities: Oxford, Cambridge and London. At one level, we are aspiring to increase the Gross Enrolment Ratio (GER) so that a larger proportion of eligible students can access the higher education system.[39] At another level, we face the problem of institutionalized mediocrity across our universities, with even postgraduate degree holders unable to get suitable jobs for want of knowledge, expertise and skills.[40] Higher education in India cannot be reformed unless we develop strong private universities that are truly non-profit, philanthropic, and committed to promoting academic freedom and institutional excellence.

The effort to promote private initiatives in higher education should go hand in hand with other equally committed efforts to strengthen and develop our public universities. Indian universities must re-examine their substantive role and contribution to promoting creativity and innovation. In the course of a quantitative leap resulting in the expansion of higher education in India, quality and excellence suffered significantly. Mediocrity has been institutionalized leading to a lack of creativity and innovation in our efforts to build world-class universities. The mere celebration of a few islands of excellence, mostly in the form of specialized single discipline institutions, is not going to address the larger problem of lack of creativity and innovation.[41]

The quality of Indian universities has to be significantly enhanced and the best of the global practices need to be brought into India, contextualizing them to our circumstances. We need to understand and appreciate the remarkable transformation in higher education that has taken place in countries in Asia, including but not limited to Japan, Singapore, South Korea, Taiwan, Hong Kong, and Mainland China.[42] The heart of this transformation in Asia is about creativity and innovation in curriculum, courses,

---

[38] Kumar, *Building World-Class Universities in India*, p. 102.

[39] Kumar, *Building World-Class Universities in India*, p. 102.

[40] Kumar, *Building World-Class Universities in India*, p. 102.

[41] Kumar, *Building World-Class Universities in India*, p. 103.

[42] *Times Higher Education* BRICS & Emerging Economies Rankings 2016.

programmes, teaching pedagogy, faculty recruitment, student admission and mobility, international collaborations, research, and publications.

A committee constituted by the Planning Commission and headed by the then chief mentor of Infosys, N.R. Narayana Murthy submitted a report that focused on the role of the corporate sector in higher education.[43] This committee acknowledged the importance of stronger private initiatives in the field of higher education and recommended path breaking measures such as free land for 999 years, 300 per cent deduction in taxable income to companies for contributions towards boosting higher education and 10 year multiple entry visas for foreign research scholars.[44] It also suggested that mandatory accreditation be made essential for Indian universities.[45]

To promote greater accessibility of higher education to the under-privileged, the committee recommended the establishment of an Rs 1,000 crore-scholarship fund with tax exemption for contributions made by the corporate sector.[46] Innovative solutions need to be found in addressing the challenges of higher education. Corporate philanthropy needs to be significantly promoted, as private wealth in India has not adequately contributed to the growth and development of not-for-profit higher education.

Role of Private Universities

The role of private universities in India has become a matter for discussion and debate. While there is the need for the expansion of the higher education sector, there has been criticism on the role of private sector, owing to the dubious and irresponsible growth of private universities and their lack of vision, academic commitment and commitment to institution building.[47] This situation, however, has begun to change and a new

---

[43] N.R. Narayana Murthy et al., *2012 Report of the Committee on Corporate Participation in Higher Education*.

[44] N.R. Narayana Murthy et al., *2012 Report of the Committee on Corporate Participation in Higher Education*, p. 8.

[45] N.R. Narayana Murthy et al., *2012 Report of the Committee on Corporate Participation in Higher Education*, p. 8.

[46] N.R. Narayana Murthy et al., *2012 Report of the Committee on Corporate Participation in Higher Education*, p. 9.

[47] Kumar, C. Raj. 'Take a Qualitative Leap.' *The Week*, 1 June, 2014; See also P.N. Tandon et al., *2009 Report of the Committee for Review of Existing Institutions Deemed to be Universities*.

generation of private universities is assuming a leadership role in raising the quality of higher education.[48]

The establishment of private universities in India did not lead to positive changes in the quality of education. Rather, private universities in general in India have been, unfortunately, equated with all the problems of the public universities. In addition, many private universities tend to be engaged in malpractices that have undermined the reputation of private university education. They have fostered a culture of mediocrity and dubiousness, both of which have led to adverse consequences for higher education.[49]

There is thus, a need for a paradigm shift in the availability of funding and resources. For example, resources for pursuing research and knowledge creation leading to publications should not be given on the basis of whether a university is public or private. It should be based upon the nature of faculty and research capacities that prevail in the university and how best to augment those available resources with a view to advancing the research agendas.

It has to be recognized that education in general and higher education in particular requires a commitment to not-for-profit engagement. Private universities established under a not-for-profit framework include O.P. Jindal Global University, Azim Premji University, and Shiv Nadar University. The founders of these universities are people who have created wealth in other businesses and are not looking at them as a source of income. Most private universities in India, however, are created as business ventures.

Some of the top universities in the world, such as Harvard, Yale, Stanford, and MIT, are private. World-class universities are not developed through government departments exercising powers over institutions; they are nurtured when faculty members, students, staff and other stakeholders are able to take decisions about the university in an independent and transparent manner.[50]

After a university is established, it needs autonomy and freedom to innovate. Such innovation, autonomy, and vision are possible in private universities. Higher education in India cannot be reformed unless we

[48] See generally Ernst & Young, *Private Sector Participation in Indian Higher Education*, 2014.

[49] See Tandon et al. *Report of the Committee for Review of Existing Institutions Deemed to be Universities.*

[50] Kumar, *Take a Qualitative Leap.*

develop strong private universities that are truly nonprofit, philanthropic, and committed to promoting academic freedom.[51]

Institutional Vision and Leadership

There is an urgent need in Indian universities to reflect upon the crisis of leadership and its inability to seek reforms relating to institution-building. Leadership is central not only for providing an institutional vision that will garner and galvanize academic consciousness among faculty and students to fulfill the goals and aspirations of the university, but also to reflect upon the larger role and responsibilities of the Indian university that connects it with the professions, government, intergovernmental organizations, think tanks, and NGOs. Leadership is also about taking responsibility and being accountable for one's decisions. Unfortunately, the existing model of governance in the Indian university system does not recognize leadership as a critical aspect of building institutions of excellence.

India's aspiration to establish world-class universities will depend upon our commitment to create and nurture transformational institutions that will inspire the faculty and students with a spirit of enquiry and instill in them the flame of imagination.

Political Leadership

Institutional leadership should be complemented by political leadership with suitable policy reforms in the country. In this context, Russia has embarked on an ambitious initiative called 'Project on Competitiveness Enhancement of Leading Russian Universities among Global Research and Education Centers'.[52] This is expected to be a transformational initiative for Russian universities to seek a stronger presence in global rankings.[53]

Project 5-100 is a bold initiative of Russian President Vladimir Putin and the Russian Federation government in order to support the

---

[51] Kumar, *Take a Qualitative Leap.*

[52] *Project 5-100: Russian Academic Excellence Project,* available at http://5top100.com, accessed on 28 May 2015.

[53] *Project 5-100: Russian Academic Excellence Project,* available at http://5top100.com, accessed on 28 May 2015.

best universities in the country.[54] Its vision, says Alexander Povalko, Deputy Minister of Education and Science of the Russian Federation, is to '... support the best universities in Russia, with a desire to see at least five of them enter the top 100 of the leading global university rankings by 2020 ... Project 5-100 is a comprehensive academic excellence initiative that unites top-tier Russian universities behind the goal of deep transformation of the institutions according to the best international models and practices'.[55] There is a collective consciousness emerging within many universities to seek excellence that will ultimately help them fare well in international rankings.[56]

Similarly, nearly 20 years ago, the Chinese government created a vision for establishing world-class universities supporting nine top universities (C9 League) out of their over 2,000 universities. This official state policy gave phenomenal results for China.[57] More recently, on 5 November 2015, the Chinese State Council released a statement which was designed to lift the status and standing and international competitiveness of China's higher education system. President of India, Pranab Mukherjee through his vision and leadership as the Visitor of 126[58] central institutions and more recently, the Prime Minister's Office (PMO) have articulated a vision for nurturing world-class universities. This culminated in the announcement of Finance Minister Arun Jaitley in his budget speech announcing an innovative policy that will enable 10 public and 10 private universities to receive autonomy and resources to become world-class institutions. Recently,

[54] *Times Higher Education World Summit Series*, http://www.theworldsummit-series.com/thebricsus2014/project-5-100, accessed on 28 May 2015.

[55] 'Push for the Top', *Times Higher Education*, 1 January 1990, https://www.timeshighereducation.co.uk/world-university-rankings/2015/brics-and-emerging-economies/analysis/push-for-the-top, accessed on 28 May 2015.

[56] Kumar, C. Raj, 'A New Imagination for Indian Universities', *The Hindu*, 20 December 2014, http://www.thehindu.com/opinion/op-ed/lead-article-a-new-imagination-for-indian-universities/article6698317.ece, accessed on 28 May 2015.

[57] Kumar, C. Raj, 'India's Tryst with World Class Universities', *Deccan Herald*, 8 August 2016, http://www.deccanherald.com/content/562954/indias-tryst-world-class-universities.html, accessed on 28 May 2015.

[58] See *The President of India, Shri Pranab Mukherjee*, http://presidentofindia.nic.in/126-central-institutions.htm, accessed on 28 May 2015.

the University Grants Commission (UGC) has come out with a public consultation document[59] on the guidelines and regulations governing the eligibility criteria, selection procedure, monitoring, evaluation, and other regulatory aspects of the proposed world-class institutions. Amongst other things, the document mandates that selected world-class institutions 'should come in top five hundred of any of the world renowned ranking frameworks (such as the Times Higher Education World University Rankings or QS or Shanghai's Jiao Tong University) in the first ten years of setting up or being declared as a World-Class Institution, and come in the top one hundred eventually over time.'[60]

While this is a welcome and much needed step, a number of issues grappling higher education in India, as elucidated in this chapter need to be urgently addressed. In the next section, it is discussed that the need for advancing multidisciplinary education is profoundly felt in India, given our strong commitment to democracy and pluralism. Thus, any discussion on the future of higher education and building world-class universities in India is incomplete without emphasizing on liberal arts education.

IMPORTANCE OF LIBERAL ARTS EDUCATION

One of the consequences of the crisis in the higher education system has led to calls for focusing on employability as the sole objective of education. In recent times, there has been a systematic attack on academic streams like liberal arts and humanities not only in India, but also in other countries where there has been an established tradition that has promoted liberal arts education including the United States.[61] A meaningful employment is one of the important goals of higher

---

[59] *Public consultation document on Policy on World Class Institutions*, 2016, available at http://mhrd.gov.in/sites/upload_files/mhrd/files/upload_document/public_consultation.pdf, accessed on 28 May 2015.

[60] *Public consultation document on Policy on World Class Institutions*, 2016, available at http://mhrd.gov.in/sites/upload_files/mhrd/files/upload_document/public_consultation.pdf, accessed on 28 May 2015.

[61] *Public consultation document on Policy on World Class Institutions*, 2016, available at http://mhrd.gov.in/sites/upload_files/mhrd/files/upload_document/public_consultation.pdf, accessed on 28 May 2015.

education, but it will be a mistake to consider this as the only goal of any educational experience.

A liberal arts and humanities education foregrounds and fosters critical thinking capacities in students—a behavioural aspect that is more and more in demand today, across industries.[62]

We no longer live in a day and age where technical skills and specialization per se are sufficient for growth in the working world.

In today's competitive world, an individual may have technical skills of a certain kind, but if s/he does not have the requisite analytical acumen to communicate and articulate views or weigh the pros and cons of complex issues, they are not going to be useful in the working world beyond a point.[63]

This is where a full rounded education in the liberal arts makes an individual a complete personality, with the ability to bring in a broad range of knowledge and insights to any task at hand.[64]

Knowledge Acquisition

Liberal arts education promotes intellectual curiosity, which is critical for the growth and development of any individual in a society. It helps in the process of creating knowledge and sharing perspectives about some of the most fundamental issues of our society. It helps people come to terms with the past, develop an understanding of the present and prepares them to charter ideas and perspectives for the future.

The need for acquiring knowledge in a range of subjects including philosophy, history, literature, sociology, anthropology, and psychology while pursuing interests in music, theatre, performing arts, and fine arts is the hallmark of a liberal education.[65]

Skill Formation

Universities should focus on raising the skills of the population and generating new knowledge. There is no question of prioritizing one over

---

[62] Kumar, C. Raj, 'Liberal Arts Education for Enlightened Citizens', *Deccan Herald*, 19 June 2014, available at http://www.deccanherald.com/content/414441/liberal-arts-education-enlightened-citizens.html, accessed on 28 May 2015.

[63] Kumar, *Liberal Arts Education for Enlightened Citizens.*

[64] Kumar, *Liberal Arts Education for Enlightened Citizens.*

[65] Kumar, *Liberal Arts Education for Enlightened Citizens.*

the other. All countries, including developing countries, need to create knowledge and contribute to research, but also need to develop significant capacities to promote vocational education, and develop various types of skill sets, which will enable and empower its populace to undertake a range of job opportunities. There ought to be greater diversity in our higher education sector.

A liberal arts education is key to enabling this. It provides opportunities for students to develop a range of skills that are essential to become lifelong learners.

In fact, the skills relating to reflective reading, critical thinking, effective writing, and verbal communications are central for professional advancement.

Liberal arts education gives due emphasis to inculcate these skills in students as these are relevant not only for the next job that the graduate of a college will aspire, but for a long time to come.

The future of education will depend upon how effectively we are able to impart knowledge, skills and perspectives that will promote versatility and will be able to empower them in a variety of professional endeavours.

Understanding Heritage

One of the important goals of education is to work towards achieving enlightened citizenship. Education needs to promote a greater degree of civilizational understanding. India has a rich and long tradition of promoting civilizational understanding through education. The inspiring institutions of higher education in ancient India—Takshashila University and Nalanda University promoted liberal arts and humanities education long before any other institution in the world.[66] Takshashila University established over 2,700 years ago had over 10,000 students from around the world and studied subjects as diversified as the Vedas, philosophy, grammar, politics, astronomy, future, music, Ayurveda, agriculture, surgery, and commerce.[67]

Takshashila University is probably the oldest liberal arts college of the world. India needs to revive this rich and inspiring cultural and educational history of promoting transnational humanities education.[68]

---

[66] Kumar, *Liberal Arts Education for Enlightened Citizens*.

[67] Kumar, *Liberal Arts Education for Enlightened Citizens*.

[68] Kumar, *Liberal Arts Education for Enlightened Citizens*.

Citizenship is about people taking responsibility and enlightened citizenship cannot be achieved unless people receive a sound and rigorous education in liberal arts and humanities.

The critical study of these values will inevitably mean a stronger focus on humanities education. It is not possible to deepen democracy without students being given an opportunity to understand these values through a serious study of humanities.

It is also important to change attitudes of all stakeholders in education, including primary and secondary education, leading to higher education.

The obsession to make choices of study and careers purely on the basis of employability and immediate financial gains and nothing else has neither led to employability, nor enlightenment.

Promoting Employability

Liberal arts education creates opportunities for students to develop knowledge and critical thinking abilities that is the hallmark of good education. Unfortunately, India does not have a large number of liberal arts colleges. Even the colleges that do have a few degree options in liberal arts and humanities do not fully understand and appreciate the pedagogical foundations of liberal education. There has been far too much emphasis on specialized education with a view to focusing on specific areas of interest and not to challenge the boundaries of knowledge and thought processes. Employers are not only looking for people with knowledge, but would expect graduates to be problem solvers; who can read and reflect effectively; who can write and communicate persuasively; and who can be sensitive and appreciate the complexities of the society that we live in today.[69] A liberal arts and humanities education equips students with the analytical inventiveness and versatility of mind, which makes many careers possible, whether in business, consulting, academia, government, NGOs, journalism, creative industries, and numerous other professions including civil service.[70]

Education Policy Recommendations for India

The current Union Minister for Human Resource Development, Prakash Javadekar, has set out an ambitious agenda to seek reforms in higher

[69] Kumar, *Liberal Arts Education for Enlightened Citizens*.
[70] Kumar, *Liberal Arts Education for Enlightened Citizens*.

education.[71] There is no greater challenge to the future of India than the urgent need to revamp our institutions of higher education. The reform that has to take place will have to address the fundamental problem of institutionalized mediocrity, deeply embedded in these institutions. It is not enough to talk about pursuing excellence; to establish and build world-class universities of excellence, the ecosystem of higher education has to change dramatically. These are some of the changes required.

Nurturing Talent

Transforming Indian universities involves a vision that will help India have a stronger commitment toward pursuing excellence. While global rankings of universities around the world have embarrassed us time and again, with no Indian university in the top 200 universities, this should not surprise us.[72] What should, however, make us ponder is how the last two decades have seen a dramatic increase in the number of universities in Asia, which have begun to figure among the top universities of the world. What is it that Singapore, Hong Kong, South Korea, Taipei, Japan, and China have done that we have not? While as individual scholars and researchers Indians have been doing remarkably well around the world, it is the inability of our own universities to nurture this talent that needs understanding. Unfortunately, most Indian universities are not spaces that are inspiring enough for knowledge creation, nor have they been designed to ensure the pursuit of serious research and scholarship. Affecting transformation involves five things: substantial resources, a progressive regulatory environment in which higher education regulators begin to trust universities, a new governance model for creating opportunities and space for research and scholarship, an enabling environment within universities that will significantly incentivize research and publications, and an attitudinal change among all stakeholders in the higher education sector.

The core emphasis has been to expand the diverse higher education sector with a view to increasing the gross enrolment ratio (GER). Mindless

---

[71] 'Qualitative Reforms in Higher Education', *Ministry of Human Resource Development*, available at http://mhrd.gov.in/qualitative-reforms-higher-education, accessed on 28 May 2015.

[72] 'World University Rankings 2014–2015', *Times Higher Education*, available at https://www.timeshighereducation.co.uk/world-university-rankings/2014-15/world-ranking, accessed on 28 May 2015.

expansion has led to a situation where there is mediocrity. Central universities may be well funded, but suffer from a crisis of governance in which over 40 per cent of faculty positions lie vacant.[73] The problem is even more serious when it comes to the state universities—they suffer from a lack of resources among other things. The new government must ensure that all faculty appointments are filled up within a time-bound framework. This will involve tactful engagement with the institutions and a creative approach to faculty recruitment. Archaic policies that have outlived their time should be dispensed with while recruiting faculty. Until the crisis of a lack of adequate infrastructure and faculty is addressed, there should be a short moratorium on establishing more central universities, IITs, and IIMs. The misguided approach of building more institutions is not only bad public policy, but also creates social expectations that get belied very quickly when it comes to the quality of education that is offered.

Building world-class, research-oriented universities involves a serious commitment to knowledge creation in the sciences, arts, social sciences and humanities. It is not enough to focus only on building laboratories and knowledge parks, promoting an industry-academia interface and pursuing research grants and creating incubators; we need to go beyond these reforms in order to create a culture of research.[74] The vision for transforming Indian universities needs to focus on a set of specific goals to nurture research. It is essential to identify a selected set of institutions to represent the best of public and private universities and significantly enhance their capacities with a view to advancing their research agendas. This will not only help in understanding the key challenges that universities face in relation to nurturing research, but will also help us learn from recurring mistakes. Institutional reform inevitably requires risk-taking and innovation.

Indian universities are generally timid in seeking collaborations, which are necessary for the development of new ideas and perspectives. There are a significant number of biases and prejudices that have led to skepticism

[73] Kumar, Brajesh. 'Govt Directs over 40 Varsities to Fill Faculty Posts', *Hindustan Times*, 26 October 2014, available at http://www.hindustantimes.com/india-news/govt-directs-over-40-varsities-to-fill-faculty-posts/article1-1278955.aspx, accessed on 28 May 2015.

[74] Kumar, C. Raj. 'Fresh Ideas, Not More Institutions', *The Hindu*, 16 June 2014, available at http://www.thehindu.com/opinion/op-ed/fresh-ideas-not-more-institutions/article6117037.ece, accessed on 28 May 2015.

in promoting any form of collaboration, even among our own universities. There is also lack of interdisciplinary teaching among different faculties and schools. The bureaucratic approach of university managements and regulators has led to the creation of too many hurdles in the pursuit of any meaningful collaboration.[75]

Existing policies relating to research collaborations both within and outside India need to be re-examined and made more progressive and inclusive. They should be made progressive *vis-à-vis* ensuring greater autonomy and freedom to universities to determine who they want to collaborate with and what the terms of collaboration should be. I do not see any reason why the knowledge, wisdom, integrity and experience of the faculty members of the collaborating universities are less important than that of the regulators. There is a need to remove the distinctions that exist in relation to public and private universities; instead, universities ought to be differentiated on the basis of their performance and contribution. There is also a need for an inclusive approach, which involves all aspects of the higher education sector in knowledge creation. This will help in developing a higher education system that will assess the quality of education through objective standards and international benchmarks rather than making private sector education subservient to public universities.

Amending Rules

The biggest challenge is to create an enabling environment to promote innovation. Archaic rules and regulations that are constantly flouted have given rise to opportunities to dubious institutions to be engaged in corruption. There is a need to seek a change in the attitude of government departments that are involved in policymaking, and regulatory bodies that are monitoring and ensuring standards in higher education.[76] The deep distrust that is prevalent among the institutions on the one hand and the government and regulatory bodies on the other has made the higher education sector static. There is little effort in seeking innovation. This has to

[75] Kumar, C. Raj. 'Fresh Ideas, Not More Institutions', *The Hindu*, 16 June 2014, available at http://www.thehindu.com/opinion/op-ed/fresh-ideas-not-more-institutions/article6117037.ece, accessed on 28 May 2015.

[76] Kumar, C. Raj. 'Fresh Ideas, Not More Institutions', *The Hindu*, 16 June 2014, available at http://www.thehindu.com/opinion/op-ed/fresh-ideas-not-more-institutions/article6117037.ece, accessed on 28 May 2015.

change, and quickly. No reform of higher education institutions is possible without a careful and calibrated effort to examine the current framework of the powers of the government and of regulatory bodies.

Increasing Research

The R&D intensity, an indicator reflecting R&D expenditure as a percentage of GDP, of India stands at 8 per cent according to a recent report of UNESCO on the rise of higher education in Asia, which is very low when compared with countries like The Republic of Korea.[77] Every international ranking of Indian universities has repeatedly underscored the woefully inadequate research that takes place in Indian universities.[78] We cannot address this problem till such time there is a systematic change and substantial increase in the R&D expenditure in Indian universities. This will also mean changing the incentive structure that prevails among the faculty members in Indian universities. It is critical to examine the different models and experiences that have shaped the increase of R&D expenditure in many universities in China and other parts of Southeast Asia.

Need for Special Education Zones in Higher Education[79]

To fulfil the vision of education and ameliorate few of the difficulties highlighted above, India needs to establish Special Education Zones (SEZs) as the new and innovative policy reforms for promoting governance mechanisms that will enable the establishment of world-class universities. The new generation of SEZs in education should nurture the creation of

---

[77] United Nations Educational, Scientific and Cultural Organization, UNESCO Institute for Statistics, *Higher Education in Asia: Expanding Out, Expanding Up*, 2014, available at http://www.uis.unesco.org/Library/Documents/higher-education-asia-graduate-university-research-2014-en.pdf, accessed on 28 May 2015.

[78] 'World University Rankings 2014–2015', *Times Higher Education*, https://www.timeshighereducation.co.uk/world-university-rankings/2014-15/world-ranking, accessed on 28 May 2015; 'QS World University Rankings', *QS*, available at http://www.topuniversities.com/qs-world-university-rankings, accessed on 28 May 2015.

[79] Kumar, C. Raj. 'Need for SEZs in Higher Edu', *Deccan Herald*, 28 November 2015, available at http://www.deccanherald.com/content/514356/need-sezs-higher-edu.html, accessed on 28 May 2015.

a knowledge development eco-system with everything that is needed to build world-class universities.

We need to evolve a new institutional imagination for such universities. Jamil Salmi in a World Bank report titled 'The Challenge of Establishing World Class Universities' had observed: 'In an attempt to propose a more meaningful definition of world-class universities, this report makes the case that the superior results of these institutions (highly sought graduates, leading-edge research, and technology transfer) can essentially be attributed to three complementary sets of factors at play in top universities: (a) a high concentration of talent (faculty and students), (b) abundant resources to offer rich learning environment and to conduct advanced research, and (c) favourable governance features that encourage strategic vision, innovation, and flexibility and that enable institutions to make decisions and to manage resources without being encumbered by bureaucracy.'

The following could be some of the unique characteristics of these SEZs in higher education that will enable the development of world-class universities in India:

Establishment

The universities that will be invited to establish institutions in these SEZs for higher education will be based on transparent criteria with the main objective of building world-class universities in India. These universities could be both Indian as well as international universities, but will necessarily need to have educational standards that are comparable to the best in the world.

There is a need for an enabling legislation at the national level that will help establish these universities in any part of the country through a Central government initiative. The legislation should have a clear mandate and autonomous institutional mechanisms that will foster the establishment of world-class universities.

Regulation

The idea of SEZs is to create an ecosystem where certain rules and regulations that are applicable elsewhere may not be applicable within this framework. While this aspect of the Special Education Zones is indeed similar to the existing Special Economic Zones, the most important rationale for creating the SEZs in higher education is to significantly advance India's aspirations to establish world-class universities. For this purpose, the existing legal and regulatory framework needs to be re-imagined through the creation of SEZs in higher education. The governance of universities in SEZs should be based upon the best global practices of the involvement of all stakeholders in the university system with little or no governmental involvement.

Funding

The funding and resources for the establishment of world-class universities through the SEZs in higher education ought to come through the private sector and the international higher education sector. One of the important requirements for building world-class universities is the need for abundant resources. This may not come from the government as its priorities will inevitably be to expand opportunities in the higher education sector and create access to a large number of individuals.

At present, the not-for-profit private sector in higher education has little or no incentives to contribute to the creation of universities in India. The SEZs in higher education need to develop a vision that will significantly attract the wealthiest individuals and corporations to establish world-class universities through individual and corporate philanthropy. The existing tax structure and corporate social responsibility regulations need to be thoroughly re-examined to enable significant incentives for establishing universities in the SEZs.

* * *

The discussion in this chapter has highlighted that the transformation of Indian universities and its impact on seeking fundamental changes in the higher education arena is critical for the future of India. This transformation needs to be based upon a new imagination of Indian universities that have hitherto not been adopted. There is a need for transformation of the regulatory environment for seeking fundamental reforms in the higher education sector.

There is little doubt that the higher education sector is crying for reform and mindless proliferation of rules and regulations with numerous approval mechanisms and inspection regimes will not help in raising the quality of higher education, nor will it foster the promotion of excellence.

The entire university system in India is based upon a command and control system that at every stage has a multilayered, bureaucratic, government-led regulatory structure that not only controls, but also scuttles the freedom and liberty of academic institutions. This needs to change. The basic framework of most, if not all regulations in the Indian university system, is based upon a deep and pervasive distrust that prevails across the regulatory bodies for the university administration and the faculty. Universities are expected to be dynamic institutions where new ideas get tested, mistakes made and lessons learnt. This process of learning and constantly reinventing is not possible if regulations are made with the purpose of exercising controls leading to obstacles and hindrances for institution building.

The only way for Indian universities to change is to give more autonomy, independence and freedom so that they can find their own institutional space within India. Promoting excellence in Indian universities is not just a goal that is worthy of pursuing, but it is a policy imperative that needs to be achieved, for economic as well as social development.

2 An Invitation to a Thought Experiment

Quality, Diversity, and the Epistemics of University

Shiv Visvanathan

This chapter is an attempt to look at the question of quality within a wider vision of diversity and democracy. It is an effort to show how epistemological approaches to knowledge and democracy help to determine the quality of knowledge, life, and well-being in a society. In such an exercise, there are two ways to create policy from social science. One is to go with the formal way and launch huge surveys and extract information/data from detailed interviews. Beyond the formal social science with its professional rituals of evaluation, is an informal social science which thrives on gossip and the anecdote, which yearns to go beyond accepted categories, to talk of the possibility of alternative worlds. Instead of the case study with empirical details, one is content with an anecdote, a fragment of wishful thinking.

I want to begin with three such anecdotes, casual as rhizomes sprouting across more linear conversations. Like rhizomes, they cut across the tap roots of hierarchical thought and produce that bit of surprise, the frisson of an idea that makes conversation memorable.

THREE ANECDOTES

The first event dealt with a parent-teacher meeting in a Bangalore club on the feasibility of liberal arts in India. The university professors, most of them trained abroad, outlined their dream of a new liberal arts college. The students were keen in their response, candid in their questions about the availability of scholarships and future careers. One or two of the parents also chimed in anxiously. Some of the parents, both consumers and professionals, were silent and then one of them spoke about her dreams and what she had dreamt of doing 30 years ago. She said 'in my time we had no such courses and our worlds were more practical. We were asked to do home science or social work. Today, there is choice and I want my daughter to make those choices.' A bit later, she added wistfully 'I envy my daughter'. I wish I could do such courses. She shrugged indicating that the university segregated people by age sets.

I asked them, many of them, whether they would like to return to the university. They laughed in delight at the possibility and then dismissed it as wishful thinking.

The second story was an offshoot of a lecture I was delivering in a training course for colonels and brigadiers, stiff in their respectability. As a peacenik, I expected hostility when I cheekily claimed that the Indian army did not know how to fight the next war or the next place. The army, I claimed is one of the great literacy machines. It made sure that an uneducated *jawan* was an oxymoron. But today given the nature of technology and equipment, the Indian soldier, I claimed, was not ready for war. Then I added that the army was not ready for waging peace either. I was aware of transitions between military and civilian life but often saw it too narrowly as occupational transition, allowing for a transfer of the army into security services or pushing those with an MBA into the middle management. The army officer and the jawan become emasculated creatures, experiencing a sense that they have lost out in the civilian world. In fact, the very narrative of the transition reinforces the stereotypes regarding the army.

One of them added that what they need was relearning not reskilling. They needed heuristics and frameworks and not just a few certificates. When I suggested that the army should return to the university so that it could be transformed into a new kind of force, one of them responded that such a move 'would add to dignity'. The soldier becomes not a slot but a person.

The third example, poignant in its own way, came from a retired management executive, a middle-level practitioner who was laid off during a downsizing programme. He was 55 and completely distraught. Without a job, he claimed a middle-class man has no identity, literally no being. He claimed he worked his way up to senior position and that he does not have a PhD or the Ivy League degrees which hang like lichens on the elite. He said 'at least abroad, they have introduced the idea of professors of practice, here we want pristine world of Oxford and Columbia'. He asked in desperation what a university is, if it makes its citizens meaningless.

ENTER QUALITY AND IQ

I admit that these are not stories one hears at the standard educational conferences. If the conference is UGC related or sponsored, one needs to collect certificates, which like boy scout badges add up for promotion. It is a world of brownie points. It reminds you of an older era where IQ was fashionable, and social sciences went hysterical finding the right measures for it. Everyone mistook IQ for intelligence. It was like confusing temperature for heat, an index for an event. But the enthusiasm over IQ destroyed education, reintroduced racism, created a false elitism in education. Today IQ has been replaced by the idea of rankings. The president of India, pretending he is fashionable, bemoans the fact that there is no Indian institution in the Times Educational Supplement (TES) list of rankings that no university, Indian Institute of Technology (IIT) or research institute figures in the list.[1] The news and the rankings, now exhumed by

[1] Pandey, Neelam. 2016. *Hindustan Times*. 'No Indian Institute among Top 200 World Universities, Experts Worried,' available at http://www.hindustantimes. com/education/experts-worried-about-lack-of-indian-representation-in-global-university-rankings/story-PnB8AeIYbrAEUxobloFpiP.html, accessed on 19 May 2017.

the Indian academe, is being treated as pathologist's report, a pre-emptive obituary for the university. The planning commission and the UGC arrange the seminars, set up committees to examine this fatal case of educational lag. The Indian elite always comes belatedly to a crisis. When Marx said 'History repeats itself twice, first time as a tragedy, second time as a farce', one almost feels he was referring to Indian educationists.[2] They never see the tragedy of Indian education but they can reduce any crisis to a farce with ritual alacrity. The reformist's response is always an attack on symptoms, where reform seeks prescriptions without aetiology. The diagnosis is knee-jerk and the cure, cosmetic.

THE KNEE JERK RESPONSE: THE IIT SYNDROME

While educational consultants and accreditation experts run rampage, the debate follows predictable lines. With every lag, the educational elite feels the umbilical cord with the West lengthening. With every crisis we become more colonial, demanding that Oxford, Harvard, or MIT be reproduced in India. These are no doubt great institutions and reflect embedded traditions and complex genealogies of knowledge. We become a race of mimic men, where every reform feeds the informal economy of consultants and tutorial colleges. At one level, our government quickly establishes a longer chain of IITs and IIMs (Indian Institutes of Management) cloning these institutions and reproducing them in literally every state. This response is cleverly tactical because it is a brilliant hybrid of the populist and the elitist. The IITs and IIMs are seen as the creamy layer of institutions, a virtual guarantee to an American university, a green card to the western world. The states are happy as they feel that there is distributive justice, an IIT in every state is a guarantee of an export house in every region. Simultaneously, the elitist nature of the IITs's reputation gives one a feeling of a democratization of quality and equality. It is a win-win situation that the world of electoral politics loves. The dreams are magical. An epidemic of IITs and IIMs should grant us some place in the future world of ranking.

No one has done a sociology of IITs to look at the human cost of an IIT. The number of suicides among the students is legendary. One of the IITs went to desperate levels of removing ceiling fans from hostels in a hope that it prevents suicides. The IITs also create an informal economy

[2] Marx, Karl. 1852. *The Eighteenth Brumaire of Louis Bonaparte*.

of coaching institutions and coaching towns like Kota, in Rajasthan, where the entrance exam becomes the holy grail. Children who do not make it, feel the stigma of exclusion for decades as their parents and siblings remind them of it. In fact, the attitude is so pathetic that recently a first rate student expressed his claims to excellence by announcing that he missed entry to IIMs by one percentile.

At another level educationists, in their hurry to turn education into an industrial world of productivity and quotas, paid little heed to the reflective comments of our former environment minister, Jairam Ramesh, who observed that IITs are hardly places to pursue research. Another scientist and a professor explained to me that IITs as an educational system, produce convergent rather than divergent thinking. In fact, he mentioned in an aside that this is the secret crisis of the IIT. He said the power of quizzes and examinations is two-fold. By turning education into a game, it destroys the sense of play. It makes education more competitive and instrumental rather than dreamy and playful. The first consequence of this for many middle-class Indians is that it destroys childhood, the sense of joy one obtains from dream time. It also destroys play and the possibility of alternatives, it creates a world of convergence where the student knows that there is only one official answer. As a result, there was no attempt to think of alternatives or even rework the question. Another leading scientist, a director of a premier physics institute said, 'We Indians are great summarizers. We are not originals but we can present someone else's original idea brilliantly. We are like an intellectual secretariat to someone else's original idea. We execute an idea but never or rarely conceive of an original one. As a result, we are not original in research but conduct an exam and we will be there. We are a nation of first class firsts'. Another great engineer, once Dean of IIT Kanpur, an expert on fluid dynamics, claimed that Macaulay was right. We are clerks to the world. What he said of literature and culture is true of engineering and the sciences. We are a technical secretariat to the world. As technologists, we are objects of outsourcing. We run the call centres of the world. The creativity and communication lie elsewhere. The scientist later added, an IIT is an intellectual plantation, a prison house of the mind for export. He dubbed it odourless, colourless, and lethal.

A sociologist who taught at one of the IITs said, the IIT is like iceberg. 'The ice cap you see is the creamy top'. He then stopped and said 'no, my metaphor is wrong. An IIT is an ant hill. Do not look at the five major

institutes, each supported by a foreign power, look at the educational ancil-
laries the system spawns', I was perplexed. He said:

> Look at the tutorial colleges, the study centres, the IIT spawns. It is the
> cult of entrance exams that makes the IITs such a monotheistic religion.
> Students do not look at any other field. But you have to admit that IITs create
> jobs. They are all in the informal economy of education. The start-ups are in
> the parallel economy. I am sure the turnover of these colleges is more than
> the value generated by all the IIT entrepreneurs put together.

THE PROBLEM OF SCIENCE

One began with the critique of IITs because at the moment of crisis, we
whip them out as an example. Deep down we have to realize that they often
integrate us into the corporate industrial complexes of the world.

One must add that the fate of science is not very different. Homi
Bhabha, the founder of Tata Institute of Fundamental Research (TIFR),
once complained that the establishment of the Council for Scientific and
Industrial Research (CSIR) had only one effect. It destroyed the pursuit
of science in the universities. It governmentalized science, destroying
the university as the place that combined teaching and research accre-
tive functions.

THE NATURE OF DISCOURSE

I began with this array of examples to emphasize that education in
India and university in particular is embedded in the wrong discourse.
In fact, the university is never read as a culture of knowledge. It is seen
instrumentally as an employment creation centre, as a relevance generating machine. In fact, one almost forgets it is a social construction of
knowledge, a classification of knowledge systems, expressing many of the
dualisms, tensions, and the creativities of knowledge. As a discourse, we
have to ask the following questions. How does the university as a classification of knowledge work? In fact, what is knowledge? How does one
look at the relation between university and state, between knowledge
and power? Are the dualisms between science and religion, pure and
applied knowledge, still valid? Is the university as a knowledge system
exclusive or does it include the infinite varieties of knowledge? What is

the role of the university in the knowledge societies of today and in the Enlightenment discourse?

As one looks at the discursive nature of the university as a representative and trustee of knowledge systems, one realizes that many of the debates that occur, fail to ask fundamental questions. Part of the reason for this, as many dissenting educationists have realized, is the colonial hangover and legacy. The debate, the narrative of university education, has been embedded within a colonial model, what social scientists would call a centre-periphery model.

THE CENTRE/PERIPHERY MODEL

The centre/periphery or the metropolis/province model is a cognitive mapping of knowledge in terms of power and creativity. The centre is the source of power, of creativity. The colony is only a place for the absorption of knowledge created elsewhere. The centre is the source of invention, the colony, the site for the diffusion of knowledge. Within such a discourse, Western knowledge is superior. As Thomas Babington Macaulay, the patron saint of every Indian Babu, claimed that not all the civilization of India was worth a shelf of western books. He dreamt of creating a nation of clerks brown in skin but bleached white in their imagination. The university system that appeared as a result of the Woods dispatch of 1854 created the universities of Calcutta, Madras, and Bombay.[3] The battle between orientalists and utilitarians ended in the victory of the latter and these three universities were colonial creations, basic embodiments of western knowledge.

THE INDIAN UNIVERSITY: A MAP

The Indian university had always been a site of contestation, a subject of debate. I think it is important we break the linear narratives of this debate where there is a clear linear line between Macaulayite contempt for India and the global idea of rankings. We have to ask what was the nature of critique as a search for equality, quality, and diversity and what were its implications? A quick map of educational critique of the Indian university

---

[3] Macaulay's Minute on Education. 1835.

would include six basic positions. In a synchronic sense, we can classify six intellectual and political viewpoints.

First, the modernizers and their siblings, the nationalists who wanted more of western education criticizing not the civilizational aspect of the university but its political economy and sociology.

Second were the colonialists themselves who lampooned the university for its mediocrity. But a third group included 'the other colonialists' who saw in India creative possibilities the West had abandoned. The metaphor of knowledge as a hierarchy now becomes a spiral. Indians, in criticizing the early wave of nationalist education, asked what would be a civilizational response to western knowledge and the university. This produced a wonderful array of questions about the relation about knowledge, adding to the quality and equality, the critical question of diversity. One will quickly outline this debate and then connect it to the later debates on globalization.

Nationalism at one level was imitative. It sought to replace the brown, with the white. It sought an equivalent competence without producing a critique of knowledge. It wanted science and technology with a vengeance. The virulence of Macaulay and the enthusiasm of the nationalism complemented each other in the search for western knowledge. Representatives of this was a voice like Har Dayal who claimed 'Benaras and Puri have had their day.[4] What is there in Benaras but fat bulls and fat priests. What is there in Puri but Cholera.' Here Western knowledge becomes the marker of modernity and the sign of quality. The colonial mentality of invidiousness enters along with mimicry. We seek to imitate the best as an act of liberation. Colonialism is separated from the enlightenment and the university becomes the repository of valid universal knowledge. In a modernist sense, epistemologically western knowledge is valid, legitimate knowledge. Traditional knowledge is now outside the domain of legitimate knowledge. It is now an 'ethno-science'.

The colonialists were not all orientalists. Complementing the Orientalists were the theosophists, who saw in the East sources of Gnostic wisdom, who waxed ... 'gnostalgic' about the lost libraries of Alexandrea. There was an attempt to rectify the hegemony of dominant western knowledge by showing how the West had suppressed the alternative ideas of knowledge in itself. The works of Besant, Blavatsky, Oliver Lodge, Goethe,

---

[4] Har Dayal, 'The Health of the Nation', *Modern Review*, July 1912, *12*: 43–9; quote on p. 48.

and Octavian Hume talked of an esoteric knowledge as a complement of exoteric knowledge.[5]

If theosophy was one variant of the other colonialisms, the work of Patrick Geddes provided a second variant constituting a formidable critique of both the Indian nationalist movement and its conceptions of the university.

ENTER GEDDES

Patrick Geddes was an ecologist not merely of nature but he extended the idea of ecology to knowledge systems. Geddes argued that the career of a university must be seen as a dialogue of knowledges, often with competing notions of knowledge present in the environment.[6] The university as an ecological system survived by providing a working synthesis between competing systems of knowledge. The university, Geddes claimed, had to have a synoptic view of knowledge. For example, the 'medieval university arose out of an attempt to reconcile the doctrines of the Christian church with the recovery of Aristotle'. The medieval university became the Renaissance by imbibing the new learning from the fugitive Greeks, and incorporating the new art of printing from wondering scholars and craftsmen. The renaissance university grew into the contemporary German university. The Germans combined the French idea of the encyclopaedia, the idea of the French philosophies breaking it into constituent articles like algebra, architecture, anthropology, and creating chairs or departments around each. The architectonic of the encyclopaedia was morphed into the architecture of the university. Geddes also pointed out

[5] Besant, Annie. 1897. *Ancient Wisdom* (Madras: Theosophical Publishing House).

Blavatsky, Helene. 1968. *Isis Unveiled* (Los Angeles: The Theosophy Company).

Lodge, Oliver. 2017. *Man and the Universe: A Study of the Influence of the Advance in Scientific Knowledge Upon Our Understanding of Christianity* (S.l.: Routledge).

Uberoi, J. P. S. 1984. *The Other Mind of Europe: Goethe as a Scientist.* (New Delhi: Oxford University Press).

Hume, Allan Octavian, S. R. Mehrotra, and Edward C. Moulton. 2004. *Selected Writings of Allan Octavian Hume* (New Delhi: Oxford University Press).

[6] Geddes P. 1904. *On Universities in Europe and India, Five Letters to an Indian Friend* (Madras: National Press).

that the best of knowledge in a holistic sense was also democratized. The Germans added to the French idea of knowledge, a Chinese invention; the examination system. Simultaneously, the ideas of liberty, equality, and fraternity were translated into the new ideas of freedom and teaching. The Germans added to knowledge, the idea of independent specialized research and the minute division of labour. They supplemented it by drawing a hyphen between the state and the university. The German University was a microcosm of the modern university.

Patrick Geddes pointed out that the Indian nationalist movement had created a sub- Germanic university by ignoring the Enlightenment University of the Germans and following the London University of the time. London University was an examination machine, a university dedicated to the idea of knowledge as a well digested summary.

Geddes, in fact, had a devastating critique of the Indian idea of a western university the nationalists, he claimed, read and imitated the wrong West.[7] It read the West of Palaeolithic mechanical era before the advent of thermodynamics and ecology as an imagination. The Indian university was based on an outdated West rather than on a reading of the new ecological West, the other West which dreamt of a post-Germanic university. By instituting a pre -Germanic university the Indian university was magnifying the pathologies of the West. Second, the Indian university had ignored its own dissenting and competing forms of knowledge. As a result, all it did was to create an unreal provincial situation where Indians were proficient in English but otherwise useless for all practical purposes. Geddes warned against this imitative logic where Indians created the Ranjit Singhis of knowledge. Geddes, however, cautioned that the great cricketer like Ivanhoe was the worst example of original knowledge. Instead, Geddes talked of the J.C. Bose's science, who not only promised new paradigms but a new cosmopolitanism of knowledge. An ecology of quality did not need the Darwinian idea of competition, advocating the survival of the fittest but an idea of diversity where varieties of knowledge niched themselves to create a new interdisciplinarity. The Indian university and its exam system created a dumbing down of knowledge which achieved neither equality nor quality. It produced mutants which marked the human disaster of the system.

---

[7] Geddes, Patrick. 1920. *The Life and Works of Jagadis C Bose* (London: Longmans, Green and Co.).

THE NEW COSMOPOLITAN: BOSE AND SRNIVASMURTHI

The scientists in the national movement like J.C. Bose, P.C. Ray, and others wrote memoirs about their efforts to teach within a colonial model of the university.[8] They realized that either one produced mediocrity or one was forced to be eccentric or exotic, pressed to create an orientalist idea of knowledge. Geddes,[9] Bose, and Tagore worked to create a cosmopolitan idea of the university and of science which involved neither a revivalist idea of Indian knowledge nor an imitation of the West. Cosmopolitanism allowed you to transcend both and the university was a vehicle for cosmopolitan knowledge. For Tagore and Bose, quality was question of creativity, invention, and content and this they tried to create in their idea of Santiniketan.

The idea of an ecology of knowledge where diversity and plurality defined both quality and content also appeared from a civilizational idea of knowledge which challenged the hegemonistic classification of the university. One of the most original epistemological attempts to create a pluralistic idea of knowledge and embody it in the idea of the university was the work of the theosophist doctor, Captain Srinivasmurthi.[10]

Srinivasmurthi as a western medical practitioner who realized that western medicine was incomplete as a theory of science, health, wellbeing, and the body. He challenged two oppositions central to the classification of university as a knowledge system. First, the opposition between science and religion and second, the opposition between western science and the other sciences. A dialogue of medical systems was to him the model of a university system, where plurality as diversity created the new fraternities of knowledge.

---

[8] Geddes, Patrick. *The Life and Works of Jagadis C Bose* (London: Longmans, Green and Co, 1920).

Ray. P. C. 1932. *Life and Experience of a Bengali Chemist* (Calcutta: Chuckervertty, Chatterjee & Co. Ltd).

[9] Geddes, *On Universities in Europe and India, Five Letters to an Indian Friend.*

[10] Srinivasmurthi. G. 1923. 'Secretary's Minute', *Report of the Committee of Indigenous Systems of Medicine* (Madras: Government Printing Press), p. 20.

I am emphasizing the debates about knowledge and the university not for historical reasons but to show their contemporary relevance of the current problems of the university. Built on the centre-periphery model, it either became revivalist, imitative, or contentious, while the debates of knowledge and creativity in the discourses of nationalism were pluralistic and original.

In the next section, we will look at contemporary debates about the university to extend the meditation on creativity in the creativity.

THE NEW DEBATES

The advent of independence limited horizons. What we created were new ideas of modernity and modernization which resulted in an idea of a standardized modern university. Once one accepted the standard paradigm of university the debates shifted to competitiveness in quality, mobility, and productivity. The university became an extension of the nation-state and industrial system. India was relegated to being a third world society with a third rate university system and debates on quality became less ecological and more bureaucratic and industrial. As a result of democratic pressures, the university became a porous system, open to reservation on grounds of backwardness and caste. By the 1980s and 1990s of the last century, one realized the rules of knowledge game had changed. The new notion of globalization and capitalist industrialism sought to incorporate the university into a factory system. Second knowledge itself became a source of wealth and intellectual property. With globalization one realized that countries like China and Korea had invested heavily in their university system, integrating economy and education. In fact, as liberalization took over standardization, economic productivity efficiency threatened the culture of old university. The new enthusiasts of reform introduced management and technocratic models of seeking to make number of measures for quality.

The debates about quality also showed a level of self-criticality. Quality and search for quality as an imitative modes were was seen as iatrogenic. In fact, the very word 'iatrogeny' which was originally a reference to doctor induced illness-raised two aspects of the search for quality. First, it was an expert-induced phenomena. Here measure and quantity were seen as impersonal indicators of the phenomena. Second, that the idea of quality could be counter-productive and in fact turn reductionist, anti-plural and monolithic. In fact, quality could become an elitist tool. The debates around the science and the university in the 1980s and 1990s of the last century captured the new context within which the quality debates and the relevance of the modern university had to be redefined.

NEW DEVELOPMENTS

First given the logic of development and the Cold War; the university as a cultural system became suspect as a domain of irrelevant ideologies and as distant from immediate and long range needs of economy. The university in the West was part of the military-industrial complex and seen as a weapon of the Cold War. Ironically as the environment of the university hardened, the nature of knowledge and knowledge systems changed.

In fact, this was a part of the cumulative charges in knowledge in the twentieth century. The nature of the university was transformed by six revolutions. This included the quantum revolution in physics which transformed the mechanical idea of the reductive observer, the linguistic revolution which created an alternative model of science, the knowledge revolution which created new questions about epistemology, validity, and heuristic power of knowledge turning knowledge holistic and interdisciplinary, the genetic revolution that created a new definition of life, the information revolution that speeded up access and storage of knowledge as a network society. This was grounded in a democratic revolution which challenged science as an expertise and reworked the idea of the citizen as a knowledge consuming and producing creative and ethical revolution which showed that cognition has to be a form of ethical competence demonstrating that the age of a value neutral science was over. New ideas of feminism, ecology, multiculturalism created new domains of interdisciplinarity which demanded new forms of dialogue and reciprocity from different sectors of the university. The idea of the university as a knowledge system had to face the following issues. First, the model of development had become violent seeking to eliminate ways of life and ways of being. Knowledge no longer could be treated as immaculate innocent or antiseptic. One needed mechanisms to protect alternative knowledges from the hegemony of science.

Second, the very attempt to technocratize or mangerialize or create economistic evaluation of knowledge turned counter-productive for old definitions of quality. In fact, the innovation chain which was seen as a paradigm of efficient, integrated technical knowledge now had to face questions obsolescence, complexity mono-cultural violence which has not been entered into the old notions of quality as accountancy. The very idea of climate change changed the idea of university as a republic of specialized knowledges.

The sense that knowledge in the university could no longer exist in an ivory tower had to face new forms of violence which could be connected to the way knowledge systems were conceptualized. Three forms of mass violence-genocide, the wilful elimination of a people or cultural extinction, the large scale disappearance of species, languages as a result of man-made violence and apocalypse triggered by science related activities demanded new dimensions of ethics beyond the face-to-face dyadic interactions.

In a cultural sense, the standardization idea of uniformity, was being challenged by new movements for diversity which not only questioned old canons but created new domains of interdisciplinarity like feminist studies, science studies, and cultural studies which had implications for a whole range of disciplines.

The democratization of knowledge challenged the hegemony of expert knowledge demanding new epistemologies of science covering domains from risk, cyberspace complexity, panarchy which demanded new synergies from the university as a classificatory system.

Spurred by all these changes a new generation of ideas challenged the old ideas of quality.

THE NEW REPONSES

One of the first responses stemmed from the old battles against colonial hegemonic notions of western knowledge. These ideas did not stem from fundamentalist groups but a third world 'critical theory' which realized that the university as a repository of western canons of knowledge might lower the quality of life and value in a multi-cultural sense.

THE MULTIVERSITY

The first was the idea of the multiversity present in the writings of scholars like Claude Alvarez, Zia Uddin Sardar, Ashis Nandy and institutionalized through the agency of civil society groups like the Third World Network (TWN) in Malaysia.[11]

Mohammed Idris, president of Third World Network, spoke for many in the third world complaining that the university was an embodiment of sterile knowledge created by colonial institutions set up expressly with the purpose of destroying our creativity and identity. It was a Trojan horse that needed re-working. It was part of a continuous process of 'occidentosis' which epistemologically conditioned people to accept forms of knowledge which were anti-nature, anthropocentric and individualistic. Rather than being an encyclopaedia of holistic, synoptic, and universalistic knowledge, it is a form of hegemonic parochialism. The western university rather than being a standard paradigm had to re-examine its relationship to the other.

The aim of the multiversity launched during the Citizens International at Penang in February 2002 was to create a set of learning opportunities which were more diverse and creative. The continuity of the colonial system was seen as anathema to many people. As Claude Alvares argued that one of ironies of the Independence movement was that our freedom fighters after fighting doggedly tiredly succumbed to uncritically pursuing the educational project that they had inherited from their colonial masters.[12] The advocates of the multiversity realize that globalization consolidates colonial processes. With the downward of globalization and WTO regimes, the current education system is getting skewed to produce workers for the global machine.

The multi-university sees the world of quality control and rankings as a hegemonic order of the market and seeks to recover the new notions of play, culture, childhood, creating new epistemologies of knowledge. Implicit in it is a critique of history and epistemology, an attempt to create new creation myths for knowledge.

---

[11] Alvares, Claude. 2006. *Multiversity: Freeing Children from the Tyranny of Schooling* (Other India Press).

Sardar, Ziauddin and Ziauddin Sardar. 1988. *Islamic Futures: The Shape of Ideas to Come* (Selangor Darul Ehsan, Malaysia: Pelanduk Publications).

Nandy, Ashis. *Traditions, Tyranny, and Utopias: Essays in the Politics of Awareness* (New Delhi: Oxford University Press, 1999).

[12] Alvares, Claude. 2006. *Multiversity: Freeing Children from the Tyranny of Schooling* (Other India Press).

First, the university must retain the culture of play and plurality which allows epistemologies, heuristics, and metaphors to be seen in an experimental sense. Plurality demands dialogue and dialogue seeks to retain the identity of each part within a more holistic world of knowledge.

Second, the notion of epistemology was not the restrictive model of the scientific validation of knowledge in the laboratory but a cultural redefinition where epistemology as a knowledge system connected life, life style, life cycle, livelihood, life systems, and life chances. From an epistemological view any form of knowledge which protects the way of life of people is valid and therefore cannot be museumized. The multiversity thus encodes a notion of cognitive justice which attempts to protect the right of knowledge systems to debate and dialogue with science, without being hegemonized, hierarchized, or subject to systems of apartheid.

The idea of such a multiversity also challenges the idea of the museumization of knowledge. It challenges the split between preserving the folk song while eliminating the way of life of the folk singer. The vision of multiversity argues that knowledge should be part of a living tradition and therefore a science that racks of death and formaldehyde cannot be part of living the life giving tradition of knowledge.

The multiversity also challenges the hegemonic narratives of knowledge demonstrating for example that western science could not have survived without the generosity of the Arabs who translated and improved upon the learning of the Greeks. Translation and dialogue substitutes this for any hegemonic notion of knowledge.

THE FRONT YARD AND BACKYARD

The idea of cultural diversity present in the multiversity is also present in other variants of the university as a knowledge system. One such vision was articulated in the writings of the novelist and socialist of universities Ananthamurthy's views are representative of another of alternative thought. Ananthamurthy differentiates between models which emphasize centre-periphery and models of backyard.[13] Such ideas of dominance eventually talk of liberation which often becomes imitative. Ananthamurthy argues

---

[13] See Sadana, Rashmi. 2012. *English Heart, Hindi Heartland: The Political Life of Literature in India* (Ranikhet: Permanent Black).

that beyond centre-periphery there is a different way to conceptualizes ideas. He uses the cultural idea of front yard and backyard.

The centre-periphery idea of the university elaborates the hegemonic idea of a system. But the idea of front yard and backyard is more folksy. The metaphor derives from the architecture and anthropology of a Karnataka house. The front yard, he observes, was the domain of the male, the formal, the official. His father met visitors, officials, strangers in the front yard. The backyard including the kitchen was the domain of women, of gossip, of the informal, and the unofficial. The model of front yard-backyard helps domesticate foreign knowledges better. The backyard is *desi* and most of India's great thinkers from Gandhi to Tagore to Nanak were desi thinkers. The backyard is the domain of dialects and vernaculars and it is the backyard that prevents the hegemonization of knowledge. Translation becomes critical.

Ananthamurthy claims such a model emphasize the vernacularization of knowledge. He claims that illiterates in India speak four to five languages and adds that the sadness of an English language university begins with the fact that convent school students speak only one language. The decline of diversity is the first sign of a hegemonic knowledge system. For the novelist the uniform nature of the modern university is tied to the uniformity of nationalism where the new social contract of the nation-state and university standardizes knowledge quality then addresses an impoverished world.

THE INFORMATION REVOLUTION AND THE UNIVERSITY

The third model of university begins with the notion of information revolution. The information revolution created a challenge to the systems of knowledge by speeding up storage, accelerating retrieval, and flattering hierarchies through networks. The first folklore idea of knowledge was a downloaded system. As access to knowledge increased teaching as a face-to-face idea confronted a crisis of communication. Second, the digital revolution demanded a differentiation of concepts in terms of life worlds of time and space as community. The university had to confront knowledge and communication on several axes. First, as knowledge, information, and wisdom. Second, it had to differentiate oral, textual, and digital forms of knowledge. Third, it had to confront the market in terms of three spaces of knowledge as public, network, and commons. The idea of knowledge was distanced from commoditization and re-located as non-hierarchical, consumption-sensitive, space where knowledge was no longer privatized but belonged to a diversified commons. The technologization of knowledge had created a new model for the democratization of university. One needed new sets of indices to mark quality, rather than being an atomistic marker. Quality became a rational term. Quality was what added to the whole which increased diversity creating a new pool of alternative knowledges, turning the university into a trustee, a commons for forms of defeated knowledges.

THE EMANCIPATIVE IDEA

The fourth model of university redefining notions of quality stem from the works of Dos Santos, Nandy, Visvanathan, and Sardar.[14] It can be applied to questions like Climate change which is seen as representing a crisis in the current form of knowledge. The epistemics of such a university goes beyond quality as a still life notion to redefine knowledge and the knowledge community. First, quality or well-being or justice demands a distinction between liberatory and emancipative knowledge. The distinction formalized in the work of Boaventura Dos Santos marks two notions of knowledge. Liberation is the overthrow of the oppressor where the oppressed in turn can turn oppressor. Liberation has no filters against turning oppressive or submissive. Nationalism is liberative knowledge. Emancipation seeks to examine the possibility of oppression. It realizes that any form of knowledge can turn dominant and seeks to build pluralist conditions against such a possibility.

---

[14] Santos, Boaventura De Sousa. 2016. *Epistemologies of the South: Justice Against Epistemicide* (London: Routledge, Taylor & Francis Group).

Davies, Merryl Wyn, Ashis Nandy, and Ziauddin Sardar. 1993. *Barbaric Others: A Manifesto on Western Racism* (London: Pluto Press).

Visvanathan, Shiv. Democracy, Plurality and Indian University. *Economic & Political Weekly* 35(40) (September 30, 2000), available at http://www.epw.in/journal/2000/40/special-articles/democracy-plurality-and-indian-university.html.

Visvanathan, Shiv. 2009. 'Towards Cognitive Justice.' 2009. *Seminar*, no. 597 (May 2009), available at http://www.india-seminar.com/2009/597/597_shiv_visvanathan.htm.

Sardar, Ziauddin, Sohail Inayatullah, and Gail Boxwell. 2003. *Islam, Postmodernism, and Other Futures: A Ziauddin Sardar Reader* (Sterling, VA: Pluto Press, 2003).

Second, emancipative knowledge fights against obsolescence. Defeated knowledge is reinvented. Notions of repair become critical and emancipative knowledge unlike modern science realizes that the other side of obsolescence is innovation. The logic of innovation haunts the university and the market and defence establishment but there are no rights for an obsolescent people and their knowledges. It is in this context that we suggest that the university develops as a fold, a generational set where the ritual cycle of a university unfolds and encloses two generations, the first between 17 and 25 and the second between 40 and 65. The learning systems of the two and the tacit knowledges must be different the university now becomes not market driven but democracy driven where citizenship and knowledge must be repaired, recycled and retreated all the time.

Third, the social contract of knowledge must be redrawn. Knowledge contracts are limited and local but by bringing nature into the social contract we redraw the epistemics of knowledge and show nature as the basis of the livelihood of marginal groups. Marginal knowledges and the diversity of nature become the new kinds of trusteeship in the university.

The university is not only an archive of oral knowledge. It transcends its boundary to understand informal knowledge. In fact as a new repository of diversity, it connects eccentric, dissenting, and marginal knowledges. Now quality is not about competition, or the Darwinian power of the brand but about sustainability, sustainability needs a new epidemics of knowledge which the emancipated university must provide.

Thus, we move from quality as measure to well-being in a lived world. In a deep sense knowledge moves to being a public good in common. The democratization of the university and the search for quality begins by redefining the demands of citizenship. The university as a knowledge system reworks the enlightenment project. One began with German and French universities with their idea of liberty, equality, and fraternity. We realized that such a university was confronted by the industrial revolution with its ideas of productivity, rationality, and efficiency. Quality and the search for quality emerged as markers, remnants from this era. The tension between quality as market marker and freedom as a public good created its own impact on the world of knowledges. The clash of the two configurations created a third relationship between plurality, sustainability, and justice. The universality as a knowledge system becomes a new vision of democracy where quality goes beyond productivity, and brand to guarantee new ways of life and well-being.

3 The Future of Indian Universities

Voices from within Beckoning for the Future

Indira J. Parikh

VOICE OF A LEARNING INSTITUTION: 'HAUNTING MEMORIES'

I have existed from time immemorial
I have witnessed generations come and go
Theories have evolved, philosophies have been born
The flow of knowledge merges into ocean of wisdom

I have stood for values of life and living
I have stood for morals and ethics
Once I stood firm and tall
With no storm or hurricane to uproot me

Then I was vanquished
Enslaved, shackled and
chained the nation forgot that
I existed
And they ran after that which was to shame them

I was lost in the debris of technology
My assets were burnt or destroyed
And slowly I was lost in the labyrinth of time
Forgotten that I ever existed
The cultural memory of me was wiped out
The social memory disowned me that I ever existed
The families followed the new
And the child never had heard of me

Such is the fate of nations
Who loose pride in what they had
And run after what they did not
Turn themselves into beggars, borrowers, adapters and adopters

Nations bemoan the scarcity of talent
They bemoan the shame and indignity they heap on themselves
They hang their heads and turn into dwarfs
Nations O nations when will you ever learn

The institutions of learning
Rich and proud with heritage
Turned into debris
A voice in the wilderness never heard

Ravagement of what once was a land of wisdom
Turn into land of ignorance
From where the learning institutions
Rise from the ashes

The time has now come to awaken
To discover the soul and the spirit of the land
And give birth to the wisdom of tomorrow
The universities will shape of what is to come

To discover the gems from the ocean of wisdom
To shape the lives of the generation
And create universities of learning
For today and tomorrow

—Indira J. Parikh

Institutions of learning, centres of higher education, and the generation of today are the tripod over which the universities of any country are founded. Universities have existed from the time the human civilization began to settle down and developed roots to create permanent spaces to live for generations. Each civilization and society created its own institutions of learning with a purpose and a meaning relevant for those times. Societies evolve and perish, traditions grow and dissolve in the tides of time, and education gets formulated and outgrows the society and the generation for which it was designed. At present, the human civilization has evolved and reached both a threshold and a crossroad where each nation individually and globally has to make choices for the education they would like to provide for each different generation.

The debate on the nature of education is raging in the country as well as across the globe. This debate has become most relevant in the country as this is the time when the country, the institutions of higher education, and the educationists pause, review, reflect, and ask the basic questions to themselves and to the generation of students who are to enter the educational institutions. Universities in some form, shape, and structure are as ancient as the human race. They have evolved over centuries and are the repositories of the continuity of learning as well as define what is to come. As soon as a child is born, learning and education begins. Over time, education gets formalized and institutions get established so as to have a focused and uniform approach to learning. The learners spend a structured time and the institutions design intensive processes of learning. This is meaningful and relevant to prepare the generation for the life and occupations which await them. Over time, universities have become the process channel where the generations enter, acquire knowledge and skills, and move onto occupations and jobs.

India as a nation has been grappling with tough dilemmas and choices about education. Universities in India date back to several millennia. The country has a rich heritage of traditions and wisdom. Over time, with the history of any nation the educational institutions are set up, they grow and then decline. Today, in the twenty-first century, the country is reflecting on what to teach, how to teach, and whom to teach. What to teach gets determined by the socio-cultural context and the needs of the era, decade, century, and the millennium. How to teach gets determined by the values and philosophy of the institution, the faculty, and the teachers. It also gets influenced by the assumptions of learning in the teaching-learning process. Whom to teach gets determined by the generation of the times and the educational policies of the government. With the universalization of education and access to learning for each child, education is available to an increasingly large segment of the young population of Indian children. With technology taking over life, educational and workspaces has changed the connectivity between the teacher and the taught. It has also changed the relationship and relatedness across multiple layers of generations. The time has come for the institutions of higher learning to ask themselves the basic and fundamental questions about themselves, the universities as well as the learning structure and existing learning process.

HISTORICAL PERSPECTIVE

India is an ancient civilization. The country has a rich heritage of wisdom cumulated over millennia translated into many streams of knowledge. The country has inherited a rich legacy creating monuments reflecting grandeur, providing the civilizations with creative and intellectual spirit. Building the monuments must have required immense precision and understanding of many streams of knowledge. As the then kings and queens, emperors and the wealthy built their massive homes, temples, churches and the mosques, palaces and castles required for beauty, form, and aesthetics. They travelled across the oceans and land to trade and discover not only new lands but also new knowledge and evolution of civilization. There must have been educated and intelligent people in the country who with their insights and perspectives wrote the Upanishads and the Vedas and other philosophical treatises. However, other than the reference and mention of some Guru-kuls and ashrams in the ancient civilization, there are very little references on mass education of the larger population of the country. In some of the writings few references are available where it is stated that education was freely available only to the royalty, the elites, and the wealthy. The caste system further narrowed it to occupation and skills but not to learning and growth. There is of course mention of the two great universities Nalanda and Takshashila which seem to have flourished but were at some point of time in history destroyed. The references talk of the enormous volumes of work, the research, and the knowledge and wisdom available in the form of books in the library of that university. There is also a mention of the number of students, the diversity of the student population, the quality of knowledge generation, the spirit of learning, and the greatness of the institution.

Somewhere in the hoary history, the socio-cultural, and the national memory of education and its institutions of higher learning for the masses has been lost and forgotten in the wilderness of time. As such we do not know if there were institutions of higher education for the masses and larger population in the country. What we do know from the history of colonization is that institutions of higher education were started about two hundred years ago for basic elementary education across the nation. The objective was for the institutions of higher education to channelize and prepare a group of trained personnel required to implement the directions and instructions of the administration to govern the nation. Knowledge and learning as such was to prepare people to follow the rules and regulations, acquire skills to perform the required tasks and basically to be implementers of instructions.

There seems to be a major gap in the memory of the country and heritage of the continuity of knowledge and wisdom of the Indian civilization. Whatever be the reason, it leaves the present understanding of institutions of learning in a bit of a dilemma. How does one understand the present without the continuity or the discontinuity of the past? The attempt to understand the present context of the institutions of higher learning, the universities of today in India, the generation of today and the state they are in, is indeed a challenge. Some answers lie in history, while others lie in the choices made by the then intellectual elites of the country and the non-choices made by the population. It is important to explore the question even if we begin by the known history and then look to the future to respond to the needs of the present. For better or worse, we can explore the present to understand the past and visualize the future by understanding the generation of today. In order to do this, one must ask some basic questions. As the focus is on the future of universities, it is important to restrict the exploration to the universities.

The fundamental questions are:

1. What is the identity of the educational institutions/the universities?
2. What is the purpose of their existence?

3. Where are the universities going?
4. Where do the universities wish to go?
5. How do the universities wish to go where they wish to go?
6. Who are the people of the university?
7. What do the universities wish to create for tomorrow?

These and many more questions need to be asked and answered if this country now wishes to contribute to knowledge creation on the one hand and educate the generation which has lost interest in the educational institutions of higher learning, on the other. Let it be understood that this is not bashing of the universities, educators, or the young generation. This is to discover what is that the education and the universities need to discover to be generators and creators of new knowledge and ensure that the present and the future generation discover the magic of learning and life.

They have lost interest in the whole process of learning due to the way the institutions of higher education in general and the universities in specific conduct themselves. This chapter is not intended to indulge or engage in bashing of institutions of higher education and the universities. The purpose of this writing is to attempt to explore the status of why the institutions and the universities are where they are and what can be done about it. Let us also be very clear, that there is never a single phenomenon which leads a nation, an institution, or an individual to where it has landed or arrived. There are always multilevel, sequential, as well as simultaneous phenomena of reality which contribute and lead an institution to where it has arrived. It is important then to explore and identify those phenomena which has contributed, and then identify those processes which would alter the present status quo, and then initiate processes of transformation which would revitalize and energize the institutions and bring about their relevance for the times and the present generation.

Education is the life and spirit of a civilization. It is through the process of generating and acquiring knowledge that the civilization moves forward. It is only through the process of learning that real growth happens. From times immemorial, man has asked questions and sought answers to the mysteries of the universe. Generations after generations explored, discovered, and saved the pieces of the puzzle and created a discovery and an understanding of some aspects of the nature of the universe. It is also in this spirit of inquiry about the human existence, that philosophical perspectives of human existence have emerged. History is also a witness to show that when an individual, institution, or nation stops exploring or asking questions about the universe and themselves he/it start to stagnate and finally decay and disappear. Growth is an ongoing phenomenon and intellectual growth with the spirit of inquiry and exploration is an integral process of it.

The seven basic questions about the universities we need to ask.

1. What is the identity of the universities in India?

The universities of India today represent monoliths and monuments. Some universities have huge structures reflecting an era of glory and of creating some giants in their respective fields of knowledge. Yet, over time these very institutions have become obsolete, outdated, and uninspiring. They have large number of students who drift in and out of these spaces, wandering, meandering, and searching for knowledge and skills which would equip them for their occupations for life. The student population of the last century faced a different economic and a national scenario. Those were the times when the country was grappling with scarcity of education, opportunities, and jobs. They were thankful for admissions and the degree which provided them jobs. Education per say, was important, not what they studied but the fact that they were in the university gave them a social and personal status and hopes and aspirations for the future. Engineering, medicine of course was sought after as the numbers of admissions in those streams were in scarcity. Those admissions had a premium and only the students with a high rank could secure admissions.

As the demand for education increased, the value of being educated increased and as the numbers of students entering the universities multiplied, the quality of education based on the quality of students tempered by the preferential admission processes , began to make their negative impact felt. As the quality of rigour in education declined, the quality of faculty declined, and the quality of education suffered. Entry into different streams was pre-determined since school (science, art, and commerce), coupled with that, the lack of new and innovative curriculum and pedagogy led the students to lose interest in the learning process and the education which was being offered. The certificate or the degree became a stepping stone to enter into higher education, graduate and postgraduate degree. However, the learning and education became secondary. The universities were relegated to being spots for past time, coffee time, and fun time with friends. Universities began to age and be reduced to monoliths and monuments, outdated and obsolete. The life and creativity of the dynamic institutions of knowledge for the coming generation did not happen.

The universities have lost their identity as the spaces for creators and generators of knowledge, new ideas, and concepts. They lost their pull to challenge the young mind to dialogue, debate, and arrive at ideological principles to discover their own identities and convictions. The universities became spaces and places to fool around and criticize their teachers and grumble about the state of affairs of the universities. The universities also became politicized and the power centres began to emerge amongst both the students and those who governed the institution. In a matter of few decades, the universities transformed from an identity of the creators of future generation leaders to an identity anchored in the past traditions and lost the potency of innovation and creativity. Once upon a time, the great centres of learning and wisdom creators of giants in the field slowly but steadily started to decline into invisibility. Students started to search for education institutions outside of the country and what started out with a trickle has now grown into large numbers valuing education outside of the country.

2. What is the purpose of existence of these universities?

Universities of any nation are created and built for a purpose. The purpose is to prepare the youth for today and tomorrow so that they can engage with life and living processes and their own identity. Universities create spaces for learning for the present and future generation where the universities provide continuity of cumulative knowledge of centuries and cultures and understanding of discontinuities from the past to the present streams of emerging knowledge. The universities provide glimpses of what is to come in the future and how to prepare for the emerging scenario of the world. The purpose is generation of knowledge, availability of stored knowledge, and where new knowledge is reflected upon, so as to assess its implications for human existence. A major purpose of existence of universities is to create spaces where the students of any generation can come together to debate, enter into a dialogue, discuss, share, and roam into the world of ancient wisdom and old and new ideas. As the times change and the transformations occur, the universities need to be the forerunners of what is to come and beckon the young generation to respond with clarity, maturity, and understanding. However, at present, the whole purpose of existence of the universities has changed given their own attitudes, values, and ways of governing the universities.

The sacrosanct nature of the universities has been replaced with economic and commercial aspects which have silenced the spirit of the universities.

3. Where are the universities going?

The universities of today in India have become frozen in time. Their governance is anchored in structures of bureaucracy and power, controls and boundary maintenance, and ensuring that there is no meandering; wandering and or discoveries taking place.

Once the students enter—a particular stream of knowledge, the universities believe that a young student must decide even if the student is not sure of what he/she must choose for life. The universities insist that a student must make a choice even if it is a wrong one, but a choice the student must make and regret perhaps, for the rest of the life. The universities have created structures through such that the streams of knowledge must flow and those who enter cannot return for there is no exit to further explore to make a choice. The universities hold onto the past knowledge and make it so sacrosanct that the choices become carved in stone. The universities seem to be caught up in reflecting internally and at their own governance and the role of providers. What they provide is not to be questioned, only received. In this process the world has transformed, the universe has transformed but the universities have stood still and frozen.

4. Where do the universities wish to go?

Universities in India have woken up from the slumber and awakened to a new reality. They are experiencing the transformations and looking at their own frozenness and captivity of their roles from regulatory bodies. There are also new institutions emerging which reflect relevance and meaning. The universities are now exploring and are looking inward and outward. There has been an increase in retreats, conferences, seminars, conventions, debates, and dialogues to explore and ask question as to what next. The universities have to confront four major barriers and gatekeepers. First is the government regulatory bodies who because of their funding monitor the rules and regulations and oversee the functioning of the universities. These have served the purpose for which they were designed. The times when these regular institutions were set up were times when educational institutions were few and the demands for educating the population was just beginning to increase. New institutions were not permitted and the norms for starting educational institutions were rigorous. The resources required were very high. Few philanthropists supported the educational institutions and many did not wish to compete with the well-established institutions of repute and/or get involved with the bureaucracy of the government. The government funded many institutions and as such had control on the governance as to how the funds were to be utilized.

Similarly, the government educational boards designed the educational policies and the content of education through its various research bodies and committees and designed the conditions of various levels of education. These were largely woven around the existing core which had served the purpose for a long time. Tampering or changing—it was indeed a difficult proposition. Moreover, the core of the educational structure, assessment processes, and recruitment of faculty and administrators were anchored in the institutions started by the British a century and a half ago and it was difficult to redesign those. The universities attempted to do incremental and marginal changes which did not have an impact.

In such a restrictive environment the universities continue to remain frozen in time but continue to add new streams which were emerging through the industry requirements. The technology continued to pressurize the universities for relevant education and new emerging requirements of knowledge and learning. At the same time, the external environment was changing and the country was maturing in its freedom, and the young generation started to show different patterns of expectations and behaviour. The education from the universities started to lose their colour and the university space became a space for time pass and fun.

In this context and transformations, the debate and dialogue of where the universities wish to go began to acquire immense significance and importance. The light seems to be emerging after darkness. The whole process of questions and attempts to seek answers for creating a new path in a new direction is beginning to be glimpsed in the horizon. The sustainability of the momentum is very important.

5. How will the universities go where they wish to go?

The Government of India, the Ministry of Education, the Ministry of Human Resource Development, the University Grants Commission, the All India Council for Technical Education, and other such institutions of higher education, the educationists, the industry, and the parents all need to have a dialogue. This is possible when a forum is created for dialogue and debate. The leaders of education need to create and gather a group of individuals across the streams of knowledge to come together to reflect and explore the possibilities and probabilities of new initiatives. In the ancient times there was a concept of a Rajsuya Yagna. The concept of Rajsuya Yagna was not only war but also a process where the society assessed itself vis-à-vis the past and the present, aligned the present with the emergent realities and reconfigured what was relevant. It then anticipated the future and laid down some anchors and coordinates relevant for the times and aligned the processes. The debate explored the nature of what was the existing and—emergent and then designed the present—while anticipating the future.

It is only when the universities create such a forum for dialogue amongst the various constituencies that new meaningful coordinates of the universities, resurfacing of the vibrancy of the universities would take place. This would require immense creativity, relevance, keeping in mind the continuity and discontinuity of both the past and the present. It would require immense resources to be invested both in the teachers and the institutions.

6. Who are the people of the university?

The constituencies of the universities are the government, the regulatory bodies, administrators of the universities, faculty, students, and staff. These are the internal members. There are also the parents, the industry, and the global context. All these have grown into islands with no connectivity. Each has created boundaries and walls around their domains and there are only rules and regulations, policies and procedures, precedents and personalized exceptions; each wanting to have a say in everything and only form their point of view. Each constituency believes that they are the only ones who know what needs to be done and they are the only ones who know what is right. However, there is little dialogue or even discussion to understand the realities of each constituency. The government faces a massive challenge as the population is young, the skills required and occupations emerging are many and the competition global. The government sets up committees to explore and come up with recommendations many of which are relevant but hardly ever implemented.

The regulatory bodies understand the need of the hour but are helpless in the face of immense pressure to conform to what is demanded. The educational institutions are negotiating the existing regulations in the name of future promises of abiding. However, monitoring and implementation are so inadequate that the watering down of the quality and excellence begins to take place. The administrators are in power positions and they are caught in the web of contradictory pulls and pushes and torn asunder between the government, the bureaucracy, and the educators.

The next set of constituency is the faculty. The faculty are few, the demands many. The faculty is over engaged or underutilized, underpaid, or commercialized. This curriculum has remained the same and the predictability and monotone has increased.

Many have lost their vibrancy and passion. Those who retain the ideology, the vibrancy, and the passion are disillusioned and disenchanted with the status quo and stagnation of intellectual growth.

The next constituency is the students. The students represent the real freedom of free India. They are the sixth generation free Indians searching for their real identity, and a learning that would pull them to invest their effort and energy. They are part of small families, born and brought up with computers, iPads, mobiles, cartoons, branded clothes, and food and are most importantly intelligent. They are looking for open challenges, intellectual growth, and idealism. At the same time they are caught amidst the multiple attractions which pulls them and the peer pressure and the peer culture. The university's role and challenge is to transform all the energy of youth and to make them partners in the process of growth in shaping the university and building the nation.

The interplay of all these constituencies creates, builds, and shapes the universities of today and tomorrow. The challenge for the university and the task ahead is to transform the free energy of the youth, the structured and controlled energy of systems and the frozen energy of the inter-relationships between the constituencies and discover that path which can be journeyed jointly/travelled together.

7. What do the universities wish to create?

This is the century, the decade and the coming decades that the universities of this nation have, to be the space and the beckoning to be the innovators, creators, and generators of new knowledge, theories, and frameworks. In the global scenario of all nations in their own ways searching for new templates of education, life, and connections, there is a space to bring forth philosophy of life and social institutions. India needs to discover its own pride, dignity, and well-being and articulate the ethos and pathos of human existence in the context of societies. There is much wisdom and knowledge stored in the intellectual minds of the learned people of India. The universities need to bring all these into coherence and convergence. The universities have to ensure that the head is open to receiving and sharing knowledge, the heart is compassionate to the diversity and multiplicity of wisdom available and the spirit is experiencing the universe in all its magnificent glory. It is in this convergence that new institutions will be created and the magic of learning and decoding the mysteries of the learning will begin to happen.

If we delve deeper into the intellectual heritage of the country then some new directions may emerge and new paths can be created. The oldest of the Upanishads date from around 500 BC. These texts encouraged an exploratory learning process where teachers and students were co-travellers in a search for truth. The teaching methods used reasoning and questioning. Nothing was labelled as the final answer.[1]

The education supported residential schools. The teachers imparted knowledge of religion, scriptures, philosophy, literature, warfare, statecraft, medicine, astrology, and history. The corpus of Sanskrit literature encompassed a rich tradition of poetry and drama as well as technical scientific, philosophical, and religious texts.[2]

Two epic poems formed part of ancient Indian education. The Mahabharata, part of which may date back to the eighth century BC, discusses human goals (purpose, pleasure, duty, and liberation), attempting to explain the relationship of the individual to society and the world (the nature of the 'self') and the workings of karma. The other epic poem, Ramayana, is

[1] Gupta, Amita, *Going to School in South Asia* (Westport: Greenwood Publishing Group, 2007).

[2] Gupta, *Going to School in South Asia*.

shorter, although it has 24,000 verses. It is thought to have been compiled between about 400 BC and AD 200. The epic explores themes of human existence and the concept of dharma.[3]

Reflecting on this structure, form, and pedagogy of earlier learning institutions give us some insights into what once was and what we can now create. The Indian intellectuals and academia has much to offer and universities are one such institution which could be the provider of a learning environment which would give birth to a new intellectual spirit of the youth.

THE FUTURE OF INDIAN UNIVERSITIES

The time has come for the Indian universities to rise to the call of the nation and the generation of today and tomorrow to contribute to the nation with new choices and directions, to nurture a spirit of inquiry in pursuit and to create such knowledge as will make a difference nationally and globally. These will be the generation who would have meandered the many streams, walked many a path, climbed many a mountain, and then put down roots to create, build, and shape a new world.

AN EDUCATIONAL PERSPECTIVE OF THE FUTURE

Dramatic innovations are happening across the globe given the transformations occurring in the basic structures of education and in the spaces of educational institutions. The future of education is going to emerge as the most turbulent in the times to come. What has existed so far is going to be history. What is unfolding is unknown. But what is certain is that the education has to evolve and emerge where the students search and aspire for learning.

What is required are the following:

Institutions and universities will need to accept the person entering the portals of the university as a total human being which means his physical, social, spiritual, emotional, and psychological self and his multiple roles in numerous systems. It is after keeping all this in mind that the curriculum design would be relevant and meaningful to the entering student. It is then only that the students will connect with the life in the university and feel

[3] Brockington, John, 'The Sanskrit Epics', in Gavin Flood (ed.), *Blackwell Companion to Hinduism* (Oxford: Blackwell Publishing, 2003), pp. 116–28.

wholesome. Besides all the streams of knowledge like science, medicine, engineering, arts, commerce, and many others, the universities need to inculcate the basic ethos and pathos of human existence. Institutions of learning and universities will need to provide spaces for students to:

1. Differentiate truth from untruth
2. Differentiate dreams from fantasy
3. Differentiate reality from imaginary
4. Give shape to the identity of the students
5. Create centres of learning where learning is for life
6. Centres for discovery and experimenting which help them make choices
7. Spaces and places to grow up with values to govern their self
8. Spaces to learn and engage with diversity to accept co-existence
9. Spaces to differentiate ideology from oppressions and compulsions

The above pedagogical objectives are key to the social, cultural, and economic well-being of future generations. However, the realization of these otherwise desirable objectives will require clear and concerted efforts in the following key areas:

1. Education has to create a space where the students would aspire to come for discovering their passion as well as their calling.
2. The students must have a real appraisal of their context (cultural, social, familial, educational organizational, and environmental). This can only happen when the universities will create and design a multidisciplinary and multi-stream curriculum of education.
3. The universities of the future will have to cater to multiple mediums of instruction as well as learning.
4. Universities will have to be techno savvy which means that the faculty, students, staff, and the administrators will have to know and understand technology so as to use it for the learning purposes.
5. Each university will discover newer models and frameworks of teaching-learning so that it contributes to generation of new knowledge.
6. Competition and complexity will be the order of the day. This will mean universities will have to strive for excellence and innovation as much as creativity and discovery of relevant and meaningful methodologies of teaching and learning.
7. The educational institutions must be centres of discovery of truths. The educational institutions must be centres of wisdom, facilitating continuity of the past as well as creators of pathways to the future.

4 The Indian University in a Comparative Perspective

N.R. Madhava Menon

The purpose of looking at Indian universities in a comparative perspective is obviously to locate it among higher education institutions across the world and to identify its strengths and weaknesses in the advancement of learning and research. By doing it, one can discern the directions for reform in order to put the university system in a competitive advantage for an emerging knowledge society. It is a matter of concern that none of the Indian universities figure in the top rankings of world-class universities. But this need not be a factor in assessing the performance of our universities because of the diversities in policies and approaches, measurement criteria and anticipated outcomes of university education in India. Nonetheless, in a globalizing world, it is necessary to make comparisons, however irrelevant in the past, because of its implications to economy, trade, and investment for the future.

UNIVERSITIES AS ORGANIZATIONS IN DISTRESS

The Indian university today is not a uniform, monolithic organization as it is the product of a highly diversified and hierarchically organized multicultural society seeking to bring about unity in diversity. There was a time in Indian history when the famous Nalanda and Takshashila Universities offered higher education to scholars across the world and created knowledge through interdisciplinary research. Somewhere down the line, India lost that tradition and became a poor cousin to the higher education system evolved in Britain in the nineteenth century. Modern university education in India is fundamentally what the British introduced in its biggest colony for producing the cadres necessary to carry on the administration and defence of its territory. Universities performed that job well with the result that when the country became independent, it inherited a civil service which could manage the transition from a colony to a democratic republic without jeopardizing the constitutional values of democracy, human rights, secularism, and the unity of the nation.

On adoption of the Constitution and the Bill of Rights, the challenge was different and the country demanded from its higher educational institutions people qualified to take the socio-economic agenda forward and create an egalitarian social order through the instrumentalities of rule of law and democratic governance. Under the federal scheme, 'education' was initially in the state list and later shifted to the concurrent list in the framework of division of legislative powers. There was no way the universities could have developed independent of the constitutional scheme. The policies of educational governance varied from state to state in the initial decades of the republic. This is reflected in the huge body of judge-made education law governing universities and the disproportionate influence of political parties, big and small, in governance of academic bodies. In the process, learning and research took a back seat in many institutions and the dominant concern was maintaining campus peace, advancing influence of ruling cliques, and expanding access indiscriminately disregarding merit at all levels. Nowhere in the world one can find repeated judicial interventions in setting norms of student union elections, ragging prevention, admissions and examination, fee fixation, attendance issues, appointments to faculty positions, capitation fee, scope of reservation of seats in technical institutions, government interference in management of unaided and minority colleges, choice of textbooks, etc., as it happens in India. This has resulted, *inter alia*, in three independent developments which adversely affected higher education in significant ways. First, university as an organization got highly politicized with unholy alliances between academics and groups which have very little to do with education, constantly keeping universities as their battle-fields for power and influence. Second, the number of politician-teachers and non-teaching teachers grew steadily deflecting the attention of the academic community including students from learning and research thereby diluting standards. Corruption increased in admissions, appointments, and promotions creating a vacuum in educational leadership, and scholarship. Third, the pattern of financing got unnecessarily cluttered in centre-state conflicts leaving the state universities to gather funds from expansive affiliation and examination routes making the system thoroughly bureaucratic and unmanageable. Many universities found no time or resources for revision of curricula or for promotion of research for long periods. Vice-Chancellors spent their time in negotiating with government offices for funds and struggling to keep order and discipline in the campus. The cumulative result of these developments was the complete surrender of university administration (in states) to the powers-that-be in government and erosion of autonomy even in academic decision-making.

In the midst of such drift and dilution of academic and governance standards in most state universities, the central government went about setting up centrally sponsored universities and technical institutes and gave them liberal infrastructure support and research funding. Many of them showed promise in quality improvement. Their products, however, mostly migrated to foreign countries leaving the state universities to fend for themselves. Research was diverted from universities by establishing a chain of research institutions with central government funding. The central government using its power to legislate for co-ordination and determination of standards in institutions for higher education and research (Item 66 of List-I) enacted legislations like the UGC Act, AICTE Act, IGNOU Act, etc., to set the standards and police the erring institutions in the states. While pursuing their mission, these regulatory agencies had to settle on common *minimum* standards and an inefficient inspection and approval mechanism which allowed mediocrity and corruption to grow everywhere. Good institutions found the environment suffocating, autonomy eroding, excellence not getting recognition, and they being looked with suspicion for alleged nurturing of elitism and exclusiveness.

Nothing would have happened to this depressing scenario in which universities were placed in the last decade of the twentieth century but for the economic liberalization and the market seeking educated people in large numbers to manage the expanding private corporate sector. Given the fat pay packages offered to the really meritorious and the increasing demand for technical and professional graduates, the private sector found it good business and set up its own universities and colleges with better infrastructure and governance systems. Some sections revolted against what they called privatization and commercialization of education. The Supreme Court declared the principle of 'education-not-for-profit' and said that profit, if made in educational enterprise, it should be invested back for improving or expanding education. Private sector soon became big players in higher education both in the states as well as at the centre through what is called the deemed-to-be-universities route. The central government brought in a series of legislations which facilitated expansion and promoted pursuit of excellence in the higher education sector which are now awaiting parliamentary approval. The whole scenario is changing, thanks to the market forces and the new economic policy, the nation is talking today in terms of the emerging knowledge society and the 'Demographic Dividend' that India is awaiting to exploit!

POLICY CHANGES PROPOSED AND INITIATIVES UNDER WAY

There is no doubt that it cannot be business as usual anymore for Indian universities. They have to change and those reluctant to change will be forced by circumstances which includes the student body, the market forces, the civil society, and the government itself. The new regulatory regime contemplated under the National Commission on Higher Education and Research (NCHER) Bill is indicative of the directions for change some of which are as follows:

1. Pursuit of excellence in education and research will be the primary goal of higher education institutions for which universities have to regain their autonomy in academic decision-making. Securing autonomy for universities and laying down a road map to achieve competitive excellence are responsibilities of NCHER.

2. Given the need for better infrastructure and resources and the continuing demand for increasing access, higher education in future cannot be managed by state alone. Therefore, private investment will become inevitable. Acceptable models of public-private partnerships will have to be evolved in coming years. There are few models already in place and the Foreign Education Providers' Bill will create more.

3. Affiliation of colleges is a practice which will be in disuse in the future. Colleges maintaining standards may become autonomous linked to universities only for award of degrees and some of them may become universities themselves.

4. State universities which occupy 95 per cent of higher education space will claim a larger share of central funds which they will get according to norms set through consultations. While the initial grant may be norm-based, continued funding will be performance-based. This will minimize the present imbalance in government funding of universities, both state and central. It will also demand greater accountability from the academic community.

5. Autonomy will be accompanied with responsibility on the part of universities and they will be required to re-organize their internal governance structures to be transparent, participatory, and efficient. This will hopefully generate a new work culture conducive to scholarship and learning.

6. Like any other public institution, universities should be open to performance assessment by internal and external agencies. As a consequence, accreditation and maintenance of standards would become obligatory on the part of the university and its leadership. Quality enhancement will become the responsibility of everyone associated with university.

7. The status of research and engagement with the society will receive greater attention on the part of the universities, public or private in the new scheme of things. In fact, it is in this sphere that universities are going to compete with each other and distinguish themselves in the years to come.

8. Technology will tend to equalize opportunities for individuals and institutions in the knowledge era. The shortage of qualified faculty in higher education will compel institutions to seek technological solutions for which policy changes will be initiated by the state.

Change is inevitable and it is happening. What is crucial for the future of higher education is the direction change is taking and how it can be influenced by well-thought-out policy. It is in this regard centre-state policies and the commitments of the academia are going to be decisive. The old mindset is still prevalent among some educators and educational administrators. Politicians play with the fear associated with change and debate endlessly on policies and state responsibilities. In this milieu, market is distorting priorities and is trying to set the agenda of university education. This is the tragedy of higher education today, where educational space is increasingly occupied by non-educationists and middle-men.

LEADERSHIP MATTERS FOR TRANSFORMATIVE CHANGE

It is said that Indians can outshine as individuals but they fail to perform as a team when it comes to managing change. The only exception possibly is defence services. Admittedly, Indian universities produce world-class scientists, engineers, doctors, managers, statisticians, and artists; but our universities are not rated world-class. Individuals graduate from Indian universities and acquit themselves creditably in organizations across the world where they are competing to perform, though not necessarily to lead. Is it a genetic problem or a cultural attribute? The argumentative Indian is a character who can explain everything without doing anything to change the course of events. And higher education is the field full of opportunities for the argumentative Indians.

Let me conclude my comments on comparative perspectives in Indian higher education with a success story in which I happened to be the team leader. Forgive me for being personal in describing the story of the National Law School Movement which revolutionized legal education in India in a short span of ten years against heavy odds and challenges.

I was a professor heading the law department in Delhi University in 1985 when the call came to establish an innovative law university in Bangalore which when established, can be compared with the best of its kind in the world and which will act as a pacesetter in legal education reforms in India. Rarely does one get such an opportunity in higher education. All my colleagues, argumentative Indians as they are, impressed upon me the overwhelming risks involved and advised me to desist from tasks considered impossible by people more knowledgeable and experienced than me. My conscience persuaded me to give it a try as the returns can be far reaching if the experiment turned out to be successful. I dreamt for several days of a university attracting talented students from all over the country pursuing a curriculum that is path-breaking in the company of a group of committed teachers dreaming with me. Once out of the dream, reality dawned on us that law is a subject which bright students seldom pursued and that good faculty may not join our institution which has no credibility or financial security yet. Funds were to be raised as we go along building the so-called world-class law school! Nonetheless, the moral support of the Bar Council of India and the patronage of Chief Justice of India as the Chancellor of the University emboldened us to take the challenge.

To cut the story short, a team of twelve teachers and few supporting staff worked with me tirelessly, determined to make a qualitative change in Indian legal education. We worked out a five-year integrated LLB curriculum, conceived several innovative methods of teaching law combining theory with practice, and developed our own brand of study materials for interdisciplinary learning. We embarked on a journey with very little infrastructure facilities and with uncertain funding support. Nobody, particularly our peers in the teaching profession, ever thought we would succeed and they dismissed us as crazy adventurists. We, however, after a long struggle, demonstrated that a well-conceived idea executed with commitment and competence can change the course of legal education not only in the institution concerned but even in every law school in the whole country. Acknowledged as the best in the country for the last thirty years and more not only by the bench and the bar but also by governments, parliament, and the private sector, the National Law School experiment is today being replicated in every other state in the country. The moral of the story is that determined leadership and some amount of autonomy can still make change transformative enough to overcome old mindsets and overbearing bureaucratic systems and build institutions for advancement of learning and scholarship.

WHY INDIA CANNOT FOLLOW FOREIGN MODELS IN HIGHER EDUCATION?

There is a demand, justifiable and desirable, to have few world-class universities in the country though there is no unanimity on the concept of what makes universities 'world-class'. It assumes global competitiveness in teaching, research, governance, and extension activities. It warrants state-of-the-art infrastructure and adequate financial support to attract the best available talents internationally to teach and research in the institution. The proposed innovation universities are supposed to fill the bill, if ever it takes place. Meanwhile, the university system in every country develops in the peculiar circumstances obtaining in that country and its transplantation to another country will not work unless there are comparable circumstances in that country as well.

The leading American universities are privately funded and have linkages with big corporate enterprises having research agendas of their own. These institutions are research-based and market driven and enjoy a lot of freedom to experiment with academic programmes without regulatory interference from anywhere. This cannot be a model for Indian universities which are not supposed to be profit-driven and market-oriented. Access, equity, and inclusiveness are key elements in our system for sustaining which compromises are inevitable even if they undermine quality and competitiveness.

Closer home the models adopted in Singapore, China, and Hong Kong which claim to have world-class universities are also inappropriate for the Indian situation. They concentrate on limited number of elite institutions with very heavy investments on infrastructure seeking to imitate the market model focusing on collaboration with foreign universities and hiring teachers globally on negotiated pay packages and service conditions.

While India can borrow some of the features of these foreign universities like research focus, industry-linkage, and autonomy in internal governance, it is neither possible nor practical to abandon or subordinate the demands of access and equity for the sake of quality. That is perhaps the reason why neither the National Education Policies nor the Five Year Plan documents on higher education have given priority to world-class focus in university development.

* * *

The University System in India, no doubt is in a state of disrepair. It has expanded since independence allowing access to higher education for almost 25 per cent of the eligible population. For some strange reason, the policy on research pursued by the government has been to put the available research funds on specialized institutions outside the university system and to restrict the entry of private enterprise in higher education, at least till recent times. Multiplicity of regulatory institutions and interference at the political and bureaucratic levels have literally killed autonomy of universities and even undermined academic initiatives at the institutional level. The internal governance structure based on nineteenth century University Acts have further inhibited academic freedom even in curricular reform, pedagogic innovations, and examination. Affiliation of colleges have made universities, particularly at the state level, mere examining and degree awarding institutions far removed from research and innovation. No wonder that the Prime Minister of India himself characterized the situation (with reference to legal education, though it applies to others as well) as 'a sea of institutionalized mediocrity with few islands of excellence'.[1]

Realizing the dangers inherent in such a situation for the future of the country, the central government initiated a series of policy changes including half a dozen legislative measures which have been introduced in the parliament. Unfortunately, neither the government nor the parliament found the time to pursue the matter and the whole system is in limbo full of uncertainties and lack of clarity on future direction. In this situation, it is too much to expect a paradigm shift in university administration and academic accountability for improving quality of higher education in the near future. One can only hope for the better. There may be few more islands of excellence in the sea of mediocrity. Otherwise, the system will continue to be enmeshed in party politics and corruption submerging quality in the name of equity and social justice. In the process, India would have lost the 'demographic dividend' about which our leaders have been talking largely to mobilize political support and publicity.

[1] Prime Minister Dr. Manmohan Singh's speech at a law conference in Vigyan Bhawan, New Delhi in 2009.

5 Strategic Management of Expansion of Higher Education in India

Key Policy Interventions for Change

Pawan Agarwal

Indian higher education has expanded dramatically in recent years. Such a swift growth is not sustainable and has resulted in many tensions and frictions. Expansion has occurred without a proportionate increase in funding and worsened the pre-existing faculty shortages. As a result, academic standards have deteriorated and the public confidence in the value of higher education has eroded. Overall, there is a rising dissatisfaction about the state of higher education in the country.

With improvements in schooling and a growing number of young people and their rising aspirations, the demand for higher education would continue to grow in India. Responding to it, the capacity of Indian higher education would have to grow further.

Current trends show a robust contribution of the private sector in creating capacities. This clearly suggests that increased enrolments can be achieved with surprisingly little direct support from the government. However, there is downside to such growth. The current growth is skewed and of poor quality. It is unlikely to meet the increasingly diverse needs of students as well as employers in future. Research and innovation has also suffered. Thus, further expansion has to be managed strategically so that it is balanced, of high quality, and done at lower costs. This requires innovative thinking and ecosystem approach.

This chapter provides a blueprint for strategic management of expansion of higher education in the country. It begins with a brief discussion on conceptual issues like systems thinking in the context of higher education and case to promote diversity in provision as the system expands. Then the chapter provides a vision for the role of higher education in the country's future followed by a brief comment on its origin and evolution. This follows an overview on the growth and funding of higher education. After listing out key problem areas, a set of policies is suggested. In doing so, lessons are drawn from the experience of other countries. This obviously keeps India's unique circumstances and culture in mind.

CONCEPTUAL ISSUES

As higher education in India expands further, we have to re-organize it in a manner that is suited to 'massive' enrolments. The provision has to connect to the needs of the society and economy. This requires thinking of higher education holistically at the system level in place of current piecemeal approach, where much of the thinking is at the institution level. Further, higher education with massive enrolments would need a variety in provision aligned with the nation's social diversity and division of labour in the economy today.

These conceptual issues are briefly discussed below.

Systems Approach

From a systems perspective, it is necessary to understand as to how various elements are put together and determine leverage points where interventions would have the best impact. Higher education system could be seen to comprise of various subsystems for funding, regulation, governance, and so on or alternatively seen to comprise of higher education institutions that are grouped as central (or national), state or private institutions. Still further, higher education institutions and programmes can be categorized by fields of study, such as engineering, management, basic sciences, humanities, social sciences, and so on.

The system as a whole meets the student demand on one hand and graduate demand from the labour market on the other within a geography after taking into account migration/migration into account. Interventions could focus on one or more elements, thus offering a variety of possibilities (see Figure 5.1).

In view of its huge size and large differences in levels of development of higher education across states, the states (rather than country as a whole) should be treated as a unit of analysis for planning and action. National system of higher education would be an aggregation of state systems. Even the central institutions should be seen as a part of state system. Medical and agriculture education (even though handled by different ministries and departments at the National/State level) should also form part of state higher education system for a holistic approach.

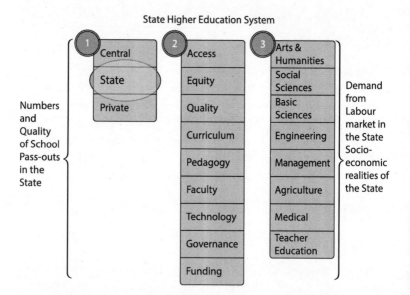

Figure 5.1 Systems Approach: Three Dimensions and Linkages

Source: Author.

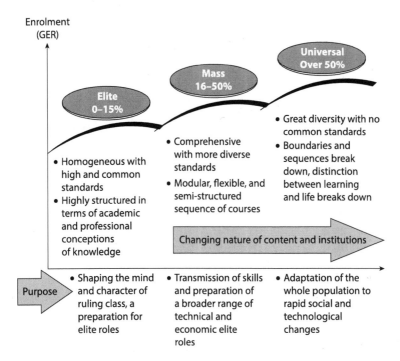

Figure 5.2 Forms and Phases of Higher Education Modern Societies
Source: Developed based on framework provided by Martin Trow 2010.

As higher education expands, there are changes in the purpose and nature of higher education. American Socialist Professor Martin Trow was the first to observe, analyse, and explain this transformation in three distinct phases. A transition from one phase to another has consequences on the internal organization of the institutions and their relations with the larger society (see Figure 5.2). It has two direct consequences. First, an expanding system requires genuine diversity in the forms of its institutions, since high costs associated with elite higher education would put a brake on expansion. Second, 'common and high standards' even though could be desired, but cannot be achieved in truly mass system of higher education.[1]

---

[1] Trow, Martin. 'From Mass Higher Education to Universal Access: The American Advantage.' *Minerva* 37 (Spring 2010): 1–26.

Enrolments in India crossed the threshold for mass higher education (15 per cent GER) recently (see Figure 5.2 for such transitions taking place in different countries).[2] Since, this transition now requires diversity in provision, it would be wrong to assume that all institutions would engage in both teaching and research. This is both unfeasible and wasteful. While, on one hand India needs world-class research universities, the country must also have a large number of sophisticated teaching institutions and a very large number of institutions that impart vocational or generic skills required in the society and economy. Quality leading institutions with innovative content and pedagogy have to emerge in each of the diverse spheres.

This recognition would require sweeping changes in the organization and structure of higher education, particularly in four areas. First, this would require vocational or skill-based education to become part of the higher education space. Second, mobility of both students and faculty would be encouraged. While, the faculty would be driven by performance and incentives to move between institutions in pursuit of a career, modular courses, credit accumulation, and transfer would help seamless student mobility throughout the system. Third, the relationship of the institutions with the governments must be redesigned and variegated to come to terms with the realities of mass higher education. And finally, there should be multiple sources of funding with institutions fiercely competing for funds among themselves.

According to Professor Philip Altbach, India needs to develop a higher education system that is 'rationally organized and differentiated in order to ensure that the increasingly diverse needs of higher education can be rationally met'.[3] For this, the government must ensure through policy and funding mechanisms that different types of institutions focus on their defined missions and together fulfil individual aspirations, and meet national goals and priorities.

India's Vision for Higher Education

A strong higher education system is essential for the country so as to develop a 'modern economy, a just society, and a vibrant polity'. A good

[2] Indian situation with wide inter-state and rural-urban disparities is somewhat complicated, but the broad argument is still valid.

[3] Altbach, Philip. 'India's Higher Education Challenges', in Pawan Agarwal, *Fifty Years of Higher Education* (New Delhi: Sage Publications, 2012).

higher education system is critical to meet the growing aspirations of its people and provide them with opportunities for upward social mobility. Accordingly, higher education should be able to equip young people with relevant knowledge and skills for current and future job roles and provide people already in employment with skills to negotiate their rapidly evolving career needs.

With its young population while the rest of world is rapidly aging, India could potentially garner a bigger share of global knowledge work if it could raise the quality of its higher education and benchmark it globally. India must also have some institutions in the global top-league in order to fulfil its aspirations to play a significant role in the emerging global knowledge economy. Thus, higher education would be central to social, cultural, and economic competiveness of India through qualified human resources, innovation and enterprise. This brings higher education at the core of the country's agenda for inclusive growth.[4]

Origin and Evolution

India had a long tradition of higher learning and was home to several famous ancient universities. However, much of it got decimated over the centuries, and there are hardly any traces of the old tradition in the country's modern higher education, origin of which can be traced to the AD nineteenth century. The country's first three universities were set up in 1857 with a view to maintain the varying standards of education in colleges that had come up in early part of the nineteenth century. The primary function of the universities was to test the teaching and learning that took place in colleges affiliated to them.

Education historians Eric Ashby and Mary Anderson note that these universities were meant 'to provide a test of eligibility for government employment and to transmit an alien culture'.[5] The examination system strongly influenced the way these affiliated colleges conducted their teaching, learning, and administration. Heavily loaded curriculum, often unfamiliar content in a foreign context, and insistence on reading and writing in English (a language culturally alien to the students) fostered rote learning

[4] Planning Commission, *Twelfth Five Year Plan (2012–17)*, vol. III (2012): pp. 89–123, New Delhi.

[5] Ashby, Eric and Anderson Mary, *Universities: British, Indian, African: A Study in the Ecology of Higher Education* (Cambridge: Harvard University Press, 1966).

and memorization. These early influences continue to dominate the higher education landscape even today.

OVERVIEW OF GROWTH AND FUNDING

Recent Impressive Growth

Indian higher education has grown impressively in recent years. On an average, about ten new institutions were set up and about 5,000 fresh students have been admitted every single day in recent years (2007–12) (see Figure 5.3). The growth has been at all levels (degree and diploma), in all types of institutions (central, state, and private), and in all subject areas alike. Engineering and management programmes at the degree level and teacher training, and nursing education at the diploma level in the private sector grew more rapidly than the rest. Proportionate share of private institutions is now 40 per cent in terms of enrolment (58 per cent of institutions). State institutions account for 57 per cent enrolment (40 per cent of institutions) and the central institutions contribute just about 3 per cent of enrolment (2 per cent institutions).

Even though, in absolute terms, India enrols the second highest number of students in its higher education system (surpassed the US's enrolment

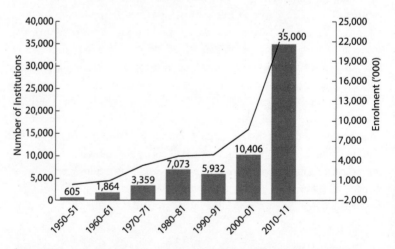

Figure 5.3   Growth of Institutions and Enrolment

Source: Compiled from various sources including Planning Commission, Ministry of HRD.

Table 5.1 Gross enrolment ratio, Private Share of enrolment, and Labour Force by Occupation

Country	Gross Enrolment Ratio	Year of 15% GER	Private Share of Enrolment	Labour Force by Occupation		
				Agriculture	Industry	Services
South Korea	103	1981	80.1	6.4	24.2	69.4
United States	95	1940s	26.1	0.7	20.3	79.0
Australia	80	1970	3.5	3.6	21.1	75.3
Russia	76	1950s	14.9	9.8	27.5	62.7
United Kingdom	60	1972	0	1.4	18.2	80.4
Japan	60	1970	77.4	3.9	26.2	69.8
Malaysia	40	1995	50.9	13.0	36.0	51.0
Brazil	26	1999	74.6	20.0	14.0	66.0
Philippines	28	1970	65.2	33.0	15.0	52.0
China	26	2003	19.9	36.7	28.7	34.6
Indonesia	23	2000	71.0	38.3	12.8	49.8
India	18	2008	40.0	52.0	14.0	32.0

Source: UNESCO & PROPHE.[6]

in 2010 and became second only to China that year), but in terms of GER (gross enrolment ratio—students enrolled in higher education as a proportion of persons in the 18–22-year age group), India's achievement is modest. GER has increased from 15.2 per cent in 2006–07 to 20.2 per cent in 2011–12. This is expected to rise to more than 25 per cent by 2017 and reach 30 per cent by 2020 (Planning Commission 2012).

Despite this growth, enrolments in India are about four decades behind the advanced nations. It must however be recognized that in most countries, higher education expanded in response to changing structure of their economy resulting in requirement for more qualified manpower, but in India, the growth has been largely in response to the rising social demand (see Table 5.1).

[6] For GER, UNESCO Institute of Statistics (Data for 2010 except Brazil-2005 and Russia, Malaysia, and Philippines-2009) available at http://stats.uis.unesco.org/unesco/TableViewer/dimView.aspx; for private share of enrolment (Data from 2004 to 2008) at www.albany.edu/dept/eaps/prophe; for 2009 or 2010, see https://www.cia.gov/library/publications/the-world-factbook/geos/rp.html.

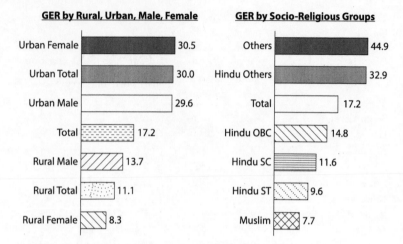

Figure 5.4   Inequity in Access: Gross Enrolment Ratio, 2007–08

Source: Twelfth Five Year Plan, Planning Commission.

Inequities and Imbalances

Despite dramatic expansion, problem of inequitable access and imbalanced growth continue to persist in the country's higher education sector. While access has improved for all social groups, including the disadvantaged, relative disparities have not reduced significantly (see Figure 5.4). In respect of access to more selective institutions, the gaps are wider.

Students from the poor households are less likely to access higher education. As in the rest of the world, the cost of higher education has escalated beyond the rate of inflation. This cost is now increasingly being transferred to the students. Thus, affordability is a key challenge, particularly for those students who come from the poor households.

Higher education has not expanded equally in all states and even within the states there are areas that continue to have no facilities for higher education. There are wide inter-state variations in enrolment and imbalances of growth within the States.

Yet, another imbalance is in terms of poorly developed vocational and doctoral education segments within higher education. Both quantitatively and qualitatively, these segments are small and under developed compared to the United States and China.

Growing but Skewed Funding

Along with expansion, expenditure on higher education has also grown. Private and household expenditure on higher education has grown fast in recent years. Government expenditure has also grown. In 2011–12, about 1.2 per cent of the country's gross domestic product (GDP) was spent by government. With nearly 40 per cent of the students that are enrolled in private unaided institutions paying full fees and 60 per cent paying at least some fees in government institutions, it is estimated that an additional 1 per cent of the GDP comes from the private sources.

Thus, India (at 2.2 per cent of GDP, 1.2 per cent public, and 1 per cent private) devotes a significant proportion of its national wealth to higher education. India's expenditure compares reasonably with that in the United States (1 per cent public and 1.6 per cent private) or Korea (0.7 per cent public and 1.9 per cent private) and exceeds that in China (0.9 per cent public and 0.3 per cent private). This suggests limited scope for further increase; even though considering very low levels of per student spending, an increased spending on higher education is fully justified. There is also a strong case for more efficient and strategic deployment of available resources.

CHALLENGES OR PROBLEM AREAS

Higher education faces a multitude of challenges. Key amongst them are contradictions in expanding higher education further, continued inequities in access, ineffective funding arrangements, quality concerns arising from legacy issues, absence of performance culture among the academia, limited research capacity and poor research performance, and finally absence of policies that foster diversity and system thinking.

At the current enrolment levels, yearly supply of graduates is about 5 to 6 million. This far exceeds the annual requirement of less than 2 million graduates.[7] Considering, India's current stage of development with over

---

[7] The figure of 2 million takes care of attrition, but could be on a higher side. As per Planning Commission estimates, requirement of qualified workers (people with graduate and above and diploma qualifications) would rise by about 1 million a year in the country over the next few years (from 44 million in 2011–12 to 49.7 million in 2016–17).

50 per cent labour force still in agriculture and a large informal sector, current enrolment levels appear to be adequate, particularly if we compare it with other countries at the corresponding stage of their development (see Table 5.1).

However, there is continued pressure to widen access to higher education. A growing number of young people, improvements in schooling, rising middle class, and their growing aspirations are all contributing to the increased demand. Thus, India is faced with a unique situation with a rapidly rising aspiration-led demand and a relative slow growth in demand for graduates from the labour market.

Recent growth has however left gaps in provision that need to be plugged. Recent efforts to achieve expanded access for disadvantaged groups have been a much-needed first step, but looking ahead, a more targeted approach is required. Ideally, the reach of scholarships and student loans need to become universal so that no student lacks opportunities for financial reasons.

Current funding arrangements are skewed and ineffective. Almost half of the colleges and one-fourth of the universities fall in the private unaided category and hence do not receive any government funding. There are large disparities in central funding. Central universities (including some deemed universities) are far more liberally funded than state universities and colleges. Funding is not linked to performance. A key challenge is to ensure that funding for higher education is efficient, effective, and also sustainable.

The affiliated college model with its several limitations continues to provide the core model for Indian higher education even over a century and half later. The language of instruction continues to be English (albeit, much less alien now). The curriculum in most cases is outdated and irrelevant since the universities are often not enthusiastic in keeping their curricula up to date and relevant. Teaching-learning practices are mostly examination-orientated with focus on rote learning and memorization. Thus, comprehensive academic reforms are urgently needed.

Many of the India's higher education institutions are too small to be viable. They are generally understaffed and ill-equipped; two-thirds do not even satisfy government-established minimum norms, and they are unable to innovate because of the rigid bureaucracy of the affiliating system that links the colleges to a supervising university. All this makes the system highly fragmented, scattered, and difficult to manage. There is a strong case for consolidation and merging small institutions.[8]

Further, a critical challenge relates to academic profession in the country. While it is true that Indian academics, by international comparisons, are relatively well paid, they are not necessarily effective. Academics, and especially college teachers, are constrained by rigid bureaucracy. Further, their work is not carefully evaluated—salary increases and promotions are awarded rather on the basis of seniority. Unfortunately, when salaries were increased in 2006, this boon was not accompanied by any reforms in the teaching profession or requirements for evaluation. A System of Academic Performance Indicators for promotion and appointment of professors and lecturers is yet to take roots.[9]

In an increasingly sophisticated labour market, employers demand specific skills and competencies rather than just degree credentials. Thus, in planning for further expansion, the focus has to be on better quality education in diverse ways to build key skills and competencies. Unfortunately, the Indian system continues to be highly centralized and driven by unrealistic myth of uniformity and a commitment to egalitarianism. We need to re-think this. Ideally, there should be heterogeneous provision that encourages diversity and quality comparisons between institutions.

Research capacity of the country's higher education is limited and research performance overall is poor. Capacity for doctorate education, particularly in science and engineering is small and has remained stagnant over the past two decades. Even though, there has been a remarkable turnaround in India's research performance over the last two decades, but it is insignificant compared to impressive developments in China. Low levels of funding, lack of performance culture and segregation of the country's R&D institutions from universities and colleges have been responsible for this. Even the country's top universities remain largely teaching focused with limited research and doctoral education. It is therefore not surprising that even the country's well-regarded institutions do not find a decent place in any of the global university rankings that primarily focus on research.

---

[8] Altbach, Philip and Pawan Agarwal, 'Scoring Higher on Education', *The Hindu*, New Delhi (12 February 2013).

[9] Altbach and Agarwal, 'Scoring Higher on Education'.

Finally, there is an absence of system level thinking on higher education. There is very little evidence of effective planning or innovation in the states that could be effective units for doing so. The states have simply tried to keep up with the demand for expansion of higher education without any holistic thinking. Most states have been primarily concerned with issues of literacy and school education and unable to provide necessary financial and policy support for higher education. Furthermore, there are growing divergences and tensions between the central and state systems of higher education that require skilful coordination and the removal of duplication and overly complex bureaucratic procedures.

STRATEGIC MANAGEMENT OF EXPANSION

As higher education capacity has to grow further in order to accommodate growing numbers of students aspiring for higher education, the country must be strategic in its approach. Focus either on enrolment expansion or increased funding would not address several problems faced by the India's higher education sector. The expansion has to occur in sync with changes in society and economy. Private sector will play a significant role in this expansion. Foreign provision could possibly supplement this.

In higher education that would be increasingly private in future, public funds have to be used in areas where private investments are unlikely such as for research or student financial aid to support poor students or for high quality but inexpensive vocational and teacher education. Further expansion has to address equity issues adequately and regulate the quality of higher education effectively. Digital technologies could potentially transform higher education. Quality improvement that would be the key challenge would require coordinated action on several fronts. In the country's strategy to expand higher education, both public and private sectors have to grow in harmony. Institutional differentiation and distinctiveness should be promoted to meet the diverse needs of the economy and society. For this, there should be a spectrum of institutions that would include multidisciplinary research universities, well-regarded teaching-focused institutions, as well as short-cycle vocational education institutions. Diversity should be encouraged in all domains of institutional functioning and should be underpinned by an emergence of leading institutions in each sphere.

While, creating additional capacity, the focus has to be to consolidate the existing institutions rather than expand the number of institutions by ensuring new institutions established in recent years reach optimum capacity rapidly, by facilitating multiple campuses of reputed institutions, and by encouraging clustering and collaboration amongst institutions.

Since the higher education in the country is highly fragmented, possibilities of merger of institutions in order to achieve the economies of scale and scope should be seriously explored. Apart from mergers that might be difficult in the Indian situation, possibilities of alliances and clusters of institutions could also be explored.

In India, skill formation through vocational education is separated from general higher education. In this binary system, vocational training is done in training institutes and training centres that do not fall within the purview of the universities. This raises serious concerns about the relevance of higher education itself. Several countries, the United States in the 1930s and almost all countries which were members of the Organization for Economic Co-operation and Development (OECD) in the 1970s and 1980s have created and supported development of short cycle skill-based higher education to respond to increased demand from wider section of society for higher education. India needs to focus on creation and development of similar programmes and build bridges with vocational education and training sector. This could be the main venue for expansion of higher education.

For further growth of private higher education, innovative ways have to be found to encourage the infusion of more private capital in the traditional not-for-profit higher education sector. At the same time, new and innovative models of Public-Private Partnerships (PPP) in higher education could be encouraged, particularly in the establishment of research and innovation institutions.

The 'not-for-profit' status in higher education should, perhaps, be re-examined for pragmatic considerations so as to allow the entry of for-profit institutions in select areas where acute shortages persist. This should, however, be subjected to the necessary oversight and accreditation to ensure quality and equity. In several countries like Brazil and China, for-profit private higher education can be taxed and the revenue from it can be channelled into large scale scholarship programme to promote equity.

While recognizing the importance of private higher education, adequate measures are needed to curb unfair practices like capitation fee by way of appropriate legislation and regulatory oversight.

Policy to enable foreign universities to establish their presence in India has been under consideration for many years. As a result of this inordinate delay, India's image has been tarnished. Clear and unambiguous policy on setting up of foreign university campuses in India is urgently needed.

In order to address the equity challenge, targeted, integrated, and effective equity related measures are needed. There is a need for a substantial increase in the level of budgetary support to equity related measures. This has to be done by careful identification and targeting of the under-served areas, vulnerable, and deprived communities and students coming from poor and rural households that are underserved by existing provisions of higher education. Finally, revamping and integration of various existing schemes is required.

As the higher education grows, of particular concern is addressing the problem of shortage of faculty. The problem is being compounded with the rapid growth of enrolments. The number of teachers will need to be doubled over the next five years. This would need a dramatic increase in capacity at the postgraduate and doctoral levels. For which massive efforts are required. State universities and colleges that have large vacancies will have to be supported to fill up the posts. Notwithstanding the fact that academics in India receive decent salaries on a comparative global scale (much higher on average than in China), the common perception is that academics is a poorly paid profession in India. This perception needs to be corrected in order to attract talent.

There is a need to focus on graduate education and research to have adequate numbers of high quality faculty and also feed into innovation, needed for economic prosperity and social well-being, and for pushing the frontiers of knowledge.

Digital technologies and organizational innovations that these technologies enable offer exciting opportunities to transform higher education. The technology could also improve governance at both the institution and system level. Easy access to existing knowledge, interesting ways to connect knowledge, and create enabling environment for collaborative work is accelerating new knowledge creation and its quick dissemination. Hence, technology could potentially accelerate research. But, most promising would be to use new technologies to improve learning. Digital technologies can make learning intrinsically motivating and teaching professionally rewarding.

By effectively leveraging the digital technologies, India could turn several higher education problems to significant advantages. For example, the affiliating college structure provides an obvious 'hub and spoke' arrangement that could ensure that lectures from the best teachers are available to hundreds of thousands of students through synchronous video-streaming. Facilitated by trained instructors located onsite to enable interaction, this method has the potential to bring about a significant improvement in teaching and learning processes in the affiliated colleges. The structure also provides opportunities for large-scale use of massive online courses.

Considerably large investment in higher education is required to deliver on multiple objectives. This investment has to come both from public and private sources and both from central and state exchequer. While government funding for higher education has to be significantly increased, but efficiency of its utilization has to be improved as well and more efforts are required to garner funds from other sources. The operating costs have to be increasingly met from enhanced tuition fees. This should however be accompanied with a significant increase in the student financial aid, both scholarships and loans.

Central plan funds for higher education need to be increased significantly and used strategically to foster desired change in the entire system. An effective way of using the larger investment by the central government would be to partner with states in deciding on schemes and priorities and increasing the proportion of funds set aside for state institutions of higher education.

While, expanding capacity, the main thrust has to be to preserve and enhance quality. Improving quality requires many interventions across the sector in eight broad areas. This is given in the framework in Figure 5. 5. Specific interventions required in each of these areas are listed and described in the annexure. Action is needed in all these areas in tandem to raise the overall quality of higher education, while also ensuring that some of the Indian institutions reach the benchmark of global excellence. In addition, the country needs a graded system of accreditation and multiple agencies to be able to review and accredit all institutions. For which, a detailed roadmap for accreditation is essential.

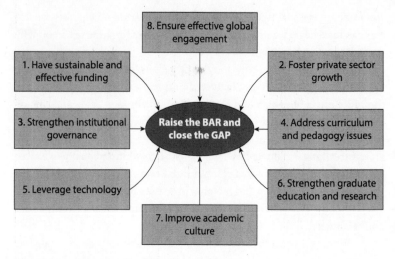

Figure 5.5   Framework to Improve Quality

IMPLEMENTATION

In order to implement above policies, seven strategic leverage points have been identified where successful action could trigger many supportive reactions throughout the system. These are:

1. Strategic central financial support to the state governments based on carefully prepared higher education plans for each state. This would also help to align central government's investment with that of the state governments in this sector and trigger a wide-ranging reform in the sector, particularly in state higher education. Rashtriya Uchchatar Sikhsha Abhiyan (RUSA) is being launched for the purpose.

2. Support equity-related measures through targeted and effective equity-related schemes, which will replace the existing maze of multiple and diffused small outlay schemes and making the student financial aid available through a single portal linked to Aadhaar. While work on linking scholarships and loans with Aadhaar has begun, concerted efforts would be required to streamline and scale up students financial aid programmes.

3. Professional development of academic staff to give students a positive learning experience through improved curriculum, better pedagogy that leverages technology and assessment aligned to learning outcomes.

Existing institutional arrangements, the 'hub and spoke' system of the affiliating system that could be very effective for cascaded capacity building and new arrangements like creating subject-based networks, setting up new 'Schools of Education' and 'Teaching and Learning Units' in existing institutions could be used. This would require new institutional arrangements.

4. Promote research excellence by supporting and nurturing pre-selected research-focused institutions and centres through competitive grants and research evaluation with provision for hiring talent globally. Also support excellence clusters, networks, and alliances amongst academic institutions, with industry and businesses for collaborative research.

5. Create, develop, and nurture an ecosystem for short-cycle skill-based and remedial higher education akin to community colleges in North America with mobility to regular degree programmes. Pilot scheme of community colleges has to be scaled up quickly to have impact.

6. Create new institutional arrangements for development of academic leadership, policy research, robust data system both for policymaking and to enable informed student choice and addressing unfair practices.

7. Learn from good practices globally and connect the country's higher education to that of other countries so that it is globally benchmarked.

Overall, there is a need for joint strategic thinking and effective policy coordination across the national and state sectors and with the growing private sector. Further, systematic approaches to the allocation of state funding (as done in the United States in the 1950s and 1960s) are needed for coordinated and robust development of higher education system.

While, recognizing that the country's higher education is now a public-private mix, further growth should leverage on the relative strengths of two. State higher education would be the main venue for planning, coordination, and action with central institutions acting as exemplars of higher quality, support, and mentor the state and the private institutions.

Various policies have to be embodied in the ongoing or the new programmes or schemes. For effective implementation, financial outlays have to be aligned to the specific interventions and the broad strategy spelt out in this chapter. New structures and institutional mechanisms are needed for coordination across ministries and agencies.

While designing new programmes or overhauling existing ones, the aim should be to interlink expansion, equity, and excellence, and focus on those activities that serve as the locus at which more than one objective intersects. It has to be recognized that fostering excellence is a multi-dimensional challenge requiring simultaneous action on many fronts. Greater flexibility should be provided to the implementing agencies by grouping schemes under umbrella national initiatives. In several areas, new national initiatives may be needed. At the state level, most policy ideas could be the part of the newly launched Rashtriya Uchchatar Sikhsha Abhiyan (RUSA).

MONITORING AND EVALUATION

In order to monitor progress, it would be necessary to develop strategic indicators against various goals that clearly identify what would be measured. Monitoring may not be confined to the flow of funds and their utilization but will also include evaluation of programmes and initiatives for outcomes and impact. Services of independent evaluation agencies and researchers could be used for the purpose. Data on institutional performance on various parameters would be collected and compiled. It is important that the practice to assess learning outcomes and conduct student experience surveys should be initiated. In order to globally benchmark Indian higher education, India should proactively participate in various international surveys and evaluations.

* * *

India's recent expansion of its higher education has been exceptional both in terms of scale and speed. Further expansion requires careful consideration of several challenges faced by the country's higher education sector.

In response to rapidly rising aspirations, the social demand for higher education far exceeds the needs of the labour market, since the country's occupational structure has changed slowly. As a result, the problem of graduate unemployment has escalated. On the supply side, this impressive growth is driven primarily by the private sector, which has its own downsides.

As India tries to build a robust system of higher education aligned to its rising aspirations and growing economy, it has to strategically manage expansion by adopting a holistic and systems thinking approach. While doing so, the imperatives of an expanding system of higher education, particularly the need for diversity in provision have to be kept in mind.

For a private-sector led growth, rethinking about the enabling policy environment and appropriate institutional structure would be needed so that the quality is preserved.

While all three 'E's—Expansion, Equity, and Excellence—would continue to be the main thrust areas in higher education, these have to be pursued differently by taking into consideration the inter-linkages between them and the current realities of the India's higher education sector.

Keeping the above in mind, this chapter has identified strategic leverage points where successful action could trigger many supportive reactions throughout the system. These interventions are required in several areas ranging from governance, funding, and regulation of the private sector to curriculum and pedagogy, technology, faculty issues, graduate education, and research, and internationalization.

This chapter outlines widespread systemic changes needed to affect a paradigm shift in the cultural, policy, strategic, and operational environment of higher education in the country. It must be understood that a nineteenth century model of higher education cannot take the country into the twenty-first century. India today more than ever needs an educational policy that adapts itself to changing times. Like the United States, India has a large population, vibrant democracy, and very enterprising people, but lacks a high quality higher education system. Higher education would be a distinct advantage for the country if it is able to develop a high quality system.

While, ideas contained in this chapter (broadly based on the country's Twelfth Five Year Plan) that seek to align central government investment with that of the state governments, align new capacity with demand, create a performance culture through deepening of competitive grants and creation of related institutional arrangements have potential to develop India's higher education as a high quality system, however, success depends on effective implementation.

ANNEXURE

Specific Interventions to Improve Quality

Raise the Bar and Close the Gap

1. *Address Curriculum and Pedagogic issues*

a. Focus on Student-Centred Model of Teaching or Learning Outcomes

Higher education should contribute to developing graduate attributes such as creativity, independent problem-solving, professional skills, critical thinking, communication skills, team work, lifelong learning, etc. For this, there is a need to adopt a student-centred learning model, where education is not a top-down process, but learning as bottom-up process. Students should be able to construct knowledge with their own activities and interpret concepts and principles in terms of schemata that they already developed. The focus on learning outcomes by actively engaging all students, not only the brightest students is a must.

Addressing issues of curriculum and pedagogy are most important and yet very difficult. Unfortunately, Indian higher education has serious problems with both content of higher education and how it is delivered. Higher education curriculum in India offers little choice for students to study subjects of their own interest due to rigidity in the combinations. A shift is needed from input-centric and credential centric approach to learner-centric approach.

b. Modularization of Curriculum and UG Curriculum Reforms

For curricular reforms, introduction of choice-based credit system, comprehensive and continuous evaluation, and regular revision of curricula for making them up-to-date and relevant to contemporary and future needs would be critical. To help institutions reform their courses, subject-specific model curricula and packaged, re-usable digitized content (such as packaged lectures and open source textbooks) could be created by instructors with the requisite expertise through subject based network of institutions. An important goal of these reforms would be to create active learning environments in colleges and universities.

c. Adopt New Pedagogic Practices

The Indian system has emphasis on easily tested (though complex) facts and simpler concepts, rather than the arguably more important assessment of complex concepts that can only be done through elaborate customized mixes of group projects, class presentations, journal-writing, and the like, that require the instructor to interact with the students during the assessment process. In research done by Carnoy et al.,[10] Indian teaching methods are found to over-emphasize the lecture method relative to instructional strategies geared to learning complex concepts. Indian institutions should adopt new pedagogic practices that focus on learning outcomes based current understanding of how students actually learn.

d. Reform Affiliating System

Affiliating system reform is central to academic reforms. It must however be recognized that the affiliating system is vast, deep-rooted and has provided a semblance of quality control since the very beginning, it is therefore neither feasible nor desirable to dismantle it altogether. However, decentralization of part of the curriculum holds great promise. With greater academic autonomy, the core courses could be retained by universities, while the responsibility for the remainder could be devolved to colleges. This would create the desired innovation culture in the colleges. Clustering and even merging colleges that are very small would be part of the necessary reforms. In addition, universities that affiliate a very large number of colleges would have to be reorganized into two or more universities, with each of them affiliating a more reasonable number of colleges in order to improve overall academic effectiveness.

2. Promote Use of Digital Technologies

e. Promote Blended Learning and Use of MOOCs

Extensive use of blended learning could be used. A new model built around Massive Open Online Courses (MOOCs) that are developed locally and combined with those provided by top universities abroad could deliver higher education on a scale and at a quality not possible before. With a decade of experience in this space and a vibrant technology ecosystem, there is every chance that India will find its way soon.

---

[10] Carnoy, M., P. Loyalka, M. Dobryakova, R. Dossani, I. Froumin, K. Kuhns, J. Tilak, and R. Wang, *University Expansion in a Changing Global Economy: Triumph of the BRICs?* (Standford, CA: Stanford University Press, 2013).

3. *Address Quality of Academic Staff and Create Performance Culture*

f. Attract and Retain Talent for Teaching

Notwithstanding the fact that academics in India receive decent salaries on a comparative global scale (much higher on average than in China), the common perception is that academics is a poorly paid profession in India. This perception needs to be corrected in order to attract talent.

g. Review Faculty Hiring and Contract Arrangements

Hiring needs to be decentralized and innovative hiring practices, such as instituting probation periods of five to seven years for young faculty members, and offering top-up salaries and variable pay to motivate the faculty could be adopted. A large portion of those in teaching profession are currently casual or part-time academic staff and this is likely to continue. However, by streamlining the system of casual hiring, improving their working conditions and engaging them in faculty development programmes, it is possible to improve their performance.

h. Develop Performance Culture

Improving academic culture based on professional ethos, merit, and competition is critical to higher education reform. This would require repositioning the academic profession to attract the best qualified people to work in universities. Furthermore, in order to enthuse and motivate college teachers as well as promote innovation and experimentation—their involvement in curriculum design, pedagogy decisions, and in examination matters is essential.

After the recent pay revision, faculty evaluation based on academic performance indicators was introduced. It is not surprising that the academic community is not very enthusiastic about it. They rightly feel that it is excessively focused on research and not suited to most of them. There is an urgent need to make these indicators robust and ensure effective implementation. Few universities conduct student evaluation of teaching and, even among those that do, it generally has little impact.

It is important that performance-based pay system (practised in many countries including the United States from 1930s and South Korea from 2010) is introduced for academic staff in India. This should ensure some (even if slight) variation by each university based on their prestige. There is very little mobility of academics between institutions.

i. Focus on Professional Development

Continued faculty development is vital to ensure that faculty are current with the best pedagogical practices. Institutional weaknesses in the existing Academic Staff Colleges (66 nos.) should be removed and a qualitative change in their content and methodology of faculty development must be brought about. Further, 'Teaching and Learning Centres (TLCs)' must be established in the country within existing universities, preferably those that have a strong research culture as well as large undergraduate programmes. In some cases the Academic Staff Colleges could also serve as a TLC.

j. Use of Adjunct Faculty

Adjunct faculty from industry and research labs could be used greater numbers. A growing pool of retired experts is now available in the country. It is possible to tap their expertise for teaching and research. They could function as adjunct faculty and also enrol for doctoral degrees, for which current eligibility requirements could be waived.

k. Provide Global Exposure to Faculty

Special focus should be on building capacity of the faculty by sending them in large numbers to the best universities of the world for orientation and exposure to best international practices in teaching and research. For this, an International Faculty Development Programme could be a launched. A programme to fund doctoral students to study at international institutions needs to be implemented.

4. Promote Graduate Education and Research

l. Attracting Talent for Graduate Education and Research

Attracting and retaining talent is critical and emphasis will be laid in creating a better research infrastructure and work environment to attract the top-talent from within the country and also bring back India's brightest graduates who left the country to pursue higher studies abroad. For this, our upper-tier institutions should be allowed to hire globally, including foreigners on permanent appointments, and provide compensatory benefits to those who relocate in a flexible manner.

m. Promote Concentration and Selectivity in Research Funding

From the earlier discussion, it is clear that it is neither necessary nor realistic to expect all institutions achieve high levels of research excellence;

however, it is absolutely necessary for a country of India's size to have some of its institutions of higher learning in the top league of research-intensive universities globally.

For this, first it is necessary to review existing arrangement for funding of research, both core funding of research facilities and infrastructure and project funding in academic institutions with a view to identify gaps and ensure a more coordinated approach in research funding. Second, a strategy is to be developed for selective approach in allocation of research support to academic institutions is to be developed in order to ensure that resources for research are used to the best advantage; and finally a framework for excellence in research could be developed to ensure that increased funding supports country's most talented researchers and most effective research institutions and departments and also to ensure that some of the country's institutions reach the global benchmarks in research performance.

n. Improve and Expand Doctoral Education

It is essential that measures to improve the quality, structure, and content of doctoral education are taken urgently to build the foundation for further expansion. Existing PhD programmes would be modernized, and new ones created, particularly in new institutions and those that require interdisciplinary efforts. This is necessary to not only alleviate acute faculty shortages, build research capacity and provide highly qualified manpower to the industry and government.

o. Promote Synergy of Research Efforts

Historically, a large proportion of research in India is done in research institutes and laboratories outside the university system. It is essential to reconnect teaching with research by creating linkages between India's large research laboratory systems with that of the university system, so as to create a vibrant research ecosystem in the country.

There is a need for Indian institutions to build a range of institutional support mechanisms such as technology incubators, proof-of-concept centres, entrepreneurship programmes, and technology transfer mechanisms within Higher Education Institutes (HEIs). Institutions should also be encouraged to build collaborative ties with private actors in the area of innovation and entrepreneurship including technology companies, venture capitalists, as well as national and international foundations.

5. *Higher Education Internationalization*

p. Ensure Policies and Support for Effective Global Engagement

India needs to work towards deeper global engagement of its higher education so as to raise its quality and benchmark it globally. For this, a clearly articulated strategy for higher education internationalization is needed. This should include faculty and student exchange, institutional collaborations, exposure to diverse teaching-learning models, and enhanced use of new technologies. Globally compatible academic credit systems and processes for mutual recognition of qualifications would be critical for effective internationalization. Curricular internationalization would promote academic collaboration through joint and dual degrees and encourage student mobility.

6. *Have Sustainable and Effective Funding*

q. Strategic Central Funding of State Higher Education

State governments' expenditure on higher education has been falling over the years in relative terms. This trend has to be reversed. The central government support to the state universities and colleges has been abysmally low. This needs to be significantly enhanced and leveraged. There is a need to shift from institutional funding to system level funding for state higher education system and the funding should be linked to desired governance, regulatory, nudge academic reforms, and focus on building overall system capacity.

r. Linking Public Funds to Performance

Tying of public funding to performance can potentially improve efficiency is use of public funds and enhance effectiveness. Funding to performance through norm-based funding. The block grants should replace line-item budgets and plan allocations should be based on long-term strategic plans developed by the institutions. Consequently, annual funding should be linked to the performance of institutions against the milestones and targets laid-down in their strategic plans. In turn, institutions need to provide complete transparency about their financial performance and use of funds by putting their financial statements online.

s. Funding through Competitive Grants

Use of competitive grants also helps in giving the best value for money. It has several advantages and could serve as powerful motivator for institutional change, empowering those within organization who advocate for improvement.

t. Raise Resources through Tuition Fees

Maintaining low levels of tuition fees is not sustainable; in fact, it is regressive since it often tends to benefit the better-off students. Thus, there is a case for raising the tuition fees to reasonable levels.

u. Put in Place Well-funded Students Financial Aid

Increase in tuition fees should be accompanied with establishing a well-funded integrated Student Financial Aid Programme addressing all tiers of society and all levels of education, and a loan guarantee programme.

v. Mobilize Funding through Alternative Sources

Institutions should be encouraged to mobilize resources through alternative sources so that student fees do not form the only source of revenue. They should be encouraged to seek funding from diverse stakeholders through external contracts/grants for research, consulting, and/or training projects.

7. *Strengthen Governance*

w. Improve Institutional Governance: Rebalance Autonomy and Accountability

Reforms in governance arrangements are needed at national, state, and institutional levels, but it is particularly important at the institutional level. To improve institutional governance, changes are needed in four areas: autonomy and relations between governments and institutions; the composition and functioning of boards and councils; internal management structures; and the quality of leadership and senior administrative staff. All these four areas require attention. Adopt new public management practices, a shift from democratization towards growing concerns about efficiency and accountability. Higher education institutions have to be more accountable and responsive, efficient and effective and, at the same time, more entrepreneurial and self-managing.

x. Focus on Creation of Alliances, Networks, Clusters, and Consortia

To supplement efforts of the central agencies like the University Grants Commission (UGC) and the All India Council for Technical Education

(AICTE) and to enhance capacity of the system to govern itself, of academic institutions amongst themselves and with the research institutions and industry would be facilitated. This would accelerate the process of change by knowledge sharing, better resource utilization (both human and capital), and complementing mutual expertise resulting in synergetic effects.

8. Revamp Regulatory Ecosystem

y. Using Accreditation at the Heart of Regulation

Accreditation should be central to regulatory arrangements. For this, the country needs a graded system of accreditation and multiple agencies to be able to review and accredit all institutions.

z. Promote Healthy Regulation of the Privatev Sector

Measures are needed to ensure that private institutions are committed to quality, equity, and transparency through reform of regulatory oversight. The current regulatory framework needs to be revamped to: (*i*) encourage serious private philanthropy and investment to innovate and provide high quality education; (*ii*) promote better availability of information on private institutions to the public; (*iii*) ensure institutions that indulge in unfair practices are dealt with swiftly. In order to provide incentives for improvement, some flexibility should also be provided to private institutions related to fee fixation, which should be accompanied with transparency and provision of credible information about quality and fee levels to potential students.

6 Building New Institutions of Excellence in India

Three Case Studies of Innovation

Pramath Raj Sinha

In this book, I am sure the opportunities and challenges in Indian higher education have been discussed threadbare. I am not an expert on higher education and certainly not qualified to comment on the sector as a whole, therefore, I have based this chapter on the stories of my personal experience.

To begin with, purely by chance and more deliberately over time, my own approach to making a positive difference to higher education in India is one of building institutions that set a very high bar of excellence for the country, and possibly the world, to benchmark against. Instead of driving systemic change through policy advocacy or large-scale capacity-building, my efforts have been directed towards the building of new institutions that address an unmet need and an unsolved problem in our country, and that aspire to be the best in the world from the word go.

Given this context, this chapter focuses on the experiences of building three different institutions and programmes—the Indian School of

Business (ISB), Ashoka University, and the Young India Fellowship (part of Ashoka University).

ISB is the oldest of these initiatives, started in 1996, leading to the launch of the institution in 2001 in Hyderabad, India. I was involved in the ISB initiative from day one, and over time became the leader of the project and then the institution's founding dean. ISB has become one of India's leading B-schools in the league of the original Indian Institutes of Management (IIMs), certainly the best private B-school, and was consistently ranked amongst the Top 20 MBA programmes in the world by the *Financial Times*, becoming the youngest institution ever to figure in the rankings. It continues to make great strides and is now a recognized leader for management research out of India, with more than 50 outstanding full-time research-based faculty. With its second campus in Mohali, ISB graduates over 1000 students a year making it the largest programme of global-quality business education in India that has contributed to improving the careers of over 25,000 young Indians since its founding. Its graduates are becoming CEOs and successful entrepreneurs of leading organizations in India and its executive education programmes have similarly become a benchmark for corporate learning and development in the region. Several Indian and foreign institutions have emulated ISB's programmes and its practices—clearly the institution is serving as a role model for others to follow, which was the intent behind creating the school in the first place. Moreover, it serves as a great example of creating a world-class institution of higher learning in a model of broad-based private philanthropy, not seen before in India. I continue to be very involved in ISB as a member of its executive board and hold the emeritus title of Founding Dean.

Inspired by the success of ISB and the need to do so much more in the context of India's higher education challenges and opportunities, I am now engaged in building a liberal arts university, Ashoka University, in the Delhi National Capital Region (NCR). Ashoka opened its doors to an undergraduate BA programme in July 2014. Our founders aspire to create an ISB-like impact, this time in the field of liberal arts education, by creating India's first university in the class of the celebrated Ivy League and the world's top-ranked universities. The aim is to provide an Ivy League-quality undergraduate education in India at a fraction of the cost. Indeed, Ashoka University's Young India Fellowship (YIF) programme has already become highly sought after by the brightest graduates in India. Partnered with the institutions of global repute, that it is inspired by, Ashoka is founded by some of the most eminent scholars and leaders of our time who studied or taught at the world's finest universities.

Over 4,000 Indian graduates applied for 300 Young India fellowships (YIF) in 2017. The one-year programme has no parallel globally and has caught the fancy of young Indians who want to make a difference to the world they live in, and want to spend a year being inspired and learning how to. The YIF is in its seventh year and its alumni are already making a difference in top companies, NGOs, think tanks, development organizations or as entrepreneurs and postgraduate students in some of the top universities of the world. Like ISB, in a very short period of time, the YIF has made a huge mark attracting some of the brightest students from across India. They spend a year studying liberal arts and becoming better problem-solvers, critical thinkers, communicators, and leaders with a social awareness and commitment to solving some of our country's toughest and most complex problems. We see the YIF as a flagship of Ashoka University's postgraduate offerings and being positioned the same way in relation to the university as the Rhodes scholarship is to University of Oxford.

In the submission requesting financial support on its founding, the University of Sussex said, 'a new university has two obligations. On the one hand, it must have due respect for the long academic traditions of its sister universities and seek to emulate their high academic standards; on the other, it has a duty, as a newcomer, to try and illuminate some of the difficult contemporary problems of higher education'.[1] They could not have said it better. In each of the three case studies described below, the emphasis has been on creating something that compares to the best in the world but at the same time addresses some of the specific challenges of contemporary Indian higher education. I believe, we are privileged to live in a time when there are many opportunities to create institutions of higher learning in India, the scale of which is unprecedented in history. As several initiatives to build new institutions are spawned and existing universities are being upgraded, hopefully, the experiences of these three case studies will provide some useful and practical insights.

[1] Mackenzie, Norman. 'Starting a New University', *Higher Education Quarterly*, vol. 15, issue 2 (2007).

THE INDIAN SCHOOL OF BUSINESS

In 1996, a small group of Indian businessmen was seized by a dream for the future: 'an international business school that would one day take its place of pride in the ranks of the best business schools of the world, yet at the same time has a uniquely Indian flavour'.

The idea of this business school, which in time came to be called the ISB, germinated from a poignant need in the country for quality management graduates. India was on the path of rapid liberalization and privatization in the 1990s, several multinationals were starting to set up shop in the country. Even as domestic players were bulwarking themselves to withstand intensified competition and everyone was looking for quality talent at all levels, businesses were struggling for lack of options in managerial talent. It was not so much about the numbers—a lot of B-schools had mushroomed all over the country by then. According to one estimate, there were 422.

All India Council for Technical Education (AICTE) approved B-schools in 1998[2]—as it was concerned about the quality of graduates that our not-so-premier B-schools were churning out. Pradip N. Khandwalla, erstwhile professor at IIM Ahmedabad, notes that there was a wide qualitative gap between top schools and the rest, and even among the top ten management schools, there are considerable variations. 'Until standards are enforced, the overall quality of management education in India may decline,'[3] he warned. Even students from India's premier business schools, such as the IIMs, though good, did not match up to international standards. As PepsiCo India's then Executive Director, Mahendra Swaroop, noted in *Business Today*'s first B-school survey in 1998, 'Students with merely excellent academic track records make only excellent management trainees ... IIM-A is producing managers today whereas it needs to produce leaders for tomorrow'.[4]

The reason for disappointment was twofold. First, most Indian business schools admitted, and continue to admit, students without prior

---

[2] Business Today B-School Rankings, 1998 (http://businesstoday.intoday. in/story/best-business-management-b-schools-of-india-2012/1/188775.html).

[3] Khandwalla, Pradip N. 'Management Education in India', *International Encyclopaedia of Business and Management*, vol. 3, p. 2805 (London: Routledge, 1996).

[4] Business Today B-School Rankings, 1998 (http://businesstoday.intoday. in/story/best-business-management-b-schools-of-india-2012/1/188775.html).

work experience. Though very bright, these students lacked something in terms of the context for the learning they were provided. In contrast, most international business schools admitted students with several years of work experience, often at a managerial level, who had the know-how and international exposure necessary to appreciate real challenges faced by companies and industries. Moreover, at that time, we felt that the programmes being offered in Indian business schools, even in the best of institutes, were too narrowly focused on India, and lacked the breadth necessary to connect the dots in a globalizing world.

Therefore, our attempt, when we started, was to bridge these two very important gaps in Indian management education. We were coalesced together by the vision to create India's first truly international business school that would build talent which met, even exceeded, industry expectations; talent which could script the story of India's liberalization and growth and do the nation proud.

None of us had been involved in a project like this before and the enormity of the task at hand dawned on us only gradually, as we painstakingly began to transform the vision into what we hoped would be an invincible institution. While my book, *An Idea Whose Time Has Come: The Story of the Indian School of Business* (2011), chronicles in detail the building of the ISB and its decade-long run, for the purposes of this chapter, I will only touch upon certain aspects that reflect the spirit of innovation, initiative-taking and risk-taking that went into creating the ISB.[5]

The one-year programme—one of the earliest decisions that we had to make while conceptualizing the ISB was the programme structure. The ISB made, quite early on, the unusual but deliberate choice of going for an intensive one-year programme, unlike the two-year MBA that is the norm in India. Although most American business schools in the late 1990s were still running two-year MBA programmes, the one-year model, such as the one used at INSEAD, Oxford's Said Business School and Cambridge's Judge Business School, was coming into vogue then in Europe. We had realized that the ISB's value proposition lay somewhere in between the quality MBA programmes that were on offer in India, such as those of the IIMs which could compete on cost but had limited capacity, and those of overseas schools, which offered world-class programmes but came at

[5] Sinha, Pramath Raj, 2011. *An Idea Whose Time Has Come: The Story of the Indian School of Business* (New Delhi: Penguin India).

a significant price. The one-year model, therefore, seemed apt for the ISB which was under pressure to keep costs down in order to be competitive with other Indian business schools, while also offering a world-class education unmatched by existing schools. One-year also meant that students could be back in the job market within a year, but with an enhanced skill set and qualifications. Effectively, students would get greater value for money with a lower opportunity cost. Moreover, initial research showed that young Indian professionals—who tend to get married earlier than their counterparts in the West[6]—were more willing to take the one-year route to professional development than the traditional two-year MBA format.

However, this was not an easy decision. While the one-year programme was certainly student-friendly, academicians were unhappy as they thought that it would mean fewer contact hours and a lower quality of education. Finally, a compromise was reached; there would be a very intensive one-year programme of the kind used in Europe with little reduction in contact hours. The programme would be divided into eight terms of six weeks each, with students taking four courses each term. Each student would take 16 core courses which would not only teach basic skills but also help to develop people and turn them into potential international leaders. Another 16 courses would be chosen from a list of optional courses to help students tailor the programme to suit their own needs. Most important of all, every course would be taught by an internationally recognized expert. The modular structure with short-term lengths meant we could rely on visiting faculty to form the bedrock of our teaching paradigm (as we will see in the next section on faculty). Even through the 12-month study course, we were confident of being able to provide 640 contact hours, equivalent to a normal two-year MBA programme, while achieving the same standard of education, or so we believed, but the AICTE begged to differ!

AICTE is the statutory body that accredits all graduate and postgraduate programmes in business and management studies in India. By the end of 2000, it was becoming clear that the AICTE disapproved of ISB's independent status. We learnt that other business schools in India were warned by the AICTE to not cooperate with us, and subsequently, we

---

[6] The average age of marriage for men in India is 26 and women 22, as opposed to 29 and 27 in the USA, 32 and 30 in France, 31 and 28.5 in the UK and 30 and 28.5, respectively, in Singapore (Source: http://en.wikipedia.org/wiki/Age_at_first_marriage).

were issued a notice that the AICTE intended to close ISB on grounds of 'commercialization'. While we knew it was not within the AICTE's power to shut down ISB, however, we were worried because it had the power to withhold accreditation of our programme, which indeed, turned out to be the case. The AICTE was critical of our one-year model and mandated that like all other Indian MBA programmes, ours be two years in length. By that point, we were beginning to question the utility (or futility) of policies that regulated only the inputs—land requirements, building plans, library facilities, computer centre and other such amenities—with complete disregard to the output, quality of instruction, and learning processes. Therefore, we eventually decided to go forth without AICTE accreditation. In other words, we proceeded on the basis that we would deliver the equivalent of a full MBA programme, but without granting an actual degree or diploma at the end. Instead, there would be a certificate, co-signed by the deans of our partner schools and the chairman of the governing board.

This was a huge risk to foot. The MBA was, after all, a prestigious degree and students coveted it. But as it turned out, our students valued the learning experience they were being offered greater than the degree they would receive at the end of the year. ISB could take the chance because, as M.R. Rao, a prolific academician and ISB's former Dean, says, 'A world-class business school requires two things; academic respectability and corporate support' and ISB had both. It should be added that we were not the only Indian business school to fall foul of AICTE and several highly-ranked institutions offer programmes that are not accredited. In the recent past, the Indian Supreme Court has ruled that the AICTE, in fact, does not have the power to approve MBA programmes. However, I have learnt since that it is wise only for professional courses to take such a bet, it only needs them to win the confidence of students and recruiters. Other undergraduate and postgraduate programmes cannot afford the gamble. For instance, at Ashoka University we have full university status under the Haryana Private Universities Act and Ashoka is fully recognized by the University Grants Commission (UGC).

As I look back, a distinctive feature that set the ISB apart was the school's ambition and drive to be world-class, from the word go. We didn't go the traditional phased route of aiming first to be the best in India, then Asia and so on, but aspired to be counted amongst the best in the world on every conceivable dimension—facilities, infrastructure, students, faculty, and research—from day one. Among other things, this meant that we needed word-class faculty for teaching and research, from day one, and this was one of ISB's biggest constraints.

In the 1990s, there weren't too many academic leaders in management in India, and the few there were, were employed in IIMs and other top-ten B-schools in India. While we could have induced some to join on board as faculty at the ISB, the executive board firmly held that we should not 'poach' faculty from within India. It was important that this did not become a 'zero-sum' exercise for India. ISB had no choice but to look overseas.

ISB's International Academic Council that was in-charge of faculty and curriculum, reached out to a large number of internationally reputed faculty of Indian origin, teaching at top business schools in Europe and North America. All liked the idea and several pledged their support. But it became clear almost at once that, while it was easy to garner support and advice for the idea, persuading the academicians to jeopardize promising careers by moving back to India to take up posts at an unbuilt and entirely unproven institution proved to be a hard proposition indeed. For one, most faculty want to work at prestigious institutions, and few are willing to take the risk of moving to an untried fledgling institution. Second, moving from America or Europe to India was, or was perceived to be, a decline in the standard of living, and lastly, our salary scale—though very good by Indian standards—was still low by Western standards, and we would be asking people to take a pay-cut. Fortunately, for ISB, there were enough faculty who, though unwilling to relocate completely, were willing to give six to eight weeks of their time in a year to support the cause of quality management education in the country.

The visiting faculty model was an innovation that would serve ISB well for many years to come. It was decided that we abandon, at least in the beginning, the pursuit to hire large numbers of permanent faculty, and instead, opt for a visiting faculty approach. Overseas faculty would come in to teach one or two courses each year, with each course compressed into a six-week period. This model allowed ISB to draw on 'superstar' faculty from across our partner institutions and elsewhere to come and teach without major disruption to their careers and family lives. The visiting faculty, by the sheer weight of their name, would lend tremendous academic cred-ibility to ISB, and we believed that this, in turn, would ease the difficulty of recruiting permanent faculty.

The model was a huge success; ISB had an impressive line-up of 23 visiting faculty from Kellogg, Wharton, the London School of Business,

Yale, Stanford, University of Chicago, University of Texas, and University of Minnesota when the school opened to its first class in 2001. The original plan was that within five years, 70 per cent would be permanent faculty and 30 per cent would be visitors. But so popular were the visiting faculty with students that we revised our original plan and resolved to continue inviting visiting faculty. We have retained a mix of core and visiting faculty till date and it has served us well. Moreover, segregating teaching and research faculties and using visiting faculty for teaching has allowed us to hire our permanent faculty with greater deliberation rather than be under pressure to hire whoever was available and interested.

Riding on our teaching reputation, in time, the reputational groundswell created by our visiting faculty helped ease some of our challenges

Visiting faculty who agreed to teach at ISB, 2001–02
(as reported to the executive board, 26 March 2001)

Name	Home Institution	Course Taught
B. Balachandran	Kellogg	Managerial Cost Accounting
Rajiv Banker	Texas	E-Commerce
Haskal Benishay	Kellogg	Microeconomics
Sunil Chopra	Kellogg	Logistics and Supply Chain
S. Deshmukh	Kellogg	Decision Models
Sumantra Ghoshal	London Business School	Competitive Strategy
Dominic Houlder	London Business School	Strategy
Anjani Jain	Wharton	Statistical Methods
Dipak Jain	Kellogg	Marketing Management
Sunil Kumar	Stanford	Operations Management
Vijay Mahajan	Texas	Marketing Strategy
Madhav Rajan	Wharton	Financial Accounting
Raghu Rajan	Chicago	Corporate Finance
Jagmohan Raju	Wharton	Pricing Strategy
Krish Ramaswamy	Wharton	Financial Engineering
Narendra Rao	Northern Illinois	Investment Analysis
Jeff Sampler	London Business School	Technology and Strategy
Harbir Singh	Wharton	Business Strategy
Jitendra Singh	Wharton	Strategy, Management and Organization
Seenu Srinivasan	Stanford	Customer/Product Planning
Raj Srivastava	Texas	Marketing Technical Products
Shyam Sunder	Yale	Knowledge Management
Akbar Zaheer	Minnesota	Business Strategy

in recruiting permanent faculty. By 2004, ISB's name was becoming well-known and young, recently graduated PhDs with prestigious degrees from American or European universities were prepared to consider ISB as a career option and faculty numbers had started to rise. M.R. Rao, then Dean of ISB and a passionate believer in research, was instrumental in the drive to build research capacity. Today, ISB has nearly 60 full-time tenure track faculty who are publishing steadily, adding to the teaching reputation that we have built over the years. In 2016, ISB made it into the top 100 list of research rankings globally conducted by University of Dallas (UTD) during 2011–2015. For a business school which has been around only for 15 years, this is worthy of respect. It is also the first Asian institution to be accredited by Association for Advancement of Collegiate Schools of Business (AACSB), an internationally accepted accreditation institution focused on raising the standards of management education worldwide.

Applied research too has begun to pick up. ISB now has nine centres of excellence, the Centre for Analytical Finance, the Centre for Emerging Markets Solutions, the Centre for Investment, the Centre for Leadership, Innovation, and Change, the Centre for Teaching, Learning, and Case Development, the Indu Centre for Real Estate and Infrastructure, the Srini Raju Centre for IT and The Networked Economy, the Thomas Schmidheiny Chair for Family Business and Wealth Management and the Wadhwani Centre for Entrepreneurship Development, and four schools in Public Policy, Healthcare Management, Manufacturing Management and Infrastructure Management which connect industry and academia to advance education, research and outreach in key areas.

GOVERNANCE STRUCTURE

ISB was the result of the collective efforts of many leading business leaders, entrepreneurs, philanthropists, and academics. Even while the new institution was merely an idea, without even a name, donors, and funders from India and abroad who had much the same vision came forward to give generously of their time and money. These heavyweight corporates on the ISB board could have been the envy of any global business school. In time, we were also able to attract leading business schools to associate with us, who served as able guides and mentors in our venture. We believe that working together with, yet working independently of, these multiple stakeholders has been the key to our success.

ISB's governance structure is characterized by a unique convergence of two worlds traditionally thought to be divergent—the industry and the academia. Our executive board is entirely composed of business people, who have always provided the strategic direction to the project and made decisions on academic and administrative matters. As the academicians who taught, planned, and oversaw the programme at ISB rubbed shoulders with the business persons who managed the school, the tension between the two groups was apparent. The academicians found it hard to accept the views of this group of business people who know very little about educational academia, and similarly, business people tended to work the business logic and were sometimes dismissive of the views of the academics. But to their credit, on the whole, they have cooperated very well, and each side recognizes the value the other brings to the institution. The business side brings the corporate support, the funding, the entrepreneurial thinking, the global aspiration; the academics deliver the results in terms of research, education, and training. The academic and business sides of ISB work collaboratively, with a certain amount of creative tension, and lots of constructive debate.

The other pillar critical to the ISB architecture is its network of academic partners and mentors. Several of ISB's executive board members had served on governing boards of international schools earlier, and saw the tremendous value that partnering with such institutions would bring to ISB, particularly since the school was starting ground-up, and not under the aegis of an established university. The founding team had already begun canvassing support amongst American schools since the beginning of 1997, and when we had decided to forge formal academic partnerships, four schools stood out—Harvard Business School, the Stanford Graduate Business School, the Wharton School (of the University of Pennsylvania), and the Kellogg Graduate School of Management (of Northwestern University). All four were big-ticket names, and any one would have given a face-lift to ISB's brand, but the school exercised enormous caution in picking its partners. First, we did not want just one partner, because that would have risked ISB becoming known as the 'Harvard of the East' or the 'Stanford of the East'. In contrast, a joint venture with several schools would allow us to maintain an independent identity. This ruled Harvard out, which wanted to be the sole partner, and

Stanford backed out for lack of resources, leaving us with Kellogg and Wharton, both of which were excellent choices for us to work with, particularly since the two already had prior experience of working together to establish the Sasin Graduate Institute of Business Administration in Thailand. The London Business School too joined in the endeavour, and together the three schools played the role of academic mentors, helping ISB plan its programme and curriculum, loaning faculty from their schools, enabling student exchanges between campuses and building a culture in ISB that was resonant with the world-class culture that existed in their schools. In time, MIT Sloan School of Management and the Fletcher School at Tufts University enriched the portfolio of our associate schools.

As I have briefly alluded to before, ISB was always keen to maintain an independent identity. As a matter of fact, we were obsessive about this, from the start. The view was that the institution was larger than any individual, partner, or corporate. Lots of people would take part in its success but no person could take credit for it. For example, we have made sure that people who have given more money than others are not more prominent. The membership of the board is such that regardless of how much a person donated to the School, they only get one vote on the executive board. As a result there is no one attributable founder of ISB; rather, there is a broad group.

We have also maintained independence from our partners. We are not a Kellogg or a Wharton in India. Although we depended on them heavily for expertise and advice, we have always reserved the right to say that we will do what we do what is best for ISB. We have also maintained fierce independence in terms of admissions. We have refrained from reserving seats, or management quotas, for board members, or playing favourites in any other way. Lastly, we have preserved our independence from the government, an unusual thing to do in India. We burnt our fingers early on in dealing with the Maharashtra state government (Mumbai was our choice of location before we moved the project to Hyderabad), which had asked for reservations for students and employees from the state. Once bitten, twice shy, we stayed clear of banking on the government for concessions of any sort, although I must admit that we got very supportive arrangements for the land in Hyderabad and Mohali.

Our independence served to anchor us in a vast sea of stakeholders and well-wishers and enabled us to do what was best for the school at every step. The reason I am emphasizing this repeatedly is that I see a lot of people setting up institutions in India today. They are usually very prominent philanthropists who turn out to be the single-largest donors of the institution they are building, and in their eagerness to leave a legacy behind, start to run the institution their way. This has not happened at ISB for the sole reason that we have always had broad ownership and truly separated ownership from the management and functioning of the institution.

SALIENT INSIGHTS

ISB has gone from strength to strength in its decade of existence. Its Hyderabad and Mohali campuses together graduate over 1000 students every year from its full-time postgraduate programme in management, in addition to offering executive education to several thousand each year. In 2008, it broke into the top 20 in the *Financial Times* Global MBA ranking. In 2009, the School was ranked fifteenth in the world; in 2010, twelfth; in 2011, thirteenth; and in 2012, twentieth. More recently, it was ranked twenty-seventh in 2016. The dream of building a world-class institution has come true. Reflecting over the last 15 or more years, and seeing how the school was founded and how it has grown, I have tried to distil from my experience key insights that have led to the present success.

We learnt powerful lessons about the faculty model while building ISB, particularly the everlasting impact extraordinary faculty have on students. To provide inspiring teachers who excite and challenge their students to be the best they can be, has been a cornerstone of the ISB model—something that we adopted into the YIF model with as much success several years later.

Even from the start, ISB had very ambitious plans of expansion. Our initial target was 120 students in each of the first two years, doubling to 240 in year three to five, and then doubling again to 480 in year six. We have by far stuck to that model, and today have an alumni network comparable to the IIMs established in the 1960s. In contrast, most people take the approach of building institutions slowly and gradually. Counter-intuitive as it may seem to the wisdom of small-class sizes and elite institutions, scale helps attract better students, better resources, and better quality. Naturally, as more alumni make their mark, more prospective students learn about the institute. Attracting bright students helps keep the pressure up on delivering quality, and an expanded incoming class translates to more resources to invest in ensuring quality, creating a virtuous cycle.

Another innovation we used—borrowing from our corporate backgrounds—was a mental model of education as an enterprise. In the early stages of the project, there were many discussions over who the real customers of ISB would be. Were students the customers? Were faculty the customers? Were recruiters the customers? Or were they all customers? Eventually, we settled on this position that the only way that we would be successful was if corporate and recruiters saw us as the best place to recruit from. That meant we, as an institution, and the students were working together collaboratively to produce the 'product' that recruiters and corporates wanted. While most academics are reluctant to think of students as the 'product', this model clarified a great deal for us. It shaped our approach to setting up the school as an organization and the processes we used. For instance, if we were going to create the best 'product' we had to get the best students. And once we had recruited them, we needed to make sure they shared in the culture of co-creation. Like any good producer, we were obsessive about quality: quality students, quality faculty, quality teaching, quality facilities, all of which would reflect in the product.

A natural extension of thinking of education as an enterprise was the thrust we laid on the placement process. Traditionally in India, the recruitment process is completely organized and led by the students themselves. They contact companies, schedule appointments, and run the recruitment office. But that did not fit with our model. If recruiters were our customers, then we should invest in building relationships with them. So we set up a recruitment office staffed by very high-quality professionals with good connections to industry, people who could go out and convince CEOs and heads of HR that there was plenty of talent to be found at ISB and they should come and recruit there. We invested heavily in the recruitment process, and that was another innovation in India.

We aimed to create a world-class business school, an ambition that was rooted since day one, and having stopped to consider what that really meant, we came to the conclusion that 'world-class' for a new school really meant top-ranked. We knew that rankings were controversial and that some top schools actually looked at rankings with disdain. There were questions about accuracy and fairness. On the other hand, getting into the rankings and especially getting high in the rankings would win us recognition. That was particularly important for us as a new business school. We had to not just *be* world-class, we had to be *seen* to be world-class.

Needless to say, each of these insights comes with a certain context, and not every strategy or every idea will work in every circumstance. We had no inkling when we were building ISB that we were creating a sort of a template, a blueprint for building world-class institutions, until nearly 15 years later, a group of philanthropic business leaders and I are drawing upon these same insights from the ISB experience to build another world-class institution, only this time, a university in liberal arts.

ASHOKA UNIVERSITY

Ashoka University was begun with an abiding belief that all Indian students should be able to receive a world-class higher-education experience in India.[7] Much like ISB, the Ashoka University, a multidisciplinary university anchored in liberal arts and a liberal education aims to bridge an important gap in the society, albeit a different one. The inspiration behind Ashoka is a combination of deep concern for the quality of higher education presently available to students in India as well as a vision for the kind of graduates and leaders that the future of India needs.

Ashoka is founded on the fundamental principle that education must be holistic and liberal, that we must move beyond, in Dr Indira Parikh's words, 'the rigidity, aridity and empty formalism'[8] of a syllabus-bound, employment-oriented educational system, and that such education is vital to producing leaders of tomorrow who can think critically, communicate effectively, and become self-aware and socially responsible.

Traditionally, the Indian higher education landscape has been characterized by strict disciplinary boundaries, rigid departmental silos, and narrow specializations. The Indian model borrows greatly from the British education system—another of the many colonial legacies—where students start to specialize very early in their academic trajectory. As they enter the threshold of under graduation, they are forced to choose their major, a choice that they have to live with for the rest of their education and life.

---

[7] Ashoka University website: http://ashokauniversity.edu.in/Home.

[8] India-OECD Collaborative Workshop on Education and Innovation: Summary Report, EDU/CERI/CD (2012)12, available at: http://www.oecd.org/india/EDU-CERI-CD(2012)12.pdf.

While this narrow focus has helped the country develop a cadre of special-ized experts in several fields, it has left Indian graduates underprepared in terms of the width of perspectives and critical thinking skills that distinguish their counterparts from around the world.

Advocating for an educational policy which contains a built-in flex-ibility, the Chairman of the 1966 Education Commission, D.S. Kothari, had forcefully expressed himself as far back as 1966 in the following words:[9]

> If I may say so, the single most important thing needed now is to get out of the rigidity of the present system. In the rapidly changing world of today, one thing is certain: yesterday's educational system will not meet todays', and even less so, the need of tomorrow.

While Dr Kothari's remark might have been aimed at the state of sci-ence education in the country, the situation in liberal arts and humanities is no different. It is important to distinguish here an education in liberal arts from a liberal education. The Association of American Colleges and Universities says:[10]

> Liberal Education is an approach to learning that empowers individuals and prepares them to deal with complexity, diversity, and change. It provides students with broad knowledge of the wider world (e.g., science, culture, and society) as well as, in-depth study in a specific area of interest. A liberal education helps students develop a sense of social responsibility, as well as strong and transferable intellectual and practical skills such as communica-tion, analytical and problem-solving skills, and a demonstrated ability to apply knowledge and skills in real-world settings.

Does the liberal education we offer in this country match up to that definition? To answer with an example, at a typical Indian university today, in the three-year BA Honours in economics programme now taught over six semesters, a student would take a total of 26 courses, roughly four to five courses a semester. Of these, 21 or over 80 per cent are required courses in the discipline of economics. Of these 19 are specified and only two are electives. The remaining five courses are in other areas

---

[9] 'Report of the Education Commission 1964–1966', *Government of India Press, Delhi* (1966).

[10] Available at http://www.aacu.org/leap/what_is_liberal_education.cfm.

with two required language courses and three elective courses outside of the economics discipline. Given the perceived importance of these five 'subsidiary' courses, they get the short shift from the students and teachers alike.

In contrast, if a student were to be admitted to the Yale University's four-year undergraduate programme, she would do a total of 36 courses, again roughly four to five courses a semester. However, there is a big, big difference! The student is only required to do 16 courses (just below 45 per cent of total) in the economics major. Also, only about half of these courses are specified subjects, the other half are electives chosen from a wide variety of economics courses. That is the extent of specialization or depth but that, too, with considerable choice. So after completing the required major courses like microeconomics, macroeconomics, econometrics, etc., one can choose to do game theory, environmental economics, anti-trust economics, economics of South Asia, and debates in macroeconomics as examples of your electives within the economics major. The remaining 20 courses, more than 55 per cent, are further split in two areas, foundation and electives (outside the major) courses, to provide a certain breadth. One recent economics graduate from Yale ended up taking English writing, ethics, astronomy, calculus, advanced calculus, psychology, sociology, humanities, philosophy, logic, advanced sociology, and political science for his 12 foundation courses. For his electives, he exercised his full freedom of choice to pick cyber law, Hindi literature, algorithms and programming, ecology, public health, international affairs, and intellectual property in the digital age and linguistics.

The contrast between the three-year BA economics honours approach and the four-year Yale University BA with a major in economics is apparent. The former is very specialized with little choice or flexibility. The latter provides tremendous breadth in that additional one year while recognizing the need for specialization. It recognizes that the economics major may go on to work in areas other than economics. It equips the student with a multidisciplinary education, helping them approach problems that they are asked to solve later in life with both flexibility and multiple perspectives. In fact, in the great universities of America this approach is not only applied to the liberal arts majors but also to professional majors like engineering, computer science, and business. Thus, when a civil engineer sets out to build a bridge he is not only approaching this from an engineering angle, but also assessing the environmental impact of building the bridge, the socio-economic impact of improved infrastructure, the financing of the bridge and possibly all the related regulatory hurdles to be overcome to get the plans approved.

This means a student, say in the famed Delhi University, studying for an undergraduate degree in economics, with 21 core courses that provide depth and specialization in economics and a mere five subsidiary papers that provide breadth and interdisciplinary learning, is getting an education in liberal arts, alright, but not a 'liberal education'. And notably, while we have colleges aplenty offering the former, there are hardly any that offer the latter. Ashoka's aim is to catalyse this important change in the education system. Therefore, Ashoka University's vision is:

> To be a premier institution of higher-learning, promoting a broad-based, liberal education for all students that prepares them to be effective, ethical, and responsible leaders in a diverse, rapidly changing world. Thus, to be a role model for liberal education that others may look to emulate and thereby help in transforming higher education in India.

Ashoka University opened its doors in July 2014. The University has forged partnerships with leading schools in the West including the School of Engineering and Applied Sciences at the University of Pennsylvania, Carleton College, and the Institute d'etudes Politique de Paris, popularly known as Sciences Po. Like in its illustrious partner institutes, Ashoka's core programme was planned to be a four-year liberal arts BA. This is because the most enduring wisdom on a liberal education recommends a two-year general education that allows students to explore breadth and a subsequent two years to provide depth. Hence, the need for four years. But this is not easy to do, and the challenges are twofold. In 2017, Ashoka is launching BSc in physics and biology to complete its offering in natural sciences. Majors in subjects like computer sciences and mathematics were already on offer.

Will Ashoka be able to hire inspiring high-quality faculty? The importance of having phenomenal faculty to inspire and stimulate students to be creative and original thinkers and develop a love for learning cannot be overemphasized. Unlike what we could do for ISB by relying on visiting faculty, we would need high-quality resident permanent faculty right from the start at Ashoka. The good news for us is that there is a sizeable class of very high quality humanities faculty and researchers in India who are looking for institutes of excellence, where they can conduct meaningful research and impart valuable life lessons, igniting the minds of the young. It is our intention to make Ashoka that place for such educators and thought leaders. In fact, at the time of writing Ashoka University has already recruited some of the best and brightest faculty from around the world and the pipeline of academics interested in joining Ashoka is strong and very high-quality. To hire faculty, Ashoka had put together an Academic Council under the leadership of André Béteille and including the likes of Ramachandra Guha, Sunil Khilnani, Kaushik Basu, Christophe Jaffrelot, and others. This year, our founding Vice-Chancellor Rudrangshu Mukherjee will be succeeded by Pratap Bhanu Mehta, a highly distinguished academic. Two years after Ashoka's inception, the Council was reshaped to include present Deans and senior professors and the erstwhile previous group was renamed the Academic Advisory Group.

Does a liberal education get you jobs? For where India is in the trajectory of economic development, it is but natural, even if disheartening, that educational pursuits are by and large guided by the desire to find high-paying employment. No wonder then that as a country we produce the highest number of engineers, and are obsessed with medicine and management as fields of study, and liberal education comes a distant last. Liberal education in India is beset with a huge perceptional challenge, that it does not get you jobs. While this is largely true, one must note though that it is not the idea of liberal education that is at fault here, but the way such an education is delivered in our colleges. In the West, graduates from liberal arts colleges go on to occupy enormously coveted leadership positions in the corporate world and this should come as no surprise because the very idea of a liberal education is to produce critical thinkers, agile problem-solvers, effective communicators, great team members and leaders, and, above all, socially sensitive and responsible citizens in a country facing enormous social challenges.

A liberal education not only sharpens the critical thinking capabilities of the graduates but they realize from studying the variety of liberal arts subjects that asking the right question is as, if not more, important than finding the right answers. Often, there are no answers. This is the heart of critical thinking and analysis that employers expect every university graduate to bring with them. It comes from the practice of the three critical aspects—reading, writing, and reasoning—that all liberal education programmes emphasize, given their emphasis on the liberal arts subjects.

Critical thought enables graduates to effectively engage and deal with ambiguous and complex problems, some of societies' toughest challenges, to which there are no clear answers. The three Rs also strengthen the communication skills of the graduates, the constant writing and debate makes them articulate their thoughts and ideas better, again, great for a successful career. And finally, given their breadth of exposure, a four-year liberal education grooms responsible graduates who are committed to solving the tremendous social, environmental, economic, and political problems we face as a world.

The idea at Ashoka is to reverse this decline in the perceived value of a broad-based liberal arts education by delivering it the right way. We are already beginning to do this through the YIF programme.

THE YOUNG INDIA FELLOWSHIP PROGRAMME

As the shape of Ashoka began to take form in our minds, and as we started putting the first pieces of it together, we realized that it would take us at least six years to put the requisite inputs together—infrastructure, faculty, students, partnerships, and graduate the first batch. However, we had already started to line up a powerful set of academic collaborations and an inspiring set of faculty from within India and abroad. Not wanting to lose time while we built and launched the university, we launched the YIF Programme as an exciting one year multidisciplinary immersion programme for young graduates who yearned to learn beyond the rigorous disciplinary boundaries they were subjected to in their undergraduate education.

The YIF is aimed at graduates from any discipline. In its first two years, YIF also offered a full scholarship to everyone selected for the YIF. Today, the YIF is 'needs-blind', offering varying amounts of scholarships depending on the candidate's ability to pay. This year, we received 4000 applications for the 300 Fellowships on offer. In a very short period of time, the YIF has become a highly sought after and very selective programme.

We have attracted some of the most inspiring 'rock star' faculty from around the world to teach on the programme, again in the ISB visiting faculty model. André Béteille (sociology), Dwight Jaggard and Kenwyn Smith (leadership), Rudrangshu Mukherjee and Gopalkrishna Gandhi (history), A.K. Shiva Kumar (economics), Mihir Shah (development economics), Amita Baviskar (environmental sociology), Devesh Kapur and Christophe Jaffrelot (political science and International Relations) are some of the faculty who teach in the YIF—they are the best and brightest globally in their fields.

Education at YIF places liberal arts at the centre of a more holistic learning experience. Key elements of the programme include:

A wide assortment of courses: Fellows take classes in a range of subject areas that cover everything from anthropology to ethics, natural sciences to climate change, art appreciation to entrepreneurship. The fellows develop new insights on some of the most complex global challenges we face and a world-view based on a broad set of core disciplines. The programme is delivered through 20 to 26 courses by the best academicians and practitioners from India and abroad. The programme structure borrows much from the highly successful (and intensive) ISB model with eight terms of six weeks each, spread over a year, lending itself well to visiting faculty.

An experiential learning module: Given that Fellows have limited professional experience prior to joining the programme, YIF has conceived the experiential learning module, or ELM, to complement their academic work with real work experience. YIF requires its fellows to undertake eight-month-long engagement with an organization after completing the first two terms of the programme. These projects are derived from different companies, organizations, and institutions across various sectors, business, academic and social, and are designed to develop basic skills of building and working in diverse teams, apply essential techniques of structuring and problem solving, gain real life experience by working on live projects with clients and create new opportunities for professional advancement with the client organization.

Mentorship: The Fellows, during their stay at YIF and beyond, have the unique privilege of being mentored by eminent leaders, academicians, and practitioners from India and abroad. These mentors come from diverse sectors spanning media, consulting, non-profit organizations, banking, IT, etc., and are committed to supporting the programme by guiding the fellows in developing insights into sectors of their interest, creating new opportunities for the fellows through their network and enriching the curriculum by giving lectures and interacting with students and teachers through seminars and other events.

A diverse student body: The student body at YIF only adds manifold to the richness of the programme. The programme has attracted some of the brightest minds in the country, from across India and abroad and multi-disciplinary backgrounds including humanities, engineering, science, commerce, design, law, management, and medicine. In what is uncommon in institutes of higher learning, the YIF student body has generally had a greater percentage of female students. We have graduated six classes, close to 900 students so far, and the Fellows have gone on to pursue careers in corporate and academic worlds apart from the development sector and entrepreneurship.

In what is very gratifying for us as founders, many Fellows have found in the YIF, a place to learn unfettered by rigid boundaries, a place where they can think freely with reason and without bigotry, a place to explore forgotten passions and quench their fertile curiosity that has long been a subject of the aridity of our higher education system. Several of them have made amazing turnarounds in their careers, for instance, an agricultural engineer who is a budding author now with a reputed publishing house; a student of law now working with tribal populations at the intersection of law and anthropology; students of engineering and sciences who have been admitted to renowned graduate programmes in public policy, economics and other social sciences, and the list goes on. Several of them have chosen to go back to their earlier chose of discipline, enriched by the vastness of insights gained at YIF and many of them are pursuing successful careers in the corporate and social sectors. Strategically, the YIF has served to prove that liberal arts majors are eminently employable, in a way easing the way for Ashoka.

* * *

While these may be three very specific and distinct case studies, they hold valuable lessons in building higher educational institutions. Whether these lessons apply to other situations will obviously depend on the context. In closing, let me reiterate some of the most powerful insights I have gained from building ISB, Ashoka, and YIF so far:

- While there is room for many, many institutions of higher learning in India and not all of them have to be innovative and distinctive, we do have the unique opportunity and privilege to build greenfield institutions from the ground-up. It is, therefore, always worth considering, and especially required when aspiring for greatness, that the institution address some unmet demand, some unsolved problem in higher education that will make it stand apart.

- Innovations in higher education come from borrowing working and successful models from the West (since they have continuously honed their model and have the experience of the past 300–400 years), but adapting and customizing them to the contemporary Indian context. Partnerships are a great support in this quest for innovation and distinctiveness.

- Governance and leadership are the two most important elements of building great institutions. This is especially true for higher education in India. Without independence—true independence from owners, investors, founders, government, and partners—achieving true greatness is difficult. The choice of the institution's leader, both, the selection process and the choice itself, is paramount in building institutions right.

- The magic in the creation of any institution happens when you bring inspiring faculty together with bright students. Ultimately, that is all that matters. If you make that happen, everything else falls into place.

- It is possible and has now been proven that one can aim to create institutions of higher learning in India that are world-class in the quality of their student-faculty interaction from day one. As our nation laments that our top universities do not figure in the global rankings of top universities, we have to believe that one day soon we will have many institutions that may not have the years behind them but can deliver education that is available in the best of universities globally right here in India. This is possible and we all have to strive to make it happen.

We are privileged to be part of a generation that has benefitted from the education we got in India and also the strong desire to learn and succeed in whatever we do. Our nation struggles with numbers and our much touted demographic dividend threatens to become a disaster if we continue to fail our young people in providing a high-quality education. It is high time we committed to building many, many more institutions of excellence in this country, institutions that are not just best in the world but also best for the world.

Indian Higher Education in a Comparative Perspective

Policy, Regulation, and Management

7 Future of Indian Universities

Need for a Liberalized Legal Regime

A. Francis Julian

The current legal regime governing universities in India consists of a plethora of central and state laws, rules and regulations framed under these laws and their interpretation by courts.[1]

Indian Parliament and state legislatures have enacted laws establishing universities and created regulatory agencies.[2] These regulatory agencies, both at the national and state levels, regulate the establishment,

---

[1] Universities being institutions of higher education, the laws relating to universities would cover several branches of law. There is no branch of law which exclusively deals with universities, though it is in the process of evolution.

[2] This is because a university as an educational institution can be created only by an exclusive law passed by the Parliament or state legislature for that purpose, unlike other educational institutions which can be established under any existing legislation which permits registration or incorporation of educational institutions.

existence, and functioning of Indian universities.[3] Superior courts in India have, while interpreting constitutional provisions in the context of higher education, laid down laws which also regulate the functioning of universities.[4] Thus, the legal regime which currently governs universities in India is multilayered and highly complex which lacks uniformity in its application to different universities. This situation has made the task of administering universities most difficult, plagued by uncertainties and very often courts have to intervene when the actions of universities are questioned as violative of constitutional safeguards, statutory protection and regulatory requirements.[5]

A degree can be awarded only by a university established and incorporated by law. *Prof. Yashpal & Anr. v State of Chhattisgarh & Ors. (2005) 5 SCC 420; Rajasthan Pradesh Vaidya Samithi v. Union of India (2010) 12 SCC 609.*

[3] There are 16 national level regulatory bodies which regulate higher education in India. They are (1) All India Council for Technical Education (AICTE) (1987), (2) Bar Council of India (BCI) (1961), (3) Central Council of Homoeopathy (CCH) (1973), (4) Central Council of Indian Medicine (CCIM) (1970), (5) Council of Architecture (CoA) (1972), (6) Dental Council of India (DCI) (1948), (7) Distance Education Council (DEC) (1985), (8) Indian Council of Agricultural Research (ICAR), (9) Indian Nursing Council (INC) (1947), (10) Institute of Cost and Works Accountants of India (ICWAI) (1959), (11) Medical Council of India (MCI) (1956), (12) National Council for Teacher Education (NCTE) (1993), (13) Pharmacy Council of India (PCI) (1948), (14) Rehabilitation Council of India (RCI) (1992), (15) State Councils of Higher Education (SCHE), and (16) Veterinary Council of India (VCI) (1984).

[4] A university falls within the definition of 'State' as being 'other authorities' under Article 12 of the Constitution of India since it is established by an Act or under it. Being a 'State' any act by it which is in violation of the fundamental rights under the Constitution of India can be challenged before the Courts. The right to education is a fundamental right under Article 21 of the Constitution of India as held by the Supreme Court of India. See *Maharshi Mahesh Yogi Vedic Vishwavidyalaya v. State of M.P. & Ors. 2013 (8) SCALE 541; Society for Unaided Private Schools of Rajasthan v. Union of India (2012) 6 SCC 1; Bharatiya Seva Samaj Trust v. Yogeshbhai Ambalal Patel (2012) 9 SCC 310; State of Tamil Nadu v. K. Shyam Sunder (2011) 8 SCC 737; Ashok Kumar Thakur v. Union of India (2008) 6 SCC 1; Mohini Jain v. State of Karnataka & Ors. (1992) 3 SCC 666; Unnikrishnan J.P. & Ors. v. State of A.P & Ors (1993) 1 SCC 645.*

[5] These involve admission of students, fee structure, reservation in admissions, disciplinary matters pertaining to students, appointment of faculty and non-faculty

Universities in India can be grouped on the basis of their origin, whether established by a central legislation or a state legislation, or on the type of ownership, whether public or private.[6] There are central universities established under central laws and state universities established under state laws.[7] Recently, there is mushrooming of deemed to be universities which have been conferred the status of university by the Central Government on the recommendation of the University Grants Commission (UGC).[8] Universities in India have also been further grouped on the basis of their ownership, whether public or private.[9] Their governance structure and the applicable laws and rules vary in accordance with their origin and the ownership.

---

members, and disciplinary matters involving academic and non-academic staff. However, courts are very reluctant to interfere in academic decisions or decisions in matters of discipline or administration of the internal affairs of a university. See *Guru Ghasidas University v Craig Macleod (2012) 11 SCC 275.* When there is a violation of statutory rules or legal principles courts will interfere. *Dr. Ambedkar Institute of Hotel management, Nutrition and Catering Technology v Vaibhav Singh Chauhan (2009) 1 SCC 59; All Indian Council for Technical Education v Sutinder Kumar Dhawan (2009) 11 SCC 726; Thapar Institute of Engineering & Technology (2001) 9 SCC 157.*

[6] Presently there are 634 degree awarding institutions in the country with Tamil Nadu leading the chart with 59, followed by 58 in Uttar Pradesh, 48 in Rajasthan, 44 in Maharashtra and Karnataka, Gujarat, Madhya Pradesh and West Bengal having 42, 36, 28, and 26, respectively. The eight states of Northeast have 40 such institutions with Assam having 10, Meghalaya, 9. Rest of the six Northeast states—Sikkim, Nagaland, Arunachal Pradesh, Mizoram, Manipur, and Tripura having 5, 4, 3, 3, 3, and 3, respectively. 'Higher Education In India At A Glance: UGC Report', *University Grants Commission,* http://www.ugc.ac.in/ugcpdf/208844_HEglance2012.pdf.

[7] There are 46 central universities out of which 28 have been established by individual enactments. See 'Central Universities', *University Grants Commission,* http://www.ugc.ac.in/centraluniversity.aspx, accessed on April 28, 2017. There are 358 state universities. See 17 'State Universities', *University Grants Commission,* http://www.ugc.ac.in/stateuniversity.aspx, accessed on April 28,20.

[8] As of 22 February 2017, there are 130 deemed to be universities in India. See 'Deemed University', *University Grants Commission,* http://www.ugc.ac.in/deemeduniversity.aspx, accessed on April 28, 2017.

[9] There are 264 private state universities currently in India. The following states have private universities: Arunachal Pradesh, Assam, Gujarat, Haryana, Himachal

The external regulatory regime on universities is complicated by the control and supervision exercised by several agencies at national and state levels. It varies depending on the nature of universities in terms of their establishment, area of academic activity, and ownership type.[10]

The UGC established by the University Grants Commissions Act, 1956, is the principal national regulatory agency that plays an overall regulatory role in the functioning of all universities in India.[11] UGC initially was envisaged as a funding agency to the universities. It has now emerged as a national level regulatory body of universities.[12]

Pradesh, Jharkhand, Karnataka, Chhattisgarh, Madhya Pradesh, Meghalaya, Mizoram, Nagaland, Odisha, Punjab, Rajasthan, Sikkim, Tripura, Uttar Pradesh, Uttarakhand, West Bengal. See 'Private Universities', *University Grants Commission*, http://www.ugc.ac.in/privatuniversity.aspx, accessed on April 28, 2017. Private universities have certain autonomy in administration when compared with public universities.

[10] In the case of a public university, the government which has established the same, exercises a higher degree of control than in the case of a private university. Similarly, the professional bodies and councils have certain regulatory power over universities conducting courses in the area in which the professional bodies have jurisdiction. Such power is given to the professional bodies by the respective statutes which have established these professional bodies. For example, universities offering law courses are under the regulatory supervision of the Bar Council of India created under the Advocates Act.

[11] The Act in its preamble states as follows: 'An Act to make provision for the co-ordination and determination of standards in Universities and for that purpose, to establish a University Grants Commission.'

[12] The statement of objects and reasons of the UGC Act is as follows: 'The Constitution of India vests Parliament with exclusive authority in regard to "co-ordination and determination of standards in institutions for higher education or research and scientific and technical institutions". It is obvious that neither co-ordination nor determination of standards is possible unless the Central Government has some voice in the determination of standards of teaching and examination in Universities, both old and new. It is also necessary to ensure that the available resources are utilized to the best possible effect. The problem has become more acute recently on account of the tendency to multiply Universities. The need for a properly constituted Commission for determining and allocating to Universities funds made available by the Central Government has also become more urgent on this account. In the second para it is said that the Commission will also have the power to recommend to any University the measures necessary

Universities which are imparting professional education such as medicine, pharmacy, technical education, dentistry, architecture, law, etc., have to satisfy the norms laid down by the respective professional regulatory bodies constituted under laws enacted by the Parliament.[13] State universities on certain aspects, in addition to the UGC, are under the regulatory supervision of respective state governments in terms of the parent legislation which had established the universities.[14]

The internal governance structures and processes of universities depend on the type of university and are mainly prescribed by the parent legislation which has established the university.[15] The internal governing structure consists of internal authorities responsible for the governance, management, and administration of universities in which members representing different

---

for the reform and improvement of University education and to advise the University concerned upon the action to be taken for the purpose of implementing such recommendation. The Commission will act as an expert body to advise the Central Government on problems connected with the co-ordination of facilities and maintenance of standards in Universities.'

[13] This is because once these regulatory bodies issue regulations under the respective statutes, the universities are bound to follow the same. *Parshvanath Charitable Trust v AICTE (2013) 3 SCC 385; Professional Examination Board v Prashant Agarwal (2010) 15 SCC 756; Vishno Devi Mahila Mahavidyaalaya v State of UP. (2013) 2 SCC 617.* Insofar as technical education is concerned the universities are outside the purview of the AICTE which is the regulatory body created under the AICTE Act, to regulate technical education. See *Bharathidasan University v All India Council for Technical Education (2001)8 SCC 676; Association of Management of Private Colleges v All India Council for Technical Education (2013) 8 SCC 721.*

[14] The Act establishing a state university being state law the state government has jurisdiction under the Act to have supervision over the functioning of that university so as to prevent commercialization and profiteering and also to ensure that the university maintains certain minimum standards. Now invariably all state enactments provide for such supervisory jurisdiction. The state laws invariably provide for membership of state officials in the university bodies, mandatory submission of annual reports and accounts, and prior permission before starting new courses and strict regulation on admission of students and collection of fees. The state enactment also invariably invests the state governments to take over the administration and in extreme cases to dissolve the university.

[15] This is done through prescription of certain structures and processes to maintain proper internal governance in universities.

interest groups including academics participate.[16] Day-to-day management and administration of universities are carried out by a group of officers, right from the Chancellor to Deans of Schools.[17] The appointment of teaching and non-teaching staff in universities including their qualifications, their service conditions, fee structure, admission of the students, disciplinary proceedings against students and faculty, the curriculum, examination process, and awarding of degrees are highly regulated externally.[18]

Recently, there have been series of initiatives at national and state levels introducing reforms by way of legislative measures.[19] The reasons for these initiatives are the growing complexities and controversies in the governance of Indian universities coupled with the urgent need to create favourable legal and regulatory environment to encourage establishment of more universities in the era of privatization and globalization. There has been increasing tendency towards commercialization of education and establishment of sub-standard educational institutions which have further necessitated reform initiatives in the area of higher education including universities.[20] These initiatives have thrown open several issues pertaining to the scope and extent of legislative powers between the Parliament and the state legislatures in the regulation of universities and have also raised questions pertaining to university autonomy and academic freedom in universities.[21] The need of the day is a liberalized legal regime with

[16] The UGC has laid down Private Universities Regulation, 2003 to regulate these universities. This is being reviewed and University Grants Commission (Establishment of Standards, and Maintenance thereof, in Private Universities) Regulations, 2014 replacing the 2003 Regulation has been approved by the UGC and the same will be brought into force soon.

[17] Ibid.

[18] There are laws enacted by the state governments providing for the norms to be followed by the universities and professional higher education institutions in the area of admission of students and the fees to be charged by them. The Central Government has also introduced legislation in the Parliament for creating regulatory bodies to regulate the universities and tribunals to deal with issues pertaining to disciplinary proceedings on the faculty.

[19] 'Private Universities Regulation, 2003', *University Grants Commission*.

[20] 'Tandon Committee Report', available at https://www.scribd.com/document/186472058/Complete-Report-on-Deemed-University-Original accessed on April 28, 2017.

[21] 'Private Universities Regulation, 2003', *University Grants Commission*.

adequate safeguards to prevent commercialization, maladministration, and exploitation of students.[22]

The following sections will deal with the legal regime which is currently governing Indian universities. First, it will briefly analyse legal regime governing the establishment of different types of universities such as central universities, state universities, 'Deemed to be Universities', state public universities and state private universities. Second, it will deal with the regulatory structure governing universities both at the national level and state level. Third, this will also cover the regulation of universities externally by professional councils and internal regulation of universities. Fourth, it will summarize some of the measures initiated by the Central Government in the form of legislative reforms to improve the functioning of universities. Finally, some of the current issues pertaining to administration of universities will be addressed. The conclusion is that the current legal regime applicable to universities in India is highly restrictive and Indian universities require a liberalized legal regime if the universities have to compete globally and achieve higher world ranking.

REGULATORY STRUCTURE OF UNIVERSITIES

There is no single general law or legal system which governs various facets of university administration in India. The universities are established and incorporated by laws passed by central and state legislatures. The organizational structure, functions, and powers of universities are primarily governed by the respective statutes under which they are established.

Definition of University

There is no law which formally defines a university. Several attempts have been made to define a university so as to distinguish it from a large number of other institutions of higher education and learning. Traditionally, the essential attributes required for an institution to be called a university are as follows: (i) incorporation by the highest authority (i.e., sovereign power); (ii) students from all parts of the world; (iii) a plurality of masters among the academic staff; (iv) teaching in at least one of the higher faculties;

---

[22] The Supreme Court also highlighted this in the context of admission of students in various higher educational institutions.

(v) residence in the institution's own buildings or near at hand; (vi) the right to confer.[23] The definition of a 'university' under the UGC Act does not provide any specific criteria to identify an institution as a university.[24] Section 2(f) of the UGC Act defines a university as follows:

> University means a University established or incorporated by or under a Central Act, Provincial Act or a State Act, and includes any such institution as may, in consultation with the University concerned, be recognized by the Commission in accordance with regulations made in this behalf under this Act.

Under this definition, an educational institution to be recognized as a university under the UGC Act, it has to be established and incorporated under an Act either passed by the Central Government or provincial government or state government.[25]

---

[23] These are the essential attributes for a university accepted in England in *St. David's College Lampeter v. Ministry of Education [1951] 1 ALL ER 559.* Now even the above attributes are undergoing changes. See D. Harrington and D. Palfreyman, *The Law of Higher Education* (Oxford University Press, 2012), p. 62. Dr Radhakrishnan in 1948 stated as follows, 'There are certain fundamental characteristics which should be inherent in any institution which is to call itself a university ... It should be a place for providing a student with opportunity for all round well-proportioned education for effective living and for citizenship, in addition to preparation for a calling. It may occur that a university shall develop special strength in some particular field, as in engineering or industrial development or in teacher-training or in forestry or fisheries. In fact, since no institution can be excellent in everything, it is desirable that areas of special strength be developed at least in all but perhaps the largest of our universities. However, these areas of special strength should be in addition to facilities for all round higher education, and should not be a substitute for such facilities.' See 'Report of the University Education Commission, 1948', *Ministry of Education, Government of India,* 1962. Traditionally, university was a word used in connection with corporations and guilds. In US the term university is used very loosely. See K.W. Alexander and K. Alexander, *Higher Education Law: Policy and Perspectives* (New York: Routledge, 2011), pp. 25–27.

[24] An additional problem is that the definition of university under the UGC Act is unique to that Act only. It is different from the word university under the Income Tax Act, 1961. See *Oxford University Press v. CIT (2001) 3 SCC 359.*

[25] A company incorporated under the Companies Act with the name university cannot be a university. *Premchand Jain v. R.K. Chhabra (1984) 2 SCC 302.*

A university is considered as 'a high-level educational institution in which students study for degrees and academic research is done'.[26] Only a university, unlike other educational institutions, can confer degrees.[27] This distinguishing feature alone has been the hallmark of a university. The Supreme Court of India has laid down the following characteristics for identifying an institution as a university:

> University is a whole body of teachers and scholars engaged at a particular place in giving and receiving instructions in higher branches of learning; and as such persons associated together as a society or corporate body, with definite organization and acknowledged powers and privileges and forming an institution for promotion of education in higher or more important branches of learning and also the colleges, building and other property belonging to such body. Other necessary attributes of University are plurality of teachers teaching more than one higher faculty and other facilities for imparting instructions and research, provision for residence and must have certain standard of instructions providing for graduate and post-graduate levels of study. It pre-supposes existence of a campus, classrooms, lecture theatres, libraries, laboratories, offices, besides some playgrounds and also sport facility for overall development of personality of the students.[28]

In spite of the above specific criteria laid down by the Supreme Court that plurality of teachers teaching more than one higher faculty and other faculties, there are a large number of single faculty universities that are functioning in India, especially in the field of professional education.[29] Now it has been universally accepted that the main characteristic of a university

---

[26] *Oxford Dictionary*, www.oxforddictionaries.com/definition/english/university, accessed on 28 April 2017.

[27] A degree is recognized only if it is granted by university constituted in terms of the University Grants Commission Act, 1956, or under any State or Parliamentary Act. *Pramod Kumar v. U.P. Secondary Education Service Commission (2008) 7 SCC 153.*

[28] *Prof. Yashpal & Anr. v State of Chhattisgarh* & Ors. (2005) 5 SCC 420; *Rajasthan Pradesh Vaidya Samithi v. Union of India* (2010) 12 SCC 609.

[29] For example, the national law schools are universities established by the respective state laws, but impart education only in law. In contrast, many state private university acts specifically state that the university should have minimum of three faculties.

is promoting research and development of higher knowledge in any discipline along with the power to award degrees.[30]

Constitutional Provisions

Schedule VII of the Constitution of India specifies the lists of items under which the centre and state legislatures have powers to enact laws. List I of Schedule VII contains the items on which Parliament has exclusive power to legislate, List II contains items on which the state legislatures have exclusive power to legislate and List III contains items on which both the Parliament and state legislatures have concurrent power to legislate. The Parliament has, in exercise of its power under Entry 66, 'Coordination and Determination of Standards in Institutions for Higher Education or Research and Scientific and Technical Institutions' in List I (Union List) enacted laws to regulate higher education including universities.[31] The topic of 'education including universities' was originally a state subject falling under Entry 11 of List II (State List).[32] By the 42nd Amendment of the Constitution in 1976, that entry was omitted from the List II (State List) and, was included in Entry 25 of the List III (Concurrent List).[33] In addition to this, Entry 32 of List II confers states the power to incorporate universities.[34] The scope and extent of power to legislate under these entries had created a conflict between the

[30] However, merely having power to award degrees will not make an educational institution a university. Many institutions of national importance such as All India Institute of Medical Sciences (AIIMS), Indian Institutes of Technology (IITs), National Institutes of Technology (NITs), Rajiv Gandhi National Institute of Youth Development (RGNIYD) and many other similar institutions established by Acts of Parliament with degree awarding functions are not universities. See *Dental Council of India v. Hari Prakash (2001) 8 SCC 61.*

[31] Most of the enactments including the University Grants Commission Act, 1956 dealing with universities are enacted by the Parliament in exercise of this power.

[32] In the United States the power is exclusively with the States. See Farrington and Palfreyman, 2012.

[33] Entry 25 of List III reads as follows: 'Education, including technical education, medical education and universities, subject to the provisions of Entries 63, 64, 65, and 66 of List I; vocational and technical training of labour'.

[34] Entry 32 of List II reads as follows: 'Incorporation, regulation and winding up of corporation, other than those specified in List I, and universities; unincorporated trading, literally, scientific, religious and other societies and associations; co-operative societies.'

Parliament and state legislatures with respect to enacting laws to regulate universities. The Supreme Court of India has resolved the conflict by holding that the power of the Parliament to enact laws conferred by Entry 66 of List I must prevail over the power of the states to enact laws to regulate universities.[35] The Supreme Court has stated as follows:

> The consistent and settled view of this Court, therefore, is that in spite of incorporation of Universities as a legislative head being in the State List, the whole gamut of the University which will include teaching, quality of education being imparted, curriculum, standard of examination and evaluation and also research activity being carried on will not come within the purview of the State legislature on account of a specific entry on coordination and determination of standards in institutions for higher education or research and scientific and technical education being in the Union List for which the Parliament alone is competent. It is the responsibility of the Parliament to ensure that proper standards are maintained in institutions for higher education or research throughout the country and also uniformity in standards is maintained.[36]

In view of this clear enunciation of the law by the Supreme Court of India, currently though universities are being incorporated by laws enacted both by Parliament and state legislatures, only Parliament has overall supremacy in regulating universities.[37]

---

[35] *Gujarat University v. Shri Krishna AIR 1963 SC 703; State of Tamil Nadu & Anr. v. Adhiyaman Educational and Research Institute 1995 (4) SCC 104; Osmania University Teachers Association v. State of Andhra Pradesh & Anr. 1987 (4) SCC 671; Dr.Preeti Srivastava & Anr. v. State of M.P. & Ors. 1999 (7) SCC 120.*

[36] Para 20, *Prof Yashpal's case.* The Supreme Court laid down these principles in a case which involved the entries before 1976 Constitutional amendments when incorporation of universities was in the state list. After the Constitutional Amendments of 1976, the position of the Parliament's power to legislate on universities has been further strengthened because of the entry being brought under the Concurrent List and in view of Article 254 of the Constitution whereby the Parliament has the primacy to legislate on an entry in the Concurrent List.

[37] In *Mahishi Mahesh Yogi Vedic Viswavidhyalaya v. State of MP*, the Supreme Court has recently held that the State has no power to regulate the courses being taught by the state university and that only the UGC has the power. The Court also reiterated the supremacy of the Parliament to regulate the affairs of the universities. However, the provisions of the UGC Act will prevail over

Central Universities

Parliament in exercise of its power to legislate on universities has enacted laws establishing central universities.[38] The Aligarh Muslim University is the oldest central university established before India's Independence in the year 1920.[39] There are other universities such as Benares Hindu University,[40] Delhi University,[41] Jawaharlal Nehru University,[42] and Indian Maritime University,[43] etc., which were also some of the universities established by individual enactments by the Parliament. In addition to these central enactments, certain central universities have been established in each state under

---

central university Acts since UGC regulations have wider amplitude and the object of the UGC Act is to maintain minimum standard of instruction and coordinate the same with other institutions. Therefore, the universities created by Central laws are bound to follow UGC regulations. *Annamalai University v Information and Tourism Department (2009) 4 SCC 590.*

[38] There are currently 42 central universities out of which 28 have been established by individual enactments. XIth Five Year Plan envisaged establishment of 16 central universities in hitherto uncovered states of Bihar, Jharkhand, Orissa (now Odisha), Gujarat, Haryana, Punjab, Rajasthan, Himachal Pradesh, J&K, Karnataka, Kerala, Goa, Chhattisgarh, Madhya Pradesh, Uttarakhand, and Tamil Nadu. Accordingly, 16 new central universities, including three state universities converted to central universities, were established under the Central Universities Act, 2009 (Act 25 of 2009).

[39] Though in the year 1877, the Viceroy laid the foundation stone for the establishment of Muhammadan Anglo-Oriental College, Aligarh, which over a period of time became a flourishing institution, the university was established by legislative Act No. 21 of 1920. See *Azeez Basha v. Union of India.*

[40] Established under the Banaras Hindu University Act, 1915.

[41] Established under the Delhi Universities Act, 1922.

[42] Established under the Jawaharlal University Act, 1966.

[43] The Indian Maritime University was established by the Indian Maritime University Act, 2008, which was enacted by the Parliament to establish and incorporate a teaching and affiliating university at the national level to facilitate and promote maritime studies and for matters connected therewith. The power has been given to the university to determine and to admit to its privilege, colleges and institutions not maintained by the Indian Maritime University, to determine standards of admission and to regulate admission of students for various courses of study in recognized institutions.

the umbrella Acts passed by the Parliament.[44] Thus, central universities have been established under the Central Universities Act, 2009, in many states.[45]

Deemed to Be Universities

In addition to the individual Acts enacted by the Parliament establishing central universities, the central government has been conferred with the power to declare, on the recommendation of the UGC, a higher educational institution as deemed to be a university under Section 3 of the UGC Act.[46] By the conferment of that status the institution will have the powers of a university. The central government confers the status of deemed to be institutions on educational institutions, which have attained a level of research status on the recommendation of the UGC.[47] UGC has framed regulations prescribing the eligibility criteria, minimum infrastructural requirements and procedure for conferring deemed university status to educational institutions.[48] Recently, there has been mushrooming of these deemed to be universities and many of them are alleged to not have necessary infrastructural facilities and research programmes and have been criticized for collecting huge capitation fees.[49]

---

[44] This is a new trend wherein by means of a single central Act several universities have been established.

[45] This is under Section 3 of the Central Universities Act, 2009.

[46] This power is given under Section 3 of the University Grants Commission Act, which states as follows: 'The central government may, on the advice of the Commission, declare by notification in the Official Gazette, that any institution for higher education, other than a university, shall be deemed to be a university for the purposes of this Act, and on such a declaration being made, all the provisions of this Act shall apply to such institution as if it were a university within the meaning of clause (f) of section 2.'

[47] There are currently 130 deemed universities.

[48] UGC (Institutions to be Universities) Regulations, 2010.

[49] There are serious complaints against some of the deemed universities on the ground that they are being run for commercial purposes without any basic facilities and that huge capitation fees are being collected for admission into these universities. A public interest litigation has been initiated before the Supreme Court of India (*Viplav Sharma v. Union of India*). A Committee appointed by the Government of India pursuant to the Supreme Court directions (Tandon Committee) has recommended black listing of 44 deemed to be universities on the ground that they have no basic facilities to be conferred the status of a university.

State Universities

The state governments have established state universities under state laws. Pre-constitutional universities such as University of Madras,[50] University of Bombay,[51] and University of Calcutta[52] were established by the respective enactments. These three universities were modelled after the University of London.[53] States have, through state laws established government state universities which are under the control of the state governments and financed by the state governments.[54]

In addition to public universities, in many states, private state universities have been established under state laws.[55] The main purpose for encouraging private universities is to attract, encourage, and promote

[50] The University of Madras was incorporated by the Act of Incorporation No. XXVII of 1857. The establishment of the university is recited to be 'for the better encouragement of Her Majesty's subjects of all classes and denominations within the Presidency of Fort St. George and other parts of India in the pursuit of a regular and liberal course of education.' The Indian Universities Act VIII of 1904, which, by virtue of its second section, is to be deemed part of the Act of Incorporation. The Indian Universities Act, 1904 increased the scope and functions of the old university but restricted its freedom of action by bringing it under the control of the government in respect of the several important matters.

[51] The University of Bombay was brought into existence by Act XXII of 1857 which received the assent of the Governor-General on 18th July. It was described as, having been established for the 'purpose of ascertaining, by means of examination the persons who have acquired efficiency in different branches of Literature, Science and Art and of rewarding them by Academic Degrees'.

[52] The University of Calcutta was the first university established under Act XXII of 1857.

[53] For the history on the establishment of three oldest Indian universities, see 'Structure of University Education in India', *UNESCO Paris*, 14 April 1952, accessed on 28 April 2017.

[54] Of around 611 universities in India, there are around 94 private universities under state legislation and about 90 private deemed universities (out of around 130 deemed universities). In other words, private universities account for about 30 per cent of the universities in India, which will see an increase over the next few years. A. Goswami, *Higher Education Law and Privately-Funded University Education in India, Towards a Vision?*, Indian Infrastructure Report, Ch 17, 2012, p. 185. Currently there are 300 public state universities.

[55] Currently there are 264 private state universities. See *University Grants Commission*, http://www.ugc.ac.in/privatuniversity.aspx, accessed on 28 April 2017.

private sector investment in higher education. The idea is to create opportunities for private entrepreneurs and philanthropists and academics to set up universities.[56] Under the private university laws, various self-financed universities have been established without financial assistance from the state.

The requirement for individual legislations to establish universities was reiterated by the Supreme Court, when an attempt was made by state of Madhya Pradesh to establish several universities through government orders. The Supreme Court mandated that universities should be established only through legislation and not by executive orders. Since several universities in the case before the Supreme Court were established through executive orders published in official gazettes, Supreme Court held that they were not universities in the eyes of law.[57]

Private universities established under state private university enactments are unitary in nature without any power to affiliate—any institution or college. Only private universities which fulfil certain conditions including number of years of existence can establish off-campuses, but with prior approval of state government and concurrence of UGC.[58] Similarly, private universities with certain number of years of existence can alone start distance education courses with the prior approval of the Distance Education Council (DEC) and concurrence of the state government.[59] The private universities are also competent to award degrees specified by the UGC. They are required to maintain minimum standards on academic

[56] In India most of the private universities are set up by promoters who fall into the above three categories.

[57] In this case the Chhattisgarh Legislature enacted the Chhattisgarh Niji Kshetra Vishwavidhyalaya (Stapana Aur Viniyaman) Adhiniyam, 2002 which allowed the state to incorporate and establish a university by issuing a notification in the gazette and permitted such university to affiliate any college or other institution or to set up more than one campus with the prior approval of the state government. Pursuant to this Act, in a short span of one year as many as 112 universities were established and many of them had no buildings and were running from one room tenements. On a Writ petition by Professor Yashpal, Supreme Court struck down the law holding it *ultra vires* and declared that all the universities set up under the law have ceased to exist. *Prof. Yashpal v. State of Chhattisgarh (2005) 5 SCC 420.*

[58] 'Private Universities Regulation, 2003', *University Grants* Commission.

[59] Regulation No. 3.3 of the 'Private Universities Regulation, 2003', *University Grants Commission.*

and physical infrastructure as laid down by the parent Act.[60] However, UGC regulates the quality and standard of programmes offered in state private universities and specifies the names of degrees which should be awarded by them.[61] The UGC has the authority to inspect, recommend improvement and in special cases, to intervene to disqualify the operations of the private university.[62]

REGULATORY REVIEW

Universities are regulated and governed both externally and internally. Universities are governed externally by national level regulations and state level regulation. Apart from these there are professional regulatory bodies which regulate universities in the respective areas in which they operate. The internal regulation and governance are done through the university authorities and officers who frame regulations in the form of statutes, ordinances, rules and regulations.

National Regulation

The UGC Act has been enacted by the Parliament essentially to make provisions for the co-ordination and determination of standards in universities.[63] The UGC was established under the UGC Act as the principal regulator of universities and higher education at the national level. The UGC Act, as regulatory measure, has prohibited unauthorized conferment of degrees and diplomas and also use of the word 'university' by institutions which had not been either established or incorporated by special legislation.[64]

---

[60] Regulation 3.6 of the 'Private Universities Regulation, 2003', *University Grants Commission*.

[61] Regulation 3.7 & 3.8. of the 'Private Universities Regulation, 2003', *University Grants Commission*.

[62] Regulation 4 and 5 of the 'Private Universities Regulation, 2003', *University Grants Commission*.

[63] The preamble to the UGC Act.

[64] Under Section 22 of the UGC Act the right to confer degrees can be exercised only by a university established or incorporated by or under a central Act or a state Act or an institution deemed to be a university or an institution specifically empowered by an Act of Parliament to confer or grant degrees. Under Section 23 of the UGC Act, no institution, whether a corporate body or not, other than a

UGC being the national level principal regulator of universities and higher education has a primary role in regard to the functioning of the universities in India. The said role is performed by UGC by way of issuing regulations from time to time framed under the UGC Act.[65] Apart from issuing regulations, UGC also issues from time to time circulars, notifications and specific directives dealing with various academic and administrative matters.[66] Any breach of these regulations or directions by universities would lead to cancellation of grant[67] and withdrawal of recognition by the UGC.[68]

State Regulation

State universities are established under the laws passed by the respective state legislatures within the territories of which the universities are located. Therefore, state governments have primary interest in regulating state universities. However, in reality, state governments have limited regulatory role in the functioning of the state universities. This is because under the power to regulate over 'co-ordination and determination of standards in higher education and research' the central government alone has the power to regulate state universities.[69]

---

university established or incorporated by or under a central Act, a provincial Act or a state Act shall be entitled to have the word 'University' associated with its name in any manner whatsoever.

[65] These regulations are binding on all universities. Being subordinate legislations they become part of the UGC Act. *Annamalai University v Information and Tourism dept. (2009)4 SCC 590.*

[66] For list of UGC regulations, see 'UGC Regulations', *University Grants Commission*, http://www.ugc.ac.in/page/UGC-Regulations.aspx, accessed on 28 April 2017.

[67] Section 14 of the UGC Act.

[68] Regulation 5 of the 'Private Universities Regulation, 2003', *University Grants Commission.*

[69] See the Supreme Court judgment in *Maharshi Mahesh Yogi Vedic Vishwavidyalaya v. State of M.P. & Ors. 2013 (8) SCALE 541; Society for Unaided Private Schools of Rajasthan v. Union of India (2012) 6 SCC 1; Bharatiya Seva Samaj Trust v. Yogeshbhai Ambalal Patel (2012) 9 SCC 310; State of Tamil Nadu v. K. Shyam Sunder (2011) 8 SCC 737; Ashok Kumar Thakur v. Union of India (2008) 6 SCC 1; Mohini Jain v. State of Karnataka & Ors. (1992) 3 SCC 666; Unnikrishnan J.P. & Ors. v. State of A.P & Ors (1993) 1 SCC 645.*

This has resulted in a peculiar situation wherein states after establishing universities have limited control over their administration and functioning.

Regulation by Professional Bodies

In addition to UGC as a regulator of universities, there are professional councils which also monitor universities which conduct courses which are regulated by the respective professional councils established by Acts.[70] These professional councils require all educational institutions including universities to obtain permission before commencing courses, prescribing the course content, curriculum, admission criteria, etc., of courses regulated by them so that universities have limited regulatory power over the administration of these courses.[71] The rationale behind such an approach is that the professional bodies, in which representatives of particular professions are members, are better equipped to regulate the relevant professional education rather than UGC.[72] Academic collaboration between Indian universities and foreign educational institutions is also subject to approval by the UGC.[73]

---

[70] For example, medical education is regulated by the Medical Council of India (MCI) established under the Medical Council Act; Legal education is regulated by the Bar Council of India (BCI) under the Advocates Act. Technical education was regulated by the All Indian Council of Technical Education (AICTE) under the All India Council of Technical Education Act. Technical education conducted by universities is outside the purview of the Act as per the decision of the Supreme Court in *Bharathidasan University v All India Council for Technical Education (2001)8 SCC 676.e.*

[71] This is because the regulations issued by the regulatory bodies will be binding on the state governments and the universities.

[72] However, in the case of technical education now the UGC has sole power to regulate in view of the recent decision of the Supreme Court in *Association of Technical Education Colleges* cases.

[73] UGC has issued University Grants Commission (Promotion and Maintenance of Standards of Academic Collaborations between Indian and Foreign Educational Institutions) Regulation, 2012 which has prescribed the requirement of prior approval and procedure for foreign and Indian universities to enter into collaborations.

Internal Regulation

Ideally, the internal governance of universities should be based on democratic principles of accountability and transparency so as to ensure academic freedom and university autonomy.[74] However, in actual practice the above ideals are not followed. There are vast differences in the internal governance structures among universities, especially, between public universities and private universities. Similarly, internal governance system between central universities and state universities varies.

The internal governance structure in universities consists of formal authorities or entities, constituted in terms of the parent enactments, which have the duty to ensure that internal administration in a university is properly carried out. These authorities are the senates/governing bodies, which are the apex statutory bodies within a university entrusted with the responsibility of policymaking and providing general supervision over the functioning of the university. The syndicates/board of management of university is mainly entrusted with the supervision of the university administration. These statutory authorities lay down the rules and regulations for internal governance in the form of statutes and ordinances. The senates or governing bodies in universities are the principal legislative authorities. The syndicate or the board of management is the principal management authority in universities. These bodies have overall supervision in the functioning of universities. There are also academic councils in universities mainly to regulate the academic matters in universities.

Besides the above statutory authorities, there are statutory officers of universities who are directly responsible for the day to day management and administration of universities. Among them, the key officers are the Chancellor, Vice-Chancellor, the Registrar and the Controller of Examinations who implement the decisions taken by the university authorities and are responsible and accountable to the university authorities. Their manner

---

[74] Governance in the context of higher education, especially university education would mean the structures and processes by which the university system is governed. See W.A. Kaplan and B.A. Lee, *The Law of Higher Education*, Student Version, 4th edn (John Wiley & Sons, Inc., 2007), p. 34. The concept of governance in the context of university will be more regarding checks and balances to ensure that the university is well managed, allocation of responsibility and has the power to fulfil the responsibility. See Farrington and Palfreyman, 2012, p. 123.

of appointment and function vary in accordance with the type of university, whether public or private and whether central or state university. In addition to the above key officers, university administration consists of deans of schools and other academic and administrative staff. Their appointment and service conditions are regulated by the statutes and ordinances laid down by the authorities of universities.[75]

The admission of students and the fee structure are normally regulated by the parent enactments or by separate laws enacted by the Parliament[76] and State legislatures.[77] The disciplinary and other student matters are part of the internal regulation of a university. However, courts have a supervisory control over these matters when the actions of universities affect constitutional or statutory rights of students.[78]

CURRENT SCENARIO

Increasing Role of UGC

Two recent judgments of the Supreme Court have brought into sharp focus the role of UGC in higher education, in the context of regulating universities. In the first case, the Supreme Court held that All India Council for Technical Education (AICTE) had no control over colleges affiliated to universities imparting technical education and only UGC has the power by virtue of the fact that they are affiliated to a university. In the second decision the Supreme Court held that UGC and not the state government can regulate the academic activities of a state university. Both these decisions have further strengthened the role of UGC in the exercise of the power to

[75] The UGC has also laid down regulations prescribing the qualification and conditions of service of academic staff in universities. See UGC Regulations on Minimum Qualifications for Appointment of Teachers and other Academic Staff in Universities and Colleges and Measures for the Maintenance of Standards in Higher Education 2009.

[76] There are laws governing reservation in admissions based on caste, domicile, and other considerations.

[77] States have passed laws regulating fee structure in various courses, especially professional ones. In the case of private universities, the particular state university laws specifically provide for reservation based on domicile.

[78] Usually matters pertaining to admissions and fee structure end up in courts and there is considerable case law on these matters.

control higher education especially in the context of universities and have underscored the importance of university autonomy.

In the first case, *Association of Management of Private Colleges* case,[79] an association of private affiliated colleges in Tamil Nadu which are conducting MBA and MCA courses challenged the jurisdiction and control of All India Council for Technical Education (AICTE) over these institutions. Their contention was that they being institutions affiliated to universities, should fall outside the control of AICTE since as per the earlier decision of the Supreme Court in *Bharathidasan University* case,[80] universities were not 'Technical Institutions', and therefore colleges affiliated to universities should also be outside the control of AICTE. The Supreme Court upheld this argument and held that colleges affiliated to universities do not come under the control of AICTE. Since this logic is also applicable to engineering colleges run by colleges affiliated to universities, UGC has proposed to regulate those technical institutions affiliated to universities by framing separate regulations.[81]

In *Mahishi Mahesh Yogi Viswavidhyalaya case*[82] a state university, Mahishi Mahesh Yogi Vedic Viswa Vidyalaya in the state of Madhya Pradesh established by the Mahishi Mahesh Yogi Vedic Vishwavidyalaya Adhiniyam, 1995 challenged the amendment to the Act which sought to restrict the power of the university to offer courses only in the field of vedic learning and also the power of the university to conduct courses in various off-campus centres. The Supreme Court upheld the challenge holding that the state government has no such power to restrict the power of the university to offer courses in off-campus centres on the ground that right to education is a fundamental right. One of the main reasons for the decision is that the field of higher education is part of the Parliament's power to legislate under Entry 66, 'co-ordination and determination of standards in higher education' in List 1 and Entry 25 'education' in List III of Schedule VII of the Constitution of India. Supreme Court consequently held that all

---

[79] *Association of Management of Private Colleges v All India Council for Technical Education* (2013) 8 SCC 721.

[80] Ibid.

[81] UGC [Approval of Colleges offering Technical and Professional Education by Universities] Regulations, 2013.

[82] *Maharshi Mahesh Yogi Vedic Vishwavidyalaya v. State of M.P. & Ors. 2013 (8) SCALE 541.*

matters of higher education including regulation of conducting courses, curriculum, teaching standards, examination, and awarding degrees are within the power of UGC to regulate and the state government has no competence to regulate the same.

These two decisions though followed earlier decisions of the Supreme Court,[83] have further strengthened the hands of the central government to regulate higher education and universities through UGC. The first decision has indirectly increased the role of UGC in regulating technical institutions hitherto regulated by AICTE[84] and the second decision has directly empowered the UGC to regulate universities in regard to academic matters by curtailing the role of the state governments which had established the universities by enacting legislations.

Reducing Role of State Governments

This would also make redundant, the efforts recently taken by some of the state governments which have amended their private university laws to introduce specific requirement of prior approval for commencing new courses.[85] If the state governments have no regulatory powers as held by the Supreme Court all these amendments would be *ultra vires*.[86] The Supreme Court has also based its decision on the fact that right to education is a fundamental right and therefore the state government cannot take away the powers of the university to impart education. This also would expose to challenge the initiatives of state governments to regulate state universities as violative of the fundamental right to education.

This also brings into focus the receding role of the state governments in the field of higher education and the increasing role of central government. The recent attempt of the central government to assume an increased

---

[83] *Bharathidasan University* case and *Prof. Yashpal's* case.

[84] See All India Council for Technical Education (Grant of approval for starting new Technical Institutions/introduction of additional courses or programmes increase in intake) Regulations.

[85] See Section 34A of the Haryana Private Universities Act which has been introduced in 2012.

[86] This is because if the UGC alone has the power to regulate courses conducted in universities, the state law prescribing its permission before commencement of courses would be *ultra vires* the power of UGC.

role in higher education through various bills,[87] which are either pending before the parliamentary committees or awaiting their introduction in the Parliament, has raised the issue of the curtailment of the state power in the field of higher education, especially, in the context of regulation of universities. This issue assumes importance in the context of low Gross Enrolment Ratio (GER) (about 18 per cent) in India which is much lower than most of the countries in the world, which necessitates establishment of new universities for promoting higher education. According to the report of the Knowledge Commission India needs at least 1,500 universities to increase India's GER to 25 per cent.[88] When state's power is limited only to incorporate universities but not having any power or control over their functioning in terms of regulating matters pertaining to courses, teaching, and pedagogy, the question would arise whether the state governments would have any interest at all to establish universities.

Globalization, Commercialization, and Privatization of Higher Education

Globalization has changed the entire higher education scenario.[89] In addition to West-based higher education providers, there is increasing competition for admission of Indian students from universities based in Eastern Europe, Australia, and China.[90] Private educational institutions with commercial motives are being established in these countries with a view to attract more students.[91] There are developments in the area of

[87] National Commission for Higher Education and Research Bill, 2011; See infra for other bills.

[88] National Knowledge Commission Report to the Nation 2006, p. 43, Government of India (January 2007).

[89] See OECD, 'Higher Education 2030, Part II, Globalization', *Center for Educational Research and Innovation, OECD, Paris,* 2009.

[90] Bashir, Sajitha. 'Trends in International Trade in Higher Education: Implications and Options for Developing Countries', *The World Bank,* March, 2007; also see, 'Indian Study Abroad Trends: Past, Present, and Future', *World Education News & Reviews,* 6 December 2013, http://wenr.wes.org/2013/12/indian-study-abroad-trends-past-present-and-future/4, accessed on 28 April 2017.

[91] In China, see L. Tao, M. Berci, and W. He, 'The Commercialization of Education', *The New York Times,* http://www.nytimes.com/ref/college/coll-china-education-005.html, accessed on 28 April 2017.

distance education, such as, massive open on-line courses (MOOCs) conducted by top universities in US to provide distance learning at virtually free of cost to students across the world.[92] In this global scenario, the regulatory structure to be formulated by UGC must be to strengthen and support the ability Indian universities to face growing global challenges from universities across the globe while encouraging them to improve global ranking.[93]

FAILED LEGISLATIVE INITIATIVES

Following various recommendations for structural changes in higher education especially in the case of universities,[94] Government of India proposed the following six legislative bills as part of higher education reform initiatives.[95]

---

[92] For a list of institutions offering MOOC, see 'MOOCS Directory', http://www.moocs.co/, accessed on 28 April 2017.

[93] It is a serious concern that Indian universities consistently fail to reach even the 200 mark in global ranking.

[94] See 'Report of the Central Advisory Board of Education (CABE) Committee on Autonomy of Higher Education Institutions', *Ministry of Human Resources and Development, Department of Secondary and Higher Education, Government of India*, June 2005; One of the recommendations of this Report is that the Ministry of Human Resources and Development should develop a central legislation in consultation with UGC, AICTE, and other professional councils to streamline establishment and governance of private universities, deemed to be universities, self-financing institutions, and establishment of foreign universities in India; see also 'Report of the Committee to Advise on Renovation and Rejuvenation of Higher Education', *Ministry of Human Resources and Development, Government of India*, 2008, http://mhrd.gov.in/sites/upload_files/mhrd/files/YPC-Report_0.pdf, accessed on 2 October 2013; See also 'Report to the Nation 2006', *National Knowledge Commission, Government of India,* January 2007. See also 'Towards a Knowledge Society, Three Years of Knowledge Commission', *National Knowledge Commission, Government of India*, October 2008.

[95] See 'Report of the Working Group on Higher Education for the XII Five Year Plan', *Ministry of Human Resource Development, Higher Education Department, Government of India*, September 2011, http://planningcommission.gov.in/aboutus/committee/wrkgrp12/hrd/wg_hiedu.pdf, accessed on 28 April 2017.

1. National Commission for Higher Education and Research Bill, 2011.[96]
2. Foreign Educational Institutions (Regulation of Entry and Operations) Bill, 2010.
3. National Accreditation Regulatory Authority for Higher Educational Institutions Bill, 2010.
4. The Prohibition of Unfair Practices in Technical Educational Institutions, Medical Educational Institutions and Universities Bill, 2010.
5. The Educational Tribunals Bill, 2010.
6. The National Academic Depository Bill, 2011.

While these legislative initiatives for reforming higher education are long awaited, a cursory look at the provisions of the six bills creates an impression that a huge legal infrastructure is being created in the field of higher education which will lead to multiplicity of litigation. Any reform initiatives in the field of higher education should be in the form of legislative measures which would promote and encourage private participation and enhance GER in the country. When the legislative measures are complex and restrictive it would only discourage private participation in this field. While it is crucial that educational institutions should promote merit and impart quality education, without commercialization, the legal measures to promote them should be simple and understandable to common man. But the above six sister legislations make the field of higher education a legislative quagmire.

A detailed look at some of the provisions in the Bills also show that the legislative measures would only curb innovation and creativity which are much needed in further strengthening our knowledge economy. A more simplified but comprehensive legislation dealing with higher education would have a more positive impact in promoting higher education than the present complex list of legislation.

---

[96] The Higher Education and Research Bill, 2011 was introduced in the Rajya Sabha on 28 December 2011. The Bill was then referred to the Standing Committee of the Parliament, which submitted its recommendations on 15 December 2012. For a copy of the bill, see 'The Higher Education and Research Bill, 2011', *PRS Legislative Research*, http://www.prsindia.org/uploads/media/Higher%20education/high%20edu.pdf, accessed on 28 April 2017.

National Commission for Higher Education and Research[97]

This bill is intended to bring higher education under one proposed regulatory authority, namely the National Commission for Higher Education and Research (NCHER). In this bill, a single regulator for higher education sector is being proposed in the place of UGC and other professional councils. However, education in the fields of agriculture and medicine are outside the purview of the bill.

Under the bill the main function of NCHER is to take measures to promote the autonomy of higher educational institutions, for the free pursuit of knowledge and innovation, and for facilitating access, inclusion and opportunities for all and providing for comprehensive and holistic growth of higher education and research in a competitive global environment, through reforms and innovation. These include specification of norms and standards for awarding degrees, developing national curriculum framework, specification of academic quality for awarding degrees, accreditation, etc., and other detailed functions specified in the bill.

NCHER, under the bill, will maintain a national registry of persons eligible and qualified to be appointed as vice chancellors and heads of institutions of national importance. Only those persons whose names are mentioned in the national registry should be appointed as vice chancellors or heads of institutions of national importance. The bill further provides for the establishment of a 'Collegium' to aid and advice NCHER on various matters specified in the bill. The 'Collegium' consists of core fellows and co-opted fellows who are persons of eminence and integrity in academia in higher education research.

Every university or institution empowered to award degrees has to obtain authorization from NCHER in accordance with the norms prescribed by NCHER. The bill has prescribed detailed procedure for granting authorization. The bill also provides for revoking authorization by NCHER in appropriate circumstances.

---

[97] The Higher Education and Research Bill, 2011 was introduced in the Rajya Sabha on 28 December 2011. The Bill was then referred to the Standing Committee of the Parliament, which submitted its recommendations on 15 December 2012. For a copy of the bill, see 'The Higher Education and Research Bill, 2011', *PRS Legislative Research*, http://www.prsindia.org/uploads/media/Higher%20 education/high%20edu.pdf, accessed on 28 April 2017.

The bill, contrary to the avowed object of promoting autonomy for universities, contains detailed provisions for regulating the administration and management of universities which are highly restrictive and retards innovation and creativity which are essential for promotion of university autonomy. What is required is to provide strict regulation at the entry level on universities, but maximum autonomy in the administration and management. Unfortunately, the bill does not provide for the same. The powers and functions of the NCHER under the bill are too broad in nature and create significant bottlenecks for universities to function in an autonomous manner.

Foreign Educational Institutions

The Foreign Educational Institutions (Regulation of Entry and Operations) Bill, 2010[98] is another reformative initiative of Government of India to regulate the entry and operation of foreign educational institutions seeking to impart higher education in India. A 'foreign educational institution' is defined as any institution established outside India, which has been offering educational services for a minimum of 20 years and proposes to offer courses which shall be taught through conventional teaching method (including classroom teaching). Under the bill every foreign educational institution intending to operate in India has to be notified as a foreign educational provider by the central government on the recommendation of the Registrar (Secretary of the University Grants Commission) in the prescribed manner. The application has to be endorsed by the High Commission of India of that country where the foreign educational institution is based.

Under the bill, the programme of study offered by the foreign educational provider has to conform to the standards laid down by the statutory authority, such as UGC, AICTE, BCI, MCI, and the quality of educational service in terms of curriculum, methods of teaching and faculty should be comparable to that offered to students in the main campus. Every foreign educational institution should publish a prospectus 60 days prior to admission which should include information about fees, deposits, and other charges, percentage of fees refundable to students, approved number of seats, conditions of eligibility and details of teaching faculty. The bill

---

[98] The Foreign Educational Institutions (Regulation of Entry and Operations) Bill, 2010 was introduced in the Lok Sabha on 3 May 2010.

provides for withdrawal of recognition in case a foreign educational provider violates any provision of the bill. The foreign educational institutions should maintain a corpus fund of a minimum of Rs 50 crore. Maximum of 75 per cent of any income generated from the fund should be utilized for developing its institution in India and rest should be put back in the fund. Revenue generated cannot be invested for any purpose other than development of the educational institution in India. The central government may exempt any institution from conforming to the requirements of the bill except the penalty provision and the revenue provision. Any person who offers admission to an unrecognized institution or makes misleading advertisements shall be liable to a minimum fine of Rs 10 lakh (up to Rs 50 lakh) in addition to refunding the fees collected. Any recognized foreign educational provider who violates the law shall be liable to a fine between Rs 10 and 50 lakh and forfeiture of the corpus fund.

The provisions of the bill are so restrictive that reputed foreign universities will not enter into India because of the liberal environments in the countries where they have been functioning. Under the bill there are no incentives for foreign universities to open campus in India. The exemption provision under Clause 9 the bill is very vague, without any guidelines and therefore will be subject to misuse. Moreover, if the vision of the bill is to enable the reputed foreign educational institutions of international standing to come to India then there is no justification for providing a classification between two categories, one subject to restriction and the other without restrictions. No provisions exist in the bill that require mandatory scholarships to economically or socially backward students.

National Accreditation Regulatory Authority

The National Accreditation Regulatory Authority for Higher Educational Institutions Bill, 2010[99] is another legislative effort by Government of India, which seeks to make it mandatory for every higher educational institution (other than institutions engaged in agricultural education) to be accredited by an independent accreditation agency in order to maintain academic quality. The bill seeks to establish a National Accreditation Authority for Higher Education (NAAHE), which shall register accreditation agencies,

---

[99] The National Accreditation Regulatory Authority for Higher Educational Institutions Bill, 2010 was introduced in the Lok Sabha on 3 May 2010.

lay down norms and policies for assessment of academic quality in higher education institutions, undertake audit on matters related to conflict of interest, disclosure of information and transparency, levy of fees, advise central and state government, and collect and disseminate information on accreditation of higher educational institutions.[100]

Under the bill, only an accreditation agency registered with NAAHE should undertake accreditation of a higher educational institution. The bill lays down eligibility criteria and the procedure of application for registration of an accreditation agency. There are provisions for suspension or revocation of registration in specified circumstances. An accreditation agency has to be a non-profit entity registered as a company under Section 25 of the Companies Act, a society or trust and controlled by the central or state government. One of its main objectives has to be to accredit higher educational institutions and should be professionally competent and financially sound. Agencies shall be penalized in case of contravention of any provision. The bill states that if an accreditation agency fails to comply with its prescribed duties, it shall be liable to pay compensation to the higher education institution, which shall be determined by the state educational tribunal. The bill further provides that the central government has the power to exempt any higher educational institution from the provisions of this law.

Prohibition of Unfair Practices

The Prohibition of Unfair Practice in Technical Educational Institutions, Medical Educational Institutions and Universities Bill, 2010,[101] is intended to protect the interest of students by prohibiting certain unfair practices in technical and medical educational institutions and universities. Under the bill 'unfair practices' include accepting capitation fee, admitting students without specified admission tests or specified merit criteria, not giving receipt for any fee charged by the institution, publishing advertisements misleading students and withholding degree or diploma to compel a student to pay fees. Each institution has to publish a prospectus containing information about tuition fee, number of seats approved by a statutory

---

[100] Currently accreditation is done by NAAC.

[101] The Prohibition of Unfair Practice in Technical Educational Institutions, Medical Educational Institutions and University Bill, 2010 was introduced in the Lok Sabha on 3 May 2010.

authority, conditions of eligibility, details of teaching faculty, minimum pay of teaching faculty and other employees, etc.

For violation of the provisions of the bill, monetary penalty is proposed to be imposed on institutions. Penalties would be adjudicated by the state and national educational tribunals. If any person contravenes the provisions of the Act, he shall be liable to imprisonment of up to three years or a fine or with both. If any person fails to pay the penalty imposed by state or National Educational Tribunals, he shall be liable to imprisonment for a minimum of one month and maximum of three years or a fine between Rs 50,000 and Rs 5 lakh or with both.

The Educational Tribunals

The Educational Tribunals Bill, 2010[102] seeks to set up Educational Tribunals at the national and state levels to adjudicate disputes involving teachers and other employees of higher education and other stakeholders such as students, universities (including foreign education providers) and statutory regulatory authorities. The bill lays down the composition and manner of selection of the members of the tribunals. Each state educational tribunal shall consist of a Chairperson and two other members (one of whom should be a woman). A member should be at least 55 years old, have knowledge and experience in higher education or public affairs for 20 years and have been vice chancellor or chief secretary in the state government. The members would be appointed by the appropriate government on the recommendation of a selection committee. The state tribunals have jurisdiction over service matters of teacher and other employees of higher educational institution and disputes over affiliation and unfair practices of a higher educational institution prohibited by any law.

The National Educational Tribunal shall consist of a chairperson and a maximum of eight members (two shall be judicial, three shall be academic, and three shall be administrative). They shall be appointed by the central government on the recommendation of a selection committee. The jurisdiction of the tribunal may be exercised by benches consisting of three members. The chairperson and judicial members shall be chosen among judges of the Supreme Court. Academic members have to be at least 55 years old, have knowledge and experience in higher education or

---

[102] The Educational Tribunals Bill, 2010 was introduced in the Lok Sabha on 3 May 2010.

public affairs for 25 years and have been vice chancellor of a university or director of an institution of national importance. Administrative members have to be at least 55 years of age, have knowledge and experience in higher education or public affairs for 25 years.

The National Tribunal shall have power to adjudicate cases of dispute between higher educational institutions and statutory authorities or higher educational institution and affiliating university (in case of central universities). It shall have appellate jurisdiction on orders of the state tribunals. Orders of the national tribunal can be appealed in the Supreme Court. An order of the tribunal shall be treated as decree of a civil court. If orders of the national or state tribunal are not complied with, the person shall be liable to imprisonment for a maximum of three.

The National Academic Depository

The National Academic Depository Bill, 2011[103] seeks to establish a national database of academic awards in electronic format, which can be verified and authenticated. Under the bill, the central government would constitute a depository as the National Academic Depository (NAD) to establish and maintain the national database. The bill makes it mandatory for every academic institution (college, university, or boards that award Class X and XII certificates) to lodge every academic award with the depository. The depository would provide training to the staff of the academic institution and recover a reasonable cost of the training. Disputes regarding cost shall be adjudicated by the State Educational Tribunal.

On a request made by the depository, an academic institution should verify within seven days that the award was issued by the institution. Any person could apply to the depository or a registered agent to verify and authenticate any specific award. The depository would inform the person within three days whether the award could be verified and authenticated. A depository has to meet certain conditions: (a) it has to be registered under the Securities and Exchange Board of India Act, 1992 or a fully owned subsidiary of such a depository, (b) its memorandum of association specifically should mention the depository service for academic awards as one of its objectives, and (c) it should fulfil other terms and conditions that may be prescribed.

---

[103] The National Academic Depository Bill, 2011 was introduced in the Lok Sabha on 5 September 2011 by the Minister of Human Resource Development.

The central government under the bill would authorize a depository to begin operations only when it is satisfied that there are (i) adequate systems for storage and retrieval of records from the national database, (ii) safeguards to ensure that its automatic data processing system is secure, (iii) adequate network through which the depository shall maintain continuous electronic communication with academic institutions and other concerned bodies, and (iv) adequate number of facilitation centres, established by the depository, to provide services. The central government would review the working of the depository every ten years. If satisfied with the working it would renew the registration for another 10 years. If not, the registration would be revoked. The central government may also revoke the appointment of a depository on certain grounds such as wilful default, breach of terms and conditions, and financial viability.

The depository under the bill, has to provide for registration of academic institutions, access to the national database to registered academic institutions, training to academic institutions to lodge and retrieve academic records, verification and authentication of any academic award in the national database and ensure that databases are designed in such a way to facilitate online interaction with the Central Identities Data Repository to be created under the National Identification Authority of India Act, 2011. The Depository also has to fulfil certain requirements such as adequate mechanisms for monitoring and evaluating controls, data recovery mechanisms and safeguards, maintain data backup and ensure a secure online connectivity. These measures would be inspected annually by a panel of independent experts, appointed by the central government. The depository should register academic depository agents to assist in providing services. These agents should be minors, be of unsound mind, hold any equity share capital or have any other interest in the depository.

ROAD FOR THE FUTURE

Relook at the Higher Education Regulation

The increasing role of UGC also brings into focus the need for a relook at the higher education regulatory scenario in the context of the need for establishing more universities, to counter the slow growth in India's GER.[104]

---

[104] National Knowledge Commission, 'Report to the Nation 2006', Government of India, New Delhi (January 2007).

There is serious entry level barrier in setting up of a university. The gestation period is more than two years, with severe bottle necks in the form of availability of land, red-tapism, governmental apathy, lack of funds, mid-stream changes in policy and need to obtain series of approvals and permissions. These constraints and bottle necks will dissuade philanthropic initiatives in setting up universities.

The slow growth in GER requires urgent attention, as India has at present the highest percentage of youth with lesser opportunities for good quality education, in addition to address India's need to improve the human resource potential available.[105] This would also bring into focus the sharp reality that when central government has lesser funds for setting up universities only state governments have to take up the responsibility of setting up more and more universities.[106] The role of UGC as the principal regulator of higher education needs to be revisited, especially when the Higher Education and Research Bill has yet to see the light. The objections raised by the state governments that the bill was against the federal structure of the Constitution of India, that the states do not have any say in the policy on education if the bill is passed and that the bill would take away the autonomy of universities are some of the reasons for its lack of progress as evident from the parliamentary debates.[107]

UGC as a Super Regulator: What Implication?

Under the University Grants Commission Act, 1956, UGC has the mandate of promoting and coordinating university education, determining and maintaining standards of teaching, examination and research in

[105] A recent Report by PriceWaterhouseCoopers on Indian higher education states as follows 'with the emergence of India as a knowledge-based economy, human capital has now become its major strength. This has put the spotlight on severe inadequacies of India's infrastructure for delivery of education, particularly higher and vocational education'. See 'Indian Higher Education Sector: Opportunities for Private Participation', *PriceWaterhouseCoopers*, 2012, p. 3.

[106] See 'Higher Education in India at Glance', *University Grants Commission*, 21 March 2012, p. 8, available at http://www.ugc.ac.in/ugcpdf/208844_ HEglance2012.pdf, accessed on 28 April 2017.

[107] Paras 2.4 and 2.5 of the Two Hundred Forty Seventh Report on The Higher Education and Research Bill, 2011 by the Department-related Parliamentary Standing Committee on Human Resource Development (Presented to the Rajya Sabha on 13 December 2012) (Laid on the Table of Lok Sabha on 13 December 2012).

universities, framing regulations on minimum standards of education and monitoring developments in the field of collegiate and university education.[108] It also disburses grants to the universities and colleges. UGC issues regulations and guidelines to carry out these functions.[109] UGC, by specifying the type of degrees which can be awarded by universities regulates the type of courses which could be conducted in universities, the duration of courses, the broad curriculum, pedagogy, the qualification and service conditions of the teachers, the examination systems and the manner of awarding degrees.[110] However, the inability of UGC to function effectively has been cited as a main reason for the proposed Higher Education and Research Bill. In fact, it was stated by the central government that the higher education sector was over regulated but under governed. The deemed universities which are directly under the supervision of UGC have been found wanting in many respects. It is fact that many of them run professional courses by collecting illegally capitation fees running to several crores of rupees. The UGC is helpless in curbing this menace. This would show that present external regulatory mechanism suffers from serious flaws which require attention.

University Autonomy: A Mirage

The role of the UGC as a super regulator of universities has to be seen in the light of the three oldest universities in India, namely University of Calcutta, University of Bombay, and University of Madras.[111] These three universities were established under the British Act of Incorporation of 1857 followed by respective universities Acts prescribing their powers.[112] These universities had been under the control of the then provincial governments and thereafter under the state governments, except for a brief period of five years during 1935–40 when it was with the Government of India. The history of more than a century and half of these universities show that these universities have been regulated well by their internal regulatory system and by the state governments and that they could maintain high academic standards. These universities were well managed much before UGC was

---

[108] Section 12 of the University Grants Commission Act, 1956
[109] Section 26 of the University Grants Commission Act, 1956.
[110] Sections 12, 22, and 26 of the University Grants Commission Act, 1956.S
[111] See 'Deemed University', *University Grants Commission*.
[112] See 'Structure of University Education in India', *UNESCO Paris*.

created. The historical reputation of these universities would be at stake if they are brought under the regulatory control of UGC with increased regulatory powers.

Internal Governance in Universities: A Distant Dream

Currently, there is an erosion of internal governance in Indian universities and there is a need for strengthening the internal governance in universities. In the context of increasing clamour for more regulation, the UGC should act more towards strengthening the internal governance of universities based on the principles of transparency and accountability so as to preserve autonomy and academic freedom in universities. The commercialization of education by few institutions should not be a justification for stricter external regulation of universities. The regulatory structure should be focused on ensuring university autonomy and academic freedom, while preventing mismanagement and commercialization. In this regard a fine balance needs to be maintained between internal regulation of the universities and their external regulation. The mechanism prescribed by UGC as an external regulator should be for the purpose of strengthening the internal regulatory structure and processes. This can be done by making the officers of the universities more accountable to the authorities of the universities based on the principle of trusteeship. The UGC has to study the internal governance structure and processes of word's top universities and suggest best models for Indian universities suitable to individual universities based on the principle of democracy and accountability.

Role of Universities and Academics: A Dream to be Fulfilled

Universities are social systems and their main function is to act as agents of liberation from structural constraints and promote social changes. They should critically examine the social and economic status in the society they exist and through experimentation suggest changes in the policymaking and administration. For this the academics in universities play key role. In the US, faculty members of top US universities play active part in government's policymaking and implementation. Some of them join the government and play key role in the administration. Many secretaries in the US Administration had been academics from top US universities. There has been a constant interchange of academics between US Government and the US universities. Such an approach has strengthened the US Government in formulating better policies, speedier decision-making and effective implementation. In turn, the US universities are also immensely benefitted by the practical experience of faculty members in governmental administration. However, in India such interactions are lacking. Universities and academics in India play very limited role in government's policymaking and administration. Indian universities, on the other hand, are regulated from outside and they are told what to teach, who to teach, how to teach and whom to teach. This has severely restricted their academic autonomy and freedom and severely retarded their growth and development. There is an urgent need to drastically change this approach if the Indian universities want to achieve global ranking. The universities should play active role in the society in bringing social changes through research and interaction with the government. Academics in India should play active role in governmental administration.

* * *

In conclusion, UGC as an external regulator needs to address the above crucial issues and strengthen the Indian universities in terms of their internal governance, autonomy, and academic freedom and make them fully competent to deal with the challenges of globalization, commercialization, and privatization. Then alone Indian universities can earn a position among the top universities in the world, which was once enjoyed by great ancient Indian universities such as Nalanda and Takshashila.

8 Global Competitiveness, Privatization, Dignified Spaces, and Curricular Reform in Indian Higher Education

Kanti Bajpai

The modern university system in India goes back two hundred years; today, it is in a nearly terminal state. In saying this, I rely on the judgment of various international university ranking systems and my own personal experience. Every ranking system rates Indian universities poorly against their Asian counterparts in China, Hong Kong, Japan, Singapore, and South Korea, and in some cases, even universities in Indonesia, Malaysia, and Thailand. This is true even for the *navratnas* of India—the IITs and IIMs. Ranking systems of course have their limitations. My own experience as a teacher at two Indian universities—one provincial (Maharajah Sayajirao University of Baroda) and one central (Jawaharlal Nehru University)—and my time in the major English-speaking systems where I studied or taught (Canada, Singapore, the US, and the UK) suggest that Indian universities are in an egregious condition. The question is why, given that in 1947 it could fairly be said that at least a dozen Indian universities were leaders in Asia and were of international repute. This chapter essays some answers. It also argues for curricular reform, in particular the introduction of public policy studies at the major Indian universities.

The Indian government, finally, is trying to improve university educa-tion. It is expanding the system and urging universities to compete with the best in the world.[1] Given the growing number of young people, especially young men, an expansion of the university system is vital if we are to maintain social peace. The government is right also to insist on competi-tion with the rest of the world.

I suggest that there are at least two other key reforms needed to improve India's higher education system and rescue it from its pathetic state—there must be more private universities; and universities desperately need to be modernized in a spatial sense.[2] In addition, Indian universities require a strong dose of curriculum reform: a key curricular investment is public policy studies.

FROM ALIENATION TO ENGAGEMENT WITH THE WORLD

There are many reasons for the shambolic state of Indian universities, and other chapters in this volume will rehearse them, but I take the view that perhaps the biggest problem is their alienation from the world. Listening to a talk by a high-level educator in India in 2013, I was dismayed to

[1] For a recent view of Indian higher education by the Minister of State for Human Resource Development, see 'Post-Kapil Sibal HRD Stint, Shashi Tharoor Slams Students' Standards', *The Indian Express* (5 November 2012), http://www.indianexpress.com/news/postkapil-sibal-hrd-stint-shashi-tharoor-slams-students-standards/1027018/, (accessed on 23 June 2013).

[2] This part of the chapter draws on my earlier essay, K. Bajpai, 'Three Big Things We Need to Do for Indian Higher Education–Or Else', in Nalini Menon (ed.), *Educating India* (New Delhi: Pearson, 2014).

hear him speak about India's poor performance in the annual global rankings.[3] The rankings were problematic, he said, for all kinds of methodological reasons. India would therefore have to devise its own ranking system. Anyway, he contended, Indian universities should not worry about the rankings game. As for learning from foreign universities, India would try to do so but should remember that it had its own genius. The educator made reference to Nalanda and India's rich history of higher education to illustrate his contention that India had a proud academic record and did not need to be overly impressed by developments elsewhere.

The educator was not entirely off the mark. Nonetheless, the tone of his remarks, at a time of such deep crisis in Indian higher education, was revealing of a more general, almost chronic sense of complacency that afflicts so many areas of public life in India. It is true, of course, that university rankings are problematic beyond a point. No one suggests that the only way to judge a university is by some aggregate measure or survey result. But quantitative measures tell you something even if they do not tell you everything. Paying attention to the rankings at a certain stage in the development of a higher education system is therefore not a bad thing. It might at least shake the system and provide a clear goal to aim for. I often hear Cambridge, Harvard, Oxford, and Yale colleagues dismiss the ranking system. That is understandable for universities sitting magisterially at the top; universities that reside solidly at the bottom cannot afford to be quite as Olympian.

To claim furthermore, as the educator did in his speech, that India has its own genius and will not mimic others was disappointing: who could disagree that every society will modify and adapt foreign systems to their own conditions and needs? The point he should have made is that mimicry is not a bad thing, at a certain point in academic time and to some degree. Many great writers and painters, for instance, have started out by mimicking those they admire. Japan built an entire technological system that profited

[3] According to the Times Higher Education Rankings 2012–13, India had only two universities in the top 400 universities! See *The World University Rankings 2012–13*, http://www.timeshighereducation.co.uk/world-university-rankings/2012-13/world-ranking/region/asia., (accessed on 14 June 2013). The QS University Rankings gave India 8 universities in the top 100 Asian universities. See QS rankings for 2013 at http://www.topuniversities.com/university-rankings/asian-university-rankings/2013 (accessed on 14 June 2013).

by mimicry. Singapore's rise as a knowledge hub has been built on rankings and imitation.[4] We in India have developed such an inferiority complex and have such a brittle sense of self that we reflexively turn away from the best practices of others—even when it is in our own interest!

The alienation of Indian universities from the world has several causes, but a major reason is that higher education in India is still stuck in an 'import substitution' view of life. For the better part of 50 years, the Indian economy held closely to the idea, and ideal, of import substitution. What this meant was that India would not import the goods it needed; it would instead make everything itself. The country would thereby save money, build industry, grow a technological base, and protect itself from malign foreign economic and political influences. The result was not growth and development but rather stagnation and inefficiency. Sadly, the same mantra was chanted over and over again in Indian universities: India would not engage with the rest of the world; it would flourish. Except that it did not flourish. It is worth remembering that all our great universities were built with foreign help—the proud universities of Delhi, Chennai, Kolkata, and Mumbai, in colonial times; and the original IITs, IIMs, and agricultural universities after Independence. This is the case too for the ancient university of Nalanda, which had many foreigners come to it and enrich it with their genius, giving as much as getting from India.[5] The role of outsiders in one's education development is not a matter of shame. The American university system was profoundly influenced by the German system. It imported not only German practices but also, at various times, German academics, especially in the nineteenth and twentieth centuries.[6] So also the British

---

[4] National University of Singapore (NUS) ranked 29th in the world and 2nd in Asia in 2013, and Nanyang Technological University (NTU) ranked 86th and 11th, respectively. See *The World University Rankings 2012–13,* http://www.timeshighereducation.co.uk/world-university-rankings/2012-13/world-ranking/region/asia. (accessed on 21 June 2013). The highest placed Indian university was IIT, Kharagpur, which was 28th in Asia.

[5] See a brief history of Nalanda and its importance in the ancient world at UNESCO, 'Excavated Remains at Nalanda', http://whc.unesco.org/en/tentativelists/5407/, accessed on 18 June 2013.

[6] Braeman, J. 1996. 'The German Influence on American Education: A Review Essay', *Journal of Higher Education* 37 (2): pp. 101–3. See also the various papers in Ulrich Teichler and Henry Wasser, eds., *German and American Universities: Mutual Influences–Past and Present* (Kassel: Centre for Research on Higher

university system adopted ideas from continental Europe at various points in its history. Historically, various European universities learned from Oxford and Cambridge and more recently from the Americans. Increasingly, East and Southeast Asia are learning from their engagement with, and often wholesale import of, foreign systems and practices, while India sticks numbingly to its own path.

Indian universities have to engage internationally if they are to improve standards in a fast-changing world that is investing rapidly in higher education. Engagement means many things. It means comparing oneself with institutions abroad. It means publishing in the highest-ranked journals.[7] Engagement entails partnering with and learning from foreign universities wherever appropriate. If Indian academics are to be in the world, they must break out of their self-imposed intellectual exile and collaborate with international colleagues. They must go to international conferences in their disciplines.[8] Foreigners should come to their conferences. Conferences held in India must be organized to world standards in terms of logistics, accommodation, and transport. Finally, and most importantly, the faculty and student body must be more international. It is depressing to go to an Indian university and see only Indian faces, usually overwhelmingly from the host state–indeed, the trend towards the provincial looks to be growing rather

---

Education and Work, Comprehensive University of Kassel in cooperation with Center for European Studies, Graduate School and University Center, City University of New York, 1992), available from the Educational Resources Information Center, http://www.eric.ed.gov/ERICWebPortal/search/detailmini. jsp?_nfpb=true&_&ERICExtSearch_SearchValue_0=ED355902&ERICExtSearch_SearchType_0=no&accno=ED355902 (accessed on 23 June 2013).

[7] On the pitfalls, though, of relying too much on high-impact journal ratings, see the recent warning on the dangers issued by the American Society for Cell Biology (ASCB) in its San Francisco Declaration on Research Assessment (DORA), http://am.ascb.org/dora/, accessed on 14 June 2013.

[8] At a recent international law conference held at the National Law School (NLS), Bangalore, widely regarded as India's premier law school, not a single paper was presented by NLS faculty! Indians from other law schools in India did present. See the 10th ASLI Conference, 'Celebrating Diversity: Ten Years of ASLI', held at NLS, Bangalore (23–4 May 2013). The conference panels and presenters are to be found at http://law.nus.edu.sg/asli/10th_asli_conf/pdf/10th_ASLI_Panel_Listing.pdf, accessed on 17 June 2013.

than reducing as India becomes obsessed with the local and the native. The word university contains within it the notion of 'universal'. The etymological root of universal is *universalis*—'of or belonging to all'—and *universus*—'all together, whole, entire'.[9] Indian universities must strive to be universalistic, diverse, and plural beyond just India. A full and exciting education at the university level in a globalizing world needs the presence of foreigners. If Indian faculty and students are to rise above petty localism and a stifling, brittle nativism, and if they are to be shocked out of the mediocrity they have sunk into, they need to be exposed to talented, energetic outsiders.

A more cosmopolitan university system will require the country to throw far more money at higher education—to improve research and pedagogical standards and to fund foreign faculty and students.[10] In a cash-strapped economy, India can only allot more to higher education if it cuts elsewhere, such as in subsidies, defence, and wasteful public sector enterprises. This will require careful thought and political courage, but it will be worth it in the long run.

FROM PUBLIC TO (MORE) PRIVATE UNIVERSITIES

The second key reform has begun but has to move ahead far more quickly: India needs many more private universities. It needs them for at least three reasons: in order to goad public universities to do better; because public universities have been strangulated by rules, regulations, and political interference and there is not much prospect of loosening the choking hold of governments unless private universities grow and excel; and to supplement government funding of higher education. By private universities, I mean teaching and research institutions offering the full suite of science, social science, and professional subjects; I do not mean the hundreds of horrible,

---

[9] Online Etymology Dictionary, http://www.etymonline.com/index.php?term=universal.

[10] Indian spending on higher education as a proportion of GDP is roughly 3 per cent which is higher than the US (2.6 per cent), and Korea (2.6 per cent). See Philip G. Altbach and Pawan Agarwal, 'Scoring Higher on Education', *The Hindu* (12 February 2013), http://www.thehindu.com/opinion/op-ed/scoring-higher-on-education/article4404687.ece, accessed on 14 June 2013. However, Altbach and Agarwal note that the absolute amount India spends relative to size of population is low.

deadening engineering, medical, and IT schools that churn out graduates no one can employ and who have had such a narrow, instrumental education that they need re-educating if they are to do any good.

If private universities are to flourish, they must be left alone by that gargantuan bureaucratic mess called the University Grants Commission (UGC). They should be chartered and accredited, perhaps by an entirely new licensing body. To live and grow, they must be given the freedom to set their own fees, salaries, and hiring practices, to offer innovative courses and programmes, and to discipline students and staff as long as they abide by the basic law of the land and by a sense of natural justice. India cannot have a university monoculture, dominated by sad, sprawling, public universities that are political in the worst way and operate as if they were in the nineteenth century. If Indian business can be opened up to the private sector and to competition, so can Indian higher learning. Private capital will flow to higher education when it can get a reasonable return on its investment. There is an allergy to private universities making a profit, but it is unclear why this is the case. A profit-making university that provides good education is not a criminal or morally abominable institution. At the very least, can private universities possibly be worse than India's public universities which are dens of corruption and inequity? This aversion to profit is visible in the foreign university bill which essentially states that a university that sets up an Indian branch will not be allowed to take back any profits. It must reinvest all its surpluses in India. Why any foreign university should invest in India in any meaningful sense on these terms is a mystery![11]

The test of private universities will largely be a market test. If private universities do not meet that market test, if they fail to provide a service that others are not providing, if in short they do not offer academic facilities and training of the kind that India so desperately needs, they will disappear.

---

[11] One possibility is that it would spread the brand name of a foreign university and get Indian students to apply to the original campus in the home country. The problem here is that a university of any standing globally will be well known to Indian students anyway. A 'branch plant' would be no value addition. Indeed, depending on how it performs in India, it might even damage the original university's name. Another possibility is that the law will eventually be changed and foreign universities will be permitted to repatriate some profits. From that perspective, foreign universities might have an incentive to invest in India at the very beginning, even if the conditions around the investment are onerous and constraining.

How they price their services must also meet a market test. If they charge exorbitantly relative to their services, they will price themselves out. On the other hand, if they provide a valuable service and if they are affordable, they will flourish and fill a gap. Their rise will goad the public universities to do better. More than government cajoling and coercing, it is the challenge of private universities that will instigate public universities to reform and improve standards. Indian higher education cannot be turned over to the private sector; neither can it be dominated by the state. There needs to be a balance.

FROM SPATIAL INDIFFERENCE TO SPATIAL SENSITIVITY

Indian universities must pay attention to the physical environments that they provide to students, faculty, and staff. As things stand, our universities are scruffy, dirty, and ugly spaces that demean anyone with the ill luck to enter their gates. Most Indian universities look like the Public Works Department (PWD) designed and built them (it probably did).

How can anyone learn anything in these abysmal spaces? Spatial conditions affect mental processes and the nature of social interactions. Squalid spaces will produce squalid people and a squalid social life. Universities need various types of spaces—poetic, rationalist, meditative, forensic, sporting, leisure, administrative, and residential.[12] In a country with as miserable a climate as India, university spaces should be designed for better temperature and light control. Passive design features should be supplemented by energy-based systems such as air conditioning and heating to make interior spaces more congenial and attractive.

Why do we in India insist that students, faculty, and staff live and work in searingly hot or numbingly cold spaces when we can mitigate their distress? Why should students and faculty be made uncomfortable to the point of exhaustion just because they have chosen the life of the mind? There is a sourness and humourlessness about the Indian public and Indian political leaders on this subject. My old university, Jawaharlal Nehru University, has in recent years built a spate of new

---

[12] On the importance of space in human existence and social life, see the classics, Lefebvre, H. *The Production of Space* (London: Wiley-Blackwell and Bachelard, 1992), G. Bachelard 1994. *The Poetics of Space* (New York: Beacon Press).

facilities—teaching and research spaces, offices, student residence halls, even faculty housing. Sadly, and myopically, it has not had the sense or courage to air condition or centrally heat any of them. India has to gradually improve the work and living spaces of its people. The bureaucracy increasingly makes sure that its work spaces are better built and are more comfortable. Why should the country not make life more congenial for educators and students?

CURRICULAR REFORM: INVESTING IN PUBLIC POLICY STUDIES

As India debates higher education reform, one of the elements of discussion must be curricular reform. There is an enormous task ahead of Indian educators here, in every field. The rest of this chapter restricts itself to making a case for public policy studies. Indian universities, public and private, must seriously consider introducing the study of public policy as a new offering. To that end, every major university should invest in a school (or department) of public policy. Public policy as an academic field originates in the US, at least in its current avatar. Indian universities can learn from the US experience and the experience of others (such as public policy schools in Asia) but should adapt the field to the needs and requirements of India.

What are public policy studies? I define public policy studies as the study of what governments actually do or should do for the common good and how they can best do so.[13] Public policy making certainly involves other actors, but in the end it is governments that take decisions, formulate policies, and implement them 'in the field'. What governments actually do may or may not necessarily be motivated by the common good. Government often enough make policies for sectional, even personal interests.

[13] For this definition and a discussion around it, see Kanti Bajpai, Scott A. Fritzen, and Kishore Mahbubani, 'Global Public Policy as a Field of Study: A View from Asia', *Lee Kuan Yew School of Public Policy: Building a Global Policy School in Asia* (Singapore: Lee Kuan Yew School of Public Policy and World Scientific, 2013), p. 161. Thomas Dye in his classic definition states that public policy is 'whatever governments choose to do or not do'. See T. Dye. *Understanding Public Policy* (New Jersey: Prentice-Hall, 1995), p. 2.

Still, policies must be presented as being in the common good. Few if any modern governments can make policy without reference to the common good. Even policies that ostensibly benefit a sectional interest—tax breaks for businesses, affirmative action for disadvantaged minorities—are defended as being for the common good: for example, tax breaks for businesses are defended on the grounds that they will stimulate investment and generate employment; and affirmative action may be justified on the grounds of raising the living standards of minority ethnic groups as well as making up for a history of discrimination and thereby constructing a happier, more resilient society.

There is a descriptive, analytical, and normative element therefore to the study of public policy. Descriptively, public policy studies tell us *what* governments do—the empirical facts of government policymaking, from agenda setting to implementation and evaluation.[14] Analytically, public policy studies delve into *why* governments and their agents do what they do and how they do it. This is the more theoretically driven element of public policy studies which attempts to 'connect the facts' and provide explanations and understandings of government behaviour. Normatively, public policy studies are concerned with what governments *ought to do* (or not do) for the common good. Public policy studies typically combine all three elements, even if some studies are more explicit and self-conscious than others about doing so.

SUBSTANTIVE DEMOCRACY AND PUBLIC POLICY STUDIES

A liberal democratic society cannot remain liberal or democratic if its governing institutions do not deliver rational, efficient, and just governance. Liberal democracies are typified by constitutionalism, rights, checks and balances, and full franchise elections. India qualifies in so far as it has all these. The quality of India's democracy is quite another matter. There is widespread agreement that while the basic structures and processes of a liberal democracy exist in India, the quality of its democracy is poor. The

[14] See Wu, Xun, M. Ramesh, Michael Howlett, and Scott A. Fritzen, *The Public Policy Primer: Managing the Policy Process* (London: Routledge, 2010), pp. 1–13 on the policy cycle from agenda setting to policy evaluation and back to another round of agenda setting, etc.

historian Ramachandra Guha has called Indian democracy 'a glass half full' for exactly this reason.[15]

Scholars of democracy distinguish between procedural democracy and substantive democracy.[16] By procedural democracy, I mean an electoral democracy characterized by a written constitution, the enumeration of rights, the division of responsibilities between various arms of government, and free and fair elections as a means of choosing political representatives and the government of the day.

India is fairly impressive as a procedural democracy, though even here its record is uneven and increasingly troubling. As a substantive democracy, its record is worse, to say the least. A substantively rich democracy is one in which the governing institutions deliver on the rationality, effectiveness, fairness, and inclusiveness of governance. By rationality of governance, I mean policies that attempt to translate preferred social and political values into implementable policies designed to give expression to those values. By effectiveness of governance, I mean that governors are able to identify a set of alternative ways of translating values into policies and are able then to implement the alternative that promises to maximize the gains and to minimize the costs to society. By fairness of governance, I mean that preferred values and preferred policies embody notions of fairness—fairness in procedures and fairness in outcomes. Last, by inclusiveness of governance, I mean the effort of the government to involve ordinary citizens in policy consultation and decision-making and to create conditions whereby they can vent their grievances.

Most commentators would give India low marks on all these counts. Indeed, perhaps a widely accepted judgement would be that while India has attempted to provide substantively rich democracy, while it has an impressive array of legislation and policies that are designed to deliver substantive democracy, and while there has been progress over the 60 years of its Independence, there is a long way to go.[17] India is marked by

[15] Ramachandra Guha, *India after Gandhi: The History of the World's Largest Democracy* (New York: Harper Perennial, 2008).

[16] Robert Dahl, *Democracy and Its Critics* (New Haven: Yale University Press, 1989).

[17] For a somewhat different notion of substantive democracy and a more positive view of India's attainments, see Stuart Corbridge, John Harriss, and Craig Jeffrey, *India Today: Economy, Politics, and Society* (Cambridge: Polity, 2013), pp. 140–57.

a high level of 'structural violence' in spite of attempts to lift the vast mass of Indians out of poverty and disempowerment.[18]

Public policy studies are important for a society that wants to move from procedural to substantively rich democracy. Procedural democracy is the preoccupation of political philosophy/theory, political science, and legal/constitutional studies. Substantive democracy, at least as defined here, is far more the focus of public policy studies.

SOCIAL COMPLEXITY AND PUBLIC POLICY STUDIES

Public policy studies are vital in a world and in a domestic realm that is increasingly complex.[19] In a simpler world and in an India that was simpler, public policy was easier to implement. India in the 1940s found itself in a world where there were only fifty independent countries. Apart from the UN, IMF, and World Bank, there were few international organizations. The country's international interactions and obligations were relatively limited. World order was defined by a Eurocentric, Westphalian diplomatic system and Cold War competition. At home, a combination of visionary and popular leaders who had thought about India's future for thirty years at the helm of the nationalist movement, a small but experienced civil service inherited from the colonial period, and a public that had been mobilized for freedom and was prepared to trust its nationalist leaders as well as make sacrifices in the service of the new nation made the job of public policy formulation and implementation easier.

---

[18] Akhil Gupta, *Red Tape: Bureaucracy, Structural Violence, and Poverty in India* (London: Duke University Press, 2012) Borrowing from Johan Galtung, structural violence, according to Gupta, refers to 'any situation in which some people are unable to achieve their capacities or capabilities to their full potential, and almost certainly if they are unable to do so to the same extent as others. ... The reason such violence is considered to be structural is that it is impossible to identify a single actor who commits the violence' (p. 20).

[19] For this and other arguments on the need for public policy education in India, see Mukul Asher, 'Why Public Policy Education is Essential in India', January 2007, http://www.inpad.org/res102.html, accessed on 22 June 2013. There is not a great body of academic, public policy writing in India. A recent work by a very well-known Indian political scientist is Kuldeep Mathur, *Public Policy and Politics in India: How Institutions Matter* (New Delhi: Oxford University Press, 2013). See also R.V. Vaidyanatha Ayyar, *Public Policy Making in India* (New Delhi: Pearson, 2009).

The end of the Cold War, while welcome, ushered in a world of much greater complexity. Since 1989, India has been embedded in a world of nearly two hundred independent states and a lattice-work of international organizations—universalist and regionalist—that are bewilderingly numerous and often overlapping. The country's international interactions and obligations are multitudinous. The post-Cold War world order is difficult to describe and define. Fareed Zakaria has called it a 'post-American world'; Ian Bremmer, more recently, sees it as a 'G-zero world' in which there is no dominant power; and Kishore Mahbubani, more optimistically, thinks the world, of necessity, is experiencing a 'great convergence'.[20] All three accept that international society is messy and uncertain in a way that few countenanced when the Cold War ended.

Domestically, India has grown from a population of 300 million souls to 1.2 billion and is likely to peak at 1.7 billion in 2050.[21] The country is organized in 35 states and union territories. In 2011, Uttar Pradesh had a population of nearly 200 million, the size roughly of Brazil, while Maharashtra, the second most populous state, with 112 million, is nearly the size of Mexico.[22] India's current leaders, with none of the political capital of the nationalist leaders who led the country immediately after Independence, have to deal with a society, polity, and economy that are four times bigger and several times more complex as a result.

This would not matter if India's capacities to deal with size and complexity had expanded. Unfortunately, they have not done so. As in so many things, India stagnates and stubbornly refuses to change. In 1970, when India's population was roughly half the size it is today, the Indian

[20] Fareed Zakaria, *The Post American World* (New York: W.W. Norton, 2009) Bremmer Ian, *Every Nation for Itself: Winners and Losers in a G-Zero World* (New York: Portfolio/Penguin, 2012), and Kishore Mahbubani, *The Great Convergence: Asia, the West, and the Logic of One World* (New York: Public Affairs, 2013).

[21] Ranjit Goswami, 'India's Population in 2050: Extreme Projections Demand Extreme Actions', *East Asia Forum* (5 April 2013), http://www.eastasiaforum.org/2013/04/05/indias-population-in-2050-extreme-projections-demand-extreme-action/, accessed 9 June 2013. By contrast, China's population is projected to be 1.3 billion in 2050. See Population Reference Bureau, http://www.prb.org/pdf11/2011population-data-sheet_eng.pdf, accessed on 9 June 2013, for Goswami's source.

[22] 'Population of India', *Indiaonlinepages.com*, http://www.indiaonlinepages.com/population/india-current-population.html, accessed on 9 June 2013.

Parliament consisted of 560 MPs. Nearly 50 years later and with twice as many people, the country still has only 560 MPs, which must be the worst ratio of political representatives to population anywhere in the world. The frontline Indian civil service consists of 4,400 IAS officers and 2,200 IPS police officers—a frighteningly low number.[23] The total number of policemen in India per 100,000 persons is 130 whereas the UN suggests that the minimum should be 220.[24] The capacities of the government to deal with complexity and the consequences of complexity are therefore very limited. At the same time, the Indian public has never been less trustful of its leaders and its patience has never been shorter judging by the rate at which elected leaders and incumbent governments are voted out of office.

EXISTING FIELDS OF STUDY AND PUBLIC POLICY STUDIES

A third reason to institute public policy studies in India is that the existing social science disciplines and humanities do not quite do the job of telling us what governments have done and why and what they should do instead. All the social sciences and some of the humanities are potentially policy sciences. Anthropology, business and management studies, economics, history, linguistics, political science (including international relations), philosophy, psychology (at least certain branches of the field), and sociology seek to understand the human condition including how human beings relate to collective life—in the family, clan, community, tribe, nation, and beyond—and how human institutions affect individual and collective life. To the extent that they do so, their insights have implications for policy.

---

[23] '30 per cent Shortage of IAS Officers: Govt', the *Indian Express* (10 May 2012), http://www.indianexpress.com/news/30--shortage-of-ias-officers-govt/947734/, accessed on 9 June 2013 and 'Over 3,000 IAS, IPS Posts Vacant', the *Indian Express* (17 August 2012), http://www.indianexpress.com/news/over-3000-ias-ips-posts-vacant/989604/, accessed on 9 June 2013. These figures were cited by the Minister of State for Personnel on the floor of the Lok Sabha.

[24] 'The Number of Policemen per 100,000 People in India is 130', *Rediff news*, http://news.rediff.com/interview/2010/feb/15/number-of-policemen-per-100000-people-in-india-is-130.htm, accessed on 9 June 2013. This figure and the UN norm was cited by G.K. Pillai, Home Secretary to the Government of India.

The social sciences amongst these, in particular business and management studies, economics, and political science, are the most ostensive policy sciences. Yet, each individually does not fill the space of public policy studies. Thus, business and management studies are focused primarily on private entities that seek profit for their owners and shareholders and are not directly and intimately concerned with protecting and enlarging the common good (though, with Adam Smith, we can agree that the private pursuit of profit can produce a collective good, namely, the generation of wealth in a society). Economics is broadly the study of how goods and services are produced in conditions of scarcity, or put differently, how resources should be allocated to different ends. Economists focus both on how the overall economy functions (macroeconomics) and how individuals and businesses make decisions (microeconomics). Political science is probably the most cognate to public policy studies in the sense that as a field it certainly is concerned with the state or government and what the state and governments do. Having said this, 'its canvas is much larger than governments and the common good. The interests and roles of individuals, ethnic communities, sectional groups (classes, associations, businesses), international and transnational organizations in shaping social reality is much more important for political studies as compared to public policy studies.'[25]

Public policy studies seek to combine the insights from business and management studies, economics, and political science 'into the service of practical problem-solving for the public good.'[26] It is this cross if not altogether interdisciplinary mix that marks the study of public policy and distinguishes it from its 'feeder' disciplines even though it is true that the feeder disciplines themselves draw on insights from each other and from other social sciences.[27]

[25] Bajpai, Fritzen, and Mahbubani, 'Global Public Policy as a Field of Study: A View from Asia', in Mahbubani, Yiannouka, Fritzen, Tuminez, and Tan, *Lee Kuan Yew School of Public Policy*, p. 162.

[26] Bajpai, Fritzen, and Mahbubani, 'Global Public Policy as a Field of Study: A View from Asia', in Mahbubani, Yiannouka, Fritzen, Tuminez, and Tan, *Lee Kuan Yew School of Public Policy*, p. 163.

[27] Bajpai, Fritzen, and Mahbubani, 'Global Public Policy as a Field of Study: A View from Asia', in Mahbubani, Yiannouka, Fritzen, Tuminez, and Tan, *Lee Kuan Yew School of Public Policy*, p. 163.

THINK TANKS AND PUBLIC POLICY SCHOOLS

Public policy studies are the mission of think tanks. However, think tanks alone cannot fulfil the larger mission of public policy studies. James McGann, in his landmark work on think tanks all over the world, has defined think tanks in the following terms:

> Think tanks are public-policy research analysis and engagement organizations that generate policy-oriented research, analysis, and advice on domestic and international issues, which enable policymakers and the public to make informed decisions about public policy issues. Think tanks may be affiliated or independent institutions and are structured as permanent bodies, not ad hoc commissions. These institutions often act as a bridge between the academic and policymaking communities and between states and civil society, serving in the public interest as independent voices that translate applied and basic research into a language and form that is understandable, reliable, and accessible for policymakers and the public.[28]

Unfortunately, India is not rich in think tanks. In 2012, India reportedly had 269 think tanks, about the same number as the UK which has a population of 62 million; half the number of China which has a slightly larger population than India; and about one-seventh the number of European Union and the US which have populations of 450 million and 313 million, respectively.[29] Even this rather low figure for India looks an inflated one. Many so-called think tanks in India are small, NGO-like institutions with very little capacity for research, dissemination of research, and policy influence.

Part of the reason for the paucity of quality think tanks is that the Indian private sector has not been supportive. In general, Indian business

[28] McGann, James G. 2012 Global Go to Think Tanks Report and Policy Advice, Thank Tanks and Civil Societies Programme, International Relations Programme, University of Pennsylvania, Philadelphia, p. 15.

[29] See McGann, 2012 Global Go to Think Tanks Report and Policy Advice, p. 35, https://www.sas.upenn.edu/irp/sites/www.sas.upenn.edu.irp/files/2012_Global_Go_To_Think_Tank_Report_-_FINAL%201.28.13_0.pdf, accessed on 12 June 2013. India is ranked fourth in the number of think tanks after the US, China, and UK. https://www.sas.upenn.edu/irp/sites/www.sas.upenn.edu.irp/files/2012_Global_Go_To_Think_Tank_Report_-_FINAL%201.28.13_0.pdf, accessed on 12 June 2013.

has been narrowly self-regarding and has not invested greatly in public philanthropy. As for funding independent-minded think tanks, Indian companies have quite resolutely steered away.[30] The private sector probably also fears the government and does not want to fund institutions that may challenge policymakers and thereby alienate or offend them. Individual companies have lobbied the government directly or have sought to influence policy through business associations such as CII, FICCI, and ASSOCHAM. They do not believe in the long-term educational role of think tanks in India. Partly this is because Indian business, like the Indian government, does not respect Indian intellectual production.

Indian think tanks at their best tend to be narrowly focused. There are few if any all-purpose think tanks such as the Brookings Institution. Internationally, too, this is the case—think tanks tend to focus in one or two related areas for the simple reason that a narrowly focused think tank may be more influential in impacting government thinking and public opinion. Yet in the real world, policy is inter-related. Policy in one area is—or should be—mindful of and connected to other areas.

Schools of public policy, by contrast, tend to be more versatile. Faculty are drawn from various disciplines. Public policy schools are larger than most think tanks, and the range of issues they can deal with is therefore more extensive. The cultures of think tanks and academia differ as well. Think tanks tend to be top-directed, and the leadership is aggressive in chalking out specializations and priorities. Think tanks are far more preoccupied with 'breaking news' and immediate policy challenges. Academic departments and schools are more decentralized. It is a rare chairperson or dean who will dictate faculty research agendas. In addition, professors take a longer view of policy. Public policy schools are led by academics, who are more self-reflective and want to account for the rise of public policy as a historical occurrence. They want to know how the notion of the 'public' originated and evolved, how it spread from one society to another, how scholarly thinking changed the notion of the public good and the role of the government, and so on. In this sense, public policy studies is not just a matter of 'problem solving' for the public good; it is also about the nature

---

[30] There are exceptions. The Mahindras are helping Gateway House, Mumbai. Siddharth Shriram has funded the Delhi Policy Group, New Delhi. Reliance helped create the Observer Research Foundation, New Delhi.

of the public good and how our understandings of it have changed and why. Public policy schools have other advantages over think tanks. They train administrators—either putative administrators, or administrators who are in harness and return to university life to reflect on their profession and wish to learn new skills, tools, and perspectives. Public policy schools also train the next generation of public policy professors who in turn will train the next generation of administrators. This is not the mission of think tanks.

CHALLENGES TO SETTING UP PUBLIC POLICY STUDIES/SCHOOLS

Setting up public policy schools is not easy. The Lee Kuan Yew School of Public Policy, National University of Singapore (NUS), is arguably the best known and most successful public policy school in Asia. In a volume that it published recently on its own rise, the School reflected candidly on its first eight years.[31]

The School had many advantages—the name Lee Kuan Yew; the attachment to a globally top-rated university; autonomy within the university as also from the government; the fact that it is located in an advanced economy with an enviable record of good governance; the leadership of a founding Dean with a global reputation; the early partnership with the Harvard Kennedy School; the existence of a public policy programme at NUS on which it could build; excellent recruitment of well-trained faculty at its founding, world-class facilities, salaries, and research funding; and a sizeable corpus. Few, if any, Indian schools of public policy will be able to count on these kinds of advantages.

India needs at least thirty schools of public policy, one per state and in the Union territories of Delhi and Chandigarh. As things stand, it has nine very small, incipient programmes.[32] It needs to grow the existing programmes into full-fledged schools with a range of master's programmes—a

---

[31] See Mahbubani, Yiannouka, Fritzen, Tuminez, and Tan, *Lee Kuan Yew School of Public Policy*.

[32] These are at the Administrative Staff Training College, Azim Premji University, Central University of Rajasthan, Indian School of Business in Mohali, Indian Institute of Management in Ahmedabad, Indian Institute of Management in Bangalore, O.P. Jindal University, Management Development Institute in Gurgaon, and TERI.

one-year programme for mid-career professionals, a slightly shorter executive programme for more advanced professionals, a two-year programme for early career professionals and fresh graduates, and eventually a modest doctoral programme as well. On top of the nine existing programmes, it needs at least twenty more public policy schools. These are best located in state capitals in order to draw public servants to the taught programmes and to access officials and political leaders, as practitioners, to help teach. Each state should have at least one public policy school because there are issues that are particular to each state as also because this will encourage a greater sense of ownership of and investment in the schools on the part of local officials, politicians, and civil society.

As suggested earlier, there are all kinds of challenges facing a putative public policy school—the relationship to the university and government, leadership of the school, founding partnerships with established schools, building on existing public policy or public administration programmes, facilities, salaries, and research funding, establishing a corpus, and so on. Let me focus on two additional challenges: the curriculum; and the consequences of interdisciplinarity.

The curriculum of a public policy school is obviously a core issue. The standard public policy curriculum, derived largely from the US programmes, is typified by core courses in microeconomics and macroeconomics, quantitative techniques, policy analysis frameworks including cost-benefit analysis, public management, public finance, leadership, and ethics. This core is then supplemented by electives in these and other areas including development policy, international relations/international trade and finance, and various areas of social policy (health, education, urban, social security, population policy, etc.).

A more sociological-historical approach would feature economics but would also expose students to insights from sociology, history, and political science/international relations. Thus, students would study, as suggested earlier in this chapter, the origins of notions such as the public realm, the public good, public policy, good governance, and global governance. How did rulers and governors come to see their role as definers of the public good and as providers of public policy and good governance? How has the idea of the public good and the proper ends and uses of government expanded or contracted? What kinds of criteria have been applied to assessing public policy apart from an economistic calculus of cost and benefit? How have rulers and governors made policy and implemented them, and how has the participation of civil society grown? How have global, extra-national actors and dynamics come to affect 'domestic' policy? How, over time, have societies grappled with complex interaction effects between the domestic and international, between the local and national, between geopolitics, nationalism, bureaucratization, urbanization, environment, demography, technology, capitalism, and migration? What kinds of policies emerge in these kinds of settings?

Beyond the broad curricular stance—economistic or sociological—anyone setting up a school of public policy will have to think about the spatio-temporal context within which the programme will exist. In an essay, I wrote with my colleagues, Scott Fritzen and Kishore Mahbubani, we made an attempt to sketch in a context for Asia, which I quote at some length here:

> First of all, socially, Asian societies are usually highly plural in terms of ethnic, religious, and linguistic affiliations. The relationship of individuals to communities is still strong. Kinship matters considerably, though with variation. How to manage this diversity in the interest of social peace and progress is a constant concern in much of Asia.
>
> Second, economically, Asia offers a heterogeneous landscape with several countries in East Asia and Southeast Asia that have advanced up to and in some cases beyond Western levels and others that are in the mid-range while yet others are at low levels of per capita income and industrialization. Still, the overwhelming number of states is in the mid or low range. Sustained economic growth over the next three to four decades and eliminating poverty constitute central challenges. Transitioning from a rural-agricultural economy to an urban-manufacturing-cum-service economy lies ahead. These are societies that are struggling to achieve higher levels of human development, build modern infrastructure and communication systems, and achieve a balance between economic development and environmental sustainability. The mid and low range economies also feature high income and wealth disparities. Demographically, they continue to grow even as rates of growth are slowing down. The demographic profile features a very large number of young people in search of education and jobs. How to manage both kinds of economic systems but particularly the mid and low range systems and to take them to higher levels of economic development while ensuring social justice and environmental stability is a huge challenge, one that is complicated by issues relating to fiscal health, the state of the global economy and of a country's trade and investment, and state regulation and simultaneously de-regulation of the economy.

Third, politically, Asia features governments that have intervened in all sectors of social and economic life as part of nation building. Asian governments have a mixed record in delivering clean and efficient administration, providing basic services, ensuring law and order, and responding to popular demands and participation. How to build institutions that carry out the will of the political leadership in these and other areas and yet empower and respect the rights of citizens is a crucial pivot of Asian politics? This basic problem of governance has not yet been definitively resolved in Asia.

Four, geopolitically, Asia features a number of conflicts which divide it and which could explode into violence. In this sense, Asia is more like Europe of the 19th century. These rivalries and conflicts pivot about border and other territorial quarrels, relative power and status, and national identity and pride. Asia has a history of war—interstate as well as internal—but it has also evolved norms and institutions to deal with its problems. Asia's explosive economic growth could be a force for integration, but it could also fuel geopolitical rivalries which outpace the ability of its normative and institutional structures to deal with conflict. Asian security is complicated by the presence of four nuclear powers—China, India, Pakistan, and North Korea—and some of the world's largest militaries. How to manage Asia's geopolitics is also a key policy challenge. Finally, Asia is home to terrorism and insurgency, with links that are transnational (both regional and global).[33]

This context suggests that a curriculum for GPP [that is, global public policy] in Asia might include courses in the following four inter-related fields:

- Managing ethnically, religiously, and linguistically plural societies.
- A sustainable transition from a predominantly rural/agricultural, regulated, and autarkic economy to an urban/manufacturing-service, marketizing, and internationalizing economy in a globalizing world.

---

[33] Bajpai, Kanti, Scott Fritzen, and Kishore Mahbubani, 'Global Public Policy as a Field of Study: Where Are We Going?' a paper presented at the GPPN Conference, Rockefeller Foundation, Bellagio 14–18 June 2011, pp. 7–8. Versions of this paper were published as 'Global Public Policy as a Field of Study: A View from Asia', *Jindal School of Public Policy Journal* 1 (1) (August 2012): pp. 8–25, and as 'Global Public Policy as a Field of Study: A View from Asia', in Mahbubani, Yiannouka, Fritzen, Tuminez, and Tan, *Lee Kuan Yew School of Public Policy*, pp. 159–77.

- Institution building in political systems that must balance government leadership and responsiveness.
- Peace and security in Asia.[34]

To this I would now add that rising Asia is increasing its outlays on social security—on health, pensions, housing, food—and therefore the fiscal viability of these systems over a long period of time, as people live longer and the number of young people decreases, is a crucial area of public policy debate.[35]

Furthermore, rising Asia is consuming vast amounts of energy and is polluting its land, rivers, and air as never before. Public policy in the continent must therefore give much greater attention to energy and environmental policy.[36] Put somewhat differently, public policy studies in Asia must contend simultaneously with both a developmental and post-developmental agenda.

In addition to curricular challenges, there are the challenges of inter-disciplinarity in pedagogy and faculty recruitment, tenure, and promotion. Few faculty members are truly interdisciplinary in terms of their intellectual training and expertise. Yet, public policy schools offer courses in economics, policy analysis, public management, political science and international relations, with the hope that students will be interdisciplinary in the sense of being able to use the various concepts, theories, methods, and modes of analysis in their studies and, later still, in their practice.

[34] Kanti Bajpai, Scott Fritzen, and Kishore Mahbubani, 'Global Public Policy as a Field of Study: Where Are We Going?' a paper presented at the GPPN Conference, Rockefeller Foundation, Bellagio 14–18 June 2011, pp. 7–8.

[35] South Asia is an exception here in as much as the proportion of young people is projected to keep growing until 2030. See World Bank, 'Investing in the Youth Bulge in South Asia: Summary of Findings and Recommendations from World Development Report 2007–Development and the Next Generation', World Bank Working Paper, Report No. 70368, disclosure date 22 June 2012, p. 1, http://www-wds.worldbank.org/external/default/WDSContentServer/WDSP/IB/201 2/06/22/000386194_20120622035429/Rendered/PDF/703680WP0P094506 B00PUBLIC00SAR0note.pdf, accessed on 22 June 2013.

[36] In the same week of 17–24 June 2013, India had to deal with the consequences of the Ganga river in spate in the Himalayas which devastated parts of the state of Uttarakhand; and Indonesia, Malaysia, and Singapore had to confront the haze that drifted over from Sumatra in Indonesia. These may well be the precursors to much larger and more sustained ecological crises.

How is this kind of interdisciplinarity to be imparted when the faculty are for the most part resolutely *disciplinary* rather than interdisciplinary in their approach and preferences? One way is to co-teach courses, that is, to have faculty from different streams conceptualize and teach courses together. Co-teaching here implies a deep immersion in the course and not simply parachuting in to deliver one's lecture never to be seen again! At the Lee Kuan Yew (LKY) School of Public Policy, we are trying increasingly to develop a deeper sense of co-teaching, with the recognition that it is no easy endeavour.

Another way of delivering interdisciplinarity in the classroom is to recruit faculty differently, namely, to find faculty that are comfortable with interdisciplinarity and can range across different fields of study. Given that the social sciences are organized overwhelmingly by disciplines, this will test any recruitment system. Recruiting doctorates from public policy schools may be a preferred way to go since PhDs from those programmes will have been exposed to an interdisciplinary course of study and will be more comfortable pedagogically with it.

This leads us to the issue of tenure and promotion. Schools of public policy must think seriously about tenure and promotion decisions in the light of the interdisciplinarity challenge. Indian universities do not have tenure systems, but they do have promotion systems, and going forward they may opt to develop something like tenure.

How does a school with quite different intellectual streams judge its faculty in respect of both their teaching and research excellence? In the US and UK, various metrics as well as external review by experts in the disciplinary subfields are used to assess faculty competence. In India, we use neither method. Indian universities rarely if ever use metrics such as citation counts and the h-index to assess research excellence. As for external review, this is supposed to occur in the promotion committee. However, few committees in India in practice have the time or application to read the work that is submitted to them. Excellence is largely judged by performance in a 30–40 minutes interview and an ineffable sense of the candidate's overall intellectual standing. While interviews and reputational knowledge can help in a promotion decision, they are not enough if there is to be a systematic and defensible appraisal of excellence.

Beyond curricular and faculty challenges, there is the challenge of student recruitment. What kinds of students should a public policy school in India recruit? This depends partly on the kinds of degrees on offer: a one-year, two-year, or nine-month master's? These are usually differentiated by the age and experience of students enrolled in them. Most public policy schools target officials of various ranks. Who should public policy studies attract beyond officials? Increasingly, the students in these programmes comprise those from the profit and non-profit sector. At many public policy schools, the student body also has students who have just graduated or who are making career transitions and want to get an additional, more professional degree. While the officials can go back to their careers in the civil service, what are the career prospects of those who come from other backgrounds? Could younger students who get a master's go on to compete successfully in the civil service examination? As things stand, a public policy degree is unlikely to help them: the subject is not on offer in the list of subjects one can be examined in. Nor is there lateral entry into the Indian civil services. Many graduates will therefore find employment opportunities in areas that other social science and humanities graduates are vying for—the non-profit sector, the media, and think tanks. Some may, in addition, find employment in the private sector or even international organizations. Some may choose to go on to do doctoral studies. At any rate, schools of public policy will have to think deeply about the kind of students they ideally want and the kinds of career placements they are preparing their students for.

* * *

Neither Indian society nor the Indian government respect the life of the mind and certainly not the university system. For all the talk in India of the ideal relationship between teacher and pupil, between *guru* and *shishya*, Indians care very little about teachers or students. Indian universities went from being amongst the best in Asia to being nowhere in Asia. As in so many things, we in India have taken fairly respectable institutions and made them into caricatures of the original and have worked assiduously to destroy them.

Today, a society that neglects fundamental improvements in higher education is courting disaster. India's future is fraught and has never been more uncertain given various internal challenges, external threats, and global changes including climate change.[37] Buoyed by a decade of high rates of

[37] See various recent books on India's 'grand strategic' challenges including Kapil Kak (ed.), *Comprehensive Security for Emerging India* (Delhi: KW Publishers

economic growth, Indians have developed an unreal sense of their future, an 'India Shining' view of what lies ahead.[38] The economic facts staring India in the face since the world economic crisis of 2008 suggests that the country may be on the cusp of a very dark period of economic and political history, especially given the array of political, economic, social, and physical challenges it confronts and given the abysmal nature of its leadership, both public and private. India must quickly create a higher education system that equips its young people with an intelligent and ethical understanding of their personal and social lives and of the natural and physical world. It needs young people who can creatively and sensibly solve collective and material problems, not just endlessly ruminate on those problems. The need is more than urgent. It is critical. And there is not much time.

---

and the Centre for Air Power Studies, 2010). Khilnani, S., Rajiv Kumar, Pratap Bhanu Mehta, Prakash Menon, Nandan Nilekani, Srinath Raghvan, Shyam Saran, and Siddharth Vardarajan, 'Non-Alignment 2.0: A Foreign and Strategic Policy for India in the Twenty First Century' (New Delhi: Centre for Policy Research, 2012); Menon, Raja and Rajiv Kumar, *The Long View From Delhi: To Define the Indian Grand Strategy for Foreign Policy* (New Delhi: Indian Council, 2010) for Research on International Economic Relations and Academic Publishing, Kumar, Rajiv and Santosh Kumar, *In the National Interest: A Strategic Foreign Policy for India* (New Delhi: BS Books, an imprint of Business Standard Limited, 2010). Rajiv Sikiri, *Challenge and Strategy: Rethinking India's Foreign Policy* (New Delhi: Sage, 2009) and Krishnappa Venkatshamy and Princy George, *Grand Strategy for India: 2020 and Beyond* (New Delhi: Institute for Defence Studies and Analyses and Pentagon Security International, 2012). See also Corbridge, Harriss, and Jeffrey, *India Today*.

[38] 'India Shining' was the National Democratic Alliance (NDA) slogan going into the general elections of 2004.

9 Challenges of Knowledge Creation for Indian Universities

Stephen P. Marks

The role of research in universities in India and elsewhere is inseparable from the aims of research as knowledge creation and from the broader context of knowledge creation in the educational process. The purpose of this chapter is to reflect on the basic purpose of knowledge creation in the university and then examine responsibilities of the university for promoting knowledge creation in a range of fields of investigation and levels of learning, as well as the ethical standards that apply. The conclusion will address the uncertain future of knowledge creation in the university and the alternative models for change.

The premise for this reflection on challenges of knowledge creation for Indian universities was captured at the March 2013, O.P. Jindal Global University Conference on 'The Future of Indian Universities: Comparative Perspectives on Higher Education Reforms for a Knowledge Society' (referred to below as the March

Conference) in the *Hindustan Times,* where Vice-Chancellor C. Raj Kumar wrote:

> Because of their indifference to research, [Indian] universities have been unable to provide solutions to social, economic, and political problems that affect India. Indian universities ought to become fertile ground for the generation of ideas. Research produces knowledge that offers clarity and a more informed understanding of the subject at hand.[1] These reflections are offered as a contribution to discussion on why and how a research role for Indian universities can be part of their potential for attaining world-class status. We begin with a broader exploration of the purpose of knowledge creation and then focus on the responsibilities of the university for promoting knowledge creation and on some of the uncertainties in the context of the evolving approaches to addressing specific challenges for universities to contribute meaningfully to knowledge creation.

THE PURPOSE OF KNOWLEDGE CREATION

The concept of knowledge creation should be a self-evident function of a university. However, that function is ambiguous in at least two ways. First, do we mean creating knowledge in the learner or generating accessible research results? While the quotation above by C. Raj Kumar underscores the concern with a university's capacity to produce research, it is also the university's function to enrich the knowledge of students and faculty through learning. Second, are we treating knowledge as an end in itself or a means toward an end? Here also the answer is 'both' in the sense that a university is a place where individuals grow intellectually and contribute to knowledge others can access.

Types of Knowledge and Intelligence

Philosophers and psychologists have developed elaborate categories of knowledge. One study enumerates the following distinctions: 'generic (or general) and domain specific knowledge, concrete and abstract knowledge, formal and informal knowledge, declarative and proceduralized knowledge, conceptual and procedural knowledge, elaborated and compiled knowledge, unstructured and (highly) structured knowledge, tacit or inert knowledge, strategic knowledge, knowledge acquisition knowledge, situated

---

[1] Kumar, C Raj, 'Still Not in a Class of Their Own,' *Hindustan Times,* Wednesday (20 March 2013).

knowledge, and meta-knowledge.'[2] These authors prefer the following four types of knowledge.

Situational knowledge: 'knowledge about situations as they typically appear in a particular domain, [which] enables the solver to sift relevant features out of the problem statement (selective perception) and, if necessary, to supplement information in the statement.'

Conceptual (previously called *declarative*) *knowledge*: 'static knowledge about facts, concepts, and principles that apply within a certain domain, [which] functions as additional information that problem solvers add to the problem and that they use to perform the solution.'

Procedural knowledge: knowledge of 'actions or manipulations that are valid within a domain [and] help the problem solver make transitions from one problem state to another.'

Strategic knowledge: 'a general plan of action in which the sequence of solution activities is laid down [and which] helps students organize their problem-solving process by directing which stages they should go through to reach a solution.'[3]

They then identify qualities of knowledge (*level* in terms of deep or superficial, *structure* in terms of isolated elements or structured knowledge, *automation* in terms of declarative or compiled knowledge, *modality* in terms of pictorial or verbal, and *generality* in terms of general or domain specific) and relate these qualities to each type, generating a matrix of 20 descriptions of knowledge.

In addition to kinds of knowledge there are also kinds of receiving minds or intelligences. Howard Gardner famously listed seven intelligences. His provisional listing may be summarized as follows:[4]

Linguistic intelligence: ability to learn and use languages

Logical-mathematical intelligence: capacity to analyse problems logically, detect patterns, reason deductively, and think logically

---

[2] de Jong, T. and Ferguson-Hessler, M.G.M. 'Types and Qualities of Knowledge', *Educational Psychologist* v 31(2): 105.

[3] de Jong and Ferguson-Hessler, 'Types and Qualities of Knowledge', *Educational Psychologist* 31(2): 106.

[4] Gardner, Howard, *Intelligence Reframed. Multiple Intelligences for the 21st Century* (New York: Basic Books, 1999), pp. 41–3.

Musical intelligence: skill in the performance, composition, and appreciation of music

Bodily-kinesthetic intelligence: using one's whole body or parts of the body to solve problems

Spatial intelligence: ability to recognize and use the patterns of wide and narrow space

Interpersonal intelligence: capacity to understand intentions, motivations and desires of peoples

Intrapersonal intelligence: capacity to understand oneself, including feelings, fears and motivations

This understanding of kinds of knowledge and intelligence helps frame the problem of knowledge creation in universities, whether it is in how students learn or how university-based scholars carry out research. However, it is useful to consider whether universities should consider knowledge as an end, a means, or a process.

Knowledge as an End in Itself

Drawing on an example from my own university for the purpose of clarifying what I mean by the concept of knowledge as an end in itself, I would cite a 2007 task force report that recently redefined the set of requirements, outside the concentration (major field of study), that all students must meet before they can receive a Harvard degree. The task force put it rather eloquently in describing a 'liberal education' as 'an education conducted in a spirit of free inquiry undertaken without concern for topical relevance or vocational utility'. The report continues in a philosophical vein:

[t]his kind of learning is not only one of the enrichments of existence; it is one of the achievements of civilization. It heightens students' awareness of the human and natural worlds they inhabit. It makes them more reflective about their beliefs and choices, more self-conscious and critical of their presuppositions and motivations, more creative in their problem-solving, more perceptive of the world around them, and more able to inform themselves about the issues that arise in their lives, personally, professionally, and socially.[5]

Such an understanding of the role of the university reflects the concept of knowledge for its own sake, of the learner's awareness of the world,

---

[5] Report of the Task Force on General Education, Harvard (2007): p. 1.

independent of what they do with that knowledge. But what they do with it also matters.

Knowledge as a Means

No one denies that the university prepares young people to become productive members of society. 'A liberal education is also a preparation for the rest of life,' according to the same report, which adds

> The subjects that undergraduates study and, as importantly, the skills and habits of mind they acquire in the process, shape the lives they will lead after they leave the academy. ... A liberal education is useful. This does not mean that its purpose is to train students for their professions or to give them a guide to life after college.[6]

So, knowledge acquired through university learning is not primarily aimed at preparing careers, but more about preparing citizens capable of critical reasoning and understanding the world. It is only after knowledge creation that it can be reproduced through education and training and translated into applications in the worlds of government, commerce, policy, medicine, and health, as well as in changing social mores and political preferences.

Knowledge as a Process

Knowledge is also a process. How is knowledge created? In the university setting, it can be considered to come from research and writing of a theoretical, empirical, evaluative or speculative, prescriptive, descriptive, or applied scientific research. One way of understanding the process is the production-re-production-translation cycle. This cycle of knowledge involves stages that loop: First, there is knowledge production, through research; then there is its re-production, through education and training; and finally its translation, which, when subject to scientific evaluation, feeds back into the production of new knowledge.[7]

---

[6] Report of the Task Force on General Education, Harvard (2007): p. 1.

[7] Frenk, Julio and David E. Barmes, 'Global Health Lecture given at the National Institutes of Health' (15 December 2009). 'Globalization and Health: The Role of Knowledge in an Interdependent World'. Frenk, Julio. *Globalization and Health: The Role of Knowledge in an Interdependent World* (Maryland: Bethesda,15 December 2009).

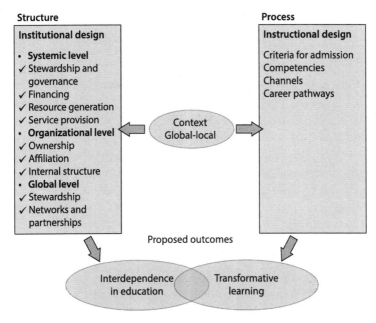

Figure 9.1 Key Components of the Educational System

Source: Frenk et al. (see note 7).

Reporting on their work for a commission on post-secondary education in medicine, nursing, and public health, Frenk et al. identified three key dimensions of education, which are relevant to all institutions of higher education (IHE): institutional design, which specifies the structure and functions of the education system; instructional design, which focuses on processes; and educational outcomes, which deal with the desired results (see Figure 9.1).[8] They also found four crucial functions that also apply to educational systems: (1) *stewardship and governance*: 'norms and policies, evidence for decision making, and assessment of performance', which ensures strategic guidance for the educational system; (2) *financing*: aggregate allocation of public and private resources for educational institution,

[8] Frenk, Julio, Lincoln Chen, Zulfiqar A. Bhutta, Jordan Cohen, Nigel Crisp, Timothy Evans, Harvey Fineberg, et al., 2010. 'Health Professionals for a New Century: Transforming Education to Strengthen Health Systems in an Interdependent World'. *The Lancet* 376 (9756) (1923–58): p. 10.

which provides resource flows and incentives to each educational organiza-tion; (3) *resource generation*: primarily external funding for faculty research and development, which meets the knowledge generation and translation functions; and (4) *service provision*: educational services primarily through instruction, which meets the knowledge transmission function.[9]

During the March 2013 Conference on 'The Future of Indian Universities', several participants argued that such a financial and institu-tional model fails to address several vital features of knowledge creation.[10] The vitality of knowledge creation is enhanced by the freedom of faculty to dissent from established wisdom or the preferences of funders of research. Innovation in teaching and generating new ideas often depend more on the audacity of members of the academic community than on established institutional incentives. Alternatives to the US model of private universities with government-funded research have emerged in Singapore and South Korea. Therefore, one of the challenges facing India is to develop its own approach to world-class knowledge creation. As one Indian scientist put it, '[g]iven that the world in the 21st century is crowded and resources in India are comparatively scarce, such institutions may not represent the best models for India to follow'.[11] He also argued that 'focus of the discussion should be on identifying the knowledge required to alleviate suffering from poverty, hunger, disease, injustice, and inequity; prevent environmental degradation; conserve the region's unique biological and cultural heritage; and meet developmental challenges'.[12]

What is said about education in general applies to research and publica-tions in particular, as research is a more narrow understanding of knowledge creation. The two types of knowledge creation (learning by students and research by faculty) are synergistic in the sense that faculty members are

[9] Frenk, Julio, Lincoln Chen, Zulfiqar A. Bhutta, Jordan Cohen, Nigel Crisp, Timothy Evans, Harvey Fineberg, et al., 2010. 'Health Professionals for a New Century: Transforming Education to Strengthen Health Systems in an Inter-dependent World'. *The Lancet* 376 (9756) (1923–58): p. 10.

[10] These observations were inspired notably by remarks made at the Conference by Professors Shiv Visvanathan, Dhruv Raina, Devesh Kapur, and Madhav Menon.

[11] S. Bawa, Kamaljit, 'India's Path to Knowledge'. *Science* 30 335 (6076) (March 2012): p. 1573. DOI: 10.1126/science.335.6076.1573-e.

[12] S. Bawa, Kamaljit, 'India's Path to Knowledge'. *Science* 30 335 (6076) (March 2012): p. 1573. DOI: 10.1126/science.335.6076.1573-e.

able to pursue research and publish works that challenge young people in 'beliefs and choices ... presuppositions and motivations,' in the words of the Harvard Task Force.[13] This is only possible if they either are paid to balance a reasonable teaching load with writing and publication, or have access to research grants. The problem here is that paying faculty to think is expensive and those with resources would rather fund research that will contribute to productivity in society, which treats knowledge as a means towards an end or even as a commodity itself.

Knowledge is transformative. In society, knowledge is acquired from experience, socialization, formal education, informal learning, investigation, exploration, and all means through which the cognitive, analytical, affective, and ethical reasoning functions of the brain are modified. The social settings are as varied as human experience. New neural connections in different parts of the brain create new understanding skills, capacities, and emotions. All these modes of acquiring knowledge continue in a university setting; however, the privileged means are one form or another of the production-re-production-translation cycle (see Figure 9. 2). Transformative change depends on possibilities that did not exist and

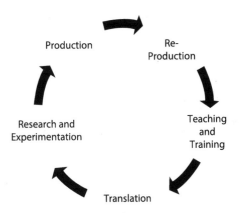

Figure 9.2   The Production-re-production-Translation Cycle[14]

[13] Report of the Task Force on General Education, Harvard, 2007, p. 1.

[14] Adapted from Julio Frenk, David E. Barmes Global Health Lecture given at the National Institutes of Health (15 December 2009). 'Globalization and Health: the Role of Knowledge in an Interdependent World'. Frenk, *Globalization and Health*.

sound research is the first step toward transformation. Thus, knowledge is both a means and an end. It is a means of innovation through research and translates evidence-based research into evidence-based policymaking.

FOUR CHALLENGES OF KNOWLEDGE CREATION IN INDIAN UNIVERSITIES

Assuming that a university is committed to knowledge as both an end in itself and as a means toward achievement, it faces four special challenges of knowledge creation, which constrain institutional instructional design. First, what is the optimal range of fields of knowledge that the university must cover? Second, what levels of education will be provided and how should knowledge creation be adapted to each? Third, what ethical standards apply to knowledge creation and how will the university enforce them? Finally, how does the university deal with the reality of politicization and commodification of knowledge?

Challenges Due to Disciplinary Fragmentation

The first challenge to knowledge creation in the university is the fragmentation of knowledge. Given limitations in available human and financial resources, each university must strike a balance among the potential academic fields. Ideally, a university should be a place of knowledge creation in all the arts and sciences but in practice very few can cover them all well. The investment required offering courses and degrees, engaging in research, and produce publications is significant in each field. Among the hundreds of fields of knowledge a university can offer, four broad groupings summarize the complexities of the challenge of selecting fields of knowledge creation.

1. *Humanities and philosophy*: aesthetic and interpretive understanding, culture and belief, ethical reasoning, etc.
2. *Natural sciences*: life sciences, physical sciences, medical sciences.
3. *Policy and social sciences*: law, institutions, management, international relations, political science.
4. *Applied sciences*: application of scientific knowledge to the physical environment, including agronomy, architecture, engineering and computer technology.

A related challenge is to encourage interdisciplinary knowledge creation, rendered all the more difficult as faculty and administrators in each of the established disciplines understandably seeks to maintain the integrity of the discipline with scarce resources. A sociology department is likely to be more concerned about surviving in a university than in creating opportunities for students and faculty to challenge sociological methods by introducing creative alternative ways of addressing the questions sociology is supposed to address. There is an unavoidable tension between specialization leading to fragmentation and unifying knowledge leading to impoverishment of disciplines.

In *Our Underachieving Colleges*, Derek Bok expressed this challenge well:

> No one has demonstrated convincingly that the drawbacks of fragmentation have outweighed the contributions to knowledge made possible by specialization. Nor has any general theory or universal methods emerged to knit the separate disciplines together. The unity of knowledge remains an elusive ideal.[15]

One attempt to reach that 'elusive ideal' was formulated in the concept of 'consilience' by E.O. Wilson. 'The greatest enterprise of the mind', he wrote, 'has always been and always will be the attempted linkage of the sciences and humanities. The ongoing fragmentation of knowledge and resulting chaos in philosophy are not reflections of the real world but artefacts of scholarship'.[16] He proposes consilience as 'the key to unification'.[17] Wilson acknowledges that consilience is a minority view 'shared by only a few scientists and philosophers'.[18] And yet he argues that 'we are approaching a new age of synthesis, when the testing of consilience is the greatest of all intellectual challenges'.[19]

What does this mean for higher education in India? Integrating fields of knowledge is not new to India. Nalanda University, operating from the fifth to twelfth centuries in ancient Magadha, is said to have been 'uniquely attractive for all seekers of pure knowledge' because of its 'ability

---

[15] Bok, Derek. *Our Underachieving Colleges* (Princeton: Princeton University Press, 2006), p. 25.

[16] Wilson, Edward O. *Consilience. The Unity of Knowledge* (New York: Vintage Books, 1998) p. 8.

[17] Wilson, *Consilience. The Unity of Knowledge*, p. 8.

[18] Wilson, *Consilience. The Unity of Knowledge*, p. 9.

[19] Wilson, *Consilience. The Unity of Knowledge*, p. 12.

to meld multiple discourses and to embrace knowledge in its entirety.[20] While those involved in re-establishing Nalanda University declare '[t]here is now a perfect opportunity to recreate the hallowed universalism of Nalanda as a centre of knowledge',[21] most Indian universities today have adapted the British or American systems of higher educational. They are thus confronted with the challenge of inter-disciplinarity in similar ways to universities elsewhere in the English-speaking world.

Professional advancement is in large part determined by identifying with and contributing to specialized disciplines and students expect to find a wide range of departments and concentrations in the humanities and philosophy, the natural sciences, and policy and social sciences, including law and management. The need to advance interdisciplinarity notwithstanding the pull toward fragmentation is addressed in the chapter by Yugank Goyal in this volume.[22] The breadth of disciplines covered is further complicated by the challenge of levels of degree programmes.

The temptation for a university concerned with its reputation in knowledge production is to focus on those areas of research where innovation is measurable and applications are needed in the industrial sector, such as the bio-sciences rather than the arts, humanities, and social sciences. There is a strong trend in this direction in India today. For example, chemical biologist Krishna Ganesh, director of Indian Institute of Science Education and Research (IISER), Pune, declared '[w]e need to find ways to attract intelligent students into science.'[23] A report on the future of scientific research in India stated that '[t]he future of scientific research in India is very promising' given the pool of professionals in such areas as genetic modification, bio-energy sources, biochemistry, atomic energy, organ donation, biomedical science, among others.[24] The research in these areas 'will determine much of the way these issues are viewed by the world in the near future.'[25]

---

[20] Nalanda's History. Available at http://www.nalandauniv.edu.in/abt-history.html.

[21] Our Vision. Available at http://www.nalandauniv.edu.in/abt-vision.html.

[22] See Chapter 14 in this volume.

[23] Quoted by Richard Stone. 'SCIENCE IN INDIA. India Rising'. *Science* 335 (6071) (24 February 2012): pp. 904–10. DOI: 10.1126/science.335.6071.904.

[24] http://www.kitesindia.org/the-future-of-scientific-research-in-india.php.

[25] Available at http://www.kitesindia.org/the-future-of-scientific-research-in-india.php.

As such, '[h]ow India handles many of the ethical dilemmas that scientific research presents will be an education for many other countries, including developed countries'.[26] The Minister for the Ministries of Science and Technology and of Earth Sciences, Shri Sudini Jaipal Reddy, takes pride in the fact that 'India is one of the top- ranking countries in the field of basic research. Indian Science has come to be regarded as one of the most powerful instruments of growth and development, especially in the emerging scenario and competitive economy'.[27]

Indeed, it is also noteworthy that the Indian Department of Science and Technology (DST) acknowledged 'the present situation of a large number of well- qualified women scientists who due to various circumstances have been left out of the S&T activities needs to be addressed'.[28] In order to address the problem, the DST has created a 'Women Scientists Scheme (WOS)'. A positive development is the agreement, announced by Alice Prochaska, Principal, Somerville College, University of Oxford, at the March 2013 Conference to set up of the Indira Gandhi Centre for Sustainable Development at Somerville College, Oxford, as a tribute to the former Prime Minister, Indira Gandhi, who was a student of Somerville College.[29] It will provide 'graduate/PhD scholarships ... specifically to Indian students at Oxford, with a cohort of Indian graduate students participating directly in research of relevance to India'.[30] This initiative is consistent with WOS and will no doubt be followed by other efforts to remove the barriers to women in science and other fields of research.

The push for science education is understandable and is likely to succeed in light of resources made available for education and research in these areas.

[26] Available at http://www.kitesindia.org/the-future-of-scientific-research-in-india.php.

[27] Available at http://www.dst.gov.in/.

[28] Available at http://www.dst.gov.in/scientific-programme/women-scientists.htm.

[29] Indira Gandhi Centre for Sustainable Development at Oxford University approved, *The Hindu*, New Delhi (7 December 2012), available at http://www.thehindu.com/news/national/indira-gandhi-centre-for-sustainable-development-at-oxford-university-approved/article4175367.ece.

[30] Indira Gandhi Centre for Sustainable Development at Oxford University approved, *The Hindu*, New Delhi (7 December 2012), available at http://www.thehindu.com/news/national/indira-gandhi-centre-for-sustainable-development-at-oxford-university-approved/article4175367.ece.

The challenges for Indian universities shifts, therefore, to finding the resources and resolve to sustain and increase knowledge creation in the humanities and social sciences. Three additional challenges further complicate the role of Indian higher education in contributing to knowledge creation.

Challenges Due to Levels of Education

Knowledge creation faces challenges that vary according to the level of education. At the undergraduate level, students need to learn methods of research and writing at a qualitatively different level than they were exposed to in secondary education. Further, the ethics of research, principally ensuring that the student produces original work and does not plagiarize in any way ideas, data, and wording of others, is a significant feature of undergraduate education. The issue of academic integrity is addressed in more detail in the next section.

At the graduate level, students are exposed to the highest level of research in their field and are expected to begin creating their own original research, by applying the most advanced methods and translating their research into publishable scholarship. At the same time, they begin teaching undergraduates, which should offer them the opportunity to appreciate how knowledge is transmitted and how to assist younger students acquire the research skills at the undergraduate level.

At the postgraduate level, students are expected to publish in peer-reviewed journals and established networks of collaboration among professionals in their field as they prepare for a career devoted to knowledge creation.

Finally, once a qualified researcher has attained faculty status, knowledge creation, reproduction, and translation becomes the core function. As mentioned above, the task of the university is to ensure the highest possible access to research funds, time away from teaching, and access to documentation through a well-stocked library and online sources.

In sum, universities need to be aware of the evolving conditions of knowledge creation across these four levels of education. They intersect and overlap but special attention must be paid to each.

Challenges Due to the Propensity towards Academic Dishonesty

Knowledge creation is clearly hampered by the blatant infringement of academic honesty in the form of deliberate or inadvertent plagiarism.

A related issue is that of academic freedom and freedom of scientific research. Each of these dimensions will be addressed briefly.

Old, well-established universities like Jawaharlal Nehru University (JNU) and Delhi University (DU) and new ones like O.P. Jindal Global University have a special responsibility to ensure that knowledge created under their auspices respects the highest standards of academic integrity, meaning that all ideas, data, findings, reasoning, conclusions, and recommendations that are not original creations of the author are properly attributed. This seems self-evident but it is easy for students and even the most celebrated senior faculty to let their hope for results or time constraints lower the rigor with which they treat their scholarship. Dishonesty and inadvertence must at all times be held in check and it is the university's responsibility to communicate to all concerned clear and imperative rules of academic integrity and institute disciplinary procedures so that there are serious consequences for misconduct. Scholars and their research assistants need to be trained properly in being meticulous about avoiding that their cut-and-pasted notes from the Internet become confused with their own prose and in avoiding other forms of academic dishonesty that fall short of blatant plagiarism.

These issues seriously affect knowledge creation in China and India. In 2010, *Nature* reported that since October 2008, 'a staggering 31% of papers submitted to the Journal of Zhejiang University–Science (692 of 2,233 submissions)' were found to have contained unoriginal material.[31] India comes second to China in the 'shame sweepstakes' of questionable research practices. In a study published in the US *Proceedings of the National Academy of Sciences*, the authors used English-language articles indexed by PubMED and found that 'China and India collectively accounted for more cases of plagiarism than the United States, and duplicate publication exhibited a pattern similar to that of plagiarism.'[32] According to an assessment of this study in the *Telegraph*, G.S. Mudur reported that 'India accounted for 3.4 per cent (30 papers) of the 889 papers retracted for fraud or suspected fraud, 10 per cent (20 papers) of the 200 retracted for plagiarism, and

[31] Yuehong Zhang, 'Chinese Journal Finds 31 Per Cent of Submissions Plagiarized'. *Nature* 467 (9 September 2010): p. 153. DOI: 10.1038/467153d. Published online (08 September 2010).

[32] Ferric C. Fang, R. Grant Steen, and Arturo Casadevall. Misconduct accounts for the majority of retracted scientific publications? *Proceedings of the National Academy of Sciences of the United States of America* 109 (42) (2012):17028–33.

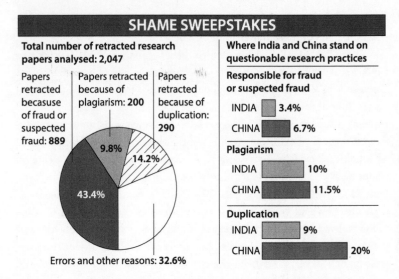

Figure 9.3   Dishonesty in Scientific Research: India and China Compared

Source: Mudur (2012, see note 33).

9 per cent (26 papers) of the 290 retracted because of duplication', noting that 'the analysis was not designed for country-to-country comparisons' (see Figure 9.3).[33] While Mudur stipulated that 'the analysis was not designed for country-to-country comparisons', he identifies a real problem, which will only increase as the pressure on Indian researchers to compete in the global knowledge creation field escalates.[34]

Similarly, an empirical study of academic integrity in law schools and colleges across India by Jonathan Gingerich and Aditya Singh concluded that 'plagiarism is a pervasive problem in Indian legal education'.[35]

[33]   Mudur, G.S. 'In Plagiarism too, China beats India, Calcutta, India'. *The Telegraph* (2 October 2012). Available at http://www.telegraphindia.com/1121002/jsp/nation/story_16042659.jsp#.UgCjRRbJ4ao.

[34]   Mudur, G.S. 'In Plagiarism too, China Beats India, Calcutta, India'. *The Telegraph* (2 October 2012). Available at http://www.telegraphindia.com/1121002/jsp/nation/story_16042659.jsp#.UgCjRRbJ4ao.

[35]   Gingerich, Jonathan and Aditya Singh, 'Writing Requirements, Student Assessment and Plagiarism in Indian Law Schools'. *India Law News* (Fall 2010);

In July 2011, in an attempt to stem the rising tide of dishonesty in research, Indian scientists convened by the Institute of Mathematical Sciences and the Forum for Global Knowledge Sharing proposed the creation of 'an office of research integrity that could detect, investigate, and punish proven scientific misconduct in the country' and would 'ensure authentic scientific output from the rapidly expanding scientific community'.[36] In the interim, an NGO called the Society for Scientific Values (SSV), established in 1986 with no legal or administrative powers, monitors cases of misconduct and speaks out.[37] One of its members, Kasturi Lal Chopra, referring to recent cases involving researchers in high-profile institutions bemoaned the fact that '[t]here's little done about this'.[38]

The pressure to publish is so intense that even the brightest succumb. The responsibility of the university to reverse this trend and to ensure academic integrity cannot be overemphasized.

A related dimension of ethical conduct of research is *academic freedom and freedom of scientific research*. Shiv Visvanathan referenced the ecology of dissent and the ecology of debate during the March Conference. For that environment to be conducive to unfettered knowledge creation requires strict respect for academic freedom, a global concept supporting freedom of inquiry by faculty members, without which the learning and research functions of a university are and should be suspect. Accordingly, scholars have freedom to teach and disseminate ideas and information, however, inconvenient to the authorities, without fear of being fired or worse, subject to repression by the state. There is a delicate balance to be struck between negative consequences in terms of promotion and renewal of contract for academics whose research is sloppy, politically motivated, or offensive, on the one hand, and pressure being placed on the academic for espousing unpopular causes or expressing unconventional research findings. At the level of policy, universities must be explicit and public,

---

p. 12. Available at: http://www.law.harvard.edu/programs/plp/pdf/Gingerich_India_Law_News_Article.pdf. I am grateful to Yugank Goyal for drawing my attention to this study.

[36] Raman, Papri Sri and T. V. Padma, 'Indian scientists call for checks on plagiarism'. *One World South Asia* (21 July 2011). Available at http://southasia.oneworld.net/news/indian-scientists-call-for- checks-on-plagiarism#.UgCTIxbJ4ao.

[37] Available at http://`www.scientificvalues.org/.

[38] Quoted by Mudur, see note 34.

while also providing legal safeguards for faculty. It is an essential feature of a knowledge creating university to maintain this highest standard of academic freedom.

Challenges Due to the Politics of Knowledge

Knowledge is power. That oft-repeated bromide is open to a variety of interpretations. The sense in which it is used here is that knowledge can be distorted through the subtle abandonment of critical analysis of underlying political and financial interests and power relations in the process of knowledge creation. Barbara Harriss-White in her chapter 'Science-Policy Interfaces in an Era of Global Commodification' draws our attention to 'abandoning the crucial critical and self-critical process through which science, and ultimately society, make progress' in the de-politicised culture where natural scientists communicate with policymakers, contrasted with that of social scientists.[39] This is part of what she calls the 'fourth culture', that is, 'an expert culture in which science, social science, and policymaking are tightly linked, and re-politicized through their joint de-politicization'.[40] She finds that the presumed de-politicization is based on the 'assumption that if the current socio-economic model cannot be changed it is not the fault of science but of political leadership'.[41] Among the politically significant results is the masking of 'relations of authority in the allocation of public resources towards the application of scientific advances to society', and of the processes of privatization and commodification.[42] In sum, Harriss-White argues, 'it makes political critique impossible' of the ways in which commodification of the knowledge society places the private interests ahead of the public interest.[43]

The challenge of the re-politicization of knowledge is part of a broader issue of the politics of knowledge. Hans N. Weiler identified four relationships between knowledge and power, namely, '... *hierarchies* in the existing knowledge order, ... *reciprocal legitimation* between knowledge and power, the *transnational division of labor* in the contemporary knowledge order, and the political economy of the *commercialization of*

---

[39] See Chapter 10 in this volume.
[40] See Chapter 10 in this volume.
[41] See Chapter 10 in this volume.
[42] See Chapter 10 in this volume.
[43] See Chapter 10 in this volume.

knowledge'.[44] The ramifications of these four relationships are extensive. The privileged status of 'hard' sciences, of elite institutions, and of senior faculty sustains hierarchies as 'a pervasive structural characteristic'.[45] Knowledge is used to legitimize power (qualifications for careers, conditions for public funding) and political decisions are made with reference to certain forms of knowledge. Regarding the international division of labour, Weiler notes that the 'international hierarchies of economic influence and political power' are reflected in a sort of 'orthodoxy of knowledge,' exemplified by the World Bank.[46] He cites Indian political psychologist and social theorist Shamans Ashis Nandy, who called for 'a new, plural, political ecology of knowledge' to challenge this hierarchy.[47] Finally, he bemoans the fact that 'creation of knowledge has come to be regarded and treated so pervasively in economic and commercial terms'.[48]

All these concerns have implications for knowledge creation in the context of the future development of Indian universities.

A related challenge is that of preventing conflicts of interest from artificially determining the focus and the findings of research. What direct and indirect factors determine what is researched and what gets published? Can a researcher in a university understand the social engineering behind

---

[44] Weiler, Hans N. 'Whose Knowledge Matters? Development and the Politics of Knowledge', *Festschrift for Peter Molt* [Theodor Hanf, Hans N. Weiler and Helga Dickow (eds), *Entwicklung als Beruf* (Baden-Baden: Nomos, 2009), pp. 485–96]. Available at http://www.stanford.edu/~weiler/Texts09/Weiler_Molt_09.pdf.

[45] Weiler, Hans N. 'Whose Knowledge Matters? Development and the Politics of Knowledge', *Festschrift for Peter Molt* [Theodor Hanf, Hans N. Weiler and Helga Dickow (eds), *Entwicklung als Beruf*, pp. 485–96]. Available at http://www.stanford.edu/~weiler/Texts09/Weiler_Molt_09.pdf.

[46] Weiler, Hans N. 'Whose Knowledge Matters? Development and the Politics of Knowledge', *Festschrift for Peter Molt* [Theodor Hanf, Hans N. Weiler and Helga Dickow (eds), *Entwicklung als Beruf*, pp. 485–96]. Available at http://www.stanford.edu/~weiler/Texts09/Weiler_Molt_09.pdf.

[47] Ashis Nandy. 'Shamans, Savages and the Wilderness: On the Audibility of Dissent and the Future of Civilizations'. *Alternatives* 14 (3) (July 1989): p. 267, cited by Weiler, note. 32.

[48] Weiler, Hans N. 'Whose Knowledge Matters? Development and the Politics of Knowledge', *Festschrift for Peter Molt* [Theodor Hanf, Hans N. Weiler and Helga Dickow (eds), *Entwicklung als Beruf*, pp. 485–96]. Available at http://www.stanford.edu/~weiler/Texts09/Weiler_Molt_09.pdf.

her options for research and be critical, where appropriate, of the role of the university in knowledge creation? Are those options limited to research that will not challenge prevailing structures? Part of the integrity of research requires disclosure of sources of funding and financial interests in entities affected by the research.

A typical definition of a conflict of interest is 'a divergence between an individual's private interests (competing interests) and his or her responsibilities to scientific and publishing activities such that a reasonable observer might wonder if the individual's behaviour or judgement was motivated by considerations of his or her competing interests'.[49] Conflict of interest disclosure is a commonly required and essential feature of research integrity in health and medical research.[50] In other fields it is voluntary and a matter of individual ethics. The Guidelines on Good Publication Practice of the Committee on Publication Ethics (COPE) stated in 2003, 'Conflicts of interest arise when authors, reviewers, or editors have interests that are not fully apparent and that may influence their judgments on what is published. They have been described as those which, when revealed later, would make a reasonable reader feel misled or deceived.'

Academic journals often require a conflict of interest statement or conflict of interest disclosure from authors, especially in medicine and public health. Similar policies would benefit Indian universities as they define their role in knowledge creation. There are other challenges to their emerging role, most of which are determined by the evolving field of Information and Communication Technology (ICT), addressed in the next section.

FUTURE OF KNOWLEDGE CREATION IN THE UNIVERSITY

Traditional modes of knowledge creation applied across the globe for centuries tend to focus on passive learning in the classroom, research in

---

[49] World Association of Medical Editors, Conflict of Interest in Peer-Reviewed Medical Journals: http://www.wame.org/conflict-of-interest-in-peer-reviewed-medical-journals.

[50] See, for example, BMJ transparency policy: http://resources.bmj.com/bmj/authors/editorial-policies/transparency-policy, ICMJE (*International Committee of Medical Journal Editors*) uniform requirements for manuscripts submitted to biomedical journals: http://www.icmje.org/urm_main.html;

libraries, labs, and field settings. The future is clearly wound up with the development of ICT. As a result, Indian universities will have to change their priorities to adapt to new technologies. Profound changes have occurred in human history with the shift from oral to written modes of recording and transmitting knowledge, to the proliferation of print media and eventually to the technology of hypermedia made possible by the web today, all of which has affected not only the classes of people who can access knowledge but the very functioning of our brain.[51] The 'plasticity of our neural pathways,' explains Carr, is such that 'the more we use the Web, the more we train our brain to be distracted. ... As our use of the Web makes it harder for us to lock information into our biological memory, we're forced to rely more and more on the Net's capacious and easily searchable artificial memory, even if it makes us shallower thinkers.'[52] The challenge for knowledge creation in higher education in the first half of the twenty-first century is to anticipate the impact of ICT and especially the web on both the classroom and the use of books as well as on the very neural circuits of our brain.

Disappearance of the Classroom

Devesh Kapur, Director, Institute of the Advanced Study of India, told the March Conference that it is impossible for India to build enough brick and mortar universities to meet demand.[53] Hence, the future of research clearly calls for the imaginative use of distance learning and other ICT advances insofar as education and knowledge creation cannot be fully accommodated in the physical plant of the universities.

Alternatives are emerging to the traditional classroom experience of the university. The appeal of massive open online courses (MOOCs) is undeniable in order to reach thousands of students with well-structured courses but without faculty or classrooms. The online courses are offered through open access, typically without academic credit or charging tuition fees. Since their launch in 2008, about 10 per cent of the tens of thousands of students enrolled in MOOCs actually completed their courses.[54] Several

[51] See Carr, Nicholas. *The Shallows: What the Internet Is Doing to Our Brains* (New York: WW Norton, 2010).

[52] Carr, *The Shallows*, p. 194.

[53] Remarks made during the first thematic session at the March conference.

[54] Marcus, Jon 'All Hail MOOCs! Just Don't Ask if They Actually Work'. *The Hechinger Report* (12 September 2013). Available at http://hechingerreport. org/content/moocs-keep-getting-bigger-but-do-they-work_12960/.

variants emerged around 2012 inside and outside universities. Students can follow courses individually at their own pace through the Khan Academy, Peer-to-Peer University (P2PU), and Udemy outside of the university system. Several major universities offer other online teaching. Among the better known is EdX, which was founded in 2012 by Harvard University and the Massachusetts Institute of Technology (MIT) and now involves some 108 members in a growing list of the major universities in the world,[55] including one in India, the Indian Institute of Technology Bombay, although it had not offered any courses by fall 2013.[56] EdX is an open online course platform through which people anywhere in the world can follow online university-level courses in a wide range of disciplines. Harvard and MIT contributed $30 million each to this non-profit project. The president of Harvard, Drew Faust met, with alumni and business leaders in Hong Kong to discuss Harvard's online learning initiative, HarvardX, and its role in EdX. 'This is a moment of transformation for education, and we want to be able to lead in a way that allows us to enhance our outreach to the world, even as it helps us understand new ways to teach our students on campus,' said Faust.[57] By 2017, EdX had reached over 11 million learners in every country in the world.[58] Faust explains,

> [t]he hunger for knowledge is so strong around the world ... I feel [HarvardX] is a magnificent opportunity, but it is also a big responsibility for us to set a standard for online learning that upholds the most important aspects of higher education and its values, and allows Harvard to play a leadership role in shaping how education changes in the years to come.[59]

One source predicted that MOOCs 'may change the university and college system forever'.[60] As a tool for learning that offers the

---

[55] EdX, available at: https://www.edx.org/schools.

[56] https://www.edx.org/school/iitbombayx/allcourses.

[57] http://news.harvard.edu/gazette/story/2013/03/harvards-hand-in-shaping-education/.

[58] Available at https://www.edx.org/schools-partners.

[59] http://news.harvard.edu/gazette/story/2013/03/harvards-hand-in-shaping-education/.

[60] Economist.com, 'MOOCs: The fall of the ivory tower?'(1 August 2013), 21:14, available at http://www.economist.com/blogs/schumpeter/2013/08/moocs-fall-ivory-tower.

advantage of reaching hundreds of thousands without requiring the expenditure on classrooms and faculty, MOOCs and EdX present a tempting trend for Indian universities. Some predict that, as established universities offer degree credits for those students who complete MOOCs, 'this will drive a dramatic reduction in the price of a traditional higher education'.[61] However, if this occurs, the students may access quality teaching but their university loses the incentive to offer its own courses in critical areas and hire faculty, thus diminishing their capacity to contribute to knowledge. On the positive side it reflects two trends in knowledge creation.

The first is based on connectivist theory, according to which learning and knowledge are not transmitted from repositories of knowledge in libraries or didactic teachings but emerge from a network of connections. The second innovative feature is the 'classroom reversal', meaning that, in place of students listening to lectures and doing assignments outside the classroom, the lectures are watched online in private at a pace than ensures the students absorb the material, and then the exercises are performed in groups, in a collaborative, problem-solving way, closer to how people use knowledge in their professional life. This way of learning is growing rapidly and Indian universities will face difficulty in deciding whether and to what extent they should participate.

The Digital Gap

But ICT is not just for teaching: perhaps more important is how dependent research is on computer technology and the Internet for access to journals; publishing online; collecting, storing, and analysing data. One of the most visible advances in the ICT field is broadband, which is transforming societies through use of the Internet in developed countries. The failure to realize the right to benefit from advances in technology is reflected in the persistent broadband divide. In developed, as well as in many middle-income countries, the cost of access to the Internet is on the decline, yet

---

[61] 'The attack of the MOOCs. An army of new online courses is scaring the wits out of traditional universities. But can they find a viable business model?' *The Economist* (20 July 2013). Available at http://www.economist.com/news/business/21582001-army-new-online-courses-scaring-wits-out- traditional-universities-can-they.

it remains unaffordable to the majority of low-income developing countries.[62] In 2011, fixed broadband penetration was 26 per cent in developed countries and only 4.8 per cent on average in developing countries.[63] As the MDG Gap report noted,

> [a]lthough the cost of ICT services has been decreasing, they remain much higher in developing than in developed countries. Costs are still prohibitive for the majority of people in some regions, especially Africa. Mobile cellular services cost, on average, about 10 per cent of per capita income in developing countries, but their cost is as high as 25 per cent of per capita income in Africa. The average cost of a fixed broadband subscription in Africa is almost three times the per capita income. In developed countries, however, the average cost per user is less than 2 per cent of per capita income.[64]

The worst off are Oceania, South Asia and sub-Saharan Africa, where fewer than one in nine people have Internet access.[65] Compared to the international average of 5.6 mbps, India provides only 256 kbps and only 260,000 broadband connections are available in rural India, in spite of 2007 being the Year of Broadband for India. Of the 100 million Internet users in India only 12.5 million have broadband compared to 450 million in China.[66]

The Economist Intelligence Unit calculates that India ranks near the bottom in broadband penetration, as show in Figure 9.4.

The importance of broadband for India's development was recognized at a Broadband Summit, organized by KPMG International, a Swiss entity,

---

[62] Nanthikesan, S. 'Trends in Digital Divide', p. 36, Background document, 2001 Human Development Report (accessed 10 July 2011), available at available at http://hdr.undp.org/en/reports/global/hdr2001/papers/nanthikesan-1.pdf.

[63] UN MDG Gap Task Force 'Millennium Development Goal 8. The Global Partnership for Development: Making Rhetoric a Reality,' United Nations, New York (2012): p. 76.

[64] UN MDG Gap Task Force 'Millennium Development Goal 8. The Global Partnership for Development: Making Rhetoric a Reality,' United Nations, New York (2012): p. 77.

[65] UN MDG Gap Task Force 'Millennium Development Goal 8. The Global Partnership for Development: Making Rhetoric a Reality,' United Nations, New York (2012): p. 75.

[66] UN MDG Gap Task Force (2010) *MDG Gap Task Force Report 2010: The Global Partnership for Development at a Critical Juncture*, United Nations, New York, p. 71, citing Data from ITU, World Telecommunication/ICT Indicators database.

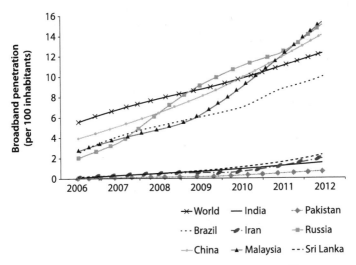

Figure 9.4   Fixed Broadband Penetration per 100 Habitants[67]

and the Confederation of Indian Industry (CII) in New Delhi in September 2012. According to the summit report, '[i]n India, the drive to facilitate widespread broadband access has been high on the national agenda since several years now.'[68] However, as their data show, '[c]urrently, broadband penetration in India is just around 10 per cent of the Internet user base and approximately 1 percent of India's population—one of the lowest in the world as compared to other economies such as Russia (11 per cent), Brazil (7.5 per cent) and China (9.5 per cent).'[69]

[67] UN MDG Gap Task Force (2010) *MDG Gap Task Force Report 2010: The Global Partnership for Development at a Critical Juncture*, United Nations, New York, p. 71, citing Data from ITU, World Telecommunication/ICT Indicators database, p. 74.

[68] KPMG International Cooperative ('KPMG International') and Confederation of Indian Industry (CII), Broadband ecosystem for inclusive growth, Broadband Summit (28 September 2012), New Delhi, KPMG, 2012.

[69] KPMG International Cooperative ('KPMG International') and Confederation of Indian Industry (CII), Broadband ecosystem for inclusive growth, Broadband Summit (28 September 2012), New Delhi, KPMG, 2012, p. 2, citing data from http://www.expresscomputeronline.com/20120331/features01.shtml3.

The future of knowledge creation in Indian universities will be disappointing until researchers and students have much better Internet access. The need to participate in online courses and access electronic journals is obvious. Conducting research also requires the need to access big data. In his inaugural lecture at the March Conference, John Wood explained how the tools of E-science are generating a tsunami wave of data.[70] The data deluge will be used for research in countries that can handle all the petabytes he talked about. If India's universities do not achieve the sort of progress achieved, for example, by universities in South Africa, it will not reach its full potential in terms of competitiveness as it might in those research fields that need such data. India for now is at a disadvantage in this dimension of knowledge creation through massive data analysis. It is likely to catch up through think tanks and advanced research institutes. However, if universities are to be able to contribute to knowledge creation of this type, a radical transformation of their ICT capacity is necessary.

Disappearance of the Book

Traditional knowledge creation involves consigning new knowledge not only to specialized journals, but also to learned tomes that line the shelves of university libraries. Hard print books have been with us since Gutenberg. The great Alfred North Whitehead wrote in 1925—and he was no doubt correct—that the 'chief tool [of education] is the printed book'.[71] But that was before computers and the Internet. We are living in a time of great change.

Indian universities need to address the issue of the purported disappearance of the book as they determine whether and how to increase availability of books for research and teaching or to shift to digital sources.

The *Wall Street Journal* reported in early 2013:

> [P]undits have assumed that the future of book publishing is digital. Opinions about the speed of the shift from page to screen have varied. But the consensus has been that digitization, having had its way with music and photographs and maps, would in due course have its way with books as well. By 2015, one media maven predicted a few years back, traditional books would be gone.

[70] John Wood's inaugural lecture in the March conference.
[71] Alfred North Whitehead, *Science and the Modern World* (New York: The Macmillan Company [edition of 1953, p. 248.)

Half a decade into the e-book revolution, though, the prognosis for traditional books is suddenly looking brighter. Hardcover books are displaying surprising resiliency. The growth in e-book sales is slowing markedly. And purchases of e-readers are actually shrinking, as consumers opt instead for multipurpose tablets. It may be that e-books, rather than replacing printed books, will ultimately serve a role more like that of audio books—a complement to traditional reading, not a substitute. ... Having survived 500 years of technological upheaval, Gutenberg's invention may withstand the digital onslaught as well. There's something about a crisply printed, tightly bound book that we don't seem eager to let go of.[72]

Books continue to be printed, of course. The number of new titles per year, per country, as of the latest year available:

United States (2010) 328,259 (new titles and editions)
United Kingdom (2005) 206,000
China (2010) 189,295 (328,387 total)
Russian Federation (2008) 123,336
Germany (2009) 93,124
Spain (2008) 86,300
India (2004) 82,537 (21,370 in Hindi and 18,752 in English)
Japan (2009) 78,555
Iran (2010) 65,000
France (2010) 63,690 (67,278 total)
South Korea (2011) 44,036
Taiwan (2010) 43,309
Turkey (2011) 43,100

...

TOTAL: approximately 2,200,000[73]

This resilience should not cloud the reality of internet-based research, where printed materials are not as important as immediate access to millions of journals and articles and books and petabytes of data. And yet

---

[72] Nicholas Carr, 'Lovers of Ink and Paper, Take Heart. Reports of the Death of the Printed Book May Be Exaggerated. Essay. Don't Burn Your Books—Print Is Here to Stay,' *Wall Street Journal* (Updated 5 January 2013). Available at http://online.wsj.com/article/SB10001424127887323874204578219563353697002.html.

[73] Available at http://www.worldometers.info/books/.

some libraries are entirely electronic. The challenge for the university is to have the bandwidth, stable grid, infrastructure, and trained staff as well as affordable data plans so that ICT will become an instrument of rather than an obstacle to knowledge creation.

* * *

Higher education has been described as evolving 'far more as a market, with university and colleges competing to supply the service of education'.[74]

In March 2013, on the first day of a weeklong visit to Asia, Harvard President Drew Faust called knowledge 'the most important currency of the 21st century,' highlighting faculty research, student engagement, and online learning as central to Harvard's global strategy.[75] During that visit, '[t]he local leaders told Faust that the continued evolution of Hong Kong's economy from manufacturing-based to knowledge-based was creating a need for new thinking in higher education, including curriculum reform shifting from three-year to four-year undergraduate degrees, along with a greater emphasis on international issues, service-oriented learning, and the liberal arts'.[76] This shift is exactly what has been proposed for India. If change is called for, it is appropriate to reflect here on what model best fits India's needs.

Two Models of Change

Hazelkorn, in her study for UNESCO on the 'Impact of Global Rankings on Higher Education Research and the Production of Knowledge' identified two models to achieve excellence in knowledge creation. Before examining her two models, it is important to stipulate a reservation regarding the obsession with rankings. Professor Shiv Visvanathan insightfully told the March Conference that 'autonomy and playfulness' are more meaningful than rankings.[77] Nevertheless, although Indian

---

[74] Newman, Frank, Lara Couturier, and Jamie Scurry. *The Future of Higher Education: Rhetoric, Reality, and the Risks of the Market* (John Wiley & Sons, 2004), p. 2.

[75] Harvard Gazette, 18 March 2013, available at http://news.harvard.edu/gazette/story/2013/03/harvards-hand-in-shaping-education/.

[76] Harvard Gazette, 18 March 2013.

[77] Shiv Visvanathan, Chapter 2 in this volume.

universities will probably continue to attach importance to rankings,[78] the value of the models proposed is that they seek to enhance the university's potential for excellence regardless of the motivation for striving towards excellence.

1. The neo-liberal model aims to create greater reputational (vertical) differentiation using rankings as a free market mechanism to drive the concentration of 'excellence' in a small number of research-intensive universities in order to compete globally. China, France, Germany, Japan, Korea, and Russia prefer to create a small number of world-class universities, focusing on research performance via competitions for Centres of Excellence (CE) and Graduate Schools. This model has two main forms: Model A, which jettisons traditional equity values (for example, Germany), and Model B (for example, Japan), which upholds traditional status/hierarchical values. The United Kingdom (UK) attempted another variation of this model by formally distinguishing between teaching and research institutions, but abandoned this by relying on the impact of performance measurement, for example, the UK Research Assessment Exercise (RAE).

2. The social-democratic model aims to build a system of horizontally differentiated high performing, globally-focused institutions, and student experiences. In contrast to an emphasis on competition as a driver of excellence, Australia, Ireland, and Norway, aims to support 'excellence wherever it occurs' by supporting 'good quality universities' across the country, using institutional compacts to drive clearer mission differentiation.[79]

Although her examples were based on the experience of advanced economies plus China, the basic options for India are not very different.

---

[78] One source commented on the 2012 rankings, 'Unfortunately, this year too, no Indian university features in the top 200 list.' Why Indian universities don't make it to world rankings. Rediff.com (15 November 2012), available at http://www.rediff.com/getahead/slide-show/slide-show-1-career-times-higher-education-worlds-best-universities/20121005.htm.

[79] Hazelkorn, Ellen, 'Impact of Global Rankings on Higher Education Research and the Production of Knowledge', UNESCO Forum on Higher Education, Research and Knowledge. Occasional Paper, no. 15 (2009): p. 7.

What Works for India?

The lessons from the application of the two models challenge India to decide which one fits best with its aspirations. Professor Ved Prakash, Chairperson, University Grants Commission (UGC), gave a partial answer when he told the March Conference about the Government's commitment to 'expansion, equity, and excellence' and its duty to be inclusive and cater to children of diverse backgrounds.[80]

The immediate future will be a test for the social-democratic model to bring India up to the level of knowledge creation and quality of research consistent with their extraordinary contribution to global civilization. Political shifts may lead a different government to consider the neo-liberal model. India is diverse enough to pursue both, with government sponsored centres of excellence along with numerous high quality universities, where outstanding contributions to knowledge emerge from intellectual curiosity and perseverance of scholars rather than focused funding of research aimed at competing with world-class research institutions in other parts of the world.

The essential change Indian universities will need to make in order to differentiate the future of knowledge creation from its past is to develop an environment conducive to research such that the finest minds of the nation will prefer to advance knowledge at home rather than abroad. The requirements for such an environment, as described in this chapter, relate to the aims of knowledge creation, the institutional setting, selection among fragmented fields of knowledge and levels of degrees, inculcation, and enforcement of ethical standards, responses to politicization and commodification of knowledge, and adaptation to new technologies. In sum, Indian universities face special challenges in cultivating knowledge as an end in itself through education that should take account of the various forms of knowledge and types of intelligence. They must have an institutional design (human and financial resources, governance, affiliations, networks, etc.) adequate to provide a solid structural foundation for research and learning and apply an instructional design that both educates citizens of the global community and prepares career pathways that draw on a sufficiently wide range of disciplines and opportunities for cross-disciplinary reflection and applications. At the same time, the

---

[80] Remarks made at the inaugural lecture at the March conference.

conditions for research must ensure academic integrity and freedom and remove perverse incentives that result from the politicization of knowledge and conflicts of interest. Finally, given that Indian universities cannot provide classroom and library structures adequate to meet the growing demand, they must be at the forefront of developments in ICT, without succumbing to fashionable trends that in the long run may not be conducive to sustained knowledge creation. Such are the challenges of knowledge creation in Indian universities as they approach an era of unprecedented expansion.

10 Science-Policy Interfaces in an Era of Global Commodification[1,2]

Barbara Harriss-White

RESEARCH AND POLICY

In 1959, in his Rede lecture, C.P. Snow famously identified two scholarly cultures and argued that the gulf between science and the humanities and the social priority and status granted to the humanities were obstacles to progress. Not long afterwards, Thomas Balogh, one of a new generation of expert policy advisers (like, the Open University, this being one of

[1] First presented at: O.P. Jindal Global University: International Conference on the Future of Indian Universities: Comparative Perspectives on HE Reforms for a Knowledge Society, 21–3 March 2013, Fifth Thematic Session: Research and Policy Impact: Universities, think tanks and international organizations.

[2] Dedicated to the memory of David Dickson (1947–2013) science and technology journalist and scholar.

Harold Wilson's enduring innovations) berated the 'humanities-based education and pre-industrial social attitudes' of his bureaucratic peers, denouncing them as 'the apotheosis of the dilettante'.[3] Ever since, the chasm between research and policy, between the specialist and the generalist, has invited bridges to be built. But it was not until the 1990s that the 'two cultures' were effectively challenged in Anglo-Saxon societies by John Brockman[4] who announced and celebrated a 'third culture' in the 'public communication' and popularization of both fundamental and applied natural sciences. In fact, this 'bridging' culture had been long in the making[5] and has proved indefatigable in its own defence against a barrage of post-modern culturalist criticism of the hegemonic power of the 'discourses of science'.

But of all the criticisms that have been levelled at this concept, the most penetrating and significant is that while the third culture has flourished it has tended to naturalise markets—as the ultimate test of institutional fitness and as the ultimate self-regulating system—to be the basis of the information society and knowledge economy[6] just as it 'culturalises' and 'marketises' nature.[7]

In fact, the central issue for science and policy today is no longer the gap between the cultures of science on the one hand and the humanities and generalist policymakers on the other, or even whether it has been bridged by a third culture. Instead it is the role of markets in the

---

[3] Cited in C. Leys, The Cynical State, in (eds) L. Panitch and C. Leys, Telling the Truth (Merlin Press, 2005), pp. 1–27.

[4] Brockman, John. The Third Culture: Beyond the Scientific Revolution (New York: Simon and Schuster, 1995).

[5] In the work for example of Haldane, Hogben, Medawar, Bronowski, and Michie, see A. Srinivasan, Donald Michie on Machine Intelligence, Biology and More (Oxford University Press, 2009).

[6] Waldrop, M.M. Complexity: The Emerging Science At the Edge of Order and Chaos (Simon and Schuster, 1993).

[7] Social memes, in the language of this third culture, use biological genes as an analogy; while biological and hydrological processes become 'ecological services' to society. See Hodgson, G. Why Economics Forgot History (London: Routledge, 2001) for this argument; see S. Zizek, 'Welcome to the Desert of the Real!', South Atlantic Quarterly, 101, 2 (Spring 2002): 385–9; for criticism of it.

emergence of a unifying culture—a 'fourth culture', if you like: that of *de-politicization*.

This de-politicized culture appears to serve the role of a *lingua franca*, seeming to overcome the technicality of the specialised languages proliferating in all research fields,[8] which makes them intelligible only to their practitioners. But the achievement of a *lingua franca* is at the expense of abandoning the crucial critical and self-critical process through which science, and ultimately society, make progress. It masks the deployment of markets to reorganize the processes and products of science in forms that can be privately exchanged. The contemporary economy is widely accepted to rest on knowledge; the 'knowledge economy' is one in which knowledge is being reconfigured so that it can be bought and sold.

The requirements of the contemporary economy-in particular the 'marketising' and commodification both of knowledge and of policy[9]—not only airbrush politics away but also rearticulate science with de-politicized and un-theorized social models—with implications as serious for policy in the public interest as they are for science and for society.

My intervention here explores this conceptual and practical paving over the epistemological chasm and its effects on both littorals. I explore the proposition that the opposition Balogh saw between the expert knowledge of the academy and the practical knowledge of the policy-maker is being realigned, in part by being de-politicized but in part by being commodified.

My method is drawn from political economy and is historical and comparative. I will use British evidence and debates[10] to generate questions which may already have been widely rehearsed in India but which may still pose challenges that the Indian intelligentsia can negotiate more effectively

---

[8] The philosopher of mind, John Searle, has concluded that language is the fundamental social institution, one ignored by most other theorists of institutions. See Searle, John R. *Making the Social World: The Structure of Human Civilization* (New York: Oxford University Press, 2010).

[9] Leys, C. *Total Capitalism* (New Delhi: Three Essays Collectives, 2007).

[10] These are drawn mainly from health, agriculture/sustainability, technology development, and education. In February 2013 these fields were used by the President of the Royal Society to exemplify core scientific research for the public good. Nurse, P. 'Making Science Work', *The Haldane Lecture*, Wolfson College, Oxford (2013).

than the intelligentsia of the former Imperial power. Two preliminary questions need to be answered:[11]

1. What models of society do physical and biological scientists and engineers operate with?
2. What models of science and of society do expert policymakers use? Are these 'fit for purpose'?

This is addressed in the first part of this chapter. The results will then turn us toward a third question:

3. How is expert knowledge and policy knowledge being commodified, and with what discursive and real effects?

In exploring this question, the second part relates the process of de-politicization to that of commodification.

Q1: How do natural scientists see society when they engage with policy?

To see how this depoliticized culture has come into existence and what it does to science and society, we first need to identify the models of society used by natural scientists when they communicate with policymakers, and their significant failure to use the models developed by social scientists—who after all do make society their subject matter. Here examples have to be used. They are drawn from three linked and self-evidently important fields of policy—the loss of biodiversity, climate change, and how the results of scientific and technological progress can best be turned to national economic advantage. These are fields that the president of the Royal Society has identified as science for the public good in which 'scientific advice must be of the highest quality'.[12]

i. *Biodiversity Loss*—Of late a number of expert 'assessments' have been published. An assessment is a term of art denoting a collective

[11] There are more. In particular the large literature on the public engagement of science is out of the current scope of this essay. See Irwin, Alan. *Citizen Science: A Study of People, Expertise and Sustainable Development* (London: Routledge, 1995); S. Funtowicz, and J. Ravetz, 'Science for the Post-Normal age', *Futures*, 25, 7 (1993): pp. 739–55 and the literature from Sussex University's Science Policy Research Unit and the journal *Public Understanding of Science*. For example, see J. Burgess, et al., *Deliberative Mapping: A Novel Analytic-deliberative Methodology to Support Contested Science-Policy Decisions. Public Understand. Sci.* 16(2007): 299–322.

[12] Nurse, 2013. It remains to disprove their representativity.

'scoping' of a scientific field for an educated audience. The reports of the Intergovernmental Panel on Climate Change are paradigmatic expert 'assessments'. In the 2012 assessment of 'Biodiversity Loss' in *Nature*,[13] after an elegant analysis of the extreme complexity of the way ecosystems function—which forms the bulk of the assessment and which scrupulously indicates where there are still areas of ignorance, scepticism, uncertainty, and controversy—there follows a description of the science needed to 'serve management and policy'. This calls inter alia for the development of 'decision support tools', of 'models at appropriate scales for policy' such as 'ecosystem service production functions', 'to explore trade-offs between services at multiple temporal and spatial scales' for 'stakeholders' who are seen as expecting 'positive returns'. Policymaking and implementation is described as having the scope of a 'natural laboratory'.

In this rational and economistic model, science is visualized as entering into the policy process in a role of service. But just as economists treat nature as an externality, so does this model of society treat power and politics as an externality too.

ii. *Population and Climate change*—In the 'Royal Society', Britain's apex learned society for science, policy work is organized around four themes: diplomacy, governance, innovation, and sustainability. Research topics are then subsumed under these organizing axes. So under diplomacy we find examples of the changing nature of global science; under governance: the implications for society of developments in rapidly developing areas of science and technology; under innovation: science funding; and under sustainability: the role of science in debates about sustainability and climate change. How are society and policy seen in this way of proceeding?

In *People and the Planet* (2012)[14] a Royal Society expert group argues with a great deal of evidence that climate change is a product of population growth, migration, urbanization and consumption and

---

[13] J. Cardinale, Bradley, J. Emmett Duffy, Andrew Gonzalez, David U. Hooper, Charles Perrings, Patrick Venail, Anita Narwani, Georgina M. Mace, David Tilman, David A. Wardle, Ann P. Kinzig Gretchen, C. Daily, Michel Loreau, James B. Grace, Anne Larigauderie, Diane S. Srivastava, and Shahid Naeem, 'Biodiversity Loss and Its Impact on Humanity', *Nature*. *http://www.nature.com/nature/journal/v486/n7401/full/nature11148.html* (2012).

[14] The Royal Society, *People and the Planet* (London, 2012).

will in turn have impacts on all these aspects of society. The recursive relationship between people and the planet needs, therefore, 'urgent reframing'. Among other policy activities that are implied by this call is the need to change existing patterns of consumption: states (i.e., governments) are assumed able to increase the consumption of the poor and to scale back that of the rich. These experts also see it as possible for energy to be decoupled from fossil fuel and economic activity to be decoupled from material inputs and from negative environmental externalities—i.e., to be de-carbonifiable and ever lighter in its footprint. In their view political leadership can change the current socio-economic model and institutions (pp. 7–8).

This is a consensus model, obviously, but from the standpoint of a social scientist it is wildly unrealistic: reductive, a-theoretical, exclusivist in its ignoring of production and the 'social manufacture' of consumption, in its disregard of the dynamic and institutions of capitalism (a veritable taboo concept). And its implication that if the current socio-economic model cannot be changed it is not the fault of science but of political leadership is a classic intellectual escape hatch.[15]

iii. *Converting scientific progress into economic progress*—The application of science involves an 'interactive ecosystem' of institutions.[16] The apex learned society for engineering has labelled the gulf that has to be bridged to convert the products of research and invention into useful commodities as the '*Valley of Death*'.[17] For the Royal Academy of Engineering, 'bridge-heads' help this valley to be spanned. Policymaking capacity and active state power are assumed to be capable of making 'strategic decisions not

---

[15] That leading scientists may concede that public policy is based on science 'and a wide range of other factors' is also an escape hatch for science (Nurse, 2013). On escape hatches, see Schaffer 'Towards Responsibility' in Clay, Edward J. and Bernard Schaffer, *Room for Manoeuvre* (London: Heinemann, 1984). Escape hatches were long ago lampooned by the Harvard mathematician and songwriter Tom Lehrer. '"Once the rockets are up, who cares where they come down? It's not my department" said Wernher von Braun.' T. Lehrer, *That Was the Year That Was* (record album) (1965).

[16] Nurse, 'Making Science Work' *Haldane Lecture*, Wolfson College, Oxford (2013).

[17] Royal Academy of Engineering, *Bridging the Valley of Death* (London, 2012); Sir Paul Nurse, 'Making Science Work,' *Haldane Lecture*, Oxford (2013).

based on cost-benefit analysis' in order to build 'sovereign capabilities' (i.e., state capacity) that will permit 'open innovation between private and public sector',[18] reduce risk, improve infrastructure, develop banks and the logistics of supply and even state procurement, and create a skilled workforce including skilled regulators themselves.[19]

The engineers' policy focus is on UK competitive advantage. On this evidence engineers see the role of engineering science as being to help policymakers improve competition policy, which they think policymakers are capable of implementing by interventions across a vast range of social and economic life.

The contrast between the models of society which all these scientists appear to have when they seek to influence policy, and the models which social scientists use, is dramatic and in more than one way painful. Social scientists see the natural scientists' models, which the latter acknowledge to be 'seat of the pants', un-theorized models, as exactly that. Social science practises a double hermeneutic. The objects of social science are social institutions and practices which reflect about, and interact with, the categories, measurements, and interpretations of the social scientist.

As Giddens puts it, '(t)he "findings" of the social sciences very often enter constitutively into the world they describe' (Giddens, 1987: 20). What follows is an unavoidable plurality of theoretical approaches to the understanding of society.[20] Not only does this mean that different social

---

[18] An example of how this may work is the reform to the world's public agricultural research system in which the products, referred to as international public goods in the guidelines on intellectual property, may be 'restricted' (read privatized) on any one of four grounds (i) if commercialization significantly enhances the scale or scope of impact on target beneficiaries (small and poor farmers) in developing countries; (ii) if it is invaluable for the further improvement or effective utilization of such intellectual assets'; (iii) to improve food security and alleviate poverty; and (iv) when there are no alternatives under no or less restrictive conditions. This gives very little intellectual basis for resisting the privatization of public assets in the name of partnership. It is a subsidy to the private commercialization of seed and other agricultural technology.

[19] By means of vivid military metaphors, and by reverse-engineering the list of desirables given here, the *absent* policy components turning the development process into a valley of death may be reconstructed and modelled.

[20] John Bellamy Foster and colleagues would add that 'because the social cannot easily be separated from ethical questions of right and wrong, this investigation

science disciplines have different models of society, but the paradigms and sub-fields within them also use different models. Progress is made through the open, critical scrutiny of assumptions, logic and predictions against empirical/historical tests.[21] Grand narratives have received much criticism but they survive because they are indispensable, as they allow a thousand mini-narrative flowers to bloom in their interstices. We live in an era of specialist sub-fields, giving rise to a complexity that makes it difficult not just to transmit the achieved knowledge of the social sciences from each generation the next, but also, and particularly, to collaborate with natural scientists whose own subfields are proliferating too—and with policymakers. As a result, almost all the grand narratives and specialist sub-fields of social science are ignored at today's science-policy interface. However they enter policy, the findings of social science do not seem to 'enter constitutively' into science. And when it comes to policymaking the sophistication and characteristic reflexivity of social science seems to go by the board, as the following example from the British Academy shows.

iv. *Social scientists and policymaking*—In a policy document entitled *'Punching our Weight'* which considers the problems of integrating social research into policy, the British Academy, the UK's apex learned society for social sciences and the humanities,[22] focuses on the weaknesses of the state's own research processes. The Academy sees public policymakers as 'fire-fighters', who would fight fire better if they made use of social science research. Hence, the BA suggests that there should be incentives for social scientists to hold dialogues with policymakers, for the activation of science-policy partnerships with social science, for policy makers to conduct long-term research, for government research to be peer reviewed, for social science researchers to be skilled in what it takes to reach out to policymakers, and for multi- and inter-departmental co-ordination in government to be organized for dealing with complex

---

inevitably implicates what is regarded as acceptable or unacceptable', and therefore 'tends to be filtered through the dominant institutions and structures of the prevailing hierarchical social order'. See John Bellamy Foster, et al., *The Ecological Rift–Capitalism's War on the Earth* (New York: Monthly Review Press, 2010), p. 20.

[21] This is at the heart of the thematic discipline of development studies which is my profession.

[22] British Academy, *Punching Our Weight* (London, 2008).

topics. Policy engagement should be a promotion criterion for academics and grounds for eligibility for high status forms of academic recognition.

The BA writes in an idiom of 'co-production'. While it recognizes that there is a difference of quality (and perhaps status) between fire-fighting research and rapid policy making on the one hand, and the open ended or long term research of the academy on the other, it sees no difference of *interest* between research and policy. Policymaking is improved by high quality research. And like the natural scientists the BA assumes that the state is rational and has wide-ranging capacity to act on the basis of whatever contribution social scientists can make.

While fire-fighting 'contingent expertise' is a necessary policy skill, Ravi Rajan's critical research on the management of industrial risk in India[23] shows that it is by no means sufficient. This is because advocacy documents like that of the BA ignore the role of social science in creating two other kinds of expertise needed by policy makers for the complex problems of what Ulrich Beck has termed the 'risk societies' of today.[24] One is conceptual expertise, which is required in order to respond creatively to drawn-out implementation processes that are replete with unintended consequences. The other is contextual expertise—knowledge of ground realities, and especially the multiplicity of informal institutions and practices that parallel those of the state in regulating any society—peculiarly relevant to India but present in all societies to a greater or lesser degree.'[25] So while there may or may not be scope in the BA's text for blue skies research, it is, or should be, inherent in social science research to criticize the main lines of policy as well as their details, from top to bottom. And while 'policymakers' are depicted by the BA as an undifferentiated bureaucratic category there is no scope for (social) science to contribute to decisions and courses of action determining outcomes (i.e., to policymaking activities) which are sited elsewhere in the state, such as in the courts, or in (civil) society such as the media, business, churches, or organized crime.

[23] Ravi Rajan, S. 'Disaster, Development and Governance: Reflections on the "Lessons" of Bhopal', *Environmental Values,* 11, 3 (2014): 193–212.

[24] Beck, Ulrich.*The Risk Society: Towards a New Modernity* (New York: Sage, 1992).

[25] Rajan, R. 2014, 'Environment and Development in India, ch. 10', in (eds) D. Davin and B. Harriss-White *China-India: Pathways of Economic and Social Development* (London: OUP for the British Academy).

Q2: *The incorporation of science by policymakers*

Governments and international agencies look to universities to undertake policy research. This does not mean the study of policies, how they are made, how they are implemented, and what assumptions they rest on. To ask these questions subverts the enterprise. Ruling institutions expect researchers to tell them what they want to know and not to be told that they are asking the wrong questions' (Gavin Williams: Keynote Address to International Conference on Higher Education and Globalization, University of Ilorin, 10 February 2010).

How in turn do policymakers, see and use science? The incorporation of scientific advice into policymaking turns out to be science-driven, moulding policy into the paradigm of a science in various ways. The oldest of these from neoclassical economics, closer to a hard science than a social science in many respects, is an approach to policy evaluation which privileges cost benefit analysis for answering the politicians' questions about value for money and policy efficiency.[26] More recently it has involved applying evidence-based procedures from hard science to policy, and especially the transfer of Randomized Control Trials and Evidence-based procedures drawn from medicine to policy, together with a step-change upwards in the placing of scientists into government as scientific advisers.

There are large literatures about the 'scientisation' of policy from which key texts and arguments about effects will be summarized here. When economic considerations are given priority over those derived from scientific and other scholarly fields such as ethics or law that cannot be measured in economic terms, or when non-economic arguments are converted into imputed dollars, controversy about purely economic factors can and does de-stabilize policy. Familiar examples of the criticisms to which this form of scientism gives rise concern missing, 'distorted' or 'guestimated' prices; putting a monetary value on un-monetary aspects of human and natural life; the assumption that there can be generalized trade-offs between one kind of valued outcome and another, or that they are substitutable for each

---

[26] See *Taking Forward the UK Climate Change Bill: The Government Response to Pre-Legislative Scrutiny and Public Consultation* (October 2007), http://www.official-documents.gov.uk/document/cm72/7225/7225.pdf for the economic reasoning behind the UK's climate change policy. (In the light of subsequent economic controversy this has been revised by its author and it would seem that economics is not proof against policy instability.)

other; the adoption of requirements of certainty for outcomes that are not certain; the choice of discount rates which are meant to represent the value of the future to the present but which involve questionable assumptions; the neglect of differing values held by different groups within a differentiated society; the limiting of technology or policy choices that are selected to undergo cost benefit analysis; the general extrapolation of results constructed for specific places, societies and times to others very different from these and so on. All legitimate points of criticism.[27]

More recently, over the last decade, a wide range of policy questions have been handled through the use of randomized control trials (RCTs), a methodology first developed in medicine.[28] The method has been transferred so as to compare the effects of interventions with what happens without an intervention (often paraphrased as a 'counterfactual'), to systematize impact evaluations, and to refine policy design.[29] The RCT method has been found to be valuable for empirical policy questions about poverty, health and education, but it is rarely sufficiently acknowledged that this tool-driven approach excludes transformative questions un-answerable through the conventions of RCTs and controls. It presupposes that the questions to be answered are the important ones, implying that the overall assumptions of policy from which they stem are sound—which in fact may

---

[27] See F. Stewart, 'A Note on Social Cost-benefit Analysis and Class Conflict in LDCs', World Development, 3, 1 (1975): pp. 31–40, and the discussions of the Stern Review on the Economics of Climate Change http://webarchive.nationalarchives.gov.uk/+/http:/www.hm-treasury.gov.uk/sternreview_index.htm; and for a taste of the kind of criticism not confined to the points made in the text here, see R.O. Mendelsohn, 'A Critique of the Stern Report', Regulation (2006): pp. 42–6; available at http://www.cato.org/sites/cato.org/files/serials/files/regulation/2006/12/v29n4-5.pdf. Space constrains discussing alternatives but large literatures exist on alternatives ranging from public engagement, and deliberative democracy to multicriteria analysis.

[28] RCTs are designed to answer two simple questions–whether the medicine/molecule/vaccine actually works and whether there are any harmful side effects.

[29] Banerjee, A. and Esther Duflo, Poor Economics: A Radical Rethinking of the Way to Fight Global Poverty (USA: Public Affairs, 2011); D. Karlan, N. Goldberg, and J. Copestake, 'Randomized Control Trials are the Best Way to Measure Impact of Microfinance Programs and Improve Microfinance Product Designs', Enterprise Development and Microfinance, Practical Action Publishing, 20, 3 (2009): 167–76. Available at: http://karlan.yale.edu/p/Crossfire%2020-3(4)%20revised.pdf.

be and often is highly questionable. James Copestake argues that RCTs are 'good for agronomy but only for a limited range of the constantly changing problems that small-scale farmers confront within diverse, complex, risky and shifting agro-ecological systems'.[30]

And for Sanjay Reddy, 'it is not possible to discuss individual fates without taking note of the macroeconomy, history, culture, and politics'. The RCT paradigm signifies that 'a focus on such interventions, as opposed to those which reshape that context, is sufficient to address poverty' (a position that Reddy criticizes). By their nature, RCTs tend to de-legitimate other ways of knowing: practical experiential knowledge, triangulation, observational, longitudinal,[31] and historical approaches.[32]

Another kind of science-derived methodology increasingly favoured by policymakers is the systematic review, also drawn from Evidence Based Medicine. Systematic reviews (SR) combine and aggregate evidence which satisfies the demanding quality conditions of positivist science. Thus, for example the early results of a meta-review of a multimillion-pound systematic review of systematic reviews at the UK's DFID reveals a substantial class of research and policy topics, framed as empirical questions, that show no cause-effect relations deemed useful for policy interventions—not because there are no cause effect relationships but because the body of data in a given policy field is deemed not of a quality to test that proposition either way.

The epistemological framework for both RCTs and SRs is technocratic—in the words of Sanjay Reddy, 'modular, reductive and mechanical'. 'It is at odds with a non-mechanistic understanding of

---

[30] Reddy, Sanjay G. 'Randomise This! On Poor Economics', *Review of Agrarian Studies*, 2, 2 (2012), available at: http://www.ras.org.in/randomise_this_on_poor_economics; and A. Bhargava, 'Randomized Controlled Experiments in Health and Social Sciences: Some Conceptual Issues', *Economics and Human Biology*, 6 (2008): 293–8.

[31] As in comparative statics.

[32] The RCT approach is not confined to quantitative evidence, however, but may incorporate qualitative evidence in statistically rigorous ways. The approach has been accused of selection and publication biases, it is claimed vulnerable to the misattribution of causes and to scaling. To prove lack of replicability is very costly but unless that is done its claims to general policy relevance may be compromised (a problem not at all confined to RCTs).

society, in which all actions are defined as well as outcomes shaped by complex and often unpredictable processes of mutual interaction.[33]

To apply SR to parts of a system under review while neglecting the whole is to neglect the interaction within a system. Moreover, since the intervener using the RCT paradigm for development usually stands outside the society s/he aims to intervene in, the way it is practiced is also often at odds with concept of social development as democratic deliberation.[34]

In the UK, all science-using departments of government, including the Treasury, now have a chief scientific adviser (CSA), drawn part-time from, and reinforcing, an epistemic community involving universities, industry and the scientific civil service; so that, as claimed by the UK government's own CSA, policy 'decisions in their departments are based on solid science and engineering'.[35] Not only do CSAs help to supply the evidence base for policy but also, networked throughout government, and supported through the British government's office for Science (embedded in the Department for Business and Skills), they 'encourage and support departments' use and management of science, as well as challenging them to match best practice across government and (where appropriate) outside'.[36] While very widely welcomed, and with direct access to ministers, the institution of CSA has received criticism for its lack of, or uneven, influence. In 2011, a House of Lords Science and Technology Committee, chaired by an eminent scientist, examined their power over public spending and their impact on policy.[37] It found that along with the adoption and co-optation of science, CSAs' evidence was sometimes neutralised: blocked, dismissed or sought too late to influence decisions.[38]

---

[33] Reddy, Sanjay G. 'Randomise This! On Poor Economics', *Review of Agrarian Studies*, 2, 2 (2012), available at: http://www.ras.org.in/randomise_this_on_poor_ economics; and A. Bhargava, 'Randomized controlled experiments in health and social sciences: Some conceptual issues', *Economics and Human Biology*, 6 (2008): 293–8.

[34] Sen, A. *Development as Freedom* (Oxford: Clarendon Press, 1999).

[35] Sir John Beddington, http://www.newscientist.com/blogs/thesword/ 2011/06/the-government-network-of-chie.html (2011). The sciences include natural sciences, social sciences, engineering and medicine.

[36] Department for Business, Innovation & Skills, http://www.bis.gov.uk/ go-science/about/how-we-work.

[37] http://www.parliament.uk/business/committees/committees-a-z/lords-select/ science-and-technology-committee/inquiries/parliament-2010/chief-scientific-advisers/.

[38] For another instance, in the 14 months to October 2013, ever since the Environment Secretary, Owen Paterson, took up his position, he had not requested a

Advice was also sometimes compromised by conflicts of interest as for example in the case where the independent science advisory committee of the Home Office had been chaired by a career civil servant drawn from the very constituency the committee was meant to use science to challenge.[39]

So the 'scientising' of policy proceeds apace, but with mixed and sometimes contradictory effects. The economisation of policy imposes a rigorous template for cost effectiveness onto policy which may have the effect of destabilizing it, since the economic parameters are contestable. RCTs are also widely recognized as a way of narrowing the field of questions considered amenable for policy and of narrowing them further through their data requirements. And despite the highly politicized nature of the selection of issues for systematic review, or the application to them of RCTs—an agenda of questions catering for, or anticipating, politicians asking 'what works?'—all these modes of relating science to policymaking are de-politicizing. The political process through which the agenda of questions is generated is excluded from consideration, as is the political context in which the policies chosen will be implemented. Yet we see from the evaluation of CSAs above that when science and policy decision-making are not aligned, policy has more power than science, and such positive impact as science might or even should have is lost.

So far we see that the scientization of policy and the 'new science' models of society are varied, rational, empiricist, metaphorical, not consensual but also—in contrast to practice in the science mainstream—not contested, either in or out of science.[40] These models are not drawn from

---

briefing from Sir Ian Boyd, the Chief Scientific Adviser at Mr Paterson's Department for the Environment, Food and Rural Affairs (Defra). http://www.independent. co.uk/news/uk/politics/environment-secretary-owen-paterson-has-yet-to-be-briefed-on-climate-change-by-chief-scientist-sir-ian-boyd-8912738.html.

[39] A considerable number of examples of lack of influence are given in http:// www.guardian.co.uk/science/2012/feb/29/scientific-advisers-ignored-lords-report.

[40] Physical and biological sciences and engineering all tend to regard the universe and the world as law abiding, non-capricious and above all, understandable. This view is then transferred to society. Economics is perceived through common sense nostrums, failing to understand that current economics is a descendant of political economy and that the discipline itself has been shaped by politics. They also fail to understand that common sense views are themselves historically manufactured through the manufacture of consent. ... Thus, they fall prey to depoliticized functionalist 'versions' of society aimed at designing social engineering policies or

social science itself. Although certain social science subfields are themselves developing de-politicized ways of modelling society and the policy process, with the exception of mainstream economics, the social sciences are benignly neglected or actively rejected by natural science, for reasons unclear. Perhaps because of their baffling plurality. But perhaps because they cannot avoid engaging with politics.

For one trait all the new models of society used by natural scientists have in common is the distinction made between science and politics. Politics, both as a social science and as the practice of power, is clearly rejected. Politics as 'ideology' is regarded as contaminating science.[41] Both science and policy are de-politicized, cleansed of politics. But de-politicization, the externalizing of politics, is itself a form of politics. How is this politics to be understood? Who gains from this extraordinary mental closure?

THE 'DE-POLITICIZED' POLITICS
OF THE SCIENCE-POLICY INTERFACE[42]

'(P)olitical conflicts and ambiguities underlie almost all technological decisions' writes David Dickson, a mathematically-trained scholar of technology and science (1984: 303). In a carefully researched and documented historical study of science, technology and policy in the US, Dickson describes a politically-driven process in which, despite Friedmanite criticism of any public funding for science, federal government expenditure has protected basic science while the individual US states have targeted funding increasingly towards fields with military and industrial applications (computing,

---

projects. In their view, society is 'messy' and requires such interventions to uphold law and orderliness. (Sanjeev Ghotge, Pers Comm, March 2013). See also Donna J. Haraway, *Simians Cyborgs and Women: The Reinvention of Nature* (London: Routledge, 1991) on the cultural constructs of science. Space here constrains development of these themes.

[41] Nurse, 'Science Needs to Be Kept Clear of Political Ideology and Religious Contamination' (2013).

[42] This section is drawn from Harriss-White, B. et al., 'Revisiting Technology and under Development: Climate Change, Politics and the "D" of Solar Energy Technology in Contemporary India', 92–127. In *Overcoming the Persistence of Inequality and Poverty*, edited by V. Fitzgerald, J. Heyer, and R. Thorp (New York: Palgrave-Macmillan, 2011).

biotechnology, materials, etc.) which offer employment and tax benefits for local populations.[43]

Dickson explains how in the US the 'government' is no mere receiver of scientific policy expertise but is instead the prime arbiter of the political economy of science and technology. This intensely politicized process involves simultaneous feedback relations between 'science' (universities and public laboratories), the 'state', and 'industry'. Demands from labour unions and environmental movements for science and technology to be socially relevant are defined, in the politics Dickson analyses, as no more than 'a cacophony, making decision making difficult'. They have been subdued by deliberate exclusion from decision processes, and by increasing secrecy.[44]

The first set of feedback relations between science and the state are as a result mediated by industry and party politics. Dickson strives but fails to refute the hypothesis that this subordinates scientific evidence to commercial interests. Policy based evidence parades as evidence based policy. Dickson shows that university establishments which may be supposed to embody at best independence, but which in practice have divided political loyalties, have moved/been moved towards a position hostile to 'state interference' and are easily captured by private funders.[45]

The second set of feedback relations are those between science and industry/business. Increasingly university science, science in state-funded labs and business all become politically unified and opposed to control by the state. 'Corporate science' then funds university research, supplementing public funds and privately appropriating the development phase of public research, the D of R and D, where ownership is key to political control and regulation. It is then a short step for industry to expand control from the development phase upstream to publicly-funded research itself.[46]

[43] Dickson, D. *The New Politics of Science* (Chicago: University of Chicago Press, 1984): pp. 2, 39, 44, 72–7.

[44] Dickson, *The New Politics of Science*, pp. 53–4.

[45] Dickson, *The New Politics of Science*, pp. 22–25, 106, Ch. 6.

[46] David Dickson, *The New Politics of Science*, pp. 66–95. For the first time in history, cutting-edge military technology develops independently of direct, formal state control (see S. Willetts, 'Weapons at the Turn of the Millennium', In *Globalisation and Insecurity*, edited by Barbara Harriss-White (New York: Palgrave-Macmillan, 2002).

The last set of feedbacks relates industry to the state. Privately appropriated technology becomes an instrument of foreign policy. Skilled labour is invited into the country, while technology is allowed to be exported if it reduces production costs and can be closely controlled—for despite patent and process protection, fees and royalties, exported technology has the potential to be used to compete with and erode the carefully constructed metropolitan 'competitive' advantage. Policymaking also comes under the aegis of economics, which develops policy as an exemplary field for cost-benefit analysis for resource allocation in the interest of national competitiveness.[47] Yet on these science-policy relationships Dickson comments: 'the value of science as a policy instrument is both limited and dangerous.' He argues that there is no neat division between facts and values and the facts of science are commonly open to more than a single interpretation.[48] The paradox Dickson describes for the USA is that with the rule of experts and science instated in public policy, scientific autonomy and the state are undermined and private interests prevail.

Dickson's account, admittedly of the USA rather than the UK, tracks hostility to state control and to politics at the interface between science and public policy. In the present era an episteme that denies politics has been built between science and policymaking and is seized on by both parties. What it is about politics to which science and the professional field of policy might be averse? While not being an easy question to answer, we saw at the outset that the 'third culture' has naturalized markets as the ultimate social and political regulators. To start building an answer to this question, we therefore turn in the last two sections of this chapter to explore the relationship between the processes of commodification of both knowledge/science and policy making on the one hand and the 'fourth culture' of de-politicization on the other.

Q3: Research and policy in an era of the commodification of knowledge.

The 'knowledge society' at the heart of this book refers to one in which knowledge is no longer confined to those who acquire and develop it but instead is made freely available, for a price, through markets. Knowledge in this situation becomes a vast collection of commodities, along with so

---

[47] Dickson, *The New Politics of Science*, p. 286 and Chapter 4.

[48] Dickson, *The New Politics of Science*, p. 299.

many other things which were previously organized or understood along non-market principles.[49] While private industrial funding for medical research in universities has a pedigree dating from the 19th century,[50] the process of commodification has already gone very far and is accelerating in reach and pace. By now most of the world's agriculture and food production has been commodified. So, as we all now appreciate after the Wall Street crisis, has risk. So too have many domestic activities, at least in middle-class households—keeping food fresh has been replaced by fridges, washing clothes by washing machines, cooking by buying precooked food and restaurant meals. Not only have farmland and fresh water supplies been commodified, but so also have parts of the oceans at an unprecedented pace (through the creation and sale of exclusive fishing and drilling rights), and even air itself (carbon trading is—in theory—a market for fresher air).[51]

Now it is the turn of knowledge. Commodification has only two levers to break it. One consists of politically determined limits—resulting from processes ranging from public deliberation to force. The second comprises non-commodifiable realms such as the family, the state or nature itself which are not produced under market conditions and yet which supply essential preconditions for capital—whether it be public infrastructure or the commons of scientific knowledge. The question then is whether scientific knowledge is like the family, and needs to be protected from commodification if it is to remain true to its nature: whether society can do without the kind of knowledge which only a non-commmodified form of knowledge production can provide.[52]

[49] U. Salam, 2015, 'Commodification, Capitalism and Crisis', in (eds) J. Heyer and B. Harriss-White, *Indian Capitalism in Development* (Routledge).

[50] Bonea, Amelia. Pers. Comm., July 2013.

[51] C. Leys and B. Harriss-White, 2012, available at http://www.opendemocracy.net/ourkingdom/colin-leys-barbara-harriss-white/commodification-essence-of-our-time.

[52] Some also argue that social institutions such as gender and ethnicity put a brake on the penetration of markets. Whether they are archaic outliers from pre-capitalist society or reworked as modern elements of contemporary capitalism is as debated an issue as whether they constrain market economy and protect market society or whether they disappear under advanced forms of capitalism. Ho's ethnography of the roles of race, gender, class, and university of origin in the hierarchical internal structuring of Wall Street investment banking seems to settle

In the scholarly subfield of the knowledge economy, it is not only knowledge itself that is to be commodified through patents and private intellectual property rights, a larger argument is being made for the worth of commodifying an entire set of institutions through which knowledge is created, acquired, and multiplied. The role of the university/higher education is then to create human capital through ever more commercializable means.[53]

Current supply and demand or 'quasi' markets will order the ownership and management of the university, its accreditation, its disciplinary structure, the curriculum, the results of examinations and certification, the nature and value of research, the way research is communicated to wider audiences, the returns to patents, and the remuneration of teachers/'instructors' so as to minimize costs and maximize profit.[54] Progress of all sorts is evaluated by money metrics. British universities are in the throes of moving from being independent institutions where knowledge is thought to be an entitlement, through a process where they house a private investment in human capital, onwards to a full consumer-driven system, in which the business model is openly competitive, and the state intervenes to incentive marketization. In teaching, the trebling of student fees has reduced the number of applications, by 7 per cent in 2012 and a further estimated 6 per cent in 2013. In research, funding for whole areas of enquiry has been blocked off, open-ended research is discouraged, transactions costs are deemed excessive for small claims on

---

these debates. Karen Z. Ho, *Liquidated: An Ethnography of Wall Street* (Durham: Duke University Press, 2009).

[53] 'The government has removed grants for subjects where private providers are able to compete, has allowed students at private colleges access to the official student loan scheme and maintenance grants, and introduced a HMRC-led consultation to exempt commercial degree providers from having to add VAT to their tuition fees.' In the UK there are only six private universities (out of about 100 universities and 159 institutions with degree awarding powers), one is for profit and another one from ten recently allowed university status is being purchased for profit by a for profit corporation. At the same time, hundreds of 'colleges' have been established since 2011 selling degrees accredited by universities all over the world–a regulatory nightmare. See A. McGettigan, 'New Universities: Will the Public Good Yield to Private Profit?' *The Guardian* (29 November 2012) and S. Collini, 2013. 'Sold Out', *London Review of Books*, 35, 20, 3–12.

[54] See for instance the Leader: 'US web education', *Financial Times* (15 March 2013).

society's research resources to be administered. Research resources become skewed towards corporate interests, patenting, and spin-off companies are actively encouraged, privatizing the results of public grants. The collective, collegial, and critical ethos of research is being actively compromised and private and public boundaries blurred.[55]

Karl Polanyi argued that a 'market society' is a contradiction in terms: markets were so destructive of conditions of social existence that a society in which market principles ruled supreme—a 'market society'— couldn't exist.[56] Without political control, markets cannot safeguard the conditions reproduction of a society. Something very similar may be said of the outcome of a generalized knowledge economy—a knowledge *society* is a contradiction in terms. In the restricted form of the subject of this chapter, research knowledge depends on public goods and collective activity. In the same way as for material goods, commodified (enclosed) knowledge, is selected for profitable development from the product of a non-commodified knowledge commons,[57] and then extracts rents from its use.

Capital—in the shape of individual firms—has no interest in paying for the 'curiosity-driven' knowledge in whose production everyone has a collective interest. But it shoots itself in the foot if it actively attacks the collective production of knowledge on which commodifiable knowledge depends. Capital however is not geared to measuring and worrying about the extent to which the conditions of existence of basic, collectively generated knowledge are being undermined. That role is played by political critique. But in the commodified and depoliticized forms of knowledge that are now common in today's science-policy exchange, there is no place for political critique.

As we have seen in the examples introduced here, official political discourse has become increasingly colonized by an economistic idiom, which is derived not strictly from economic theory proper, but rather from the language of management schools, business consultants and

---

[55] See Nurse, 2013. Asked to fill activity time-sheets in a detail of minutes per day prior to the retrospective release of research funds, the current writer is imagined by funding agencies to be well and truly Taylorized.

[56] Polanyi, K. *The Great Transformation* (Boston: Beacon Press, 1957).

[57] Salam, U. 2016. '"Knowledge as Development": A Critique of the Knowledge Economy', D Phil Thesis, Oxford University.

financial journalism'.[58] I have argued here that it is not just a language that is imported from economics but also a set of practices. 'The language of the market saturates much of public discourse, including the practice of a large part of the social sciences, and even the functionings of the state could be said to resemble a marketplace, in which political decision-making is itself a product'.[59]

RESEARCH AND POLICY UNDER THE COMMODIFICATION OF THE CORE FUNCTIONS OF THE STATE

'(I)f other parts of the public sector were to be market-tested, policy, too, should be open to contestability' observed the British Cabinet Secretary in 2012.[60] When commodification directly engages the state, a set of political changes are triggered. They include the social re-valuing of the provision of public goods and services, the incentivization of private sector involvement through state-underwritten capital investment and the subsidy of risk, the reconfiguring of the workforce as one from which profit can be made and the transformation in physical terms, as well as in the public consciousness, of public services into private commodities.[61] The process is not being confined to the privatization of textbook public goods and services (defined as non-excludable and non-rivalrous (like the army) but expands towards the privatization of goods and services about which there is a social (democratically established) consensus that they should be in public ownership (India's *Essential Commodities Act* seems to have passed both this test and the test of time). Blind to consequences, commodification even includes the processes of policymaking and 'political decision-making' themselves. Each component of policymaking is commodified: policy advice is subcontracted out to management consultancies, policy formulation may go to commercial legal drafting companies. Universities

---

[58] Collini, S. 'From Robbins to McKinsey', *London Review of Books,* 33, 16 (2011): 9–14, and Collini, *What are Universities For?* (Penguin Books Ltd, 2012).

[59] Salam, 2016.

[60] Quoted in J. Dudman, *Guardian Professional,* Tuesday 6 March 2012.

[61] C. Leys, *Market-driven Politics: Neoliberal Democracy and the Public Interest* (London: Verso, 2011).

are drawn in. They compete with more or less 'interested' think-tanks and private lobbies to capture the agenda and to store information essential to the decision process. The consequences are that conflicts of interest in regulation are deliberately embedded in the state, that the state has a short-term rather than long-term institutional memory, and that data origins and quality are increasingly hard to evaluate for evidence based policy decisions. Data are less secure too.

In this process the credit rating agencies (themselves commercialized) which 'regulate' global financial markets then set severe limits on the scope of the whole field of contestable public-interest policy. Policymakers need qualities of 'entrepreneurialism' rather than a capacity for the dispassionate sifting of debated evidence.

Balogh's 'dilettante', or, more realistically, the higher civil service 'mandarinate', originally conceived as the state's defence against the corruption of special interests, is becoming obsolete. In the New Labour era, from 2004–8 half the top civil service positions in the UK were drawn from outside, mainly from business. Under (2013) coalition government, about half the senior civil service now have their salaries paid to their own private companies, significantly reducing their tax obligations.[62] High level policy entrepreneurs develop the capacity to encourage a 'direction of travel' towards internal markets, and/or external privatization, to exclude incompatible futures, to manage the transactions costs of commissioning and subcontracting core policy activities. So the normalized social networking and 'revolving door' which give bureaucrats direct experience of business pre- and post-retirement and vice versa also embeds conflicts of interest and further erodes the boundaries between the public and private spheres and their interests. The public is surrendering to the private.

This is the context in which many scientists and policymakers now find themselves operating. The 'fourth culture' is the result. As it consolidates, the mutual de-politicized discourse between science and policy develops into something that is both un-scientific (restricting disinterested enquiry) and often bad policy, if we accept the need for, and value of, the public sphere.

---

[62] The evidence can be found in C. Leys, 'The Dissolution of the Mandarins', *Open Democracy* (2012) http://www.opendemocracy.net/ourkingdom/colin-leys/dissolution-of-mandarins-sell-off-of-british-state.

Public policy and the public interest must then be redefined as the sum total of private interest. But to define the public interest as the sum of private interests is manifest nonsense since the latter conflict—the theme of every political philosopher since Hobbes—if not before.

This is a political project indifferent to certain kinds of evidence—for example, the British Treasury's ignored case, published in 2003, against the privatization of healthcare.[63] It is a project in which flawed evidence may be mobilized—for example, the subsequently much criticized case of the costs and performance of a US healthcare corporation used against the British National Health Service.[64] It is one in which policy based evidence (working backwards from an already decided policy, selectively 'cherry picking' to generate supporting evidence) rather than evidence based policy is invited.[65] In the case of the health reforms being rammed through the UK, the budget for marketized health has new wedges to cover (i) repayments for public-private partnered infrastructure, (ii) transactions and co-ordination costs for outsourced private services, (iii) fraud and litigation not to mention (iv) profit. The opportunity cost of all of these private cost components is public health care. It is far too early in the process of privatization for outcome or impact statistics,[66] but one effort to mimic a private company in the form of a single

---

[63] Price signals don't work in relation to health care; the consumer lacks the necessary knowledge, creating a risk of overtreatment; there is a potential abuse of monopoly power; it is hard to write and enforce contracts for medical treatment; and 'it is difficult to let failing hospitals go bust—individuals are entitled to expect continuous, high-quality health care wherever they are' (HM Treasury, 2003, 12–14) (9). http://renewal.org.uk/articles/the-plot-against-the-nhs/.

[64] A. Talbot-Smith, et al., 'Questioning the Claims from Kaiser', *British Journal of General Practice*, 54 (2004): 415–21.

[65] House of Commons Science and Technology Committee, *Scientific Advice, Risk and Evidence Based Policy Making*, paras 89 (2006): 95–6; and see Nurse, 2013; and S. Player and C. Leys, *The Plot against the NHS* (London: Merlin, 2011), for systematic PBE in the drawn-out privatisation of British healthcare.

[66] The question is frequently asked without introducing the element of time. It is another point that the privileging of a utilitarian conception of impact crowds out many other useful factors about research (e.g. learning) (Nurse, 2013).

Foundation Hospital Trust has led to the preventable deaths of between 400 and 1,200 patients over four years.[67]

In the commodification of policymaking, curiosity driven research, justifiable in utilitarian as well as civilizational terms,[68] is increasingly less valued by official research funding councils. To illustrate with another example, in one of the 15 international agricultural research centres co-ordinated in a global network and reformed through the Consultative Group on International Agricultural Research, funding for blue skies research declined from 30 per cent to zero over the six years from 2006. Research themes were increasingly prescribed by donors,[69] influenced by business rather than frontier science, shattered into hundreds of normal research projects, with new research and employment contracts becoming time-bound and 'performance-related'. To be eligible for funding inside these constraints, inspired discovery science has to develop a deliberate strategic vagueness. Or curiosity-driven research must be cross-subsidized inside that subset of institutions that values and can resource it. And the result may be illustrated in a London University institution, which acts as the guardian of many rare academic disciplines and fields, where a new academic cultural abyss is opening up *within* social science and humanities, alienated from the 'fourth culture', between rare disciplines with few students, able to retain an independent critical research culture, and popular, heavily subscribed disciplines, dominated by the requirements of market-mediated mass-teaching, the latter cross-subsidising the former and having far less time for research.

For science to be useful for policy it has to manage a contradiction. Not only does it have to be able to be plugged into the politics of

---

[67] The case of Mid Staffs Hospital, the object of the 31 month enquiry resulting in the recent Francis Report; http://www.guardian.co.uk/society/2013/feb/06/mid-staffordshire-report-sweeing-changes.

[68] The utilitarian argument being that most of the significant inventions of the twentieth century have been found to have emerged from blue skies research (see http://www.ucl.ac.uk/EarthSci/research/blueskies/background.html not just for the facts but also for the suggestion that private 'venture' funds can underlie future discovery science). For the civilizational case see Nurse (2013).

[69] Minimizing transactions costs of research approvals may be a superficial reason for top-down control but this practice is consistent with enabling the research agenda to be restricted.

commodification—hence the proliferation of new and profitable industries of translation, standardization and de-politicization, but it also has
to preserve the capacity to criticise social processes in order—at the very
minimum—to preserve the non-commodified base essential to society
and economy, the very base that commodification works to undermine.

* * *

We have argued that when communicating with policymakers, most
physical and biological scientists and engineers (with a public interest
conception of natural sciences) operate with un-theorized and ad hoc
models of society not drawn from social science; that they neglect or
reject politics entirely; that expert policymakers are transferring certain
modes of reasoning from science that fulfil a narrowly defined set of policy
questions—'fit for very limited purposes'—and also reject the rigorous
study of power in their own policy processes, prominent among which
are expressions of powers hostile to the public interest; finally that both
expert knowledge and policy knowledge is being commodified. This is
the 'fourth culture': an expert culture in which science, social science,
and policymaking are tightly linked, and re-politicized through their joint
de-politicization.

We saw the processes at work in the 'knowledge society' which must
depend in practice upon a knowledge commons that is not part of the
knowledge economy. One of the conditions for progress in both science
and policy is the freedom of un-commodified and critical research. But
this freedom is confronted by the de-politicized science-policy interface.
We have argued that the process of de-politicization is so systematic that
it cannot be a random accident and must therefore be open to interpretation as a political intervention which serves social purposes. So the final
question concerns the interests that are served.

We have seen that depoliticized models of society/policy form a *lingua
franca* in the face of baffling terminological complexities in both science and
social science. The *lingua franca* is a translational device. Even the concept
of policy, distinct from politics, is a feature of the English language. Few
other languages permit it. This depoliticized discourse strives to wrench
clarity from uncertainty when clarity is thought to be needed for policymakers. But the *lingua franca* makes political critique impossible. And
in so doing it does injustice to science. Since the idea of science serving

policy depends on the excellence of science (as argued by the President of the Royal Society, quoted earlier), it therefore does injustice to policy. So the final significance of this de-politicization is that it is quite *unable to halt the process of commodification and the supplanting of the public interest by private interests.*

Not acting as a brake, or indeed even nurturing commodification, may even be the socially engineered purpose of the fourth culture, but that proposition would go further than our argument and evidence here. It is certainly its unintended consequence. Whatever its intentionality, the 'fourth culture' attacks its own nutrient base, its necessary preconditions.

Three urgent actions follow from the argument of this chapter. First, scientists and social scientists need to define what is needed to ensure the survival of a non-commodified knowledge base, given where higher education is headed. Second, non-commodified science and social science need to be well-articulated with policymaking in ways that are not mutually damaging and inform the public interest.[70] Third, in this interpretive role, policy decisions must be viewed from at least three standpoints—that of the proponent (the (in)vested interest), that of the state, and that of the larger public interest.[71]

ACKNOWLEDGEMENTS

Though I am responsible for all errors here, this essay benefited from conversations about it—in their private capacities—with Dr Amelia Bonea (history of technology), Professor Sanjeev Ghotge (technology, energy, policy), Dr Alfy Gathorne-Hardy (agriculture and environment), Dr George Kunnath (political anthropology), Dr Peter Larsen (environment and anthropology) Prof Colin Leys (politics and health), Dr Nafees Meah

---

[70] 'An instrumentalist perspective, for better or worse, is a necessary condition of policy making ... I want to be able to use the outputs of social science research instrumentally and that requires dialogue and discussion with social scientists ... Policy makers arguably instantiate the Marxist notion of 'praxis' (A UK policy-maker, Pers. Comm. May 2013).

[71] This is the adventurous call made in the 2013 report *'Benefits and limitations of nuclear fission for a low- carbon economy'.* See European Commission, *Benefits and limitations of nuclear fission for a low-carbon economy* (Brussels, 2013).

(chemistry, energy, climate change); Dr Ruhi Saith (medicine and public health), Prof Ashwin Srinivasan (computer science), and Professor John Wood (materials engineering) who know how grateful I am to them. It was written from reading and experience over a period in which I was employed on an ESRC-DFID funded project: 'Resources, Greenhouse Gases, and Employment in India's Informal Economy' but in no way commits either funding agency to its arguments or conclusions.

11 Creating Educational Excellence

The Role of Culture at the Indian Institute of Management, Ahmedabad

Shailendra Raj Mehta

This chapter looks at the process of creation of culture at the Indian Institute of Management–Ahmedabad (IIMA), India's leading business school, and one of the highest ranked business schools in the Asia-Pacific region and in the world.[1]

There are several things that are of interest about the Indian Institute of Management–Ahmedabad. First, it is by far one of the most selective

---

[1] See the details of the rankings both Indian and foreign at the following location: http://www.iimahd.ernet.in/institute/about/rankings.html.

educational institutions in the world, admitting fewer than one out of several hundred students that apply for each available seat–so it has maintained very high standards for its student intake.

Second, it was set up in 1961 but as noted by Mohan,[2] as early as 'in December 1967, a USAID survey team rated IIMA the best management institution in India. It also found that industry in India felt the same way'. So it achieved excellence rather quickly and maintained its top rank in India fairly consistently. For example Misra[3] notes 'IIMA remains "best-of-all" in the minds of prospective students'. Even the Dean of IIM-Calcutta (IIMC), one of IIMA's closest rivals, was to write that 'over the years, the Indian Institute of Management at Ahmedabad has acquired a halo around it' and 'IIMA has been ranked the topmost management institute in the country'.[4]

Third, its founding philosophy and the process has been documented very thoroughly, more thoroughly in fact, than any other educational institution in India or even anywhere else. Over a hundred people have written about its founding and about the particular approach to institution-building there. This range is very much reflected in the selection of the bibliography of this chapter. What is interesting is that these writings span the full half-century of its existence. By contrast, precious little exists about the institution-building process at its closest competitors–IIM-Calcutta (IIMC), IIM-Bangalore (IIMB), or the Indian School of Business (ISB), hardly more than a book or a paper or two in each case. Even globally, the founding of the Graduate School of Industrial Administration at Carnegie-Mellon in 1949 (renamed since 2004 as the Tepper Business School), whose process of founding was equally thoughtful and recent, has not been documented in as much detail. And of course, business schools such as Harvard Business School and the Wharton School at the University of Pennsylvania,

[2] Mohan, T. T. R. *Brick by Red Brick* (New Delhi: Rupa Publications, 2011), p. 112.

[3] Misra, S. 'Institutionality of IIMA: Retrospect and Prospect', in V.S. Chand and T.V. Rao (eds), *Nurturing Institutional Excellence: Indian Institute of Management* (Ahmedabad: Macmillan Publishers India, 2011), p. 152.

[4] Chaudhuri, S. 'Institution Building at IIMA: Key Aspects, Experiences and Reflections', in V.S. Chand and T.V. Rao (eds), *Nurturing Institutional Excellence: Indian Institute of Management Ahmedabad* (Macmillan Publishers India, 2011), p. 198.

were founded more than a century ago, and the founders and the founding team have long passed into history without leaving behind much formal/academic documentation.[5] In this sense, IIM-Ahmedabad is extremely unusual and fortunate in having such a diverse and long-standing stream of reflections on its founding and evolution. This formal documentation provides a unique opportunity to think through what is required to create educational excellence. Finally, like all living institutions, IIMA continues to evolve and learn from its own past as it adapts to its changing environment and reinvents itself for an even brighter future, being embedded as it is in one of the largest and fastest growing economies in the world.

Nor, must it be understood that the lessons afforded by the example of IIMA are only relevant to business schools. Now, at one level the fact that IIMA is a business school, means that its challenges and opportunities are different from those of a full-fledged university. Yet, the differences should not obscure the fact that the goals of all serious educational institutions are very similar—they all need to maintain excellence in research, teaching, and service to the community at large. The process of institution building is remarkably similar across a wide variety of institutions of higher learning. While the funding model may be different in a small liberal arts college, or in a medical school, or indeed in a large, global, integrated university, and outwardly they may be controlled by the State, by a self-perpetuating Trust or indeed a religious order, the challenges that they face nearly always include how to attract the best students and faculty, how to maintain academic freedom, how to fund the enormous amounts by way of subsidy that higher education invariably requires and how to build an enduring culture in an institution that measures its life not in years or decades but centuries. As such many, if not most learnings, are those with very broad resonance and not just limited to India, to emerging economies or indeed to business schools.

Yet there is something that is uniquely Indian in how IIMA was sought to be built, even though right from the drawing board onwards, IIMA was fully global in its orientation. One observer, Mrinalini Sarabhai, who had a ringside view of the founding of the institution, said 'this institution, was really built with the highest ideals of our Indian culture and civilization,

---

[5] The Harvard Business School Centennial year in 2008 brought forth a lot of outpourings of memories but very little formal work on how the institution was created and nurtured. See the archive at: http://www.hbs.edu/centennial/

using for once the right technology from the West, not imitating, but innovating and finding new methodologies, new ways of management, new ideas' and as such represents a unique experiment in combining Indian and global methods.[6] This too lends a certain poignancy to its example.

The plan of the chapter is as follows. In the next section, we formally define culture. Then we operationalize the concept in the context of educational institutions and provide a typology of cultural forms. The section after that explores how culture was built at IIMA. Multiple facets of this process are examined and contextualized. The final section concludes and summarizes the learnings.

THE CULTURE FRAMEWORK

Formal Definition of Culture

A formal analysis of the role of culture in organization design is relatively recent. Though inspired by social anthropology, it dates primarily from Schein's work at MIT in the early 1980s. Schein's definition of culture is 'a pattern of shared basic assumptions that was learned by a group as it solved its problems of external adaptation and internal integration, that has worked well enough to be considered valid and, therefore, to be taught to new members as the correct way to perceive, think, and feel in relation to those problems'.[7]

These perceived patterns include:[8]

- 'observed behavioural regularities'
- 'group norms'
- 'espoused values'
- 'formal philosophy'
- 'rules of the game'
- 'climate'
- 'embedded skills'
- 'habits of thinking, mental models, and linguistic paradigms'

---

[6] Sarabhai, M. 'Ravi Matthai in the Eyes of Others' (*IIMA Alumnus* (May) 1984).

[7] Schein, E.H. (ed.), *Organizational Culture and Leadership* (3rd. edition), vol. 2 (John Wiley & Sons, 2004), pp. 17.

[8] Schein (ed.), *Organizational Culture and Leadership* (3rd. edition), pp. 12–13.

- 'shared meanings'
- 'root metaphors or integrating symbols'
- 'formal rituals and celebrations'

In an earlier definition, Geertz defines culture by writing, 'Man is an animal suspended in webs of significance he himself has spun. I take culture to be those webs, and the analysis of it to be therefore not an experimental science in search of law, but an interpretive one in search of meaning.'[9] As we shall see in a later section, even earlier were the definitions of organizational culture formulated by Ravi Matthai, the first full-time director of IIMA, in his speeches and talks. Unfortunately, he never formalized his work in the form of a book or scholarly paper and so the numerous insights that he had into the process of organization building through the creation of a vibrant organizational culture, were largely lost to the scholarly community.

Clearly culture is the perspective with which one approaches the world around us. As such it has a tremendous role in shaping how we interact with it.

Source of Competitive Advantage

Culture is one of the key factors contributing to excellence in organizations.[10] It can also be an enduring source of competitive advantage. For this to happen culture must satisfy three conditions—it must be valuable, rare, and imperfectly imitable according to the standard framework that is used in strategic management.[11] A culture is valuable if its presence contributes to the achievement of excellence in organizational functioning. It is rare if it is not commonly found in other institutions that compete with it. And it is imperfectly imitable, if either the culture is difficult to observe, or if observable it is difficult to copy.

---

[9] Geertz, C. *The Interpretation of Cultures: Selected Essays*, Vol. 5019 (Basic Books, 1973), p. 5.

[10] Peters, T.J. and R.H. Waterman, *In Search of Excellence: Lessons from America's Best-Run Companies* (HarperCollins, 1982). R.H. Waterman, T.J. Peters, and J.R. Phillips, 'Structure Is Not Organization', *Business Horizons*, 23, 3 (1980): 14–26.

[11] Barney, J. 'Firm Resources and Sustained Competitive Advantage', *Journal of Management*, 17, 1 (1991): 99–120.

Culture certainly satisfies all three attributes. This is especially the case with culture because it consists of, as indicated above, norms, values, philosophies, rules of the game, and shared meanings.[12] Since these are in the minds of the members of the organization they are very difficult to observe. Very rarely, would an organization have taken the trouble to document its culture. Most of the time, this has to be pieced together from the disparate accounts of the participants. Further, culture exists as a system of interlocking and mutually sustaining parts. Copying one or even a few of these systems is not sufficient to reproduce it even to a partial degree. The system must exist a whole, or it exists very imperfectly. So, even if an organization wanted to copy the culture of another it would face formidable challenges. Merely recruiting senior leaders from that organization would not be enough. One would have to replicate the interlocking system that created the original culture also. This is never easy, as to do so would be to go against the grain of the existing culture of the organization. This invariably breeds resistance. Therefore, culture is very hard to copy. Culture, once established, is also very hard to change.

How Culture Is Formed

Culture is formed, in two ways. First, 'spontaneous interaction in an unstructured group gradually leads to patterns and norms of behavior that become the culture of that group'. Second, it can be endowed by a leader who creates any new organization be it a company, a cult, a division of a company or even a political party. This person 'will have certain personal visions, goals, beliefs, values, and assumptions about how things should be'. These are initially imposed on the group, in a process that is called 'a primary act of leadership' but by itself it does not lead to the production of culture. Initially it only leads to compliance. 'Only if the resulting behavior leads to "success"—in the sense that the group accomplishes its task and the members feel good about their relationships to each other—will the founders' beliefs and values be confirmed and reinforced, and, most important, come to be recognized as *shared*.'[13]

When new members join this group, they figure out for themselves some part of this culture, but not all. The remainder is picked

---

[12] Barney, J.B. 'Organizational Culture: Can It Be a Source of Sustained Competitive Advantage?' *Academy of Management Review*, 11, 3 (1986): 656–65.

[13] Schein (ed.), *Organizational Culture and Leadership* (3rd. edition), p. 16.

up through a process of feedback provided by the old members to the new members when they experiment with different behaviours.[14] Clearly the founders can have an outsize influence on the development of an organization.[15]

We will see how the thinking of these founders of IIMA and others, and the conscious choices that they made, along with institutional dynamics, coalesced over time into a very definitive culture.

FOUNDATIONS OF IIMA CULTURE

Conceptualization

The role of a leader is critical in the founding of an institution. As it happened, not one but three individuals had a major role in the founding of Ahmedabad. They were Vikram Sarabhai, Kasturbhai Lalbhai, and Ravi Matthai. All three of them helped form and crystallize the culture of IIMA. It may be useful to look at their backgrounds to get a better understanding of what they accomplished.

Vikram Sarabhai was born in Ahmedabad in 1919. The Sarabhai family was one of the most prominent industrial families in the country. The remarkable thing about this family was not that it was rich, but that it was also immensely cultivated. Along with other industrialists of Ahmedabad, the Sarabhai family worked very closely with Mahatma Gandhi to advance the cause of India's freedom. In fact it is said that the first donation that Gandhiji received to set up his ashram came from Vikram Sarabhai's father, Ambalal Sarabhai. Early on, the Sarabhais came across the pioneering work of Maria Montessori and decided to set up a school following her principles in Ahmedabad. It was called 'The Retreat' and was exclusively for the eight Sarabhai children for whom there were a dozen teachers including three PhDs, three graduates of universities in Europe, a dance teacher from Tagore's Shantiniketan, a Sanskrit teacher, and a poet. The curriculum included sciences and arts, and such practical skills as being able to help in the cowshed, in the kitchen, to manage funds, and to take care of guests.[16]

---

[14] Schein (ed.), *Organizational Culture and Leadership* (3rd. edition), p. 19.

[15] Schein, 'The Role of the Founder in Creating Organizational Culture', *Organizational Dynamics*, 12, 1 (1983): 13–28.

[16] A. Shah, *Vikram Sarabhai: A Life* (Penguin, 2007), p. 19.

After a brief stint at Gujarat College, Vikram Sarabhai moved to Cambridge University to pursue a Tripos in physics. A recommendation letter for him was written by none other than Rabindranath Tagore.[17] After finishing his degree in 1940 he returned to India and began a hectic period of scientific experiments at the Indian Institute of Science, Bangalore, under the Nobel Laureate CV Raman. He returned to Cambridge in 1945 for his PhD which he completed in 1947. With his impeccable pedigree, scientific and otherwise, it is not surprising Vikram Sarabhai had the complete confidence of Jawaharlal Nehru (his fellow Cambridge-man) who was also his father's friend. He was charged with, among other things, setting up India's space program. But that was not all. Vikram Sarabhai was an institution builder par excellence. From 1947, the year of India's independence to 1971 when he died, it is said that he set up one institution every year. His loss, and that of his friend and colleague Homi Bhabha in the prime of their lives, constitutes one of the tragedies of modern India.[18] He founded institutions as diverse as institutes of management and design, scientific research laboratories, mining corporations, organizations to house parts of India's atomic energy program, academies for performing arts, textile research, popularization of science, and many others. In this aspect, he has no peers in India and very few worldwide. A moon crater in the Sea of Serenity is named after him.[19]

Vikram Sarabhai spent a lot of time identifying leaders to put in place to lead these institutions. When it was time to choose the leadership of the Ahmedabad Textile Industry's Research Association (ATIRA), Vikram Sarabhai waited for years to get the right individual to head it. On the other hand, for the Physical Research Laboratory, the Director was selected even before the Institute was established. As he was quoted saying 'the human relations side of a man that is necessary in order that he might fit in our environment' was always uppermost in his mind.[20]

Vikram Sarabhai was a very versatile individual and remarkably far-sighted. In their book on India's information revolution, Singhal and Rogers

---

[17] Shah, *Vikram Sarabhai: A Life*, p. 37.

[18] S. Ganesh and P. Joshi, 'Institution Building: Lessons from Vikram Sarabhai's Leadership', *Vikalpa* (Oct-Dec 1985): p. 401.

[19] Available at http://www.isro.gov.in/about-isro/dr-vikram-ambalal-sarabhai-1963–1971.

[20] Ganesh and Joshi, 'Institution Building: Lessons from Vikram Sarabhai's Leadership,' p. 402.

dedicated it to the memory of Vikram Sarabhai 'who saw a revolution coming, and helped make it happen.'[21] Vikram Sarabhai was clearly one of the creators of modern India. It was Vikram Sarabhai who saw the opportunity to create a management school in India.[22]

The idea of bringing modern management education to India, was in fact being discussed quite openly. As it happened, the first management school in Asia, IBA, had already been set up in Karachi, Pakistan, in 1955 in collaboration with the Wharton School. A study was commissioned by the Ford Foundation as part of which Dean Robbins of UCLA recommended that two business schools be set up, one in Calcutta and the other one in Bombay, no doubt reflecting that these two cities were the leading industrial and commercial hubs of their time.

However, the government of Maharashtra did not show much interest and was reluctant about offering land close to the city.

In fact at that time, a cadre of trained management experts hardly existed. The industry hired functional specialists such as chartered accountants or engineers if they needed experts in finance or in manufacturing or any other technical discipline respectively. Sensing an opening, Vikram Sarabhai moved fast and made sure that Ahmedabad was chosen as the location instead of Bombay. He lined up the support of Ahmedabad industry with whom, of course, he was well-connected. The person that he most depended upon was Kasturbhai Lalbhai.

Now, Kasturbhai Lalbhai was amongst the most prominent industrialists in India of his time. Ahmedabad was the centre of the textile industry in India and Kasturbhai Lalbhai was the founder of Arvind Mills. He came from a family which was given the title of *nagarseth* (city chief) by the Mughals. That was quite fitting since one of his ancestors, Shantidas Jhaveri, was a royal jeweler of Akbar. Between them, Vikram Sarabhai and Kasturbhai Lalbhai lined up the support from the government of Gujarat as well as the Government of India. The support from the latter was shortly facilitated

[21] Singhal A. and E.M. Rogers, *India's Communication Revolution: From Bullock Carts to Cyber Marts* (Sage, 2001).

[22] Bhattacharyya, S.K. 'The Early Years of Institutional Development', in R.J. Matthai, S.K. Bhattacharyya, S.S. Rao, H.N. Pathak, et al. (eds), *Institution Building: The IIMA Experience. Volume 1: The Early Years* (Ahmedabad: Ravi Matthai Centre for Educational Innovation. Indian Institute of Management-Ahmedabad, 1993), pp. 8–9.

by the fact that both of them knew Jawaharlal Nehru intimately. Vikram Sarabhai played a major role in negotiating with the central government while Kasturbhai Lalbhai worked to rally the support of local industry.[23]

IIMA was one of the first Public-Private Partnerships (PPP) in the country.[24] It was a genuine partnership between the governments of India and Gujarat with Indian industry and the Ford Foundation, thereby bringing into its ambit the Centre, the State, the local industry and a well-respected global foundation. The Government of India provided the recurring expenses for IIMA. By contrast IIM Calcutta had very little local involvement of industry. Similarly, the IITs were established by an act of Parliament and had no participation by industry. They were entirely funded by the government. This unique collaboration, quite unprecedented in India, or outside, had a significant role in the evolution of IIMA.

Ford Foundation gave IIMA $ 2 million over a seven-year period—an enormous sum of money more than half a century ago. Indian industry raised Rs. 30 lakhs. The contribution of the government of Gujarat was valued at Rs. 26 lakhs for the 68 acres of land that they donated to IIMA.

The exchange rate of rupees to the dollar was 4.7619. In 1966 it changed to 6.3591.[25] So depending on how you think of it, the Ford Foundation gave between Rs. 1 and 1.2 crores in Indian terms. Of course, its value was even more than the nominal amount because foreign-exchange was very scarce and rationed.

Ford Foundation therefore had an outsized impact on the formation of IIMA. They also tried to dictate the choice of partner and were rooting for UCLA whom they had chosen unilaterally. Vikram Sarabhai wrote back noting that in a partnership, 'no one party in this cooperative venture goes ahead and makes commitments without prior consultation with the whole group'.[26] Ultimately the Ford Foundation relented. This insistence

[23] Matthai, R. 'Vikram Sarabhai and IIMA', in N. Sheth (ed.), *Occassional Speeches and Writings of Ravi Matthai* (Ahmedabad: Centre for Educational Innovation. Indian Institute of Management Ahmedabad, 1989), p. 156.

[24] Anubhai, P. 'Role of Values in Institution Building: The IIM-A Experience', paper presented at the 8th Annual Lecture of the Godrej and Tata Central Archives, *Royal Bombay Yacht Club* (30 November 2012).

[25] Available at http://fx.sauder.ubc.ca/data.html.

[26] Anubhai, 2012, 'Role of Values in Institution Building: The IIM-A Experience'; J.R. Dee, 'Engaging the Six Cultures of the Academy' (review), *The Review of Higher Education*, 34, 3 (2011): p. 4.

on principle, even when Vikram Sarabhai had 'a very weak hand', then became a norm at IIMA and created a culture of dealing with all parties, including the government, on an equal footing. Among other things they managed to persuade the Government of India to keep it away from the purview of CAG audit.[27]

The Ford Foundation made available large grants for bringing in Louis Kahn as the architect, Balakrishna Doshi as his Indian counterpart, additional grants for the library, the campus and especially for faculty development.

But more than just preparing the ground, literally and figuratively, for IIMA, it was Vikram Sarabhai's ability to properly conceptualize and build institutions that set them apart.

Just what was Vikram Sarabhai's approach to institution building?[28] Matthai et al. indicate that there are two approaches to institution building.[29] The first is the Master Plan Approach. Here there is a template which exists at some central level where the details of practices pertaining to administration and organization, and the funding model are laid out. Everything flows from this template. This is the approach taken by the University Grants Commission (UGC). This, however, is the classic one-size-fits-all approach and is only minimally responsive to the specific circumstances of the individual environment. The other approach is called the Organization around Man Approach. In India, both Homi Bhabha and Vikram Sarabhai followed this approach in the multiple institutions they set up. Chowdhury quotes Homi Bhabha as saying that this is the philosophy that built the famous Max Planck Institutes in Germany. She adds that the philosophy came from the Kaiser Wilhelm Society which believed that it 'shall not first build an Institute for research and then seek out the suitable man, but shall first pick up an outstanding man and then build an Institute for him'. The prototypical institution built in this fashion

[27] Anubhai, 2012, 'Role of Values in Institution Building: The IIM-A Experience'.

[28] K. Chowdhry, 'Institution Building: Two Approaches in Contrast', in R. Matthai, U. Pareek, and T.V. Rao (eds), *Institution Building in Education and Research* (New Delhi: All India Management Association, 1977), p. 12, p. 14.

[29] Matthai, R., Pareek, U., and T.V. Rao, *Institution Building in Education and Research* (New Delhi: All India Management Association, 1977).

by Homi Bhabha was the Tata Institute of Fundamental Research (TIFR) and of course, the institutions built by Vikram Sarabhai–including IIMA—clearly fit this pattern.

Kamla Chowdhry, who worked very closely with Vikram Sarabhai and echoed his sentiments,[30] believed that 'the application of the scientific method by fresh and trained young minds would be able to produce better results ... than the applications of "previous experience" gained'. This was the approach that was followed at IIMA.

S. Ganesh and P. Joshi[31] sum it up by saying that Vikram Sarabhai employed three different strategies to build institutions. He built clusters of individuals at multiple levels of the organization that he interacted with on a regular basis. He created a climate of trust by providing freedom to individuals and emphasizing peer control. And finally, he created a climate of caring by remaining approachable and by having open communication channels.

BUILDING THE CULTURE

The key individual that Vikram Sarabhai found and developed at IIMA was Ravi Matthai. He was the first full-time Director of IIMA.

He was the one who had the largest impact on IIMA. This was because as the first full-time Director who stayed in his job for eight years, he was the one who instituted the various policies, routines, and structures that enabled the right culture. He also modeled for others the attitudes and mindsets that he expected of them. It is to him and to his policies that we now turn.

Ravi Matthai

Ravi Matthai was the son of John Matthai, the first finance minister of independent India. It is interesting to note that John Matthai resigned from his post on a matter of principle on account of a disagreement with Jawaharlal Nehru. Like Vikram Sarabhai, he too was born into a life of privilege and like his father obtained a BA in politics, philosophy, and economics from

---

[30] Chowdhry, K. *Change in Organizations* (Lalvani, 1970), pp. 137–8.

[31] Ganesh and Joshi, 'Institution Building: Lessons from Vikram Sarabhai's Leadership', p. 410.

Balliol College, Oxford. Thereafter, he did what legions of Oxbridge students have done in India, he became an executive with one of the leading English industrial houses in Calcutta. He was apparently quite successful as a manager but he was bored with that life. So when the Indian Institute of Management Calcutta was set up and the word was put out that they were looking for people with corporate experience to teach, he jumped at the opportunity. In the short span of less than two years, he developed quite a reputation as a 'go to person' for understanding corporate issues. He also made his mark in executive education. When Vikram Sarabhai started looking for a full-time Director to replace himself in his capacity as part-time Director of IIMA, he heard of Ravi Matthai. Upon learning that he was delivering a program in Srinagar, Vikram Sarabhai went to see him there and made him an offer on the spot. It took some time, and Ravi Matthai eventually relented and came on board as the first full-time Director of IIMA. It can be said that Ravi Matthai and Vikram Sarabhai were the true founders of IIMA in thought, word, and deed.

The initial reception of Ravi Matthai at IIMA was not solicitous. In Calcutta, the business organization that he headed had just gone through a restructuring since it was making heavy losses. Ravi Matthai had to ruthlessly cut down manpower in the company. This reputation preceded him at IIMA where he was billed as 'Ravi the Butcher'.[32] Perhaps for this reason, or for other reasons not fully understood, the student reception of Ravi Matthai was distinctly hostile. As he puts it, the students had 'become dissatisfied and disturbed–gone berserk'.[33] To rectify the situation Ravi Matthai began a ritual that was repeated around dusk. He would pull up a chair and sit before the students who would be arrayed around him and patiently listen to their concerns, not grandstanding but only gently speaking to them, until he saw their 'angry buzz fading'. That he was able to overcome this limitation and accomplish what he did was therefore doubly creditable.

What really helped him with his sterling qualities? 'Ravi Matthai remains in my mind as one who represented the best values of an older era–cool, impartial, institutionally loyal, with a clear sense of self discipline,

---

[32] Halse, M. 1993. 'To Ravi with Respect and Affection', in R.J. Matthai, S.K. Bhattacharyya, S.S. Rao, H.N. Pathak, et al. (eds), *Institution Building*, p. 78.

[33] Halse, M. 'To Ravi with Respect and Affection', *Institution Building*, p. 79.

a certain temper beneath the velvet exterior.'[34] It is difficult to find a better statement of the ideal institutional man. Ravi Matthai set about building IIMA right in earnest.

The Most Important Contribution

The most important thing that Ravi Matthai helped build at IIMA was its culture. In fact, Udai Pareek once asked Ravi Matthai: 'A question I may like to ask you in the beginning is what is the most important thing in institution building? What contributes to institution building?' Ravi Matthai replied, 'As far as the Indian Institute of Management Ahmedabad (IIMA) is concerned, I think the single most important aspect was building a self-regulating culture within the Institute through building people'.[35] As it happened, 'self-regulation was also developed through the way in which committees functioned, the way in which individuals took responsibility without authority'.[36] The idea of discharging your responsibility without asking for the corresponding authority was a key innovation. It meant that faculty were able to take ownership of the Institute and to do whatever was required at the appropriate moment without too much by way of bureaucracy coming in the way. It also helped build a self-regulating culture which stood IIMA in good stead subsequently. It has survived in good and bad leadership as well as weathered the storms that would have otherwise sunk most normal institutions.

Ravi Matthai's Definition of Culture

The issue of culture in organizations came to the attention of management theorists starting in the early 1970s.[37] It really hit its stride with the work of Schein starting in the early 1980s[38] and through his textbook which went through several editions.[39] Ravi Matthai, of course, had started to

---

[34] De, B. 'Ravi John Matthai and the Early Years of IIMC', *IIMA Alumnus* (May 1984): 11.

[35] U. Pareek, 'Institution Builder: A Great Leader', in U. Pareek (ed.), *Organisational Leadership and Power* (ICFAI University Press, 2007), p. 94.

[36] Pareek, 'Institution Builder: A Great Leader', in U. Pareek (ed.), *Organisational Leadership and Power*, p. 95.

[37] Geertz, *The Interpretation of Cultures: Selected Essays*, vol. 5019.

[38] Schein, 1983. 'The Role of the Founder in Creating Organizational Culture.'

[39] Schein (ed.), *Organizational Culture and Leadership* (3rd. edition).

implement many of these ideas much earlier, starting with his appointment in 1965. Through application, refinement, and reflection he came up with several articulations on the importance of culture which are worth quoting. For example, in a convocation address in 1979 at the National Institute of Design[40] (NID), he has a definition of culture which is worth repeating:

> [B]y culture I mean the set of values, the beliefs, the norms, the attitudes which determine the patterns of behavior within an organization; attitudes towards the institution, attitudes towards tasks, attitude towards working relations, attitude towards your peers, attitudes towards the environment, to its creativity, innovativeness, imagination, attitude towards power and the use of authority, attitude towards leadership—all these intangibles which go to make the character of an institution as much as they go to make the character of the people within that institution.

R. Matthai indicates how one must be very careful in borrowing templates from one field to another.[41] IIMA could have inherited the culture of universities from the PhDs that it hired in its early years, but that would have been a mistake because universities are not tasked with the application of knowledge. Similarly, on account of the fact that the government had a large role to play in the founding of IIMA, it could have inherited bureaucratic rules and procedures of functioning. Both of these if adopted would have choked off the institution right at its inception.

No Preconceptions

Ravi Matthai was asked as to what was his main strength as an institution builder. His surprising reply was 'my main strength was my ignorance'. By this he meant that he had no 'preconceptions'. However, he did come into IIMA with what he called 'attitudinal biases'. He had developed a particular point of view based on his experiences as a student, an executive, and for a brief while, a faculty member at IIMC. The causal chain that he built for

[40] Matthai, 'Learning and Organizational Culture', Convocation address delivered at the National Institute of Design, Ahmedabad on 23 April 1979, in N. Sheth (ed.), *Occasional Speeches and Writings of Ravi Matthai* (Ahmedabad: Centre for Educational Innovation. Indian Institute of Management Ahmedabad, 1989c), p. 117.

[41] Matthai, 'Learning and Organizational Culture'. Convocation address delivered at the National Institute of Design, Ahmedabad on 23 April 1979', in N. Sheth (ed.), *Occasional Speeches and Writings of Ravi Matthai*, pp. 121–2.

himself was that creativity and innovation required freedom of expression which was built on self-discipline, which required self-confidence which required self-esteem and mutual self-respect. So these were the qualities that he tried to inculcate at IIMA.[42]

The Core

The core qualities at IIMA are based on the causal chain that Ravi Matthai built for himself. The first part of it is Peer Culture which helped build mutual self-respect and self-confidence.

Peer Culture and Collaboration

Visitors to IIMA are surprised that in a hierarchical society such as India, the hierarchy amongst professors at IIMA is minimal. Professors, junior and senior, young and old, are equal members of all committees and freely express their views. A young assistant professor may be called upon to become the chairman of an area. All faculty offices are similar and housing is largely allocated on the basis of tenure at the institute and not rank. In interviews with faculty, several indicated that this was one of the most striking things that they noticed when they first came to IIMA. Another professor found it interesting that at IIMA, all the faculty address each other by their first names. The junior most colleagues, too, call the Director and the Deans by their first names, something that people in other educational institutions in India would find sacrilegious.[43]

Monappa recalls the early days of the Institute when the newly recruited faculty used to converge on a specific quadrangle to share late-night coffee with the students.[44] There were attempts to form bonds with research assistants as well. The result of all of this was that the students related to each other particularly well. Another area of

---

[42] Pareek, 'Institution Builder: A Great Leader', in U. Pareek (ed.), *Organisational Leadership and Power*, pp. 103–4.

[43] T.V. Rao, 'Change at IIMA', in V.S. Chand and T.V. Rao (eds), *Nurturing Institutional Excellence: Indian Institute of Management Ahmedabad* (Macmillan Publishers India, 2011), pp. 437–50.

[44] A. Monappa. (1994). 'Memories of a Transition'. In V. Vyas, I. Patel, N. Sheth, et al. (eds), *Institution Building - The IIMA Experience. Volume II—The Subsequent Years*. Ahmedabad: Ravi Matthai Center for Institutional Innovation—Indian Institute of Management Ahmedabad, p. 62.

bonding as Saha indicates, was that people came together through the bridge and badminton clubs.[45]

There was a lot of interaction between students and faculty.[46] Given that everybody lived on the campus including both students and faculty as well as a significant amount of the administrative and blue-collar staff, it is not surprising that there was a lot of interaction after class. Students would invite faculty members for dinner and likewise, faculty members would invite students for a meal. Lifelong relationships and mentorships were consequently formed.

The work of IIMA was done in committees where, as we have already indicated, multiple individuals 'took responsibility without authority'.[47] This meant that no individual could impose his or her will on others but had to persuade them to go along. This attribute is a key requirement for effectiveness in a matrix organization. Today, most global multinationals stress this as a fundamental attribute that must be possessed by their executives. But Ravi Matthai was emphasizing it long before this became fashionable and written about in recent years as in A.R. Cohen and D.L. Bradford's, *Influence without Authority*.[48]

S. Chaudhuri describes the decision-making process at IIMA as consensus-based and says that he could hardly remember any major decision that required voting.[49] He describes the intense participation that the faculty has in all aspects of decision-making at the Institute, so much so that the Institute is not only 'faculty governed' but actually 'faculty administered and governed'. This naturally led to an enormous sense of ownership on the part of the faculty.

In his NID convocation address in the 1960s, which was published only much later, Ravi Matthai articulates a phrase that was used in the design of

[45] J.R. Saha, 2011. 'IIMA's Quest for Excellence', in Chand and Rao (eds), *Nurturing Institutional Excellence*, p. 30.

[46] A. Ghosh, 'IIMA As I have Experienced it', in Chand and Rao (eds), *Nurturing Institutional Excellence*, p. 184.

[47] Pareek, 'Institution Builder: A Great Leader', in U. Pareek (ed.), *Organisational Leadership and Power*, p. 95.

[48] A.R. Cohen and D.L. Bradford, *Influence Without Authority* (Wiley, 2011).

[49] Chaudhuri, S. 2011. 'Institution Building at IIMA: Key Aspects, Experiences and Reflections', in Chand and Rao (eds), *Nurturing Institutional Excellence*, p. 204.

the NID—'joint responsibility'—and says this means that no individual can act alone but that they must act in groups that work harmoniously together and multiple points of view are not only tolerated but encouraged and where, whenever possible, discussion proceeds until a commonality emerges. He continues:

> it is easier said than understood. And one of the greatest problems in any institution is trying to bring about this commonality. If there is ambiguity, it must be discussed. It must be discussed threadbare until there is understanding. What in (sic)understanding, we have to be able to listen to others. It is common to be aware but we do not hear. It is common that we hear but do not listen. It is common that we listen but will not or cannot understand.[50]

What is required is 'listening with the third ear' to appreciate the point of view of the other. He adds, 'if the institution legitimizes the fact that the argument should take place then implicitly it is accepted as part of its educational philosophy that its educational program must be constantly reviewed and changed circumstances warrant such change'. These were insightful observations that remain as relevant as ever.[51]

Saha talks very movingly about how as a young research assistant at IIMA he was pulled into a consulting project by Professor S.K. Bhattacharya, a very senior and renowned professor at the Institute.[52] However, he was expected to contribute as an equal, to voice his opinion and to critique the opinion of others. He was even roped in to help actually make a part of the final presentation to the Board of the company they were working with.

Saha indicates that fierce arguments would break out in faculty meetings.[53] Strong positions were strongly expressed and people would disagree vehemently. Yet when consensus was achieved, everybody willingly accepted the final decision. These disagreements did not carry over into personal relationships.

---

[50] Matthai, 'Learning and Organizational Culture', in Sheth (ed.), *Occasional Speeches and Writings of Ravi Matthai*, p. 118.

[51] Matthai, 'Learning and Organizational Culture', in Sheth (ed.), *Occasional Speeches and Writings of Ravi Matthai*, p. 120.

[52] Saha, 'IIMA's Quest for Excellence', in Chand and Rao (eds), *Nurturing Institutional Excellence*, p. 27.

[53] Saha, 'IIMA's Quest for Excellence', in Chand and Rao (eds), *Nurturing Institutional Excellence*, p. 30.

All this was only possible in an environment of trust, and this was something that Ravi Matthai and the system that he built exuded in a large measure. In fact, N. Ravichandran indicates how trust was built into the core of the Institution. Both administrative as well as academic procedures were heavily simplified and resulted in an environment, where it was a joy to work.[54]

Saha also talks about how when the early executive education programs were launched, nobody just did his or her bit and quietly walked away.[55] They hung around the program venue, sat in on each other's classes and would convene a meeting every Friday evening to review what went well and to plan the week ahead. Similar opportunities, presented themselves during case writing, which was often done collaboratively. Another source of bonding came from trips that the faculty took together, for example, to conduct admission interviews in different parts of the country. It also helped build collaboration.

In a similar vein, P. Chandra talks about returning to India after teaching in the United States.[56] He found a culture at IIMA unlike anything that he had seen. As he puts it, the faculty 'shared their stories, cases, and notes, encouraged me to experiment with new topics and new courses (and participated without any trepidation), discussed cases before and after class, went on plant tours, wrote cases with me as equals, and initiated me into the world of executive education (and it meant first and foremost education on the issues facing executives)'.

Faculty bonding came from joint programs, projects or activities. Projects such as the India Population project brought people together. The 3 Tier Program, which required several dozen faculty from IIMA to come together and collaborate to teach, was also a bonding opportunity. The admissions committee also provided ways in which people came together because people would be on the road together conducting interviews for long periods of time.[57]

[54] N. Ravichandran, 'Reflections on the Evolution of IIMA as an Institution', in Chand and Rao (eds), *Nurturing Institutional Excellence*, p. 230.

[55] Saha, 2011, 'IIMA's Quest for Excellence', in Chand and Rao (eds), *Nurturing Institutional Excellence*, p. 30.

[56] P. Chandra, 2011 'Behind the Red Bricks: Underpinnings of an Academic Culture', in Chand and Rao (eds), *Nurturing Institutional Excellence*, p. 220.

[57] W.G. Tierney (1988). 'Organizational Culture in Higher Education: Defining the Essentials', *The Journal of Higher Education*, p. 11.

Self Discipline

The second part of the core culture was self-discipline. R. Matthai indicates why self-discipline is so important to the functioning of IIMA.[58] He writes:

> if it was accepted that the institute's work would result in changes outside, then the Institute itself must have a culture of innovation and change. This could best be achieved by trying to provide within the Institute a sufficiently high degree of freedom so that individual and group creativity would have the greatest chance of expression. If freedom is not to degenerate into license, there must be a discipline within the academic community of the Institute. But it was believed that such discipline should be self-imposed and not thrust upon the faculty by hierarchical authority. It was felt, therefore, that norms should evolve in a self-regulating community rather than having large volumes of rules and regulations, which would constrain individual behaviour. The working of such a culture, therefore, rested on the selection of competent and balanced people capable of such sophisticated behaviour. The basis of the institutes' internal functioning, therefore, was to give the faculty the freedom to act, trust them to do their job well, provide facilities for these to be accomplished and to evaluate their performance.

This was, of course, a masterful statement of what a properly functioning, normally governed institution should look like. However, there is a significant danger here. If these norms are not set just right, one could tip in one extreme direction or another. Similarly, there is another danger that some of the norms or the nuances of these norms are not quite appropriate. If they are not corrected in the early days of institution building, they can ossify and harden into something that is dysfunctional. Such indeed, was the norm around what constituted research, as we shall see shortly.

Another name for self-discipline was balance. It was a question of avoiding extremes. Freedom could not become license, frankness could not become rudeness and the expression of opinions could not become self-righteousness. The way in which individuals traversed this continuum was of utmost importance at IIMA. By experimenting and making mistakes and getting feedback, in many cases from Ravi Matthai himself, a culture was built that valued and developed consideration, sensitivity and

---

[58] R. Matthai, U. Pareek, U., and T.V. Rao, *Institution Building in Education and Research* (New Delhi: All India Management Association, 1993), p. 1.

understanding. The way to build this was through group work and through shared experiences of working in teams.[59]

Innovation and Self-Expression

The third part of the core values is innovation and self-expression. It is well known that innovation, creativity, and self-expression thrive in an arena of diversity and openness.

To aid this key aspect of institution building, as S. Misra indicates, was how Ravi Matthai went about recruiting a very diverse faculty.[60] They came from all parts of the country from the North, the South, the East, and the West. Unlike IIMB, where most of the faculty tend to be from South India, and IIMC where most of the faculty were Bengali, no group from any region of India ever came close to being dominant at IIMA. This pan-India group brought in a refreshing diversity of thought and approaches and to this day, no one regional group dominates IIMA. It was not just a regional diversity that was celebrated but also individual diversity to the point of celebrating eccentricity.

P. Chandra talks about several maverick professors at IIMA.[61] They dressed differently, spoke differently and did things differently. Such people were not only tolerated, but actually encouraged and admired. Over the years, many such professors have made a mark for themselves and for the Institute.

Experimentation was de-rigueur. P. Chandra says, 'Go and try it' was the motto.[62] Often there were vigorous debates about whether a new course should be offered or not and then people on both sides of the debate would go and offer the new course together, learn from it, revise it and make it bigger and better together. The autonomy in the Institute meant that wide spaces were available to individuals to do their own thing.

Koshy talks about how with the increase in student intake, it became very difficult to schedule all the first year classes together for each of the

[59] Pareek, 'Institution Builder: A Great Leader', in U. Pareek (ed.), *Organisational Leadership and Power*, pp. 96–7.

[60] Misra, 'Institutionality of IIMA: Retrospect and Prospect', in Chand and Rao (eds), *Nurturing Institutional Excellence*, p. 149.

[61] Chandra, 'Behind the Red Bricks: Underpinnings of an Academic Culture', in Chand and Rao (eds), *Nurturing Institutional Excellence*, p. 222.

[62] Chandra, 'Behind the Red Bricks: Underpinnings of an Academic Culture', in Chand and Rao (eds), *Nurturing Institutional Excellence*, p. 221.

sections.[63] This simultaneity was required because a key part of the teaching system at IIMA was surprise quizzes. It was also important to administer the same set of quizzes to everyone at the same time to reduce variability and to ensure fairness, but with classes following a morning and afternoon shift, this meant that the quizzes could only be administered late at night when all the classes had been completed. But this brought on its own set of challenges since the afternoon sections did not have as much time to prepare for those quizzes as those in the morning. It also created a problem with the scheduling of extracurricular activities and altered the social dynamics of the cohort. Noticing all these problems, the new system was scrapped and a way was found for all the sections to be taught in the morning itself. This ability to experiment and to rapidly correct the mistakes has long characterized IIMA. Egos were often set aside and decisions made primarily with the view to rapidly learn from mistakes.

The flipside of this was a culture where mistakes were expected as part of experimentation and readily owned up to. Saha talks about how a culture of owning up to one's mistakes was deeply embedded at IIMA.[64] This was modeled most directly by Ravi Matthai himself, who would personally call up individuals and apologize if he had erred in any way.

But he sounds a note of caution:

> Articulation is no substitute for doing. And by doing, you discover much more than new facets of knowledge and problems of implementation. By doing you discover your own capabilities or the lack of them. By doing you discover as to whether you have the capability of making the leap from the point where analysis ends to the point where solutions begin, whether you have the capability of making the leap from the point where the systematic ends and where the creativity begins. Have you the capacity to bridge the gap from where knowledge ends and inspiration begins? Have you the capacity to bridge the gap from where Science ends and Art begins? This is the value of doing: to learn what no book can provide–the discovery of your own capabilities.[65]

[63] Koshy, A. (2011). 'The Post Graduate Program: An Introspective Commentary', in Chand and Rao (eds), *Nurturing Institutional Excellence*, p. 279.

[64] Saha, 'IIMA's Quest for Excellence', in Chand and Rao (eds), *Nurturing Institutional Excellence*, p. 30.

[65] Matthai, 'Learning and Organizational Culture', in Sheth (ed.), *Occasional Speeches and Writings of Ravi Matthai*, pp. 121–2.

So the emphasis was always on doing and in doing so, IIMA made sure that great ideas were translated into practice.

Teaching

The area where the emphasis on doing flourished most was in teaching, and the culture that got built emphasized excellence.

Teaching Preparation, Faculty Grading, and Student Feedback

Chaudhuri indicates the thoroughness with which the faculty at IIMA approach the teaching.[66] He says:

> in the early days, faculty members spent a lot of time preparing for class. They would prepare the course outline after a lot of discussion on the objective of each session, read the case several times, discuss teaching strategies with co-teachers, prepare board plans in great detail, sit through each other's classes and after class, discuss the teaching experiences, and identify areas where improvements could be made. A lot of time was spent choosing appropriate cases that match the stated objectives of the sessions. Many faculty members asked for midterm feedback from the students, so that they could make midcourse corrections that might include the addition of new cases, change of cases, and addition of new topics is possible, and change in pedagogy, if required.

This thoroughness of approach in terms of teaching is unprecedented in India at least and borders on the sacred.

Another faculty member indicated that he never found any institution anywhere else in India or internationally for that matter, where so much energy was devoted to good teaching.[67] Another alumnus of IIMA, who went on to do a PhD in one of the leading business schools in the world, is currently a Chair Professor in another leading business school after having taught in other leading business schools, and a thought leader in the management profession, indicates that he has never found better teaching than at IIMA (personal communication).

---

[66] Chaudhuri, S. 'Institution Building at IIMA: Key Aspects, Experiences and Reflections', in Chand and Rao (eds), *Nurturing Institutional Excellence*, p. 207.

[67] T.V. Rao, 'Change at IIMA', in Chand and Rao (eds), *Nurturing Institutional Excellence*, p. 447.

Teaching always came first at IIMA. S. Bhatnagar indicates how he had to give up the opportunity to discuss a million-dollar grant to IIMA at a meeting in Delhi, because it clashed with the previously scheduled executive education program in Goa.[68]

All this indicates the seriousness with which good teaching was approached at IIMA.

Case Method

One of the key aspects of teaching at IIMA was the use of the case method.

IIMA pioneered the use of the case method in India with the help of Harvard Business School. It should be emphasized, contrary to popular belief, that this method of teaching is still not very widespread in India even in business schools. None of the other IIMs emphasize the case method quite as much. The reason is quite simple, that it takes a lot of preparation on the part of everyone concerned, most of all, the faculty member. Not everyone is willing to put in this much effort, time and energy to make it all work. It also requires training and support services of the highest order.

In the case method the process is not teacher centric but student centric.[69] In fact the students are always referred to as 'participants' because through their participation, they co-create the learning environment in class.

Hold Oneself Accountable to All Stakeholders and Ethics

There has been a tradition at IIMA of holding oneself accountable to all stakeholders.[70] Once, the students complained to the Director saying that while he was known to the world, the students on campus hardly knew him. Rather than being defensive, his response was to invite the students over for tea in small groups.

---

[68] Bhatnagar, S. 'Reflections of IIMA Culture: A Personal Perspective', in Chand and Rao (eds), *Nurturing Institutional Excellence*, p. 170.

[69] Chaudhuri, S. (2011). 'Institution Building at IIMA: Key Aspects, Experiences and Reflections', in Chand and Rao (eds), *Nurturing Institutional Excellence*, p. 201.

[70] Bhatnagar. 'Reflections of IIMA Culture: A Personal Perspective', p. 175.

Social Conscience

From the start IIMA has always had a social conscience. It did not just focus on business and industry but also in agriculture.[71] IIMA developed very innovative programs for the cooperative sector, while working very closely with Amul, the milk cooperative in Gujarat.[72]

IIMA has had a nearly unbroken history since its founding of running Faculty Development Programs (FDP) which have dramatically helped catalyze the creation of a cadre of management faculty members, who have been employed by leading business schools in India and abroad. Indeed it may be said that the broad expansion in the Indian management education sector has been made possible in part by seeding participants in IIMA's FDPs.[73]

And, the institution has always championed out-of-the-way social projects. Matthai put it beautifully:

> many organizations can use your help such as hospitals, schools, colleges, and social work projects dealing with slum clearance, family planning, sanitary conditions, and nutrition. Even municipalities and corporations dealing with the infrastructure of established communities can use your help. How many of you would spend your annual leave in a village? To do all this does not require a vast organization or the explicit sponsorship of the Institute. If you want to be useful, just use your initiative to decide your destination, arrange logistics, and the just board the train with your bedding roll and a dream.[74]

This is what Ravi Matthai did with the famous Jawaja project.

[71] Desai, D.K. 'Centre for Management in Agriculture: An Innovation', in R.J. Matthai, S.K. Bhattacharyya, S.S. Rao, H.N. Pathak, et al. (eds), *Institution Building: The IIMA Experience. Volume 1: The Early Years* (Ahmedabad: Ravi Matthai Centre for Educational Innovation. Indian Institute of Management-Ahmedabad, 1993), p. 64.

[72] Desai, 'Centre for Management in Agriculture', in R.J. Matthai, S.K. Bhattacharyya, S. Rao, H.N. Pathak, et al. (eds), *Institution Building*, pp. 66–7.

[73] Chand, V. S. 'IIMA and Its Faculty Development Mission', in Chand and Rao (eds), *Nurturing Institutional Excellence*, p. 338.

[74] Matthai, 'Tasks Before Management Institutions', Convocation Address delivered at the Indian Institute of Management Calcutta (15 April 1974), in Sheth (ed.), *Occasional Speeches and Writings of Ravi Matthai* (Ahmedabad: Centre for Educational Innovation. Indian Institute of Management Ahmedabad, 1989h), p. 49.

A look at the papers collected in Matthai's book[75] indicates that he personally took an interest in, and prepared notes on entities as diverse as: the National Institute of Design,[76] National Chemical Laboratory,[77] Mahatma Phule Krishi Vishwavidyalaya, Rahuri,[78] Northeastern Hill University,[79] the Doon School, Institute of National Planning in Cairo[80] to name but a selection. Unlike most other notes of this type that are formulaic in their thinking, they attempt to look with fresh eyes at existing problems. In each case, the note is thought provoking and relevant even today. This is but a small sample of what Ravi Matthai had personally contributed to national building in India and outside India. Of course, the contributions of others at IIMA on this score have been enormous.

Resisting Pressure

Samuel Paul has written that the autonomy of the Institute was absolute and even the Chairman had very little ability to influence the core processes of the Institute.[81] The example that he cites is that of the Chairman's grandson who was denied admission to IIMA. He writes how he got a call from the Chairman's daughter-in-law who wanted to speak to

[75] R. Matthai, 'Vikram Sarabhai and IIMA', in Sheth (ed.), *Occasional Speeches and Writings of Ravi Matthai* (Ahmedabad: Centre for Educational Innovation. Indian Institute of Management Ahmedabad, 1989i).

[76] Matthai, 'National Institute of Design: The Organization (A)', in N. Sheth (ed.), *Occasional Speeches and Writings of Ravi Matthai* (Ahmedabad: Centre for Educational Innovation. Indian Institute of Management Ahmedabad, 1989f).

[77] Matthai, 'National Chemical Laboratory: Problems of Working Together', in Sheth (ed.), *Occasional Speeches and Writings of Ravi Matthai* (Ahmedabad: Centre for Educational Innovation. Indian Institute of Management Ahmedabad, 1989e).

[78] Matthai, 'Mahatma Phule Krishi Vishwavidyalaya, Rahuri', in N. Sheth (ed.), *Occasional Speeches and Writings of Ravi Matthai* (Ahmedabad: Centre for Educational Innovation. Indian Institute of Management Ahmedabad, 1989d).

[79] Matthai, 'North-Eastern Hill University', in Sheth (ed.), *Occasional Speeches and Writings of Ravi Matthai* (Ahmedabad: Centre for Educational Innovation. Indian Institute of Management Ahmedabad 1989g).

[80] Matthai, 'The Institute of National Planning, Cairo: Note on Reorganization', in Sheth (ed.), *Occasional Speeches and Writings of Ravi Matthai* (Ahmedabad: Centre for Educational Innovation. Indian Institute of Management Ahmedabad, 1989b).

[81] S. Paul, *A Life and Its Lessons: Memoirs* (Public Affairs Centre, 2012), pp. 119–20.

him about a confidential issue. When she met him she confided that her son had been unable to get through to IIMA and she had come not to complain about the decision but only to seek his advice about what his son should do instead.

Saha makes a similar point about how conflicts of interest were handled in the course of admission interviews where people sought a change of panels if the candidate was known to them, or if close relatives were going to be interviewed, how the faculty members recused themselves completely from the admissions process that year.[82]

Khandwalla mentions an instance where the Prime Minister's Office tried to help a student who was admitted to the PGP program but could not join because his exams had been delayed at his university and so he could not finish his degree.[83] The Director's office successfully rebuffed this directive. Over time though, the tradition of noninterference has become so well-established, that one rarely hears about any such attempt made in recent years by anyone.

Limitation of Term

One very significant aspect of IIMA's culture is the notion that a director serves one term of five years and then reverts back to the faculty.[84] This was the precedent that was set by Ravi Matthai himself when he stepped down from his position as Director and assumed his duties as an ordinary faculty member.

Empowerment

IIMA built a culture of empowerment. Barua indicates that Ravi Matthai believed that in an academic institution, the leader should behave like the conductor of a classical music orchestra, that is, as a coordinator.[85] He indicates 'as a leader, he practiced the art of never having to exercise his authority'. Through this process, he achieved remarkable harmony. Empowering

[82] Saha, 'IIMA's Quest for Excellence', in Chand and Rao (eds), *Nurturing Institutional Excellence*, p. 31.

[83] Khandwalla, P. 'Institution Building at IIMA', in Chand and Rao (eds), *Nurturing Institutional Excellence*, p. 20.

[84] Bhatnagar, 'Reflections of IIMA Culture', p. 174.

[85] Barua, 'IIMA at 50: In Retrospect', in Chand and Rao (eds), *Nurturing Institutional Excellence*, pp. 5–6.

individuals carried with it many risks of mistakes committed in the short run. However, in the long run it strengthened the institution and removed its dependence on any one individual or on a small group of individuals. This was, in fact, a way to build resilience.

Barua indicates that mutually reinforcing processes and culture were built at IIMA.[86] Two of these values were equality and openness. Knowing that both did not come easily in the context of a very hierarchical Indian social system in which IIMA was embedded, he found a simple method of reinforcing equality–he insisted on everyone addressing him using his first name, as has been indicated earlier.

CONSEQUENCES

One example of the resilience of the culture of IIMA is its ability to cope with crises of which there have been many in the history of Ahmedabad.

Pillai indicates that the processes at IIMA were resilient enough to withstand several major shocks.[87] On Republic Day in 2001, Gujarat was hit by a severe earthquake, one of the worst ever, while Chaos, the student-run festival, was on. Large numbers of students had come on campus from outside of Ahmedabad. Many buildings on campus including houses of both faculty and staff, and dorms were badly damaged. Many staff members who commuted to work at IIMA, were rendered homeless because their houses had collapsed. He adds:

> Managing all this was a Herculean task, but the community as a whole rose to the occasion. Students who came from other educational institutions were sent back; temporary tents were put up to accommodate students, staff and their families; volunteer bodies were formed which visited the staff houses outside the campus and assessed the damage; several staff members staying outside the campus were given shelter inside the campus. Institute staff especially from engineering, stores, and housekeeping worked a day in and day out, and in record time and repaired the damage to the buildings and normal life was restored.

[86] Barua, 'IIMA at 50', in Chand and Rao (eds), *Nurturing Institutional Excellence*, p. 5.

[87] Pillai, N. V. 'The Impact of Administrative Actions on the IIMA Culture', in Chand and Rao (eds), *Nurturing Institutional Excellence*, p. 181.

Another crisis erupted in 2003 when the CAT admission test paper was leaked and the exercise had to be conducted all over again. The government ordered a CBI inquiry and the strong media spotlight was on IIMA. The inquiry found no wrongdoing at the Institute which weathered the storm without a hiccup. The most severe crisis, of course, erupted in 2004 when the Ministry of Human Resource Development (HRD) decided to unilaterally change the fee structure at IIMA. This too was weathered by IIMA.

A TALE OF TWO INSTITUTES

It is now interesting to examine a case study to see how the culture built up at IIMA paid handsome dividends.

Outside of IIMA and IIMC, it is a little known fact that these two institutions were set up within a year of each other. What is even more interesting is that IIMC is the older of the two institutions. In the early 1960s, if you had been asked to predict which of the two institutions had a brighter future, the answer would have been IIMC. During that period, Calcutta was the clear intellectual centre of India almost across the board and especially so in the various disciplines of the social sciences. Bengal was the centre of the Indian Renaissance and its early contact with the British and with their institutions of learning meant that it had a head start in all academic matters. Many of the leading intellectuals of India were, and are, of Bengali origin. It had storied institutions such as Calcutta University (with such world-famous colleges such as Presidency College—now a university all by itself), Jadavpur University and the Indian Statistical Institute among others. By contrast, Ahmedabad simply did not have front rank academic institutions at that time nor was it a major cultural centre.

Calcutta was also the hub of heavy industry. On account of its location near eastern India's coal and iron ore mines, as well as its proximity to a major river and a large seaport, that is where the early heavy industrialization of India happened. Many of the large Indian and British manufacturing firms were located there. By contrast, Ahmedabad was one of the two hubs (the other one being Bombay) of the Indian textile industry and had some chemical plants, but was nowhere near as central in India's industrial landscape. The Sabarmati river was seasonal and the nearest port was quite far away.

As a result, for sometime after its founding, many people at IIMA had a huge inferiority complex vis-à-vis IIMC.

It was very much on the minds of the faculty.[88]

> When I joined the Institute in 1964, one of the themes which the faculty group constantly discussed was the inherent advantages of Ahmedabad compared to Calcutta where academic luminaries such as William Kennedy, Shiv Gupta, Ravi Matthai, Ishwar Dayal, Kamini Adhikary and Ashok Mitra were members of the faculty. Each of these persons brought with him or her to IIMC solid professional track record in a particular functional field. At Ahmedabad, we were deeply awed by the stellar cast of the Calcutta faculty and bemoaned that we would not be able to attract the right kind of students or evoke industry and government support due to our lesser luster in the curriculum vitae.

Vikram Sarabhai helped 'confront this myth'. He asked 'whether our apprehensions and concerns were based on purely academic considerations or because of the fear of the inadequacy of our insights and understanding of the management process.' He indicated that the first consideration was ultimately dependent on the second.

Therefore he suggested that 'we immerse ourselves in the business stream, try and understand the context of Indian business and then relate this understanding to the academic process and in turn our products would be more insightful about management processes rather than turn out to be academic geniuses.' Warren Haynes supported Vikram Sarabhai by adding that,

> management related insights are developed, nurtured and refined by writing cases, exposing such cases to the cut and thrust of case discussion and distilling from this writing and teaching process new insights and understandings. These were much more fundamental in their content and valuable in their application compared to all the theories available inside the covers of the management books.

This grounding of the faculty translated into grounding of the students in the real-world empirical problems and their solutions, and translated into far greater acceptability in the corporate world leading to higher salaries, which in turn led to a much higher 'application to admission ratio' for IIMA as compared to the other business schools. This set in place a virtuous cycle, which has paid dividends over the years and created an unassailable barrier to entry for later entrants into the management education field.

---

[88] Bhattacharyya, 'The Early Years of Institutional Development', pp. 12–13.

But this was not all. IIMA did something else that was to have a far-reaching impact on the evolution of the institution. Vikram Sarabhai and his close collaborator in this endeavour, Professor Kamla Chowdhry, was very clear about putting in place processes that would help create cohesiveness amongst the faculty at IIMA. He decided that the early faculty would come from a wide variety of backgrounds, from government and industry, from practice and academia and from Indian and foreign universities. So how was a cohesive culture created from such a diverse mass of individuals?

One of the most interesting processes by which culture was built at IIMA was through the International Teachers Program (ITP) at Harvard University. This was a program which brought faculty members from around the world for one academic year. Talking about the nine-month training program at Harvard, Ravi Matthai said 'the faculty was sent to the program in groups of six or seven and it was hoped that these groups, in living and working together in a new environment, away from the pressures of their institutional responsibilities, would develop a cohesive camaraderie which would provide the foundation for a stable and mutually understanding and supportive faculty community at the Institute'.[89]

Participants took some MBA courses, attended seminars, had discussions with HBS faculty members, saw how case teaching was done and also participated in doctoral seminars. There were, in addition field trips to major US cities, and institutions, both in the public and in the private sector, were on the itinerary. The funding for the program was usually picked up by an international agency and in the case of IIMA participants, it was the Ford Foundation that picked up the tab. 'The common approach fostered by the exposure to HBS and the sense of camaraderie amongst faculty who had spent time together contributed in a big way.' It created 'a shared sense of purpose'.[90] Dayal mentions that IIMA's young faculty was significantly strengthened in its self-confidence on account of the one-year training program at Harvard.[91] 'The experience of learning and living together forged among them a common perception about education and this factor helped in developing the educational activities of the Institute.'

[89] Matthai, 'Vikram Sarabhai and IIMA', Sheth (ed.), *Occasional Speeches and Writings of Ravi Matthai*, p. 158, 1989i.

[90] Mohan, *Brick by Red Brick*, p. 38.

[91] Dayal, 1993. 'Early Years at IIMA', in R.J. Matthai, S.K. Bhattacharyya, S.S. Rao, H.N. Pathak, et al. (eds), *Institution Building*, p. 61.

One of the professors who went on the ITP indicates that his own group consisted of eight faculty members who while they were abroad interacted with each other and developed the cohesion that would stay with them for the rest of their professional lives.[92]

But S. K. Bhattacharyya reveals a dark secret about the ITP in that it was:

> unorganized and the participants were treated almost as poor second cousins from developing countries. The whole tenor of the ITP was fluid, as the participants neither had the status of learners in the MBA or Executive Development Programmes on campus nor were they accorded the recognition as scholars which accrue to those who are attached to the doctoral program. By and large, they were pretty much left to fend for themselves and had no moorings in the total order of things in school.[93]

But this was precisely what was so interesting about this program. It was so unstructured that it created an enormous amount of anxiety. To deal with this anxiety, the participants from IIMA bonded with each other and became one large support group for one another. This was not so different from basic training in the Armed Forces. The principle there is the same—throw a small group of people together in a hostile, uncertain environment for a defined period of time and let them deal with it. In the process of dealing with adversity and in the process of helping each other, an immense bond develops amongst the members of the small group and allows *esprit de corps* to emerge later on in the organization as a whole.

By contrast, IIMC faculty went to MIT Sloan School individually on their own schedule and in any case it is interesting that very few IIMC faculty took advantage of the offer to go to the US in the first place. Many of them were quite eminent and well-established in their careers, already had PhDs from leading US and other Western schools, and no doubt thought it *infra dig* to attend a program so basic. Those who did go, went and came back individually, according to their own timetables and no group bonding consequently occurred. When they did, they had status as faculty members. By contrast, at HBS, IIMA faculty members were treated as participants in programs.[94]

---

[92] Vora, 1993. 'Some Reflections on Institution Building', in R.J. Matthai, S.K. Bhattacharyya, S.S. Rao, H.N. Pathak, et al. (eds), *Institution Building*, p. 90.

[93] Bhattacharyya, 'The Early Years of Institutional Development', pp. 12–13.

[94] Vora, 'Some Reflections on Institution Building', p. 90.

Two Approaches to Institution Building Again

In truth, there was a deeper issue–a fundamental difference in the educational model of the two institutions. M.N. Vora as a faculty member worked in both IIMC and IIMA and also at the Ford Foundation in Delhi with three MIT professors, who were advisors to IIMC. He spoke very perceptively about IIMC and how it differed from that of IIMA. Knowing that he would be treading on something sensitive, he wrote: 'Some of these views might not be acceptable to my colleagues. I would like to request them to pardon me for expressing my views in this manner.'

He indicates that IIMC believed that the way to build the institution was to attract very well-known professors.[95] The belief was that if half a dozen such faculty members could be persuaded to join, then they in turn could attract other individuals to join them and work with them in small groups. That is what IIMC went about doing–namely recruiting the academic stars in India's social science firmament. However, the star professors turned out to have very big egos and even the Director found it very difficult to handle them. Often they wanted their way even on seemingly minor issues and threatened to leave if they did not get their way. Given that many of these individuals believed that they were lending honour to the institution rather than vice versa, they did not feel that they needed the Institute very much. This led to a very unstable situation, and before long many of these eminent faculty members left; in any case they all had very good alternative offers on account of that stature. In turn, the junior faculty members who came expecting to work with the leading lights were stranded. Faculty who left IIMC included Yoginder Alagh, Ishwar Dayal, T.N. Krishnan, and Ashok Mitra.[96]

By contrast, at IIMA there was no attempt to recruit stars. There was also a conscious attempt to recruit people with industry work experience. These individuals demonstrated a lot of commitment to the Institute. It was the Institute which gave them the 'image' rather than vice versa. The turnover amongst such faculty was much lower and indeed if anyone did leave, the departure had little impact on the Institute. Naturally, there was an enormous emphasis on teamwork and on learning together. No one came with strong ideas about how things should or should not be done.

---

[95] Vora, 'Some Reflections on Institution Building', pp. 84–5.

[96] De, *Ravi John Matthai and the Early Years of IIMC.*

Therefore, working collectively, they were able to choose the best path forward.[97]

But there was a further problem. At IIMC, the faculty were quite eminent in their fields and had a strong disciplinary orientation. They wanted to spend the majority of the time in teaching subjects the way they were taught in universities. Not surprisingly, half to two thirds of the time would be used on teaching theory. The curriculum was drawn, in most cases, from academic journals and articles. There were no people who could champion functional areas such as finance, marketing and so on.[98]

By contrast, at IIMA faculty members were clearly told to first identify the management problem that was to be addressed and secondly, to identify an example of companies that faced that problem, and then illustrate that problem with the case, preferably, of an Indian company. A lot of emphasis was placed on preparing teaching notes that exemplified how Indian companies have developed their own responses to the problems that they faced. Requiring IIMA faculty members to go through this exercise meant that they became very aware of the challenges facing managers in India as well as of the nuances that characterized Indian organizations. Equally importantly in the early days, there was a 'mock teaching' exercise that was followed whereby new cases written by faculty members were tried out on their colleagues and research assistants, who acted as the audience. This practice surely made them better teachers and it exposed them to multiple points of view. It also generated camaraderie and *esprit de corps*.[99]

This problem was compounded by how foreign faculty members contributed to the two institutions. Vora indicates that the first set of foreign faculty members who came to stay at IIMA were doctoral students from HBS.[100] This meant that they were young and could relate to the young faculty members at IIMA. There was a true exchange of views on account of the fact that the doctoral students were not yet set in their ways and were approachable. Senior HBS faculty members came as well, but those were for brief periods of 2 to 3 weeks at a time, when they taught in executive education programs, interacted with the faculty and in general provided guidance on the many aspects of institution building. By contrast, the MIT

---

[97] Vora, 'Some Reflections on Institution Building', pp. 85–6.

[98] Vora, 'Some Reflections on Institution Building', p. 88.

[99] Vora, 'Some Reflections on Institution Building', pp. 89–90.

[100] Vora, 'Some Reflections on Institution Building', p. 86.

faculty members who came to IIMC were much more senior and hence more established in their respective areas. IIMC faculty did not find it easy to talk to them. Similarly, at IIMC there were many Indian faculty members who were already well-established, and they felt no need to talk to the foreign faculty members.[101]

Innovation too, is a collaborative activity that is very much influenced by the culture of an institution. It is not surprising that Hill mentions that innovation was often thwarted at IIMC.[102] They mentioned the example of a one-year program for junior executives that was ultimately abandoned. By contrast, IIMA's 3 Tier Training program was mentioned as an example of a significant innovation. Of course, many such examples of successes at IIMA could be given.

The consequences were there for everyone to see. Hill wrote in the early 1970s that 'since 1965 IIMC has no more than held its own and perhaps even suffered some decline in competence as a result of faculty attrition.[103] The Ahmedabad Institute, in contrast, has been characterized throughout by a slowly but steadily increasing technical capacity, and we see no reason to doubt that this trend will continue.' On the dimension of Normative Commitment they said that 'we would rate the Ahmedabad Institute high on the scale and well above IIMC, which organization may be seriously deficient as regards the commitment of its members to any common set of norms.'

In a few short years, IIMA raced forward fairly and squarely and has never looked back.

LACK OF A CULTURE OF RESEARCH

With all these advantages, IIMA was able to quickly bring itself to the front rank of institutions in India. It is been able to stay there for the past four decades at least. However, it has not been able to catapult itself to the front ranks of management institutions globally. To be sure, there are global

---

[101] Vora, 'Some Reflections on Institution Building', p. 87.

[102] T.M. Hill, W.W. Haynes, H.J. Baumgartel, and S. Paul, *Institution building in India: A study of International Collaboration in Management Education* (Boston MA: Harvard University, Graduate School of Business Administration, 1973), p. 281.

[103] T.M. Hill, W.W. Haynes, H.J. Baumgartel, and S. Paul, *Institution building in India*, p. 280.

rankings in which IIMA has done reasonably well, but those put an inordinate amount of emphasis on student quality and placement. This is where, IIMA absolutely excels. It is perhaps the most selective educational institution in the world as has already been noted above. It also has outstanding teaching. What then causes IIMA to lag behind in global rankings? The answer is clearly a marked lack of research. Samuel Paul bluntly indicates that enough importance was not given to research.[104] This lack of research is well documented.[105] He indicates that the culture of academic seminars never really took off at IIMA. Attendance was sparse in seminars and the comments not constructive. Dayal writes that people shied away from open interaction and from an open critique of the ideas of others (see note 105). Rao (see note 43) also laments that there was poor attendance at seminars.

Why was this the case? Chandra makes some very interesting points about research at IIMA.[106] Given the recent rise of India, post-liberalization, it would not be an exaggeration to say that the eyes of the world are firmly on India (and the BRIC countries in general). It goes without saying that along with growth there are numerous problems that are crying for attention. Why then is more high quality research not happening at IIMA? There has been a debate at IIMA about whether it is desirable to publish in globally peer reviewed journals in the first place. These journals are perceived to be USA centric and therefore biased against researchers from emerging economies. Research and teaching are also perceived in some quarters to be substitutes, where excellence in one precludes excellence in the other. And most interestingly, India is evolving its own methods and frameworks that the world is keenly observing. His reasons are that IIMA has never demanded research, rarely incentivized research, left salaries low which forced people to go in for consulting, penalized bad teaching but never penalized lack of research, accepted the view that both research and teaching are not required for a complete faculty member, and generally not provided the right expectations. There have also been few role models doing outstanding research.

---

[104] S. Paul, 'Building on a Solid Foundation', in R.J. Matthai, S.K. Bhattacharyya, S.S. Rao, H.N. Pathak, et al. (eds), *Institution Building: The IIMA Experience. Volume 1: The Early Years* (Ahmedabad: Ravi Matthai Centre for Educational Innovation. Indian Institute of Management—Ahmedabad, 1993), p. 97.

[105] Dayal, 'Early Years at IIMA', p. 56.

[106] P. Chandra, 'Behind the Red Bricks: Underpinnings of An Academic Culture', in Chand and Rao (eds), *Nurturing Institutional Excellence*, pp. 223–4.

V. Vyas also indicates that the main reason was 'the failure of the Institute's leadership in establishing a relevant research agenda and giving due rewards an appropriate recognition to good researchers'.[107] I. Patel adds that this is because IIMA has always emphasized the 'how' of things as opposed to the 'why'.[108]

Clearly, a culture took root at IIMA, which emphasized teaching and consulting ahead of research. However, the people cited above do not really indicate how such a dysfunction developed in the first place.

The reasons are not far to seek. It has to go back to the founding of IIMA and to the two choices that were made then—the collaboration with Harvard and the choice of Ravi Matthai. At one level these choices could not be faulted. HBS was then, as it is now, one of the most prominent business schools in the world. Yet, at that time in the early 1960s, it did almost no research as it is commonly understood today. This meant that rather than publishing in scholarly journals, HBS faculty wrote cases and published in practitioner-oriented outlets such as Harvard Business Review. However, they had an unmatched consulting profile and were influential advisers to many of the large corporations around the world. As a result, the balance of their energies were invested outside of the world of ideas and of scholarly influence. That at least was the situation in the 1960s. It took HBS right up until the early 1980s to rectify the situation and then too at the cost of a lot of internal turmoil. One of the leaders in this movement at Harvard was Michael Porter. Kiechel quotes him as saying 'Before me everybody had a DBA … After me … I wouldn't hire you in my group unless you had either business economics or some economics training. We were going to bring a new level of rigor in.'[109]

It did not help that Ravi Matthai came from industry and did not have a PhD. He had indicated, as we saw above, that ignorance was his prime virtue and that it allowed him to try things in a new way. However,

[107] V. Vyas, 'My Years at IIMA', in V. Vyas, I. Patel, N. Sheth, et al. (eds), *Institution Building—The IIMA Experience. Volume II—The Subsequent Years* (Ahmedabad: Ravi Matthai Center for Institutional Innovation—Indian Institute of Management, Ahmedabad, 1994), p. 5.

[108] I. Patel, 'The IIMA in 1984—At the Crossroads?' in V. Vyas, I. Patel, N. Sheth, et al. (eds), *Institution Building*, p. 20.

[109] W. Kiechel, *Lords of Strategy: The Secret Intellectual History of the New Corporate World* (Harvard Business Review Press, 2013), p. 136.

precisely because of his background, he did not know what he did not know—namely what does it take to create a culture of research. With regard to teaching management, he could draw upon his experiences as a student, and as a CEO, but with regard to research, it seems he had no direct experience and was largely unaware of what he was missing. It is interesting that in his many papers and books nowhere does he talk about what it means to do research as it is conventionally understood in academia. After stepping down as Director, when he initiated the Jawaja Project he approached it as an NGO rather than as a scholar. The appropriate systems to encourage research were simply not in place. Ravi Matthai simply did not know what he was missing out on. The real question is why Vikram Sarabhai, who was a first-rate scientist and researcher of worldwide eminence, failed to notice this, and if he did notice it, why it was not rectified right in the beginning.

This failing has plagued IIMA to this day, and to a large extent the other IIMs as well, given that they have been heavily influenced by its example.

The flipside of the lack of research is an excessive emphasis on consulting.

At IIMA, it was expected that the consulting assignments that the faculty took up would be novel and consequently would contribute to the development of new cases. Over time however, consulting became a routine activity for earning additional income, and as such many of the assignments that were taken up were non-novel and contributed very little to the furtherance of the objectives of the Institute.[110]

Consulting was not seen originally as primarily a moneymaking venture. It was more about helping faculty get in touch with the ground reality of management and consequently was expected to be a way for them to identify new and interesting research problems to work on.[111] Bhattacharya

---

[110] V.S. Chand and T.V. Rao (eds), *Nurturing Institutional Excellence: Indian Institute of Management Ahmedabad* (Macmillan Publishers India, 2011); J.S. Chhokar, 'Personal Reflections on Institution Building at IIMA', in Chand and Rao (eds), *Nurturing Institutional Excellence*, p. 143.

[111] Patel, 'The IIMA in 1984—At the Crossroads?' in V. Vyas, I. Patel, N. Sheth, et al. (eds), *Institution Building—The IIMA Experience*, pp. 20–1.

indicates, however, that over the years consultancy began to be viewed as a right and as a way primarily to enhance the earning capability of the faculty.[112]

This meant a further diversion of faculty energies from research.

SIX INSTITUTIONAL CULTURES

How does the culture of IIMA relate to other academic organizations? W.H. Bergquist and K. Pawlak identify six institutional cultures in academic settings.[113]

The first is the Collegial Culture. Here the institution is an arena which focuses on knowledge—its production, discussion, and transmission. Secondarily the focus is on the inculcation of values and character amongst the student body.[114]

The second culture is Managerial Culture where the meaning is found by the participants in the effective supervision and management of the various university processes and in goal-directed behaviour. Consequently the emphasis is on the proper definition and measurement of objectives. For students too, the focus then shifts to specific skills and attitudes that lead to success in the real world.[115]

The third culture is Developmental Culture. Here the meaning lies in the meaningful way in which growth and development happens in the entire educational ecosystem and how students, faculty and administrators moved towards maturation of cognitive, emotional and conative functions.[116]

The fourth culture is that of advocacy. In an Advocacy Culture the meaning lies in the special attention paid to the egalitarian character

---

[112] Bhattacharyya, 'The Early Years of Institutional Development', p. 15.

[113] W.H. Bergquist and K. Pawlak, *Engaging the Six Cultures of the Academy: Revised and Expanded Edition of The Four Cultures of the Academy* (Wiley, 2008).

[114] Bergquist and Pawlak, *Engaging the Six Cultures of the Academy*, p. 43.

[115] Bergquist and Pawlak, *Engaging the Six Cultures of the Academy*, p. 43.

[116] Bergquist and Pawlak, *Engaging the Six Cultures of the Academy*, p. 73.

of the policies in force as well as the procedures that promote fair play. Here the worry is about perpetuating a culture of haves and have-nots.[117]

The fifth culture, Tangible Culture: where meaning is found in face-to-face interaction and in a campus that has a significant or dominant residential component. The focus here is on building community values. In short, this is the model of the great research universities and the old liberal arts colleges.[118]

In a Virtual Culture, the sixth and the final culture, the meaning is in being open to interactions with the world. Here, knowledge moves online and the knowledge networks become global, shared, real-time and responsive. In many ways this is the model for the new digital age.[119]

Collegial and managerial cultures are quite old and go back several centuries.[120] The tangible culture is also quite old and goes back to the original organization of the University form. By contrast, developmental and advocacy cultures are much more recent and owe their birth to the countercultural movements of the 1960s. The virtual culture is even more recent and is taking shape largely in response to the exponential growth in communication technologies.

In a presentation Pawlak puts the six cultures along three dimensions. The first dimension mentioned is one which has collegial culture at one end and developmental culture at the other.[121] The second dimension is one which has managerial culture at one end and advocacy culture at the other. The final dimension is one which has tangible culture at one end and virtual culture at the other. This seems to me to be a good way to organize the six cultures. Clearly, every institution of higher learning has different combinations of these six cultures.

---

[117] Bergquist, W., and K. Pawlak (undated), 'Sustainability through Leadership in the Six Cultures of Contemporary Collegiate Institutions', p. 111.

[118] Bergquist and Pawlak, *Engaging the Six Cultures of the Academy*, p. 185.

[119] Bergquist and Pawlak, *Engaging the Six Cultures of the Academy*, p. 147.

[120] Bergquist and Pawlak (undated) 'Sustainability through Leadership in the Six Cultures of Contemporary Collegiate Institutions'.

[121] Pawlak, 'Six Cultures of the Academy'.

If we look at IIMA through these lenses, it becomes very clear that IIMA has a culture that is managerial as opposed to collegial, developmental as opposed to advocacy and tangible as opposed to virtual.

As IIMA navigates the future, it needs to move further along each of three dimensions in the direction of Collegial, Advocacy and Virtual if it is to increase its scholarly footprint and its impact on the world in ways other than through its students.

* * *

When looking at the development of IIMA over half a century of its existence, it is clear that culture played a central role in its development. It was also recognized as being crucially important and as such was formally as well as informally nurtured by all the key founders of IIMA who led by example. In fact, their example became hardwired into the DNA of the organization. The importance of developing the appropriate culture was recognized by all the key founders of IIMA. In particular the institution was very fortunate in having as its first full-time Director, Ravi Matthai, who was unusually attentive to this dimension, and had the self-confidence and the ability to experiment until he got things right.

How then should we summarize IIMA culture? It is characterized by several attributes that, compared to other organizations certainly in India, make it less hierarchical and more informal than is the norm, where there is an emphasis on broad involvement of all the principal stakeholders in major decision making. There is an emphasis on group work, an emphasis on academic excellence in teaching and on the part of students. It is characterized by absolute integrity and transparency and noninterference in the recruitment of students. Further, there is an emphasis on industry contact as well as an emphasis on social commitment. The development of creative courses and projects is emphasized. There is a huge emphasis on autonomy. The clear objective was to build self-sustaining processes at the Institute.

But this perspective should be supplemented by a clear appreciation of its principal failing which is lack of emphasis on globally visible, published research that can be the basis of research for other scholars. In fact, significant, globally published research is the major component missing in IIMA's portfolio and unless this problem is addressed head on, IIMA's educational mission would be incomplete.

In the years to come, this will be the principal challenge at IIMA.

ACKNOWLEDGEMENTS

I thank Bhavesh Sherasiya and Sujatha Jayprakash for excellent research assistance. All remaining errors, however, are my own.

12 Challenges of Creating a World-Class Global Private University in India

Perspective of an Administrator

Y.S.R. Murthy

In the first part of this chapter, state obligations relating to the right to education are reviewed while the second part deals with the higher education scenario in the country. In the third part, the vision and mission of O.P. Jindal Global University have been discussed while impediments in the way of creating a world class global university are covered in the fourth part. In this part, an attempt has been made to analyse the challenges in the backdrop of state obligations. The final observations have been presented in the fifth part.

NORMATIVE CONTENT OF RIGHT TO EDUCATION

Education is both a human right in itself and an indispensable means of realizing other human rights.[1]

Referring to the importance of education, the United Nations Committee on Economic, Social and Cultural Rights observes that *'a well-educated, enlightened and active mind, able to wander freely and widely, is one of the joys and rewards of human existence'.*[2]

The Universal Declaration of Human Rights, 1948 proclaims that *'education shall be directed to the full development of the human personality'.*[3] This assertion is echoed in the International Covenant on Economic, Social and Cultural Rights, 1966 which further states that education shall be directed to the human personality's 'sense of dignity'. Further, it shall *'enable all persons to participate effectively in a*

---

[1] Committee on Economic, Social and Cultural Rights, General Comment 13, The right to education (Twenty-first session, 1999), U.N. Doc. E/C.12/1999/10 (1999), reprinted in Compilation of General Comments and General Recommendations Adopted by Human Rights Treaty Bodies, U.N. Doc. HRI/GEN/1/Rev.6 at 70 (2003). The General comment 13 further says that, 'As an empowerment right, education is the primary vehicle by which economically and socially marginalized adults and children can lift themselves out of poverty and obtain the means to participate fully in their communities. Education has a vital role in empowering women, safeguarding children from exploitative and hazardous labour and sexual exploitation, promoting human rights and democracy, protecting the environment, and controlling population growth. Increasingly, education is recognized as one of the best financial investments States can make.'

[2] Committee on Economic, Social and Cultural Rights, General Comment 13, The right to education (Twenty-first session, 1999), U.N. Doc. E/C.12/1999/10 (1999), reprinted in Compilation of General Comments and General Recommendations Adopted by Human Rights Treaty Bodies, U.N. Doc. HRI/GEN/1/Rev.6 at 70 (2003). The General comment 13 further says that, 'As an empowerment right, education is the primary vehicle by which economically and socially marginalized adults and children can lift themselves out of poverty and obtain the means to participate fully in their communities. Education has a vital role in empowering women, safeguarding children from exploitative and hazardous labour and sexual exploitation, promoting human rights and democracy, protecting the environment, and controlling population growth. Increasingly, education is recognized as one of the best financial investments States can make.'

[3] Article 26(2) of the Universal Declaration of Human Rights, 1948.

free society, and promote understanding among all 'ethnic' groups, as well as nations and racial and religious groups.[4] We need to be mindful of these laudable educational objectives set out in the core international human rights treaties.

Article 13(2)C of the International Covenant on Economic, Social, and Cultural Rights stipulates that, *'Higher education shall be made equally accessible to all, on the basis of capacity, by every appropriate means, and in particular by the progressive introduction of free education'.*[5] While elaborating the normative content of right to education, the Committee on Economic, Social and Cultural Rights stated that education in all its forms and at all levels shall exhibit the following interrelated and essential features viz., availability,[6]

---

[4] See Article 13(1) of the International Covenant on Economic, Social and Cultural Rights which states that, 'The States Parties to the present Covenant recognize the right of everyone to education. They agree that education shall be directed to the full development of the human personality and the sense of its dignity, and shall strengthen the respect for human rights and fundamental freedoms. They further agree that education shall enable all persons to participate effectively in a free society, promote understanding, tolerance and friendship among all nations and all racial, ethnic or religious groups, and further the activities of the United Nations for the maintenance of peace.'

[5] See Article 13(1) of the International Covenant on Economic, Social and Cultural Rights which states that, 'The States Parties to the present Covenant recognize the right of everyone to education. They agree that education shall be directed to the full development of the human personality and the sense of its dignity, and shall strengthen the respect for human rights and fundamental freedoms. They further agree that education shall enable all persons to participate effectively in a free society, promote understanding, tolerance and friendship among all nations and all racial, ethnic or religious groups, and further the activities of the United Nations for the maintenance of peace.'

[6] Availability-functioning educational institutions and programmes have to be available in sufficient quantity within the jurisdiction of the State party. What they require to function depends upon numerous factors, including the developmental context within which they operate; for example, all institutions and programmes are likely to require buildings or other protection from the elements, sanitation facilities for both sexes, safe drinking water, trained teachers receiving domestically competitive salaries, teaching materials, and so on; while some will also require facilities such as a library, computer facilities and information technology.

accessibility,[7] acceptability,[8] and adaptability.[9] When considering the appropriate application of these 'interrelated and essential features', the Committee held that the best interests of the student shall be a primary consideration. While interpreting '[P]rogressive introduction of free education', the Committee noted that while *States must prioritize the provision of free primary education, they also have an obligation to take concrete steps towards achieving free secondary and higher education*.[10]

[7] Accessibility-educational institutions and programmes have to be accessible to everyone, without discrimination, within the jurisdiction of the State party. Accessibility has three overlapping dimensions:

Non-discrimination-education must be accessible to all, especially the most vulnerable groups, in law and fact, without discrimination on any of the prohibited grounds (see paras. 31–37 on non-discrimination);

Physical accessibility-education has to be within safe physical reach, either by attendance at some reasonably convenient geographic location (e.g., a neighbourhood school) or via modern technology (e.g., access to a 'distance learning' programme);

Economic accessibility-education has to be affordable to all. This dimension of accessibility is subject to the differential wording of Article 13(2) in relation to primary, secondary and higher education: whereas primary education shall be available 'free to all', States parties are required to progressively introduce free secondary and higher education;

[8] Acceptability-the form and substance of education, including curricula and teaching methods, have to be acceptable (e.g., relevant, culturally appropriate and of good quality) to students and, in appropriate cases, parents; this is subject to the educational objectives required by Article 13(1) and such minimum educational standards as may be approved by the State (see Article 13(3) and (4));

[9] Adaptability-education has to be flexible so it can adapt to the needs of changing societies and communities and respond to the needs of students within their diverse social and cultural settings.

[10] For the Committee's general observations on the meaning of the word 'free', see paragraph 7 of General Comment 11 on article 14.' Free of charge. The nature of this requirement is unequivocal. The right is expressly formulated so as to ensure the availability of primary education without charge to the child, parents or guardians. Fees imposed by the Government, the local authorities or the school, and other direct costs, constitute disincentives to the enjoyment of the right and may jeopardize its realization. They are also often highly regressive in effect. Their elimination is a matter which must be addressed by the required plan of action. Indirect costs, such as compulsory levies on parents (sometimes portrayed as being

All human rights treaties impose three types of obligations on states parties: the obligations to respect, protect, and fulfil. In the context of right to education, the obligation to respect requires states parties to avoid measures that hinder or prevent the enjoyment of the right to education. The obligation to protect requires states parties to take measures that prevent third parties from interfering with the enjoyment of the right to education. The obligation to fulfil incorporates both an obligation to facilitate and an obligation to provide. The obligation to fulfil requires states to take positive measures that enable and assist individuals and communities to enjoy the right to education.[11]

HIGHER EDUCATION SCENARIO IN INDIA

India's higher education sector is the largest in the world in terms of its size.[12] It has registered significant growth in the past two decades. There are over 38,000 formal degree/diploma granting higher education institutes. Sixty-four per cent of the total number of higher education institutions in the country are private. The total number of universities in the country as on 26 November 2014 is 693 of which, 325 are state universities while there are 128 Deemed to be universities. There are 45 central universities and 195 private universities.[13]

---

voluntary, when in fact they are not), or the obligation to wear a relatively expensive school uniform, can also fall into the same category. Other indirect costs may be permissible, subject to the Committee's examination on a case-by-case basis. This provision of compulsory primary education in no way conflicts with the right recognized in article 13.3 of the Covenant for parents and guardians 'to choose for their children schools other than those established by the public authorities'.

[11] Committee on Economic, Social and Cultural Rights, General Comment 3.

[12] Third largest education system in the world, in terms of enrolment, and the largest by total number of academic institutions the India, see ASHE 2014. Currently, about 687 universities and 37,204 colleges constitute the country's higher education sector.

[13] See University Grants Commission 'Annual Status of Higher Education in States and UTs in India (ASHE)', *Ministry of Human Resource Development (MHRD), Government of India* and *Confederation of Indian Industry* (2014), http://cii.in/PublicationDetail.aspx?enc=/z6B6nKIqSaHCwm+0ZNgb5TZYvB WuFf+ZTbQX6RN2bL7LuoRBe84gws7QT1SgfMKOiBsKPSTNta2jos8O9uc b65w5E1QLYb+GiWcBna2Qzo4c11rwgmQWiRe/pmfbBii89kLoTcz+AFdv9n

India has a low Gross Enrolment Ratio (GER) of 20 per cent as compared to many developed countries.[14] Likewise, the higher education spending in India at 1.1 per cent of GDP is also less as compared to many other developed countries.[15] There is an urgent need to increase GER as well as higher education expenditure in a significant manner.

With regard to the higher education sector, the National Knowledge Commission (NKC) underscored the need to focus on three key aspects of expansion, excellence and inclusion. It has recommended increasing GER in higher education to 15 per cent and above by 2015 by adding that in addition to increased public spending, '*this would involve diversifying the sources of financing to encourage private participation, philanthropic contributions and industry linkages*'.[16] Towards this end, NKC recommended the creation of 1500 universities by 2015. It is a matter of deep regret that this goal is still a long way off.

Referring to the inadequacy of government funding to the higher education sector, NKC stressed the need to stimulate private investments as a means of extending educational opportunities in higher education. In order to overcome impediments in the way of expansion, NKC recommended setting up an Independent Regulatory Authority for Higher Education (IRAHE), which would be at an arm's length from all stakeholders and would accord degree granting power to universities. To ensure quality, NKC called for reform of existing universities to ensure frequent curricula revisions, introduction of course credit system, enhancing reliance on internal assessment, encouraging research, and reforming governance

---

0984a3NGBnVQfV6RuQw1tcrx60sjdKBryieV9BLSNvKTEOuY2, accessed on 6 May 2015.

[14] US has GER of 84 per cent while it is 59 per cent in the UK, 55 per cent in Japan, and 28 per cent in China. See Report of NR Narayana Murthy Committee on Corporate Participation in Higher Education, Planning Commission, New Delhi, 2012, see Foreword.

[15] US has GER of 84 per cent while it is 59 per cent in the UK, 55 per cent in Japan, and 28 per cent in China. See Report of NR Narayana Murthy Committee on Corporate Participation in Higher Education, Planning Commission, New Delhi, 2012, see Foreword. The US spends 3.1 per cent of its GDP on higher education while South Korea spends 2.4 per cent of its GDP on the same.

[16] See 'Report to the Nation 2006–09,' *National Knowledge Commission, Government of India* (2009): 14–15.

of institutions.[17] All these issues identified by NKC are noteworthy while reviewing the context of higher education scenario in the country.

Keeping in view the steady growth in student enrolment in the past ten years, Narayana Murthy Committee notes that the demand for higher education will 'increase at a compounded rate of 11–12 per cent till 2022 and will require an additional capacity of about 26 million seats over the next decade. This would result in increased demand for institutions to educate and make employable the vast number of students who would join the system' in the coming years.[18]

Referring to the problems afflicting the higher education sector, Narayana Murthy Committee cites, 'inadequate number of institutions to educate eligible students, poor employability of the graduates produced by the universities,[19] low and declining standards of academic research, an unwieldy affiliating system, an inflexible academic structure, an archaic regulatory environment, eroding autonomy and low levels of public funding, to name a few'.[20] In terms of graduates, while their absolute number looks impressive, there exist serious questions regarding their employability. Each one of these issues needs to be addressed in a mission mode and in a concerted manner. It is important to bear these in mind while discussing the context of higher education in India.

In addition to the above, the number of vacant posts in the higher education sector is staggering.[21] Student-faculty ratio is much worse than the

---

[17] See 'Report to the Nation 2006–09.'

[18] See 'Report to the Nation 2006–09.'

[19] 'Report to the Nation 2006–09', 14–15. According to NASSCOM, only 25 per cent of the pool of graduates available for IT/ITES industry is readily employable. Similar challenges are faced across engineering as well as other disciplines and industries, including public institutions.

[20] 'Report to the Nation 2006–09', 14–15. According to NASSCOM, only 25 per cent of the pool of graduates available for IT/ITES industry is readily employable. Similar challenges are faced across engineering as well as other disciplines and industries, including public institutions.

[21] 'Report to the Nation 2006–09', 14–15. According to NASSCOM, only 25 per cent of the pool of graduates available for IT/ITES industry is readily employable. Similar challenges are faced across engineering as well as other disciplines and industries, including public institutions. According to the FICCI-E&Y report, '45 per cent of the positions for professors, 51 per cent positions for readers, and 53 per cent positions for lecturers were vacant in Indian universities in 2007–08'.

desired norm of 15:1[22] and pales into insignificance when contrasted with the best institutions in USA and elsewhere. As regards quality of physical infrastructure, one study has noted that 73 per cent of colleges and 68 per cent of universities in India fall under medium or low quality.[23] When one evaluates academic standards, outdated curricula, and ill-equipped libraries, among other things, present as serious challenges. [24]

The resources of National Assessment and Accreditation Council (NAAC) are stretched. Only a small fraction of higher educational institutions have been accredited thereby leaving us with the problem of a large number of unaccredited institutions.[25] The quality of NAAC certification itself is contested by many.

According to Annual Status of Higher Education in States and UTs 2014 (ASHE 2014), 'The rapid growth witnessed in the higher education

---

[22] 'Report to the Nation 2006–09', 14–15. According to NASSCOM, only 25 per cent of the pool of graduates available for IT/ITES industry is readily employable. Similar challenges are faced across engineering as well as other disciplines and industries, including public institutions.. *'According to statistics from the Ministry of Human Resources Development, the student to teacher ratio in an average higher education institution is 26:1, compared to the norm of 15:1. It is also quite adverse in comparison to national and international benchmarks. This ratio is 11:1 for the Indian Institutes of Management. According to The Princeton Review, it is 7:1 for Harvard University and 5:1 for Stanford University'.*

[23] 'Report to the Nation 2006–09', 14–15. According to NASSCOM, only 25 per cent of the pool of graduates available for IT/ITES industry is readily employable. Similar challenges are faced across engineering as well as other disciplines and industries, including public institutions. A study by UGC of infrastructure quality of 1,471 colleges and 111 universities revealed deficient physical infrastructure.

[24] 'Report to the Nation 2006–09', 14–15. According to NASSCOM, only 25 per cent of the pool of graduates available for IT/ITES industry is readily employable. Similar challenges are faced across engineering as well as other disciplines and industries, including public institutions. *'As per the FICCI-E&Y report, the number of books per student in the library of an average higher education institution in India is just 9 compared with 53 at IIT Bombay and 810 at Harvard University.'*

[25] 'Report to the Nation 2006–09', 14–15. According to NASSCOM, only 25 per cent of the pool of graduates available for IT/ITES industry is readily employable. Similar challenges are faced across engineering as well as other disciplines and industries, including public institutions. *As of March 2011, only 161 universities and 4,371 colleges had been accredited by the National Assessment and Accreditation Council (NAAC).*

sector has generated numerous challenges with the key ones being maintaining quality, improving equity and providing access to each and every student based in any part of the country. In terms of global exposure and achieving internationalization, our country has a long way to go'.[26]

ASHE 2014 cites a number of factors as responsible for the growth of higher education in India. More than 50 per cent of India's population is under 25 years of age and this crucial demographic indicator is a major driver besides 'widening demand-supply gap; increasing dominance and public trust on private sector institutions; fast growing IT services sector leading to demand for skilled talent pool; rising FDI in the manufacturing and affiliated sectors and the recent thrust provided by the government on online education'.[27]

The National Knowledge Commission has estimated that India needs an investment of about US$ 190 billion to achieve the GER target of 30 per cent by 2020. Keeping in view that just 1 per cent of the GDP being spent on higher education currently, ASHE 2014 strongly advocates for a crucial role for private sector to achieve this daunting task.[28]

Referring to the Yashpal Committee Report of 2009, ASHE 2014 observes that '*lack of coordination and communication among the statutory authorities, along with the existence of multiple regulators in the sector, has been identified as one of the primary challenges for the higher education sector. The complexity of overlapping mandates has further been compounded by archaic regulations that have little or no relevance in the dynamic business environment prevailing today*'.[29]

Private institutions as well as government-run institutions suffer from a dearth of adequate resources for faculty improvement and quality upgradation. These inadequacies impact students. ASHE 2014 strongly argues in favour of 'raising the overall quality of institutions therefore, irrespective of their lineage, is going to have a huge economic benefit as well'.[30]

Highlighting the need for increased private sector participation in the higher education sector, ASHE 2014 underscores the need 'to simplify prevailing regulatory framework and overall higher education ecosystem'.

[26] 'Annual Status of Higher Education in States and UTs in India (ASHE)' (2014).

[27] 'Annual Status of Higher Education in States and UTs in India (ASHE)'.

[28] 'Annual Status of Higher Education in States and UTs in India (ASHE)'.

[29] 'Annual Status of Higher Education in States and UTs in India (ASHE)'.

[30] 'Annual Status of Higher Education in States and UTs in India (ASHE)'.

Rashtriya Uchchatar Shiksha Abhiyan (RUSA) also advocates the enactment of new policies and regulations to encourage private investment.[31]

Not a single university from India figures in the Top 200 Universities of the World in Times Higher Education, QS and other major rankings as of 1 March 2013. All higher educational institutions in India need to ponder over this issue as to how to achieve excellence and get into top positions in these rankings. This is a serious challenge which needs to be addressed.

If one takes a careful look at the series of important recommendations made the Narayana Murthy Committee, the problems bedevilling the higher education sector become self-evident. The Committee made recommendations towards creating enabling conditions to make the higher education system robust and useful to attract investments. They include, among others, the following:

1. *Autonomy*—in financial, regulatory, academic and administrative aspects
2. *Resources*—ensuring availability of land, infrastructure and connectivity
3. *Fiscal incentives*—to encourage investments and attracting funding
4. *Enabling environment*—(such as visas) for free movement of faculty and students to promote collaboration with world-class institutions abroad
5. *Freedom to accredit*—with global accreditation agencies to put Indian institutions on par with the best
6. *Access to funds*—through scholarships to enable students to pursue their chosen fields of study'.[32]

The Committee made the following specific recommendations towards corporate participation in improving quality by enhancing research focus and faculty development.

1. '*Enhancing research focus*—through dedicated funding for research, sponsored doctoral programmes, and part-time Masters and PhD programmes.
2. *Faculty development*—by increasing the talent pool of faculty from corporates (working and retired), faculty development programmes, and sponsorships of visits by expert faculty'. [33]

---

[31] 'Annual Status of Higher Education in States and UTs in India (ASHE)'.

[32] Report of NR Narayana Murthy Committee on Corporate Participation in Higher Education, Planning Commission, New Delhi (2012), see Foreword.

[33] Report of NR Narayana Murthy Committee on Corporate Participation in Higher Education, Planning Commission, New Delhi.

As regards fiscal incentives, Narayana Murthy Committee made a far-reaching recommendation. It suggested that 'contributions made by a corporate or a foundation or any other grant-making entity to a university or to a research centre or a centre of excellence (being part of a university or higher education institution) or a new university approved by the government or an approved programme under a university-industry partnership, should be eligible for deduction from taxable income to the extent of 300 per cent of such contribution.'[34] Though this recommendation was made in 2012, the Government of India has still not acted on it.

To give fillip to private initiatives in higher education, the Committee in its wisdom recommended free land for 999 years. It has also recommended the establishment of Rs 1,000 crore scholarship fund with tax exemption for contributions made by the corporate sector in order to cater to the needs of the under privileged.[35]

The Narayana Murthy Committee observed that by '*easing current norms, overcoming systemic challenges, creating a conducive environment for higher education to thrive in and focusing on quality of the institutions and the outcomes (students, research output)*', a select group of Indian higher education institutions could be transformed by the government into world-class institutions and attract investments for new institutions.[36] The committee underscored the need to address these issues to ensure productive participation from the corporate sector and further emphasized the need by the government to 'transform itself from a provider of higher education to play key roles in enabling and establishing an appropriate regulatory framework to set quality standards for higher education.'[37]

Referring to the reform of the higher education, the Vice-Chancellor of O.P. Jindal Global University, Professor Raj Kumar argued that it 'cannot be reformed unless we develop strong private universities that are truly non-profit, philanthropic and committed to promoting academic

[34] Report of NR Narayana Murthy Committee on Corporate Participation in Higher Education, Planning Commission, New Delhi.

[35] Report of NR Narayana Murthy Committee on Corporate Participation in Higher Education, Planning Commission, New Delhi.

[36] Report of NR Narayana Murthy Committee on Corporate Participation in Higher Education, Planning Commission, New Delhi.

[37] Report of NR Narayana Murthy Committee on Corporate Participation in Higher Education, Planning Commission, New Delhi.

freedom'.[38] Pointing out the 'one-size-fits-all' policy followed by the regulators, he observes that 'there is little scope for institutions to be differentiated by the regulators in relation to their own goals and Aspirations'.[39] Professor Kumar laments the fact that 'higher education regulations and institutional mechanisms have, unfortunately, created opportunities for corruption, nepotism, and abuse of power'.[40] Instead of acting as facilitator and institutional mentoring to promote excellence, regulators in India are taking recourse to inspector raj, monitoring, shaming and imposition of sanctions. In the process, they miss the central objective of attaining excellence.[41]

VISION AND MISSION OF O.P. JINDAL GLOBAL UNIVERSITY (JGU)

The vision of establishing JGU is to impart high quality education with a view to produce world-class professionals, scholars, business leaders and academics in law, management and other disciplines. Globalization has opened various opportunities and challenges which have created the need for competent academics, scholars and professionals. The JGU seeks to fulfil this need by equipping its students and faculty with the knowledge, skills, scholarship, and vision to meet these challenges and demands of globalization. India, which is on the verge of becoming an economic superpower, requires world-class professionals, scholars, and academics to compete globally. It is fairly self-evident that excellence in education leads to economic growth and development.[42]

The motto of O.P. Jindal Global University is 'A Private University Promoting Public Service'. The vision of the O.P. Jindal Global University highlights its aspiration to become 'a role model for institutional excellence in higher education among leading institutions in the world as a multidisciplinary, research driven university fostering excellence in teaching, research, community service, and capacity building and nurturing socially responsible leaders through an eclectic and sustainable approach serving the local and

---

[38] Kumar, 'Take a Qualitative Leap', The Week (1 June 2014).
[39] Kumar, 'Take a Qualitative Leap'.
[40] Kumar, 'Take a Qualitative Leap'.
[41] Kumar, 'Take a Qualitative Leap'.
[42] University Brochure 2014', O.P. Jindal Global University.

regional communities.[43] The vision document further notes that through its work, the university will '*build bridges across nations, working with national, international, and governmental organizations, and NGOs, and business organizations*'.[44]

Its vision document recognizes that education is about empowerment of youth and the quality of life and the environment leading to meaningful careers and enriching lives of our students with the central objective of enabling them to become caring and responsible members of society making constructive contributions in the service of humanity. In this context, O.P. Jindal Global University (JGU) aspires to be recognized among the top universities in the world for its excellence in teaching, research, community service and capacity building. The vision of JGU relates to five principal areas of institution building.[45]

First, the university aspires to equip its students to become outstanding global citizens with honesty, personal and professional integrity, and rectitude, having acquired through imaginative pedagogy and a stimulating academic environment, knowledge, skills, and aptitude needed for leadership positions, nationally and internationally, in all communities and professions in which they may choose to serve.[46]

Second, with its focus on applied research outcomes, the university aspires to be a leading knowledge creating institution, benchmarked against international standards, promoting cutting-edge, interdisciplinary research leading to publications which have an impact and thereby extending the boundaries of scholarship and professional practice.

Third, the university aspires to be recognized nationally and internationally as a socially responsible institution *par excellence*, serving the local and regional communities and building bridges across nations, working with national and international governmental and business organizations, NGOs, and such other organizations and enterprises and equipping practitioners from governments, corporations and civil society organizations, in India and abroad, with policy-oriented skills and comparative knowledge of good practices, firmly grounded in professional ethics.[47]

---

[43] See 'Vision Philosophy', *O.P. Jindal Global University*, http://www.jgu.edu.in/JGU/CMS/Overview/VisionMissionCoreValues, accessed on 6 May 2015.

[44] See 'Vision Philosophy'.

[45] Shah, Aman. *JGU Internal Background Paper Relating to Draft Vision.*

[46] Shah, *JGU Internal Background Paper Relating to Draft Vision.*

[47] Shah, *JGU Internal Background Paper Relating to Draft Vision.*

Fourth, the university aspires to be the preferred institution for all stakeholders by engaging in good practices and promoting a culture of excellence in all areas of its work.[48]

Finally, the university aspires to be recognized as a model institution of higher education in the region promoting excellence in institution building and thereby contributing to India's nation building efforts.[49]

Public funds available in India are hardly adequate to meet the needs of higher education. In this backdrop, it is fairly obvious that there is a need for a significant infusion of private funds. The funding gap in higher education could be met through corporate and individual philanthropy. JGU's mission is implemented through corporate philanthropy and commitment to corporate social responsibility of the Jindal Group, which is a multinational Indian corporate business house. JGU is a unique example of providing new opportunities in the field of private, non-profit higher education. To achieve the vision of providing globalized education in India, JGU has recruited the best faculty from across the globe, besides entering into collaborations, exchange programmes, research partnerships, and other forms of engagement and interaction with top universities and institutions across the globe. JGU aspires to build upon the experiences of the past and the innovations in teaching that are taking place at present to create for the future an institution of global excellence.[50]

In pursuit of its Vision, the O.P. Jindal Global University inter alia seeks to;

- Promote a global perspective through a global faculty, global courses, global programmes, global curricula, global research, and global collaborations in an intellectually rigorous research environment, ensuring academic freedom and creative scholarship with functional autonomy.
- Provide an enriching, intellectually exciting, and discovery-based learning environment for students with innovative pedagogy and outcomes based teaching and learning strategies, including opportunities for engaging in interdisciplinary research, summer internships in leading organizations, semester abroad, participation in community service projects, and in national and international academic, cultural and sports events.

[48] Shah, *JGU Internal Background Paper Relating to Draft Vision*.
[49] Shah, *JGU Internal Background Paper Relating to Draft Vision*.
[50] 'University Brochure 2014', *O.P. Jindal Global University*.

- Conduct capacity building and executive education programmes for practitioners from governments, corporations, and civil society organizations to enhance their leadership qualities and skills, management capacity, and commitment to professional ethics.
- Function as a fair and caring employer by promoting equity and diversity and an opportunity for personal and professional growth and development among faculty and staff.[51]

THE CHALLENGES FACED IN CREATING A WORLD CLASS GLOBAL UNIVERSITY

In what follows, various impediments in the way of realizing vision and mission of JGU have been described. There are various challenges faced by a private university in its day-to-day operations.

The private universities don't get any monetary support from either the central or the state government. On the other hand, the regulatory framework hinders the capacity of private universities to operate in an autonomous manner. Real autonomy includes functional as well as financial autonomy.

It is fairly obvious that a university, be it a state or private, must have the freedom to decide on the courses it will offer. This is a decision which its Academic Council or Board of Studies are best suited to make. External regulatory agencies ought to have no role whatsoever in the matter as the university is expected to work out human, financial, and other resources required to offer a particular course. Alas, that is not the case.

The Haryana Private Universities Act, 2006, was amended in 2012. The amended legislation requires a university which wishes to offer a new course to take the approval of the state government.[52] The government will specify the manner in which the university will commence the enrolment of students for the course and shall give 'authorization' to the university to start the course and also 'approve' the procedure thereof. The university

---

[51] See 'Mission', *O.P. Jindal Global University*, http://www.jgu.edu.in/JGU/CMS/Overview/VisionMissionCoreValues, accessed on 6 May 2015.

[52] The exact provision is as follows:

34A. - (1) The university intending to start a new course or programme of study, shall intimate such intention to the government, along with an assessment report as prescribed under the bye-laws.

shall not commence first enrolment of students without specific authorization of the government.

The government may, if it is satisfied that the university is not in a position to efficiently discharge the duties and obligations imposed, cancel the permission to continue the course after making such inquiry, as may be specified by bye-laws.

If the government were to decide issues such as these, what then is the role and relevance of the Academic Council, Board of Studies, and other similar structures in the universities?

After the Haryana Private Universities Act was amended in 2012, JGU started several new courses after obtaining necessary approvals. These include the bachelor's programmes in liberal arts and humanities and global affairs. To be fair to the senior officials in the Department of Higher Education in the Government of Haryana, they cleared these courses after several visits to the state capital. They showed required maturity and sagacity in appreciating the scope of these new courses. It is not difficult to visualize what would be the state of affairs if a dishonest person were at the helm of affairs. Why should a university run from pillar to post in the state capitals and waste precious time when its own bodies should be empowered to make such important decisions? At stake are critical issues concerning institutional autonomy, speed, flexibility to respond to the demands of time, and offer appropriate courses.

In case any degree programme is not properly delivered owing to poor faculty or any other reasons, the students will not get placed thereby endangering future admissions. Market forces have a way of correcting institutional infirmities, if any. Professor Raj Kumar argues

---

(2) *The government shall specify the manner in which the university shall commence enrolment of students for such course or programme of study and* **shall give authorization to the university to start the course or programme of study and also approve the procedure thereof.**

(3) *The university shall not commence first enrolment of students without specific authorization of the government. In no case, the application for authorization be kept pending beyond 120 days, whereafter it shall be deemed to have the concurrence of the government to start the course or programme of study.**

34B. **Power to cancel a course**. - *The government may if it is satisfied that the university is not in a position to efficiently discharge the duties and obligations imposed, it may, after making such inquiry, as may be specified by bye-laws, cancel the permission to continue the course or programme of study.**

that one ought not to make policy keeping in view a few fly-by-night operators among private universities. That would be doing disservice to the efforts of many good private universities seeking to contribute their mite to nation-building.

The revenue model for the private universities is restricted as well. Under the Haryana Private Universities Act, there is a 25 per cent reservation for persons belonging to Haryana domicile[53] based on merit-cum-means and be as follows:

- 1/5th of the 25 per cent shall be granted full fee concession.
- 2/5th of the 25 per cent shall be granted 50 per cent fee concession.
- The balance 2/5th of the 25 per cent shall be granted 25 per cent fee concession.

When the private universities are not funded by the state, what is the justification for restricting the revenue on the lines mentioned above? Aggrieved by such provisions, a private university in Haryana has even moved a court of law challenging these retrograde amendments.

There are problems faced by the private universities in recruiting foreign faculty members which is regulated by legislation. In the interests of global engagement and internationalization, there is a need to attract foreign faculty members. However, the capacity of private universities in this regard is constrained by several factors. Current visa regulations

[53] Section 36 of the Haryana Private Universities Act. 'Fee structure.—(1) The university may, from time to time, prepare fee structure and shall send it for information to the Government, at least 30 days before the commencement of the academic session.

(2) The fee structure for the 25 per cent of the students who are domicile of Haryana shall be based on merit-cum-means and be as follows:

   (i) one-fifth of the 25 per cent shall be granted full fee concession;
   (ii) two-fifths of the 25 per cent shall be granted 50 per cent fee concession;
   (iii) the balance two-fifths of the 25 per cent shall be granted 25 per cent fee concession.*

Provided that in case of the universities having collaboration with reputed foreign or international universities or other institutions of other similar nature, the government may approve different percentage of students eligible for 100 per cent, 50 per cent or 25 per cent fee concession.

(3) The university shall not charge any fee, by whatever name called, other than that prescribed as per sub-sections (1) and (2) above.'

require the payment of a minimum salary of US$ 25,000 per annum. Our own personal experience is that a lot of precious time of senior administrative staff of the university is wasted in chasing Indian Embassies and High Commissions to expedite the issue of visa when in fact all their efforts should be concentrated on academic and other institution building aspects.

The Government of India, Ministry of External Affairs and their embassies, consulates, and missions have a stake and role in promoting our competitive edge and improving higher education in India rather than thwart the efforts of institutions to attract best talent from the world over without proper application of mind and a lack of vision.

Narayana Murthy Committee Report has recommended that 'all academic and research visitors (faculty, students, staff, administrators, and researchers) should be exempt' from the minimum salary requirement of $ 25,000 per annum. However, it is a matter of deep regret that this recommendation has still not been accepted by the government despite a lapse of more than three years.

At the same time, there are also problems in holding international seminars and inviting foreign scholars to participate in them. In the past nearly six years of its operations, the O.P. Jindal Global University has organized scores of international conferences involving distinguished academics from abroad often in collaboration with leading universities of the world. One has to run from pillar to post to get necessary security clearance, political clearance, and clearance from the nodal ministry. At times, some international scholars are unable to negotiate this exacting regime, fail to obtain their visas on time thereby leaving the organizers in the lurch at the last minute scrambling for their replacements.

The Narayana Murthy Committee in its Report observed that 'the existing visa regime is a significant impediment to free exchange of ideas and movement of faculty and students that is essential to building world class institutions'.[54] It therefore recommended a '10-year multiple entry visa for multiple visits of six months duration for each visit for all academic and research visitors (faculty, students, staff, researchers, administrators, and visitors for conferences) should be issued within 24 hours of the

---

[54] See N.R. Narayana Murthy, et al., *Report of the Committee on Corporate Participation in Higher Education* (2012).

application. A visa for five-year visit should be issued within 5 working days.' As with many other progressive recommendations of that Committee, it is yet to be acted upon.

The conservation of environment requires hardly any over emphasis. There is a need for sustainable development and there is a responsibility cast on us to leave the Earth in a safe manner for the use of future generations. Under the Environment Protection Act, certain authorities have been created like the State Pollution Control Board, State Environment Impact Assessment Authority, State Expert Advisory Committee, etc. In 2009, the O.P. Jindal Global University applied to Haryana State Environment Impact Assessment Authority in advance for necessary environment clearance. Though rules stipulate time bound disposal of such proposals, this is very often used as a Damocles' sword over institutions, sapping the energy and time of senior officials. Vice Chancellor and Registrar of JGU have had to make numerous visits to sort out issues related to environment clearance when in fact their creative energies were required for institution-building. When we consider labour, fire, building, town and country planning, and other clearances, the cup of woes is complete with the system plagued by delays, arbitrariness, and at times corruption.

The second part of this chapter has clearly brought the need for private sector participation in the higher education sector. It is an open secret that many private universities in India are not self-sufficient. However, they are systematically discriminated against by the state while allocating funds, be it for research or for other purposes. In fact, they are treated as 'pariahs' or 'untouchables' when it comes to funding. JGU's own difficulties in this regard are worth reflecting upon. Recognition under Section 12(b) of the UGC Act entitles a University to receive funding by the UGC. JGU applied for it four years back. After a protracted and lengthy correspondence and many visits, the matter has not been taken to its logical conclusion. At the senior leadership level in the University Grants Commission, there is maturity and sagacity while at the level of lower bureaucracy, there is apathy, indifference, stonewalling tactics. Even if a query raised by the regulatory agency is answered, it comes back again either in a rephrased form or much less in the same form. It makes one truly wonder as to what the intentions are. There are several questions regarding the modalities of a peer review or inspection of the institution by 'experts'.

Insofar as NAAC accreditation process is concerned, the same sordid story repeats itself. While on paper, modalities of assessment process appear to be fine but in practice, it is again mired in a bureaucratic and non-transparent process. This fact can be corroborated by many private higher educational institutions which have been through this process.

Narayana Murthy Committee recommended a series of fiscal incentives to promote private initiatives in higher education. JGU made a number of attempts to secure concession under Sections 35 and 88 of the Income Tax Act. Though it submitted all relevant documents and though a lot of time and energy of senior officials was spent in this effort, it is a matter of regret that, this effort has not yet succeeded.

In this part, a few challenges in the way of creating a world-class global university have been described but it is only an illustrative sample and the list is by no means an exhaustive one.

* * *

The importance of education in general, and in particular, higher education requires hardly any overemphasis. It empowers individuals, lifts marginalized people out of poverty, empowers women, promotes human rights, democracy and environment, and besides leading to many other positive spin-offs. Of the many competing demands on resources, education is regarded as one of the best financial investments states can make. In addition, the need for private investment in higher education has been noted in the interests of promoting access and improving quality. States have a positive obligation to create an enabling environment for the private efforts in higher education to succeed and flourish.

Provision of education is not an act of charity or welfare. It is indeed a human right. Under core international human rights treaties, states have clear obligations to respect, protect, and fulfil the educational needs of its people. In particular, the International Covenant on Economic, Social, and Cultural Rights which has been signed and ratified by India, requires it to take specific measures. These include, among other things, positive measures that enable and assist individuals and communities to enjoy the right to education and to avoid measures that hinder or prevent the enjoyment of the right to education.

The need for encouraging private sector initiatives in the field of higher education has been noted. The imperative is to stimulate private investments as a means of extending educational opportunities in higher education. However, in practice, there are determined efforts on the part of regulatory agencies to thwart these efforts in many cases.

The exercise of creating a world-class global private university in India is beset with numerous challenges. Though it is indeed a lofty ideal, there are many practical difficulties at every stage. The government, academia, legislators, and other sections of the general public need to ponder over critical issues discussed in this chapter and make concerted efforts to create a truly enabling environment.

13 Deconstructing the Discourse on University Social Responsibility

Anamika Srivastava

In the Conference of University Leaders 2016, Craig Mahoney, vice-chancellor of the University of the West of Scotland in the United Kingdom, remarked that 'If we're not socially responsible, then there is no future for our universities'.[1] While he also pointed out that 'having a socially responsible institution is actually a common sense',[2] it becomes interesting to explore what governments and universities mean when they highlight being socially responsible as a separate objective in their policy and mission

---

[1] Weiss, Brennan, 'The Rise of Social Responsibility in Higher Education, University World News', issue no: 423 (12 August 2016), http://www.universityworld-news.com/article.php?story=20160811095808959.

[2] Weiss, 'The Rise of Social Responsibility in Higher Education, University World News', issue no: 423 (12 August 2016), http://www.universityworldnews.com/article.php?story=20160811095808959.

statements. Since 2015, India is deliberating upon its New Education Policy by organizing number of consultation meetings at the state and the national level. One of the sub themes discussed in these consultation meetings is 'linking higher education to society'.[3] This included discussion on how universities and colleges reach out to their community and how students can contribute to their community, not only when they are pursuing their degrees but also once they are employed. One of the pertinent questions is can higher education ever be delinked from the society? And if not so then why do we need to discuss this topic today? 'The decisive tension is that universities around the world are being encouraged by governments to assume greater responsibility for economic development and to translate knowledge into products and services for the market—whilst at the same time being tasked to work with communities in alleviating the social and economic excesses of the market.'[4] This chapter is an attempt to understand the discourse on the linking of higher education to society, which in the contemporary era is often referred to as the 'university social responsibility' (USR). In particular, this chapter makes an attempt to deconstruct the concept of USR and other related constructs, discuss the origin of the linkages between university and society and put forth the current national and international discourse on USR. The chapter also makes an attempt to understand the reasons behind the rise of USR approach in higher education. The chapter concludes by arguing that the *raison d'être* of a university is to be linked to the society and thereby it would be meaningful for the Indian universities of the future to embed social goals in its core activities of teaching and research rather than relying on a few of its departments to reach out to the community.

'UNIVERSITY SOCIAL RESPONSIBILITY' AND OTHER RELATED CONSTRUCTS

Although community-university linkages can be traced back to the origin of the university itself, some overlapping constructs related to USR

[3] Ministry of Human Resource Development, *Themes and questions for Policy Consultation on Higher Education*, accessible at http://mhrd.gov.in/sites/upload_files/mhrd/files/upload_document/Themes_questions_HE.pdf.

[4] Bourke, Alan, 'Universities, Civil Society, and the Global Agenda of Community-engaged Research', *Globalisation, Societies and Education*, vol. 11, no. 4 (2013): 498–519.

have emerged in the recent times. The following section deals with such constructs.

Civic Learning

During the 1980s, the Carnegie Foundation for the Advancement of Teaching propounded that the most important role of higher education is to prepare students for committed citizenship.[5] This was in response to the decreasing interest and attention of young citizens in the voting process. As a result there was a rise of civic learning initiatives in the university campuses. Service learning and experiential learning, two forms of Civic learning, emphasize on the involvement of the community in classroom learning. According to a definition, civic learning is 'any learning that contributes to student preparation for community or public involvement in a diverse democratic society ... we have in mind here a strict interpretation of civic learning-knowledge, skills, and values that make an explicitly direct and purposeful contribution to the preparation of students for active civic participation.'[6] Although the concepts of civic participation and good citizen are variedly understood,[7] in the 1980s the emphasis was on political participation of the youth in the voting. However, by the 1990s it was realized that civic learning separated from core activities of universities, does not lead to any lasting impact on the students. Although, students were interested in voluntary participation but not in traditional political participation.

Scholarship of Engagement

While it is often argued that social responsibility is embedded in the core activities of universities, recently, universities have established separate departments for this purpose. Barker (2010) provides a list of centres involved with civic engagement rather than just civic learning, in particular,

[5] Newman, Frank, *Higher Education and the American Resurgence: A Carnegie Foundation Special Report* (New Jersey: Princeton University Press, 1985).

[6] Howard, Jeffrey, Service-Learning Course Design Workbook, *Michigan Journal of Community Service Learning*, Edward Ginsberg Center for Community Service and Learning at the University of Michigan with support from Campus Compact, Ann Arbor (2001).

[7] Stanford Encyclopedia of Philosophy, *Civic Education*, http://plato.stanford.edu/entries/civic-education/.

established in the United States and the United Kingdoms.[8] It is due to the terminology of 'scholarship of engagement' used in these civic engagement centres, these centres adopt different approach from the pre-existing civic learning initiatives of universities.[9] The focus here is to emphasize upon the traditional activities of the universities, that is, teaching and research with rigor and clarity, in the process, produce knowledge *for* the community and *with* the community.[10]

Ernest Boyer, a former president of the Carnegie Academy for the Advancement of Teaching and Learning describes scholarship of engagement to be used inclusively 'to describe a host of practices cutting across disciplinary boundaries and teaching, research, and outreach functions in which scholars communicate to and work both for and with communities.'[11] As argued, scholarship of engagement responded to the hitherto existing dominance of mainstream academic scholarship. Barker (2010) points out three reasons for it. First, due to excessive specialization and thereby, production of highly technical research output, mainstream academic scholarship cannot be communicated to the public at large. Second, invoking the problems of positivist epistemology, the scholarship of engagement points out that the much celebrated value neutrality and objectivity of mainstream research, in effect, turns a blind eye towards real world problem of rather value laded politics and society. Third, with the growing corporate influence on the culture of higher education, universities have been delinked from the society and thereby, need to engage with the community directly. Barker has identified five common practices within scholarship of engagement-public scholarship, participatory research, community partnerships, public information networks, and civic literacy scholarship.

[8] Barker, Derek. 'The Scholarship of Engagement: A Taxonomy of Five Emerging Practices', *Journal of Higher Education Outreach and Engagement*, vol. 9, no. 2 (2004): 123–37.

[9] Barker, 'The Scholarship of Engagement: A Taxonomy of Five Emerging Practices', *Journal of Higher Education Outreach and Engagement*, vol. 9, no. 2 (2004): 123–37.

[10] Barker, 'The Scholarship of Engagement: A Taxonomy of Five Emerging Practices', *Journal of Higher Education Outreach and Engagement*, vol. 9, no. 2 (2004): 123–37.

[11] Barker, 'The Scholarship of Engagement: A Taxonomy of Five Emerging Practices', *Journal of Higher Education Outreach and Engagement*, vol. 9, no. 2 (2004): 124.

University Social Responsibility

The origin of the idea of university social responsibility can be linked to the concept of Corporate Social Responsibility (CSR) which emerged within the corporate for profit business models since 1960s. 'While pressures to make profits are higher, stakeholders expect ever increasing standards of accountability and transparency. Business responsibility–and its relationship to the community in which it operates and seeks to serve–is more important than ever.'[12] CSR can be defined as 'the continuing commitment by business to behave ethically and contribute to economic development while improving the quality of life of the workforce and their families as well as of the local community and society at large.'[13] CSR is now extended to university space whereby universities are expected to, as any other economic organization, lay out their strategy as to how they bore USR. According to one definition, USR is 'a policy of ethical quality of the performance of the university community (students, faculty and administrative employees) via the responsible management of the educational, cognitive, labour, and environmental impacts produced by the university, in an interactive dialogue with society to promote a sustainable human development.'[14] Thus, theoretically, USR has emerged as an overarching construct subsuming all other related constructs. In practice, however, the emphasis is on human capital formation and knowledge creation to solve the problems of the community.

THE RISE OF 'UNIVERSITY SOCIAL RESPONSIBILITY'

While USR discourse is recent in origin, the university-community connection at the policy level dates back to the eighteenth century United States

[12] Vasilescu, Ruxandra, Cristina Barna, Manuela Epure, and Claudia Baicu, 'Developing University Social Responsibility: A Model for the Challenges of the New Civil Society', *Procedia-Social and Behavioral Sciences*, vol. 2, no. 2 (2010): 4177–82, 4178.

[13] Watts, Phil, and Lord Holme, *Corporate Social Responsibility: Meeting Changing Expectations*, World Business Council for Sustainable Development, (Geneva, 1999).

[14] Shu-Hsiang Chen, (Ava), Jaitip Nasongkhla, J. Ana Donaldson, 'University Social Responsibility (USR): Identifying an Ethical Foundation within Higher Education Institutions', *The Turkish Online Journal of Educational Technology*, vol. 14, no. 4 (2015).

of America and Europe in the wake of industrial revolution and changing need of the economy and the society.

International Discourse

The concept of peripatetic university-led universities like Oxford and Cambridge to extend themselves and reach out to the common masses.[15] It was increasingly realized that academic knowledge generated, can no longer remain within the walls of the ivory tower and must be disseminated to the middle and the working class in general and to the woman in particular. Consequently, James Stuart, fellow of Trinity College, Cambridge, England gave lectures to women associations and working men club.[16] Understandably, the University Extension movement was supported by the women's movement, promoters of middle class and the advocates of founding new colleges in provinces.[17] The overarching objective of this movement was to take education to those sections of the society which are not able to pursue formal education for various reasons. The emphasis was to popularize demand for university education across the country using lectureship method.

In the United States, the history of university involvement with the community can be 'traced back to the Morrill Act (1862), the Agricultural College Act (1890), and the Smith–Lever Act (1914)'.[18] The Morrill Act (1852) and the Agricultural College Act (1890) provided fund via land grants to establish educational institutions to teach agriculture, military tactics, and the mechanic arts as well as classical studies so that members of the working classes could obtain a liberal, practical education.[19] The Smith-Lever Act in 1914 underlined the importance of industry-university

[15] Welch, Edwin, *The Peripatetic University: Cambridge Local Lectures, 1873–1973* (Cambridge: Cambridge University Press, 1973).

[16] Welch, *The Peripatetic University: Cambridge Local Lectures, 1873–1973* (Cambridge: Cambridge University Press, 1973).

[17] Harrison, John Fletcher Clews, *Learning and Living 1790–1960: A Study in the History of the English Adult Education Movement* (Routledge, 2013).

[18] W. Mark Hearn, James L. Thomas, and Richard Cobb, 'University Outreach Programs: Service to the Surrounding Communities while Developing Faculty,' *Research in Higher Education Journal*, vol. 16, no. 1 (2012).

[19] M. Christopher Brown and James Earl Davis, 'The Historically Black College as Social Contract, Social Capital, and Social Equalizer', *Peabody Journal of Education*, vol. 76, no. 1 (2001): 31–49.

linkages and institutional resource generation by formalizing off-campus service orientation and encourage faculty to engage in translating scientific research into actual practice which could be used for commercial application.[20] Such efforts were continued by the government and universities over the twentieth century. All these efforts were directed towards taking out universities' core activities out to the community, be it teaching or research.

More recently, in 1998, the UNESCO World Declaration on Higher Education for the Twenty-First Century recognized that social responsibility should be one of the goals of higher education institutions. It emphasized that there is a need to strengthen 'co-operation with the world of work and analysing and anticipating societal needs'.[21] The declaration points out, 'Higher education institutions should give the opportunity to students to fully develop their own abilities with a sense of social responsibility, educating them to become full participants in democratic society and promoters of changes that will foster equity and justice'.[22]

The Global University Network for Innovation (GUNI), currently a network of 210 members from 78 countries, was established in 1999 as one of the joint follow-up actions of the 1998 World Conference on Higher Education held by UNESCO and the United Nations University (UNU).[23] GUNI claims that their 'mission is to strengthen the role of higher education in society contributing to the renewal of the visions and policies of higher education across the world under a vision of public service, relevance, and social responsibility'.[24]

UNESCO Chair in Community-based Research and Social Responsibility in Higher Education was established in 2012 for a period of four

---

[20] Hearn, W. Mark, James L. Thomas, and Richard Cobb, 'University Outreach Programs: Service to the Surrounding Communities while Developing Faculty', *Research in Higher Education Journal*, 16, 1 (2012).

[21] UNESCO, World Declaration on Higher Education for the Twenty-First Century (1998), http://www.unesco.org/education/educprog/wche/declaration_eng.htm.

[22] UNESCO, World Declaration on Higher Education for the Twenty-First Century (1998), http://www.unesco.org/education/educprog/wche/declaration_eng.htm.

[23] Global University Network for Innovation website, http://www.guninetwork.org/.

[24] Global University Network for Innovation website, http://www.guninetwork.org/mission-and-objectives.

years. This UNESCO Chair is located in two institutions, namely, the Society for Participatory Research in Asia (PRIA) in New Delhi, India and at the Community Development Programme in the School of Public Administration at the University of Victoria (UVic) in Canada.[25] The objective of the co-chair was to build capacity and support policymakers for community-university research partnerships.

International agencies like Organisation for Economic Co-operation and Development (OECD), World Indigenous Nations Higher Education Consortium (WINHEC), International Association of Universities (IAU), World Federation of Colleges and Polytechnics (WFCP), and the United Nations University (UNU) took a lead in emerging as forerunners of international community engagement agencies. While the OECD emphasized that there is a direct benefit of the core activities of teaching and research on the society, the WINHEC focuses on preserving indigenous languages, cultures, and homelands. The IAU advocates on behalf of the universities about the idea that universities pursue knowledge for its own sake and its benefit accrue to all members of the society. The WFCP aims at training workforce for development and the UNU endeavours to learn local knowledge to promote sustainable development.

Recently, commitment to USR has also brought together universities to forms networks. Twelve universities which had come together in Hong Kong to discuss broad issues on social responsibility in a summit,[26] formed a group for advancing the objective of social responsibility.

Globally, universities have come forward and have more explicitly embedded 'social responsibility' in their mission and activities. However, different universities have adopted different conception of the umbrella term 'social responsibility'. These conceptions are driven by the very nature of the university-public/private, for profit/not for profit, professional/liberal arts and the context within which they are situated. Some of these universities are responding the recent rise of the discourse on social responsibility and others have reinvented their age old commitment to community outreach

[25] UNESCO website, http://www.unesco.org/en/university-twinning-and-networking/access-by-region/europe-and-north-america/canada/unesco-chair-in-community-based-research-and-social-responsibility-in-higher-education-986/.

[26] The Second Summit on University Social Responsibility cum Inaugural International Conference on Service-Learning, 19–21 November 2014 at the Hong Kong Polytechnic University. See more at http://www.osl.polyu.edu.hk/usrsl2014/.

within the brand name of USR. For instance, the University of Manchester, a public research university, delivers its commitment towards social responsibility by producing research and students, engaging communities and by promoting environmental sustainability. The University of Edinburgh, a public and an ancient university, promotes social responsibility by supporting culture of exchange, pursuing excellence and innovation and working collaboratively as part of the local and global community.[27] The University of Phoenix, a for profit university in the Unites States claims to give back to the society through social responsibility. They do this through education related philanthropy and volunteerism.[28] University of Barcelona (UB) claims[29] that since it was founded in 1450, it has been committed to fulfilling its role as a public university at the service of society and the nation. In 2009, however, the values of social responsibility were formally incorporated into the daily management of the University. As a part of their social responsibility activities, they identified relevant stakeholders of the UB which included teachers, students, university administration, Catalan and Spanish society, the public administration, the business sector and their network of suppliers, and consulted their issues. This included communication between Office of the Vice-Rector for Students and the UB's students regarding concern for high fee and insufficient financial fund responding to which the Office of the Vice Rector has come up with various financial assistance options.[30] Some other issues that were addressed are-budgetary constraints on teaching staff and lack of training in the staff. The UB established mechanisms to address problems that may arise from the participation of stakeholder groups.[31] University extension programme at Harvard served as a community resource to the city of Boston since its founding in 1919 when A. Lawrence Lowell formed the Commission on Extension Courses, and coordinated the ten institutions with the Harvard program, offering

[27] Social Responsibility and Sustainability,' The University of Edinburgh website, http://www.ed.ac.uk/about/sustainability.

[28] 'Corporate Social Responsibility,' The University of Phoenix website, http://www.phoenix.edu/about_us/corporate-social-responsibility.html.

[29] 'The University of Barcelona website,' http://www.ub.edu/responsabilitat-social/en/index.html.

[30] Report on social responsibility, University of Barcelona 2013–14, http://www.ub.edu/responsabilitatsocial/docs/en/memoria2013-14_ang.pdf.

[31] Report on social responsibility, University of Barcelona 2013–14, http://www.ub.edu/responsabilitatsocial/docs/en/memoria2013-14_ang.pdf.

a wider range of subjects, and both men and women to teach the coeducational courses.[32] These programmes were non-traditional and operated in the night, thereby, the history of the institutions often ignores this very important aspect. *Harvard after dark*[33] was meant for the early movement in adult education and university extension in the early twentieth century America. The Harvard community connection continues till date, apart from the public lecture series, it focuses on issues of community participation in university programme/events like Community Football Day, local youth invited to explore educational and career opportunities, development of the Harvard Ed portal that provides learning and exploration platform for the entire Boston facilitating community and Harvard connections.[34]

Quacquarelli Symonds, an international university rating/ranking agency came up with QS stars ratings of universities which assesses universities' social responsibility by measuring 'how seriously a university takes its obligations to society by investing in the local community and environmental awareness'.[35] They chose to rate universities on community outreach activities akin to corporate social responsibility rather than the university extension programmes emerged in the nineteenth century and twentieth century. The parameters included community investment and development, charity and disaster relief, regional human capital development and environmental impact.

National Discourse

In the pre-independence era, higher education in India has been the privilege of the elite. While university education was out of the reach of the common masses, university extension programmes as a separate endeavour was uncommon in the pre-independence era.

It was in 1960, when Kothari Commission first mentioned about three pillars of university-teaching, research and extension.[36] Influenced

---

[32] Shinagel, Michael, *'The Gates Unbarred': A History of University Extension at Harvard, 1910–2009* (Harvard University Press 2009). Hereinafter Shinagel (2009).

[33] The phrase 'Harvard after dark' highlights that the university extension programmes were run in the night. See more in Shinagel (2009).

[34] Harvard University, Community Connections, http://community.harvard.edu/.

[35] QS website, http://www.topuniversities.com/qs-stars/qs-stars/rating-universities-engagement-qs-stars.

[36] Ministry of Education, Government of India, *Report of the Education Commission* (1964–66), http://krishikosh.egranth.ac.in/bitstream/1/2041424/1/CCS270.pdf.

by the Kothari Commission report, National Policy on Education, 1968 put forward the importance of community outreach:

> *The school and the community should be brought closer through suitable programmes of mutual service and support, W[w]ork experience and national service including participation in meaningful and challenging programmes of community service including participation in meaningful and challenging programmes of community service and national reconstruction should accordingly become an integral part of education. Emphasis in these programmes should be on self-help, character formation and on developing a sense of social commitment.*[37]

The University Grants Commission (UGC) Policy Statement of 1977 included extension programme that led to the institutionalization of such programmes in different universities and colleges. Following this the UGC prepared guidelines of Adult and Continuing Education and Extension Work and circulated to all universities in India in 1982. Through this, universities, students and faculty members were expected to reach out to the community by disseminating knowledge, bringing in social change and doing action based research with the community. In the coming years, many related programmes were introduced in the university with emphasis on varied objectives. Adult education became popular in this era with the launch of National Adult Education Programme in 1978 for removing illiteracy in 15–35 age group. The Population Education Clubs were started in the year 1984, where students were made aware about population dynamics and appreciate the small family norm and the problems of rapid population growth. In the 1990s, the emphasis was on adult literacy. During the ninth plan period (1997–2002), the concept of non-formal education was brought into the fore front. This was followed by efforts in developing the discipline of andragogy (adult education), vocational career oriented courses, leadership and human resource development for out of school youth and girls during the tenth and the eleventh plan period.

Although there was no direct mention about community-university linkages, National Policy on Education, 1986 (as modified in 1991) mentioned about 'delinking degrees from job' by creating job specific courses

---

[37] Ministry of Human Resource Development, Government of India, *National Policy on Education (1968)*, http://mhrd.gov.in/sites/upload_files/mhrd/files/document-reports/NPE-1968.pdf.

for candidates who cannot pursue graduate degrees.[38] The policy also gave provisions for rural university to promote micro-planning at the grassroots level for the transformation of rural areas.[39] It advocated inculcation of environmental consciousness in schools and colleges.[40]

As per the ongoing XII Five Year Plan (FYP), the UGC will establish a Centre for Fostering Social Responsibility and Community Engagement (CFSRCE) in university campuses.[41] Terminologies like 'social responsibility', 'community engagement', 'service learning', and 'experiential learning' are ubiquitous in the document. While the hitherto understanding of community-industry linkages in the previous plan period was retained, the XII FYP turned out to be a comprehensive policy including other education policy initiative within its ambit. The CFSRCE scheme includes the element of Choice Based Credit system and the existing Academic Staff Colleges were recommended to include the community engagement in their course structure.

In the State Education Ministers' Conference held in February 2012, it was realized that skill based short duration courses are more useful for the rural learners looking for employment or self-employment or better employment locally. It was accepted that such skills are not available in the formal system. Thus, it was proposed that a flexible and an open system with value-added multiple entry and exit options should be made available. The Community College Model scheme was adopted in the XII FYP. The main objective was that higher education should be made available to the larger community, however, the objective of education here should be access to

[38] Ministry of Human Resource Development, Government of India, *National Policy on Education (1968)*, http://mhrd.gov.in/sites/upload_files/mhrd/files/document-reports/NPE-1968.pdf p. 20.

[39] Ministry of Human Resource Development, Government of India, *National Policy on Education (1968)*, http://mhrd.gov.in/sites/upload_files/mhrd/files/document-reports/NPE-1968.pdf p. 20.

[40] Ministry of Human Resource Development, Government of India, *National Policy on Education (1968)*, http://mhrd.gov.in/sites/upload_files/mhrd/files/document-reports/NPE-1968.pdf p. 28.

[41] Planning Commission, Government of India, XII Plan Guidelines for Establishment of Centre for Fostering Social Responsibility and Community Engagement in Universities (2012–17), *Twelfth Five Year Plan (2012–17), Social Sectors*, Vol III, Annexure II to item no. 4.01, http://www.ugc.ac.in/pdfnews/4750386_Guidelines-for-Establishment-of-CFSRC.pdf.

employment opportunities. Thus, within the National Skills Qualifications Framework (NSQF) and National Occupational Standards, Community Colleges will be created.

The National Assessment and Accreditation Council (NAAC) in India, an autonomous institutions of the UGC to assess and accredit institutions of higher education in the country, includes the component of extension activities and institutional social responsibility as one of the assessment criterion.[42] This component carries a weightage of 4 per cent in total assessment. Although, the description of what exactly counts as 'extension' or 'social responsibility' have been kept open but the NAAC did come out with reports on the best practices in community engagement in the country.[43]

The National Institutional Ranking Framework, MHRD, which was introduced in the year 2015, came out with its maiden rankings in April, 2016, includes 'Outreach and Inclusivity' as the as one of the parameters based on which institutions are ranked. This component carries a weightage of 10 per cent. Interestingly, this component does not include university social responsibility in tandem with the discourse on extension programmes in the country. It includes elements of regional diversity, enrolment of women, and economically and socially challenged students and facilities for physically challenged students.

WHY 'UNIVERSITY SOCIAL RESPONSIBILITY'?

One may argue that as public universities are funded by taxpayers' money, they should produce output that are relevant to the society at large. However, by that logic, private institutions need not be 'socially' responsible as they do not depend on tax payers' money. Taking this argument forward, private universities should be 'privately' responsible to their own students as they are funding the universities. This is the business logic of being accountable to one's funder. Then why is it the case that the entire higher

[42] Guidelines for Assessment and Accreditation, NAAC, http://mhrd.gov. in/sites/upload_files/mhrd/files/document-reports/Manual_for_Universities_23012013.pdf.

[43] Community Engagement, Case Presentations, NAAC (2006), http://naac. gov.in/docs/Best%20Practise%20in%20Community%20Engagement.pdf.

education including the private institutions are often grappling with the debate about their relevance and credibility[44] in the society?

The fact that universities need to prove their linkages with the society, is a matter of concern in itself. To point out the macro issues grappling the contemporary times today, higher education has ismorphically emulated the current economic paradigm of development. This includes the rise of knowledge capitalism within which universities are expected to be restructured and adopt the neoliberal values. Within this framework, economic development is depended upon the production, appropriation, profitization, and distribution of knowledge. When knowledge becomes capital, its dissemination in the society, out of benevolence of faculty members and students, becomes questionable. Thus, in the age of globalization, while higher education institutions are integral to the continuous flows of people, knowledge, information, technologies, products, and financial capital,[45] they are expected to show their commitment to community development, separately. It is because the linkages between the economy and, the universities' core activities of teaching and research and universities' core actors faculty and students have become strong as never before, their linkages with the community and society at large have become blurred which is now needed to be proved.

As a result there has been various forms in which the 'social responsibility' elements that have got institutionalized within the university space. Some of the driving factors have been international rankings, reputation building exercise of universities (especially the new-the private ones), and seeking legitimacy in higher education landscape and in society. Within this context, it is important to make a distinction between the rise of extension programme in the 1970s and the current thrust on university social responsibility in India.

CRITIQUE OF 'UNIVERSITY SOCIAL RESPONSIBILITY'

While the discourse on USR has become quite dominant, universities are yet to come up with ways that will meaningfully deliver benefit to

[44] Tandon, R., and Wafa Singh, 'Transforming Higher Education through Community Engagement', *University World News*, no. 335 (20 February 2015).

[45] Marginson, Simon, and Marijk Van der Wende, 'The New Global Landscape of Nations and Institutions', *Higher Education*, vol. 2030, no. 2 (2009): 17–57.

the larger community. Community based research, teaching, and learning are often an outcome of compulsion. These compulsions are enforced by alumni, professional bodies and more relevant in the Indian context, through regulatory framework and political will. Rarely, it is an outcome of faculty interest out of spontaneity. In the Indian context, due to top down approach of the implementation of such schemes, success of such initiatives is dependent on the intrinsic motivation of the faculty. In the absence of such motivation, such schemes are implemented as rituals, for the sake of ticking the check-box. However, the lack of motivation on the part of the faculty can be attributed to the larger regulatory issues grappling the higher education sector as a whole. Due to the lack of finance and autonomy, faculty is unable to dispense their core activities of teaching and research, effectively and efficiently. Implementation of the community-university linkages schemes turns out to be added burden. It never becomes a part of the day to day culture of the university. While the traditional academic scholars in India, especially in the social sciences, who have carried out various research relevant to the community, making theoretical and empirical contributions to disciplines like sociology, political science, and even history, however, not falling within the ambit of scholarship of engagement *per se*, have not been acknowledged within the institutionalized 'social responsibility' discourse.

There is a merit in the involving students with the community. They become reflective of others and in the process, explore their own identities and what it means to contribute to something larger than their individual lives. However, participation in community service will more likely grow into commitment if it is direct, of high quality, and integrated into an evolving sense of self.[46] There is no clear understanding on the likely impacts of the current forms of 'community services' institutionalized in higher education institutions-on servers and served.[47] There have been mixed results on whether education-based community service has demonstrable educational benefits with its impact on faculty,

[46] Jones, Susan R., and Kathleen E. Hill, 'Understanding Patterns of Commitment: Student Motivation for Community Service Involvement', *The Journal of Higher Education*, vol. 74, no. 5 (2003): 516–39.

[47] Jones and Hill, 'Understanding Patterns of Commitment: Student Motivation for Community Service Involvement', *The Journal of Higher Education*, vol. 74, no. 5 (2003): 516–39.

students and communities.[48] In the dearth of interested faculty and students, there are concerns with 'mandatory volunteeristic' nature of these schemes.[49]

While there is a merit in USR discourse, where an explicit emphasis is provided on community-university linkages, there are some concerns as well. These concerns arises from the observation that most often on the university campuses today, initiatives of community-university linkages, do not complement but substitute the larger goal of inculcating citizenship and increase democratic participation. In the context of USA, Derek Bok put this idea in the following words:

> Of course, they do work in homeless shelters but what they don't do on too many of our campuses is have an opportunity to reflect on their experience at homeless shelters and put that experience into a wider context. They don't learn why there are homeless shelters in the world's richest country, what has been tried in the past to supply housing, why it hasn't worked, how a combination of mental health policies, economic policies, housing policies, drug policies have combined to put several hundred thousand people on the streets with no roof over their heads. Lacking that knowledge, students work in shelters but still regard government as irrelevant.[50]

In the age of social networking and 24 hours news channels, popular imagery has over powered sensibility. So much so that they deal with human interest and not substance.[51] And if an educated student who has also been a member of the Community Engagment Cell of the university ended up being trapped within the popular narrative and is unable to make distinction between reality and sensation, university has failed in dispensing its social responsibility, in its truest sense.

---

[48] Eyler, Janet, Dwight E. Giles Jr, Christine M. Stenson, and Charlene J. Gray, *At a Glance: What We Know About the Effects of Service-Learning on College Students, Faculty, Institutions and Communities, 1993–2000*, Third Edition (Vanderbilt University, 2001).

[49] Stukas, Arthur A., Mark Snyder, and E. Gil Clary, 'The Effects of "Mandatory Volunteerism" on Intentions to Volunteer', *Psychological Science*, vol 10, no. 1 (1999): 59–64.

[50] Bok, Derek, 'Universities and the Decline of Civic Responsibility', *Journal of College and Character*, vol. 2, no. 9 (2001).

[51] Bok, 'Universities and the Decline of Civic Responsibility', *Journal of College and Character*, vol. 2, no. 9 (2001).

Isn't student accountability a component of social responsibility of universities? Is social responsibility of universities independent of their core activities of teaching and research? To address a few of these questions, it would be meaningful to go back to the pages of history. In his book, 'The idea of a university', published in 1852, John Henry Newman, an Anglican priest, underlined the importance of a liberal arts education in catholic universites. It was an intellectual manifesto for the minority catholic group who were oppressed in erstwhile Britain. He propounded secular humanist education which would be based on scientific approach and utilitarianism. In the education policy parlance, he was advocating knowledge creation, access and social equity. While he supported the idea that education should be available to all and should not be the prerogative of a few elite, he emphasized on scientific temperament in research and excellence in education. He argued that the training of the intellect is beneficial not only to the individual himself but also to the society. This is because, according to Newman, if there is any practical end associated with a university, it would be that of training good members of the society. Newman describes the benefit of university education and creating 'good' members of the society in the following words:

> It is the education which gives a man a clear conscious view of his own opinions and judgments, a truth in developing them, an eloquence in expressing them, and a force in urging them. It teaches him to see things as they are, to go right to the point, to disentangle a skein of thought, to detect what is sophistical, and to discard what is irrelevant. It prepares him to fill any post with credit, and to master any subject with facility. It shows him how to accommodate himself to others, how to throw himself into their state of mind, how to bring before them his own, how to influence them, how to come to an understanding with them, how to bear with them.[52]

* * *

In the current economic paradigm of knowledge capitalism, how does one break the dichotomy between working for self and working for the society? There is a need to emphasize on the maturation role of higher education where students and teachers are working on behalf of the society—whether

---

[52] Newman, John Henry Cardinal, *The Idea of a University: Defined and Illustrated* (Regnery Publishing, 1999), pp. 59–64.

in teaching, research or any community engagement. Further, there is a need to inculcate the shared value structure in the educational institutions with a sense of collective responsibility and to the institution on behalf of the society. For this, the focus should be on the vision and the mission of higher education institutions where a sense of social commitment is foremost. Strong leadership (role model) which upheld the vision and guide the path, in achieving the mission of the university, can be instrumental in achieving this objective. Leadership along with the governance structure of the university which promotes shared governance values should be put forth. Thus, 'Linking higher education to society', one of the sub-themes of public consultations on the 'New Education Policy' of India, should, in fact, be a theme that should run through all other sub-themes be it on quality, access or governance. This would be a broader approach to community-university linkages than the USR approach. Immediate action should be taken to address patronage and networking in the appointment of top leadership in universities. Rather, these appointments should be more democratic and no more political. Governance structure of the university should encourage shared governance structure where the vision and mission of the institution is deep rooted within its own context. Faculties should have a sense of belongingness to their institution. This calls for immediate check on adhockery in public universites.

Social responsibility is universities' prime responsibility which should get manifested not only in their core activities but also in their governance structure and institutional environment.

Pedagogy of Interdisciplinarity

Law, Humanities, and Global Studies in India

14 The Phoenix of Interdisciplinarity in Higher Education

Yugank Goyal[1]

We are not students of some subject matter, but students of problems.
And problems may cut right across the borders of any subject matter or
discipline.[2] (Emphasis Original)

The aim of this chapter is to *(re)claim* the position of interdisciplinarity
in the context of higher education, with particular reference to India.

[1] An earlier version of the chapter was presented at the Jindal-Rollins Seminar on Globalisation and Governance in Asia and Curriculum Development Workshop for Liberal Arts and Humanities, in Sonipat, May 2013. The author would like to thank the participants of the conference for commenting valuably on the chapter. In particular, he would like to thank C. Raj Kumar, Luiz Martinez, Keerti Nakray, Aseem Prakash and Thomas Lairson. He would also like to thank Stephen Marks and Padmanabha Ramanujam for their valuable suggestions on an earlier draft.

After throwing light on what constitutes interdisciplinary teaching and research in the first part, I will discuss in the second part of this chapter how the disciplines emerged and what kinds of forces fossilized the hierarchical structures of pedagogical classifications. This section demystifies the sanctity of disciplines and offers a strong case against the necessity of disciplinary education. In the third part, I will illustrate the desirability of interdisciplinarity reflecting in both its supply and demand. The fourth part explores in detail, the higher education landscape in India and locates interdisciplinarity therein. Policy steps for encouraging interdisciplinarity are analysed and proposals for institutionalizing interdisciplinarity are discussed in the fifth part. The sixth part concludes the essay.

WHAT IS THIS PHOENIX?

Much as self-explanatory the term appears; there is no reason to bypass a definitional start.) Klein has illustrated in great detail, the formal understanding of interdisciplinarity.[3] She summarizes interdisciplinarity as an approach that integrates and/or blends two or more disciplines (in contrast to multidisciplinarity which is achieved through the juxtaposition of disciplines that remain separate). Gibbon's famous Mode one and Mode two of knowledge production can be used to describe a rather functional view. Mode one observes specialized disciplines as natural outgrowths of the knowledge production process, which exemplify supply side dynamics. Mode one is therefore, an internal account of knowledge production.[4] Mode two on the other hand, refers to a demand driven process, which attempts to fill in the epistemic blind spots that emerge and widen in ever specializing Mode one disciplines.

The author appreciates the excellent research assistance from Preksha Malik and Punkhuri Chawla. All errors and omissions remain the author's alone.

[2] Popper, K.R. *Conjectures and Refutations: The Growth of Scientific Knowledge* (New York: Routledge and Kegan Paul, 1963), p. 88.

[3] Klein, J.T. *Interdisciplinarity: History, Theory and Practice* (Detroit: Wayne State University, 1990); J.T. Klein, *Humanities, Culture and Interdisciplinarity* (New York, Albany: State University of New York Press, 2005).

[4] Gibbons, M. et al. *The New Production of Knowledge* (London: Sage, 1994). See also, Kuhn, who has been one of the most important theorist focusing on Mode 1 (Kuhn, T.S. *The Structure of Scientific Revolutions*, 2nd edn [Chicago: University of Chicago Press, 1970]).

To understand interdisciplinarity (and the lack thereof), we need to understand disciplines and their genesis. Disciplines have never been old heroes of intellectual history (in fact it is not clear whether they are heroes in the first place). They emerged in late nineteenth and early twentieth century, when society was going through intense socio-political challenges, driven by a post-industrial revolution period. Problems of labour, industries, workers, unemployment, social classes, and extreme poverty were challenges that society had to deal with.[5]

This was followed by the Depression and the New Deal. Thus emerged a period of 'double institutional transformation' that linked research universities with welfare state in the West, where latter generated problems and former segregated them into disciplines.[6] While disciplines mirrored industrial specialization of labour prevalent then, they got permanently frozen in time.

Interdisciplinary approach to thinking, as a frontier of innovation in higher education and a locus of new scholarship and teaching, is generally considered to have arrived in 1960s–70s.[7] By then, policy researchers and educators had become increasingly dissatisfied in restricting ever-changing knowledge to the *old* and consequently irrelevant, disciplinary boundaries.[8]

---

[5] Skocpol, T. *Protecting Soldiers and Mothers: The Political Origins of Social Policy in the United States* (Cambridge, MA: Belknap Press of Harvard University Press, 1992).

[6] Miller, C.A. 'Policy Challenges and University Reform', in R. Frodeman, J.T. Klein, and C. Mitcham (eds), *The Oxford Handbook of Interdisciplinarity* (New York: Oxford University Press, 2010), p. 336.

[7] See, however, Klein (2005). It can be said that with emergence of area studies, American studies and comparative literature in the 1930s and 1940s, the stage for interdisciplinarity had been set much earlier. Other observers have noted that the first push of interdisciplinarity appeared with the creation of Social Science Research Council in USA, in 1923—Charles Merriam, the Chicago political scientist and one of the key players for conceiving the council called for 'closer integration of the social sciences themselves'. See Calhoun, C., and Rhoten, D. 'Integrating the Social Sciences: Theoretical Knowledge, Methodological Tools, and Practical Applications'. In R. Frodeman, J.T. Klein and C. Mitcham (eds) *The Oxford Handbook of Interdisciplinarity* (New York: Oxford University Press, 2010), pp. 103–18.

[8] That is why many policy-oriented schools were opened in USA during 1960s–80s. See Miller, C.A. 'Policy Challenges and University Reform'. In R. Frodeman, J.T. Klein and C. Mitcham (eds) *The Oxford Handbook of Interdisciplinarity* (New York: Oxford University Press, 2010), pp. 333–44.

The major impetus was drawn from cross cutting topics, life experiences (such as black studies, women's studies, ethnic studies in 1960s–70s) or simply from the problem solving approach, which is often-invoked in crime and environment domains.[9] Post World War II, heavy funding from government on research oriented towards technology, engineering, and medicine helped these fields to attract an interdisciplinary mode of problem-solving and gave rise to bioengineering, environment studies, nanotechnology, plasma physics, atmospheric chemistry, and the like.[10]

Conditions in the world today are characterized by the age of Big Data, where we comfortably perch on our phones and laptops, oblivious to the sea of data that we float in continuously. A recent IBM commercial shows how our daily data generation exceeds all knowledge contained in all of the world's libraries. Frodeman et al.wonder if this is a cause of celebration or concern.[11] Indeed, accumulation of more knowledge may not be the answer to our problems. What is required is a better understanding of the relationship between different knowledge points, so that knowledge production can be selectively employed for achieving socially desirable goals. Interdisciplinarity is one of the essential tools required to accomplish the same.

Studies in interdisciplinarity can easily flourish through multicultural curricula and inclusive pedagogies. In addition, the emergence of the Internet and instructional technologies are indicators of encouraging signs for the growth of interdisciplinarity. In culturally diverse countries like India, which have also achieved a very high degree of Internet and information technology penetration, interdisciplinary approaches should be natural occurrence. Yet, little has happened in this regard (as the article shows later). Proliferation of interdisciplinarity cannot take place unless pedagogical shift occurs from mastery of content to mastery of competencies. This can only happen if there is intellectual will and academic freedom. Path dependence, viscous regulatory processes, and rigid institutional structures render any effort in that direction painfully futile.

[9] Klein, *Humanities, Culture and Interdisciplinarity*, pp. 77–8.

[10] Miller, 'Policy Challenges and University Reform', in R. Frodeman, J.T. Klein, and C. Mitcham (eds), *The Oxford Handbook of Interdisciplinarity*, p. 337.

[11] Frodeman, R., J.T. Klein, and C. Mitcham. (eds). 2010. 'Introduction', in *The Oxford Handbook of Interdisciplinarity* (New York: Oxford University Press), pp. i–xxxix.

REVISITING OUR *DISCIPLINARY* OBSESSIONS: HOW DID THE PHOENIX REDUCE TO ASHES?

Looking at it closely, our lives are shaped by our careers, which in turn are modelled mostly on the disciplines we study. Instinctively, one's knowledge of the world should depend upon one's aggregate experiential observations. Unfortunately, we have been reduced to understanding the world by viewing a part of it through specific lenses. And over time, the part we are exposed to has only shrunk.[12] Disciplines act as frames of references, and these frames get narrower in time, perhaps to respond to the fast growth they have received in last 200 years.[13] What a discipline does is: first, it creates hierarchies of and within disciplines, where some disciplines dominate and marginalize others; and second, they cease to act as communities of communication, and comprehensible only to those who speak that language. Disciplines are powerful towers of intellectual territory from which their fiefdoms are run, rather dictatorially, and unilaterally. The arrogance does not emerge from any millennium old compelling thought process, but from various social pressures that became path dependent in merely two centuries.

The disciplinary boundaries were never strict and merely aided to carve out an approach of gaining knowledge, rather than an ordering of subject matter—as it happens today. In fact, all social sciences emerged in a pre-disciplinary context—as Calhoun notes,

> Hobbes and Locke could integrate politics and psychology without need for an interdisciplinary field of political psychology. Vico and Montesquieu informed anthropology, history, sociology, and political science in equal measure ... Adam Smith was not one to distinguish theoretical from applied economics, just as he saw the intimate connections of both to the 'moral sentiments' and other concerns of what would later be called psychology and sociology.[14]

[12] For instance, the Deutsche Physikalische Gesellschaft (German Physics Association) has formed 29 subsections since 1951 and Gesellschaft Deutscher Chemiker (Society of German Chemists) has split into 21 specialized groups.

[13] Weingart, P. 'Growth, Differentiation, Expansion and Change of Identity: The Future of Science', in B. Jörges and H. Nowotny (eds), *Social Studies of Science and Technology: Looking Back Ahead* (Sociology of the Sciences Yearbook, Vol. 23) (Dordrecht: Kluwer Academic Publishers, 2003), p. 188.

[14] Calhoun, C. 'Foreword', to K. Worcestor. *History of the Social Science Research Council*. New York: SSRC, 2001).

All this changed in late nineteenth and early twentieth centuries when major departments were created in America and Europe, partly by dividing existing disciplines. For example, in America, economics was stripped off from history, which was the parent discipline. Later, economics ejected sociology from itself, and political science was branched out of history again.[15] This was complemented by imitation of categories from education systems around the world.

Various disciplines around the world acted as repositories of accessible knowledge and had no social function. Hence, even though universities were structured in faculties defined by the disciplinary categories and there was a sense of hierarchies (for instance, law, medicine, and theology were above philosophy,[16] it only served as administrative segregation. Professors only viewed them as vertical career progression, ascending through different departments and therefore teaching in various disciplines. There is little doubt that the disciplines were relatively unimportant until the end of eighteenth century.[17]

Three things happened that created the institutional inertia of disciplines and hierarchization of scholarly attention. First, the thrust of industrial revolution began laying greater emphasis on sciences that could directly or indirectly produce suitable workforce.[18] The structuring of universities in departments, sorting out students who attend classes in a timely fashion with each department run on administrative lines produced. a fertile ground for most students to receive and accept an industrial state of the world, rather than a place where creativity and cross-disciplinary ideas are nurtured. Second, there was an ever-increasing surge of data in existing disciplines, which created a pressure on scholars to develop new ways of ordering the new data, to 'limit the realm of possible experience'.[19]

---

[15] Ross, D. *The Origins of American Social Science* (Cambridge: Cambridge University Press, 1991).

[16] Weingart, 'A Short History of Knowledge Formations', in R. Frodeman, J.T. Klein, and C. Mitcham (eds), *The Oxford Handbook of Interdisciplinarity* (New York: Oxford University Press, 2010), 4–5.

[17] Stichweh, R. *Zur entstehung des modernen systems wissenschaftlicher disziplinen: Physik in Deutschland 1740–1890* (Frankfurt am Main: Suhrkamp, 1984), 14–15.

[18] Bridgstock, M. et al. *Science, Technology and Society: An Introduction* (Cambridge: Cambridge University Press, 1998), 111.

[19] Weingart, 'A Short History of Knowledge Formations', in R. Frodeman, J.T. Klein, and C. Mitcham (eds), *The Oxford Handbook of Interdisciplinarity*, 5.

The third and the most important reason was the fossilization of American style of fashioning their departments, which was quickly borrowed by most of the modern world. Although various intellectual traditions developed around the world through history,[20] the Western (American) model of higher education, mainly transported through colonization, has replaced earlier systems, committing what Gandhi would call epistemic violence.[21] Therefore, to understand concepts of interdisciplinarity in Indian higher education context, it is far more important to view the history of education in the West than to peep into ancient and medieval India.

Germany created systems of *Bildung*, which was characterized by high level of scholarship, personally cultivated through individual chairs (*Ordinarien*) that would be controlling the faculties and research institutes.[22] Since there were many small, independent universities and academic careers were advanced by patronage of chairs, interuniversity moves were common even in different departments,[23] and candidates often took doctorates in generic fields (more in arts, rather than economics or English).[24] France had similar system except that (a) it lacked a research institute structure, (b) had a profound influence not just of chairs, but also patronage groups/clusters that crossed several organizations.[25] Clearly, continental Europe exhibited no specific allegiance to a

[20] With Aristotelian idea of categorizing human knowledge between *scientia* (*episteme*) as the knowledge about cause and reasons, *dosa* as mere opinions, and *techne* (technology) and *ars* (arts) used for construction (see note 19); the 'classification of sciences' have continued to evolve, rather discontinuously. For a long time, education systems around the world—since more than two millennium ago—could be segregated into Christian, Islamic, Indian, and Chinese groups, which developed distinct from each other, in different fashion. The instructions (in both content and style) were essentially religious and understanding the nature around them in different styles of categorization (see note 21).

[21] Sharma, S. *History and Development of Higher Education in India*, vol. 5 (New Delhi: Sarup & Sons, 2002), pp. 234–7.

[22] McClelland, C. *State, Society, and University* in *Germany, 1700–1914* (Cambridge: Cambridge University Press, 1980).

[23] Ben-David, J. and R. Collins, 'Social Factors in the Origin of a New Science!' *American Sociological Review* 31 (1966): 451–65.

[24] Abbott, A. *Chaos of Disciplines* (University of Chicago Press, 2001), p. 124.

[25] Weisz, G. *The Emergence of Modern Universities in France* (Princeton: Princeton University Press, 1983).

disciplinary mode of thinking. England was not very different either even though their universities at the turn of twentieth century were highly 'anti-professional, and more often than not, anti-research'.[26] They were dominated by colleges within them, which also provided the patronage for academic careers. The emphasis on small intellectual communities as hinges of education was clearly not a fertile ground for disciplines to emerge and grow.[27]

American universities adopted these styles in different ways. Like Germany, the US had numerous decentralized universities focused on research. At the same time, the US brought the structures of undergraduate education from UK. This gave them a dual function, which called for internal organization. Democratic America could not accept hierarchical departments like in continental Europe. And hence were born, departments of equals. In addition PhD degree (borrowed from Germany) changed from PhD to 'in something'.[28] Right at the same time, national disciplinary societies were formed which exacerbated the inter-department separation.[29] Therefore, it can be argued that the emergence of disciplines was a result of historical accident, rather than a planned intervention.

One of the two prominent reasons for heaviness of disciplines and their durability in America lies in what Abbott calls 'dual institutionalization'.[30] Disciplines act as macrostructure of labour market for faculty thereby embedding careers within discipline rather than within the same university. At the same time, disciplines constitute microstructure for each individual university. Due to this duality, no university could have

[26] Abbott, *Chaos of Disciplines*, pp. 124–5.

[27] For a general discussion on English university system and in particular of that of Oxford, see V.H.H. Green, *A History of Oxford University* (London: Basford, 1974).

[28] Abbott, *Chaos of disciplines*, p. 125.

[29] For historical development of US universities, see L.R. Veysey, *The Emergence of the American University*, vol. 596 (University of Chicago Press, 1970), Ross, *The Origins of American Social Science*, and Oleson and Voss (eds), *The Organization of Knowledge in Modern America* (Baltimore: Johns Hopkins University Press, 1979).

[30] Abbott, A. *Chaos of Disciplines* (University of Chicago Press, 2001), pp. 125–6.

challenged the disciplinary system without eroding the career prospects of its own graduates. In other words, disciplinary system is perpetuated by locating the university hiring practice within the system, rather strictly. This view is also shared by Turner who maintains that disciplines are economic cartels that create and regularize internal labour markets of higher education.[31]

The second reason hovers around the construction of undergraduate majors.[32] Undergraduate education in late nineteenth century was dominated by electives, and majors emerged as a response. Almost right away, they became institutionally sticky, even when the study of majors has 'never really been the subject of serious pedagogical debate'.[33] And indeed, there could be no majors without disciplines. Over time, these majors and disciplinary structures become unshakeable because of institutional isomorphism,[34] where universities follow a certain pattern of disciplines, simply because other universities do it, and thereby maintain legitimacy.[35] Clearly, American universities evolved into how we know them today through a process of unplanned and sudden period of development during late nineteenth and early twentieth century.[36] And because the world came to follow their model, disciplines became global territories.

[31] Turner, Stephens, 'What are Disciplines? And How Is Interdisciplinarity Different?'. In Peter Weingart and Nico Stehr (eds), *Practising Interdisciplinarity* (Toronto: University of Toronto Press, 2000).

[32] The history of majors is described in some detail in Ellingson, 'The Emergence and Institutionalization of the Major-Minor Curriculum, 1870–1910', Unpublished paper, Department of Sociology, University of Chicago (1995), which has been frequently cited and referred to in Abbott (2001).

[33] Abbott, *Chaos of disciplines*, 127.

[34] P. DiMaggio and W.W. Powell, 'The Iron Cage Revisited: Institutional Isomorphism and Collective Rationality in Organizational Fields', *American Sociology Review* 48, 2 (1983).

[35] See C. Sa, 'Interdisciplinary strategies in U.S. research universities', *High. Educ.* (2008), who advocates interdisciplinarity by asserting that disciplines are sustained through isomorphic pressures. See also, J.D. Frank and J. Gabler, *Reconstructing the University: Worldwide Shifts in Academia in the 20th Century* (Stanford, CA: Stanford University Press, 2006), who address the argument favourably in some detail.

[36] Veysey, *The Emergence of the American University*, vol. 596.

OBSERVING CONTEMPORARY TRENDS: IS THE PHOENIX RISING?

We can imagine Butterfield's famous work, categorizing historical accounts into 'Whig' and 'Tory' style.[37] Since Whigs defeated the King on behalf of the Parliament, Whig histories are told from the standpoint of winners. They produce *central* accounts that comfortably convince us of all good reasons why things have turned out as we see them today, and ignore every other account that does not fit into their narrative. The counterfactual historiography, exhibited by silences and indignation belongs to Tories, who lost defending the King.[38] They decline to believe the inevitability of their defeat and there is no reason to doubt their party may be reinstated. The silence of interdisciplinarity lost in the cacophony of disciplines is exactly how Tory's voices got lost in Whig's accounts. And hence, the lack of interdisciplinarity in the version of history described above is exactly the reason why we need to treat interdisciplinarity not as a lost cause but as a lost voice, with a need for a reclaim.

This muteness is visible in the lack of theoretical literature that establishes the dual propositions that disciplines hamper knowledge development and interdisciplinary knowledge is more valuable than its disciplinary counterparts.[39] In such a case, my instinct is to rely on empirical observation and see whether forces of interdisciplinarity have been significant or not. And I find that indeed, the move towards interdisciplinarity has been fairly swift. The widespread attention that university systems, government agencies and private foundations are giving to interdisciplinarity is telling. This has particularly manifested in the practice of hiring academicians who conduct interdisciplinary research,[40] providing seed money for

---

[37] Butterfield, H. *The Whig Interpretation of History* (New York: W.W. Norton, 1965).

[38] Fuller, S. *Kuhn vs. Popper: The Struggle for the Soul of Science* (Cambridge: Icon Books, 2003), p. 51.

[39] Jacobs, J.A. and S. Frickel, 'Interdisciplinarity: A Critical Assessment', *Annual Review of Sociology*, 35 (2009): 48.

[40] From 2008 to 2011, University of Michigan approved 101 new positions solely for interdisciplinary faculty members, clustered in 25 interdisciplinary teams. For proposals approved, see http://www.provost.umich.edu/faculty/faculty_initiative/funded_proposals.html (accessed on 10 August 2013).

interdisciplinary projects,[41] funding through government grants[42] and promoting cross-disciplinary training.[43] Jacobs and Frickel refer to a survey, where 70 per cent of 1,353 college and university faculty members in the US preferred interdisciplinary knowledge to knowledge obtained in single discipline.[44]

Interdisciplinary courses and their surge in American academia is a measurable and powerful indicator of observing trends in interdisciplinary supply. National Centre for Education Statistics data shows that multi/interdisciplinary Bachelor degrees conferred increased from 6,324 in 1970–1 to 42,228 in 2010–11. This is an increase of about 567 per cent, more than five times the increase in *all* Bachelor's degrees. During the same period, at Masters level, the total number of degrees increased by 210 per cent while multi/interdisciplinary degrees conferred increased by 630 per cent (from 924 in 1970–1 to 6,748 in 2010–11). The rise was noticeable in doctoral degrees as well. The increase in multi/interdisciplinary doctoral degrees was more than six-fold, while total number of doctorate degrees awarded increased only by 2.5 times. Figure 14.1 shows the increase in the percentage share of multi/interdisciplinary degree types in total degrees of the three levels. Note that this increase is also indicative of perceptive absorption of interdisciplinary graduates either in the market or in higher degrees.

---

[41] Last year, Stanford concluded a fundraising programme that collected $ 6.2 billion for 'a new model of interdisciplinary research designed to help scholars contribute solutions to some of the world's most intractable problems.' See http://annualreport.stanford.edu/2012/year (accessed on 10 August 2013).

[42] National Science Foundation in 2006 funded the Integrative Graduate Education and Research Traineeship (IGERT) (http://www.igert.org)—an interdisciplinary training. In 2007, the National Institutes of Health funded nine interdisciplinary research consortia, see http://commonfund.nih.gov/interdisciplinary/overview.aspx, accessed on 10 August 2013.

[43] The Mellon Foundation Grants offer fellowships in the humanities and social sciences the opportunity to faculty members for 'acquire systematic training outside their own disciplines'. See http://www.mellon.org/grant_programs/programs/higher-education-and-scholarship/new-directions-fellowships (last accessed on 10 August 2013). S. Brint, S. 2005. 'Creating the Future: "New Directions" in American Research universities', *Minerva* 43: 23–50.

[44] Jacobs and Frickel, 'Interdisciplinarity', p. 46.

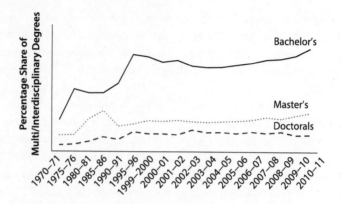

Figure 14.1 Increase in the Share of Multi/Interdisciplinary Degrees in Total Degrees Granted in USA

Source: Author's compilation from U.S. Department of Education, National Center for Education Statistics, Higher Education General Information Survey (HEGIS), 'Degrees and Other Formal Awards Conferred' surveys, 1970–1 through 1985–6; Integrated Postsecondary Education Data System (IPEDS), 'Completions Survey' (IPEDS-C: 91–9); and IPEDS Fall 2000 through Fall 2011, Completions component.

Another way to measure the penetration of interdisciplinarity is to look at the epistemic location of research centres of the universities.[45] Jacobs and Frickel estimate that there are around 100 research centres per leading university, and therefore there are more often, more research centres than university programmes in a good university.[46] When their content is examined, it was found that vast majority of these centres were perceivably interdisciplinary. In this way, they appear to serve as 'organizational counterweight to academic departments',[47] creating research at the frontier which comfortably slips into the other disciplines' domain and producing an alloyed body of research and knowledge.

Research dissemination is a pivotal exercise of the research infrastructure and hence, looking only at the research centres will yield an incomplete

---

[45] Surprisingly, this has largely been missing in topics related to interdisciplinarity. See, for example, J.T. Klein, *Crossing Boundaries: Knowledge, Disciplinarities, and Interdisciplinarities* (Charlottesville: University Press, 1996), chapter 6.

[46] Jacobs and Frickel, 'Interdisciplinarity', 53–4.

[47] Jacobs and Frickel, 'Interdisciplinarity', pp. 53–4.

picture. Academic journals help disciplines create an identity of their own, subsume newly discovered ideas into their own domain, specialize and in a way, legitimize necessary partial knowledge. They are the sites of disciplinary formation and insulation with loyal followers, inaccessible language, and limited circulation. It is at this very site, that interdisciplinary journals can contest and surface themselves. While by the 1950s, such interdisciplinary journals were rare, by the 1980s, they were attracting scholarship from eminent academics.[48] Later, we witnessed a rise of interdisciplinary journals of their own accord. Jacobs and Frickel also find that nearly 8,000 articles which carry the term 'interdisciplinarity' in the title have been published till date—with majority in the fields related to education, health and psychology.[49] The number of such articles has consistently increased over time (more than 150 in 1990 to close to 400 in 2007.[50] To estimate the interdependence between disciplines, Van Leeuwen and Tijssen, in their classification of 2,314 journals in 119 disciplinary categories find that 69 per cent of references are cross disciplinary.[51] All of the above give us fairly convincing evidence towards rising importance of interdisciplinary efforts of American universities. Indeed, these trends are reflected in most Western countries.[52]

[48] Klein, *Humanities, Culture and Interdisciplinarity*, p. 74.

[49] Jacobs and Frickel, 'Interdisciplinarity', pp. 46–7. They drew their data from Thompson Scientific, 1956–2007. ISI Web of KnowledgeSM. Web of Science®. Science Citation Index. Philadelphia, PA: Thompson Scientific Corporation. Available online at http://isiknowledge.com.

[50] Jacobs and Frickel, 'Interdisciplinarity', pp. 46–7. See also T. Braun and A. Schubert, 'A Quantitative View on the Coming of Age of Interdisciplinarity in the Sciences 1980–99', *Scientometrics*, 58, 1 (2003).

[51] Van Leeuwen, T., & Tijssen, R. 2000. 'Interdisciplinary Dynamics of Modern Science: Analysis of Cross-Disciplinary Citation Flows'. *Research Evaluation*, 9(3): 183–87. National Science Foundation performed something similar with 11 disciplinary categories. They found that biology and psychology reported more than a third of their citations from outside their disciplines. Social Science fell in the middle (22.7 per cent) within which Economics was the most insular. See National Science Foundation. 2000. *Science and Engineering Indicators—2000*. Arlington, VA: Natl. Sci. Found. http://www.nsf.gov/statistics/seind00/pdfstart.htm (last accessed on 11 August 2013).

[52] Newell, W. and J.T. Klein, 'Interdisciplinary Studies into the 21st century', *Journal of General Education*, 45, 2 (1996).

Since the analysis has been focused only on supply of interdisciplinarity, there is merit in observing demand separately. An interesting proxy for demand is the area of doctoral theses. Doctoral theses are always sourced from interests of the doctoral students, and as such, they act as a reflection of what kind of knowledge production an early career academic, who is not yet drowned deep into the disciplinary ocean, wants. It can help us explore hidden demand that surfaces in the form of doctoral dissertations and is untouched in the highly granular research of established disciplines. Ni and Sugimoto undertook an extensive survey of doctoral dissertations across more than a century[53] to examine interdependence of (highest producing thirty) disciplines, to examine the level of interdisciplinarity ingrained in the dissertations. They show that dissertations were largely single-subject driven until the 1980s, after which multiple-subject dissertations began to dominate the scene. Figure 14.2 is interesting. It shows that (a) there has been a surge in multi/interdisciplinary inspiration for doctoral dissertations

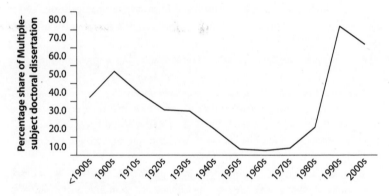

Figure 14.2   Decline and then sudden increase in the share of multiple-subject doctoral dissertation across a century in 66 countries

Source: Author's compilation from Ni and Sugimoto (2012).

[53] Ni, C., and Sugimoto, C. R. 2012. Using Doctoral Dissertations for a New Understanding of Disciplinarity and Interdisciplinarity. *Proceedings of the American Society for Information Science and Technology*, 49(1): 1–4. Data is drawn from ProQuest dissertation database and covers 2.3 million dissertations from 1848 to 2009, across 66 countries. The dataset contains subject category (inter alia), which helps authors identify whether the dissertation could be considered to lie in single subject or multiple-subject (multi/interdisciplinary) domain.

in last three decades, and (b) elements of interdisciplinary thinking declined during early part of twentieth century, just when disciplines emerged as rigid categories. Clearly, the force of interdisciplinarity in doctoral dissertations is a compelling reason for us to lend it serious thought in education policy.

THE CASE OF HIGHER EDUCATION AND INTERDISCIPLINARITY IN INDIA: HOW DOES THE PHOENIX LOOK LIKE IN INDIA?

Historical Antecedents

Historically, Indian education structures have been very different from that of the Western societies, and even within Indian subcontinent, there was a marked diversity.[54] However, colonialism forced India to go through major institutional and epistemic shifts, and created uniform education structures with pockets of elitism.[55] So little does the formal structure in which disciplines are organized in Indian universities today carry any institutional memory of pre-British era that the exercise to dwell on history doesn't merit my attention here. Since post-independent policies have only strengthened the foothold of borrowed institutions from the West, the preceding discussion on emergence of disciplines in the West is more promising to understand where we come from.

Higher education in India structured on modern university lines was cultivated from Wood's Despatch of 1854 (sent by Charles Wood, President of the Board of Control of the East India Company), which laid down guidelines for founding of a university system modelled on the lines of University of London (established in 1836). This means that the university would affiliate colleges and confer degrees. It prescribed opening of

---

[54] See, for ancient Indian education, (Mookerji, R.K. *Ancient Indian Education: Brahmanical and Buddhist.* 2nd edn [Delhi: Motilal Banarsidass, 1951]). In her impressively detailed account, she understands theory and processes of education in Brahmanical and Buddhist social structures by looking at ancient educational institutions, religious books and accounts of visitors like Fa-Hein and Heun-Tsang.

[55] S. Seth, *Subject Lessons: The Western Education of Colonial India* (Duke University Press, 2007). A. Basu, 'Indian Higher Education: Colonialism and Beyond', in P.G. Altbach and V. Selvaratnam (eds), *From Dependence to Autonomy: The Development of Asian Universities* (Chestnut Hill, MA: Center for International Higher Education, Boston College, 2002), pp. 167–86.

universities in Bombay, Calcutta, and Madras—which happened in 1857, on the lines of University of London. All universities established thereafter[56] simply copied the structure in 'isomorphic fashion',[57] without realizing the intent of university education purported by the British. England at the time had no policy for universal higher education. The reason East India Company began investing resources on higher education in India was to supply itself with English educated small class of Indians who could act as in Macaulay's words, 'interpreters between us and millions who we could govern; a class of persons Indian in blood and colour but English in taste, opinions, in morals and in intellect'.[58] Hence, their top-heavy and lop-sided efforts concentrated on urbanized upper and middle class and led to the neglect of mass education. Education emphasized on those subjects borrowed from University of London which would fulfil the aims of British. Hence, the curriculum was biased in favour of language and humanities but ignored science and technology.[59] This was because of exclusive employment of British personnel in departments of engineering, irrigation, railways, ordnance factories, and posts and telegraphs. There was little provision for vocational training as well. Learning English was in a way, considered to be the aim of education. Mechanical lessons imparted on English encouraged people to memorize rather than think,[60] which killed creativity and thirst for interdisciplinary engagements. Such institutional implants uprooted the indigenous concept of education and created pockets of concentrated and 'modern' elitism.

The University of London was predated (and constituted) by University College London (UCL) and King's College London (KCL), and therefore these two colleges had an intellectual bearing on how the University of

[56] Universities established later in Punjab (1881), Allahabad (1887), Mysore (1916), Patna (1917), Osmania (1918), Aligarh (Aligarh Muslim University) (1920), Lucknow (1921), Dacca (1921), Delhi (1922), Nagpur (1923), Andhra (1926), and Agra (1927), pretty much followed similar structures. Universities that opened after independence became a victim of this institutional isomorphism again.

[57] Jayaram, N. 'Higher Education in India: Massification and Change', in P.G. Altbach and T. Umakoshi (eds), *Asian Universities: Historical Perspectives and Contemporary Challenges* (Baltimore, Johns Hopkins University Press, 2004), p. 86.

[58] Sharp, H. (ed.), *Selections from Educational Records, Pt I: 1731–1839* (Calcutta, 1920) p. 22.

[59] Jayaram, *Sociology of Education in India* (Jaipur: Rawat, 1990), pp. 45–59.

[60] Basu, A. *Essays in the History of Indian Education* (New Delhi: Concept, 1982), pp. 65–6.

London (and therefore that of Madras, Calcutta, and Bombay) developed. No wonder therefore, disciplines of University of London got permanently etched in Indian universities. In the nineteenth century, UCL had pioneered subjects like chemistry (physics and astronomy came much later); English (and German and Italian), and opened departments of geography, medicine, civil engineering, public health, and fine arts.[61] Later, new departments like phonetics and psychology were established. And only in 2012 a bold interdisciplinary degree—bachelors in arts and sciences—was established.[62] King's had a similar background and established conventional degrees, which were soon institutionalized in India. While University of London's model ensured that higher education in India was *secularly* established (unlike Oxford and Cambridge), it also brought with it, Western patterns, with little scope for innovative customization for India's society.

As merely an administrative body, the University of London received criticisms for its lack of commitment to teaching and research. This led to passing of University of London Act in 1898. Shortly thereafter, Indian University Act (1904) was passed. Inspired by the University of London Act 1898, the Indian University Act 1904 increased the role of the university in promoting study and research, appointment policies and the like. Universities had to prescribe textbooks, set courses and their standards, conduct examinations, inter alia. But primarily as Lord Curzon's policy to check political discontent arising out of English education, the Indian University Act diverged from its London counterpart, to bring down heavily, the education system under government control.[63] During the early twentieth century, the British attempted to resolve the problems of *centrality*[64] of educational implants but could not get far.[65]

---

[61] See http://www.ucl.ac.uk/about-ucl/history#1860 (accessed on 11 August 2013).

[62] See http://www.ucl.ac.uk/about-ucl/history#1860 (accessed on 11 August 2013).

[63] Basu, A. *The Growth of Education and Political Development in India* (Oxford University Press, 1974) highlights that the Act was followed by government screening of text books (pp. 6–12) and appointment and dismissal of teachers on political grounds (pp. 36–42).

[64] Sadler Commission in 1917 commented that the Indian University Act 1904 made the Indian universities among the most completely government universities in the world.

[65] Tickoo, C. *Indian Universities: A Historical, Comparative Perspective* (Bombay: Orient Longman, 1980), p. 34.

While today University of London Act follows its 1994 avatar and many of its colleges have the power to confer their own degrees, in India, even now, the government vests its direct control on university administration.

State of Higher Education in India and State of Interdisciplinarity

Government's intervention and poor governance has brought higher education in India to a dismal state today. Kapur and Mehta (2008) have argued that the crippling state system and weak governance of regulatory agencies has resulted in a de facto privatization of higher education, which in turn has failed the promises of education. While numbers seem to be impressive,[66] issues related to quality and the signalling potential of universities in India are depressing. Political forces have damaged the university systems through (a) rent-seeking by controlling appointments of faculty and administrators, admissions of students, building contracts, and discretionary grants to government-aided institutions, (b) partisan politics, (c) 'entrepreneurial' Parliamentarians, many of whom have started colleges/ universities themselves, which are primarily a source of classified incomes and commercial enterprises with little respect for quality, and (d) making colleges sites of politics (ibid., pp. 131–4). The quality and infrastructure of most Indian universities is so deplorable that they have embarrassingly earned the sobriquet *academic slums*.[67]

---

[66] During Independence, India had 20 universities, 500 colleges (which was easily one of the most sophisticated higher education systems in the developing countries at the time), and in 1951, had 80 students per 100,000 population. By 2004–5, there were 229 universities (both central and state), 95 deemed universities, 16,000 colleges and 9,228,000 students, reaching 854 students per 100,000 populations (Debroy, Bibek. 'Higher Education: Regulation and Control', in K. Basu and A. Maertens (eds), *The New Oxford companion to Economics in India* (New Delhi: Oxford University Press, 2012, p. 336). Student enrolment grew at 5 per cent annually for last two decades, which is 2.5 times population growth (Kapur and Mehta, 2008: p. 103). However, the gross enrolment ratio of around 11 per cent (which varies considerably across states) is far lesser than Asia and OECD countries (Kapur and Mehta, 2008: p. 103). While this shows an excess demand, B. Debroy (2012) that at macro level, the total enrolment is far short of capacity hinting at excess supply.

[67] Jayaram, 'Higher Education in India: Massification and Change', in P.G. Altbach and T. Umakoshi (eds), *Asian Universities*, p. 92.

Cemented in a discipline-driven history and deteriorating quality, any innovation with regard to interdisciplinarity in Indian higher education is an unrealistic hope. With some primary research, I find that this is indeed true. We went through the websites of 70 central and state universities from across India, and drew information on the degree courses offered in these institutions. The choice of the 70 universities was governed by the aim to represent universities in most states and of varying age established from 1882 (Punjab University) until 2010 (Karnataka Sanskrit University, Bangalore).[68] We estimate that of all the courses, around 8.3 per cent courses are interdisciplinary, while the remaining 91.7 per cent fall into the standard disciplines. Almost two-thirds of these universities have information related to students enrolled in their degree programmes. Estimating their numbers, we realize that for latest year that they have uploaded the data, merely 5.3 per cent of students enrolled in the interdisciplinary degree programmes, while the rest chose to stick to standard disciplines. Not all of these universities have research centres (and many of them do not display they information on their rudimentary websites), which is equally disappointing. But from those that have it, we found only 16.8 per cent of them having a multi/interdisciplinary research centre.

Derivative Reasons for Lack of Interdisciplinarity in Higher Education in India

The lack of interdisciplinary approaches to higher education in India is made clearer if we look at the research output of Indian universities. Interdisciplinarity is the product of cross-disciplinary research, which in turn builds on the state of disciplinary research. In India, the latter itself has a disappointing record. In a study conducted by Thomson Reuters, published in a leading national daily,[69] it was found that merely 3.5 per cent of the global research output was from India, with the highest figure

---

[68] It was found that the websites of most universities seem incomplete or outdated. In fact, University Grants Commission, the highest regulatory body in India for higher education, requested some essential information from the universities for updating its own website. UGC dispatched a letter requesting the information recently. See http://www.ugc.ac.in/pdfnews/7454149_chairmenletter.pdf (last accessed on 11 August 2013).

[69] Sinha, K. 'India Accounts for Just 3.5 Per Cent of Global Research Output,' *Times of India* (1 October 2012).

ceiled at 6.5 per cent (chemistry), and only 0.6 per cent in social sciences. The woeful research culture and inadequate infrastructure is a result of the structures of higher education that have emerged post-Independence. By any indicator, the quality of Indian universities is abysmal. The QS World Education Rankings (2012) does not feature a single Indian university in their list of top 200 universities of the world. The indicators it uses to evaluate universities consist of academic reputation, citation per faculty, faculty-student ratio, employer reputation, and international faculty and students.[70] No Indian university figured in the top 200 of the Times Higher Education Rankings (2012–13) either, which based its score on similar indicators.[71]

The result of this institutionalized mediocrity is that the few colleges, which are considered to be of relatively better quality, become the site for a 'Darwinian' struggle for aspiring students to get admissions into, through competitive examinations.[72] The selection ratio (percentage of successful candidates) in Indian Institutes of Management and Pre-Medical Tests (for premier medicine schools) is less than 1 per cent, while for Indian Institutes of Technology and National Institutes of Technology it is from 1 per cent to 3 per cent respectively.[73] Despite the fact that none of these colleges are comparable to the top 200 in the world, the intense competition to secure admissions creates an artificial elitism associated with them. The quality of the students admitted, rather aesthetically inflates the reputation of these institutions even while their teaching and research quality remains deplorable. The elitism of these handful institutions breeds complacency. Innovation in pedagogy and research takes a back seat. Uninspired as they become

---

[70] This was also mentioned by the President of India, Pranab Mukherjee, in his address during second convocation ceremony of Central University of Rajasthan in July 2013. http://articles.timesofindia.indiatimes.com/2013-07-10/jaipur/40490816_1_president-pranab-mukherjee-top-200-universities-education-sector (accessed on 11 August 2013).

[71] http://www.timeshighereducation.co.uk/world-university-rankings/2012–13/world-ranking (accessed on 11 August 2013).

[72] D. Kapur and P.B. Mehta, 'Higher Education', in K. Basu and A. Maertens (eds), *The New Oxford companion to Economics in India* (New Delhi: Oxford University Press, 2012), p. 334.

[73] Kapur and Mehta, 'Mortgaging the Future: Indian Higher Education', in S. Bery, B. Bosworth, and A. Panagariya (eds), *Brookings-NCAER India Policy Forum*, vol. 4 (New Delhi: Sage Publications, 2008), p. 116.

in their ivory towers, little efforts are made to introduce interdisciplinarity, which could serve as a fertile ground for research and development on an emerging economy with unique problems.

Another reason why disciplinary boundaries are stronger in India than in the Western universities is because a large majority of universities, owing to their poor performance, cease to act as signals of skill-development. As Kapur and Mehta note that Indian university degrees serve only a formal purpose, 'which could mean anything in quality'.[74] This means that to the prospective employer, all degrees (barring those coming from top hand- ful of institutions) are fairly homogeneous in their mediocrity. In such a case, universities would be deterred to offer an interdisciplinary course, which carries a risk of being undervalued by a market that does not value the standard disciplinary degree of the university in the first place. In the face of appalling pedagogy and curriculum of standard disciplines, it is not surprising that interdisciplinary programmes are practically non-existent in most universities.

The problem is coupled by absence of qualified teachers. While exact estimates are difficult on account of lack of systematic official surveys, shortage of faculty in Indian universities is deemed to be around 35–40 per cent.[75] In 2011, the Task Force on 'Faculty Shortage and Design of Performance and Appraisal System' coordinated by University Grants Com- mission (UGC) reported a shortage of more than 300,000 in the system and estimated the number to increase by 100,000 faculty every year during coming decade.[76] From several accounts, this puts the figure of shortage at 54 per cent, pushing the faculty-student ratio to 1:20.9 from the recom- mended 1:13.5.[77] Regardless of whether such acute shortage could stem, in part, from India's economic success in recent years (which attracted college

---

[74] Kapur and Mehta, 'Mortgaging the Future', p. 134.

[75] C. Sen, 'A Framework for Analysing Demand and Supply of Faculty and the Quality of Higher Education', *Working paper number 350, Indian Institute of Manage- ment, Bangalore* (2011): 3. Available on http://www.iimb.ernet.in/research/sites/ default/files/WP%20No.%20350.pdf (last accessed on 11 August 2013).

[76] http://pib.nic.in/newsite/erelease.aspx?relid=74188 (last accessed on 11 August 2013).

[77] Tandon, A. 'Faculty Shortages in Colleges, Varsities a Whopping 54 Per Cent', *Tribune* (11 August). http://www.tribuneindia.com/2011/20110810/main2.htm (last accessed on 11 August 2013).

graduates who could have chosen academia),[78] or from the downgrading of teaching as a prestigious, lucrative and satisfying profession, it has a negative bearing on prospects of development of interdisciplinary mode of thinking. Faculty members are cornerstones of research and innovation in any university. During shortage, teaching responsibilities swell and they are saddled with administrative work, leaving little room for creativity and interdisciplinary discourse.

Entry of Private Players

It may be pertinent to assume that in the ailing public higher education, private sector would have emerged to fill the demand gap. This has indeed happened, but not necessarily as a response to address the gap, but to provide an opportunity for securing rents,[79] and arguably, exhibits another reason for lack of interest in interdisciplinarity in India. In India, almost two-thirds of students are enrolled in the arts and sciences, while one-sixth in commerce and management. The bulk of the remaining enrolment for technical (engineering, management and pharmacy) and professional (medicine, teacher training, and law) courses, has risen and is absorbed by a mushrooming private sector in recent years.[80] Kapur and Mehta refer to National Sample Survey data to show a significant reduction of the government's share in overall education expenditure (from 80 per cent to 67 per cent) between 1983 and 1999 while private sector's share grew ten-fold during almost same period.[81] A closer look at these institutions reveals that 'majority of these institutions have been supported or made possible by the direct involvement of politicians'[82] who are interested in extracting 'capitation fees' and forcing profits out of the system, at a crippling cost to quality. There is hardly any academic vision, pedagogical innovation or research investments in these private institutions. The governance crises

---

[78] Neelakantan, S. 'In India, Economic Success Leaves Universities Desperate for Professors', *Chronicle of Higher Education* (12 October, 2007) (last accessed on 11 August 2013).

[79] Kapur and Mehta, 'Mortgaging the Future: Indian Higher Education', p. 136.

[80] Pawan Agarwal, 'Higher Education in India: The need for Change', *ICRIER Working Paper no. 180* (New Delhi, India: Indian Council for Research on International Economic Relations, 2006).

[81] Kapur and Mehta, 'Mortgaging the Future: Indian Higher Education', p. 122.

[82] Kapur and Mehta, 'Mortgaging the Future: Indian Higher Education', p. 136.

in public universities (which dominate arts, sciences, commerce courses) become governance practice in private universities (which dominate management, professional, technical courses). The result is an utter lack of interdisciplinarity and novel approaches to problem solving.

POLICY RECOMMENDATIONS FOR INDIA: HOW CAN WE HELP THE PHOENIX RISE?

Location of Interdisciplinarity in Ongoing Discourse

From a theoretical standpoint, interdisciplinarity is located in different spaces. Abbott for instance, views it emanating 'immediately' from the 'unbreakable' structures of disciplines.[83] For Whitley, interdisciplinarity is a natural process of interdependence of disciplines on each other—something that has always been occurring.[84] A far more central view of interdisciplinarity is given by Fuller ho suggests that today's disciplines began as interdisciplinary social movements, and therefore, interdisciplinary approaches can be communicated to the society by inter-penetration of disciplines and changing their structures, and not by merely building on the insights of disciplines.[85]

The complexity of the Indian society and the uniqueness of the contemporary problems faced by it call for nothing less than a la-Fuller interdisciplinarity. Even though proposals to incorporate interdisciplinary teaching and research appears to be secondary to many other more pressing problems that ail India's higher education system, it is this hopelessness that presents an opportunity to an interdisciplinary enthusiasts. With higher education reform on the agenda, India may soon arrive at a juncture marked by an institutional shift. It is in these junctures that new institutions can be implanted, rather swiftly. India, in its wave of reforming higher education can divorce itself from its past, and assimilate interdisciplinarity in the relevant policy design that may ensue. The new face of higher education in India therefore will carry interdisciplinarity from the start. Even if

---

[83] Abbott, A. *Chaos of Disciplines* (University of Chicago Press, 2001), pp. 131–2.

[84] R. Whitley, *The Intellectual and Social Organization of the Sciences* (Oxford: Clarendon, 1984), p. 292.

[85] Fuller, *Kuhn vs. Popper: The Struggle for the Soul of Science* (Cambridge: Icon Books, 2003).

reformation is not underway, the efforts to incorporate interdisciplinarity will be a small step towards solving greater problems.

Current Efforts

The economic impetus currently being experienced in India is suggestive of the likelihood of acceptance of interdisciplinary courses by the market. Rise in the number of Indian students who travel abroad to study such courses—as I often observe in my own interactions with many such students—shows growing demand of such courses among students and growing second order demand of companies in hiring these graduates. The lead for starting interdisciplinary programmes needs to be taken by premier institutions, which have the capability and resources to do so, since poorly performing colleges will simply not have courage to do so in an unrecognizing market.

The University Grants Commission appreciates the value of interdisciplinarity, and has made piecemeal efforts by proposing guidelines that encourage incorporating interdisciplinarity in academic thought. For instance, until 2007, UGC had proposed separate grants for institutions with 'potential for excellence'. Bu in the XI Plan (2007–12), the UGC 'keeping with rapidly changing times and requirements' came up 'with a new venture, in which multidisciplinary approach' were to be 'groomed and nurtured'.[86] Of the universities chosen for such grants, around half were given to multi/interdisciplinary approaches.[87] Yet, there is a lack of consistency of aims. For example, the same plan had another Scheme, titled, 'Epoch Making Social Thinkers of India: Buddha, Gandhi, Nehru and Ambedkar,' which extended financial support to, inter alia, proposed/existing centres on Buddhist studies. However, the scheme mentions that this fund will be allotted only if there is a centre for learning Pali or Sanskrit,

---

[86] See the XI Plan Guidelines for Centres with Potential for Excellence in Particular Areas, University Grants Commission. http://www.ugc.ac.in/oldpdf/xiplanpdf/centerpontentialexcellence.pdf (accessed on 12 August 2013).

[87] Focus areas like Biomedical Science, Sports Science, Himalayan Studies, Behavioural Cognitive Sciences, Environmental Sciences, Biodiversity for Centres and Biochemistry/Biotechnology, Herbal Science, Nanoscience in Biology, and Bioscience and Area Studies for Universities. See http://www.ugc.ac.in/page/Centres-(CPEPA).aspx and http://www.ugc.ac.in/page/Universities-(UPE).aspx (last accessed on 12 August 2013).

in absence of which, the centre should be 'attached to another appropriate department such as history, philosophy, sociology and ancient Indian culture'[88] thereby cordoning off any other (inter) disciplinary engagements with Buddhist studies.[89] Similarly, UGC has been particularly interested in Area Studies, evinced through their funds for such programmes,[90] but one of the objectives of the scheme is to 'bring knowledge of regions of the world to the core of intellectual disciplines'.[91]

Recent efforts are promising. The XII Plan (2012–17) announced funds in its scheme for what they term as 'Innovation Universities'.[92] Identifying 'new issues ... that defy the existing divisions and protocols of knowledge', UGC continues to observe that 'no single discipline will be able to generate adequate and complete knowledge about the inter-related phenomena and to provide solutions to the problems of the real world'.[93] The scope covers new types of degrees and courses, interdisciplinary and cross-border research, and shared (cross disciplinary) research facilities. The Research Project for Teachers in the same plan encourages research in areas that 'cut across disciplines and subjects'.[94]

Yet, with little information on how exactly these schemes are materialized, nothing can be said conclusively about efficacy of the efforts. At multiple levels, the UGC is said to be overly stretched, guiding universities in everything ranging from construction of hostel blocks to floating new programmes. In doing so, they tend to miss forest for the woods. A procedure-centric approach of UGC makes it develop an oversight to its primary purpose.

[88] Guidelines for the Scheme available at http://www.ugc.ac.in/oldpdf/xiplan-pdf/epochmakingsociathinkers1.pdf (last accessed on 12 August 2013).

[89] This is exactly how it was worded in the X Plan, indicating a disinterested carrying over of previous schemes.

[90] Available at http://www.ugc.ac.in/oldpdf/xiplanpdf/areastudyprogramme.pdf (accessed on 12 August 2013).

[91] Available at http://www.ugc.ac.in/oldpdf/xiplanpdf/areastudyprogramme.pdf (accessed on 12 August 2013).

[92] See the Scheme http://www.ugc.ac.in/pdfnews/3155745_InnovationUniversity.pdf (accessed on 12 August 2013).

[93] See the Scheme http://www.ugc.ac.in/pdfnews/3155745_InnovationUniversity.pdf (accessed on 12 August 2013).

[94] Available at http://www.ugc.ac.in/mrp/ (accessed on 12 August 2013).

This is worsened by increasing politicization of its mandate, with each scheme assuming a site for rent seeking. In the next stage of reforms, the government is considering National Higher Education Commission (that will do away with all regulatory agencies in the Indian higher education context), but there is no reason to believe that it will also (like the UGC) not outlive its purpose.[95] Universities need good governance, and this cannot be effectuated from New Delhi. Universities must be carved out in substance, and once done, they should be granted autonomy.

Funding Structures

Funding mechanisms need to change dramatically. The UGC specifies in detail how funds should be spent, without considering intellectual and academic freedom. Such straightjacketing effect leads to shortfalls and unutilized funds simultaneously, seriously impacting the research output. Most grants are specified for measurable managerial and administrative intervention that the university makes—which is also the reason why fund allocation and grant parameters are kept strict. But research and pedagogical innovations—particularly in the social sciences—do not happen in an instant, nor can their intellectual delivery be observed precisely. And for what can be observed, is largely ignored. There is hardly any research reward scheme that exists for citations, publications into (interdisciplinary journals), or impact factor (or an indigenous equivalent) of journals published by Indian universities. Also, individual grants are focused on encouraging diversity in scholarship and are targeted at people belonging to backward communities or regions. While this is welcome, there is a need to cultivate good research by sponsoring research that has interdisciplinary scope and promise. This could also be given to a team of scientist/scholars from different universities–something usually not done. One of the ways in which Western institutions have emerged as the most prestigious research units in the world is through a very sophisticated style of funding research that rests on the principles of academic freedom, long term benefits, and openness to new ideas.

[95] Debroy, B. 'Higher Education: Regulation and Control', in K. Basu and A. Maertens (eds), *The New Oxford Companion to Economics in India* (New Delhi: Oxford University Press, 2012), p. 338.

Autonomous Research Centre and Programmes

Suggestions on altering funding mechanisms from UGC are akin to fixing a light bulb in a house without power. The main recommendation of this chapter hinges on a bottom-up approach—where universities themselves become engines of interdisciplinary changes, rather than it being dictated from New Delhi. Such intellectual construction crucially rests on administrative engagements, crafted by visionary and entrepreneurial Deans/Directors and Vice Chancellors. They—as thought leaders of today—need to devise mechanisms by way of which interdisciplinary programmes can be started, focusing on the development of problem solving skills of the students and the enhancement of their utility in the market. Creation of programmes must be preceded by establishing research centre(s) on the interdisciplinary approach sought. These centres must be made nodal and autonomous departments for producing research, courses, advocacy, and industry-linkages for few years. Once established and branded, they can spin off and become centres of interdisciplinary excellence, and nurture similar centres in other universities.

The interdisciplinary programmes could borrow faculty from various departments and instruct students in multiple disciplines. Incentives to faculty for working in an interdisciplinary centre could be given by offering them joint appointment in the research centre and department. The centre directors should have a representation in the Senate and Governing Body Meetings, to lend seriousness to their endeavours. The faculty and students associated with such centres and programmes must be empowered to undertake active interest in practices emanating from their efforts. For instance, they could start a newsletter, which can later culminate into a journal. They, in their own identity as interdisciplinary entities, could consult government's agencies in varying capacity, in addition to other NGO-related policy initiatives. A working paper series where problems specific to the region/issue are addressed through the newly evolving methodology, could be put up on web sites and libraries. Improving visibility through such initiatives will draw more innovative means of bolstering the centres/programmes, as well as increase market visibility.

Currently, several think tanks and research organizations work in India, which could immensely benefit from knowledge creation of this kind. Benefits could come in the form of students of interdisciplinary centres/programmes interning in these organizations or working with these organizations on joint research projects. The collaborative arrangements have a great deal of fertility, if viewed in the international context. Universities from the US in particular, and the West in general, are aggressively looking forward to set up broad range of academic ties with Indian institutions at multiple levels. They not only aspire to be part of the economic vigour that India has shown in last decade, but also want to tap the burgeoning Indian middle class which has increasingly started going abroad for higher studies.[96] Interdisciplinary research centres and programmes can become the linking bolts through which the collaborations can be hinged. Since interdisciplinary programmes are more robust and sophisticated abroad, India can greatly benefit from the knowledge spill overs that will follow.

Cultivating Interdisciplinary Scholars

One way to address challenges faced by interdisciplinary scholars and early career academics in the field is to observe how they themselves view the field, once they achieve success. Many have mentioned it to me that while interdisciplinary studies appeals to doctoral candidates and early career academics because of elements of novelty, lesser competition, social conscience, holistic approach, broad networks, exciting field experiences, community connections, and evolving discourses; the later difficulties surface in the form of reduced recognition by disciplinary scholars, fewer peer-reviewed journals, disparaged rigorousness, light infrastructure, fewer honours, and disadvantages in promotion.[97] By checking the disadvantages that interdisciplinary academics face after their doctoral studies, we can enhance the perception quotient of the decision ex ante. Faculty promotion could be based not just on publications and teaching but also on integration of knowledge and knowledge discoveries. Since interdisciplinary scholarship usually involves multiple authors, it should not be scored lower than a single author publication. Given that fewer journals cater to interdisciplinary research, more weightage should be given to them.

Cultivating such scholars through valuing their linkages in diverse fields is a good start. Lee and Bozeman (2005) show that scholars typically spend 50 per cent of their time working with members of their own

[96] Kapur and Mehta, 'Mortgaging the Future: Indian Higher Education', p. 126.

[97] Pfirman, S. and P. Martin, 'Fostering Interdisciplinary Scholars', in R. Frodeman, J.T. Klein, and C. Mitcham (eds), The Oxford Handbook of Interdisciplinarity (New York: Oxford University Press, 2010), pp. 387–403, 391.

department, 25 per cent with outside collaborators, 15 per cent working alone and 10 per cent with others.[98] Clearly, there is a lot of scope for interdisciplinarity to be ingrained in the university's social fabric. Since interdisciplinary scholars work with even broader scale of communities, they should be encouraged to lecture and debate with disciplinary scholars. This will not only make the former more rigorous, but also raise consciousness in the latter of how immaterial her problem is in the larger context of social challenge that is being addressed. Interdisciplinary scholars have a synthesizing skill, and even if it comes at the cost of deepest engagement with the issue, the benefits of having bird's eye view of a complex problem greatly outweighs the costs.

Philanthropic Initiatives

Injecting interdisciplinarity into the broken system of India's university education will be like loading an old gun with new bullets, which cannot be fired accurately. Hence, the reformation of university system is an urgent priority. One way in which this could be done is by encouraging private philanthropic initiatives. Debroy notes that India has more places of worship than educational institutions and hospitals combined.[99] Barring few, which were constructed in ancient and medieval era, nearly all places of worship are constructed and managed privately (with some major ones that are under government control). The philanthropists need to be attracted to the social sector. The problem is that bureaucratic and political forces have hijacked the meaningful agenda of earlier philanthropists in India, and post-Independence, the share of philanthropy in India has fallen from 17 per cent to less than 2 per cent.[100] Most premier private universities in the world (including Harvard, Stanford, and Yale) emerged as private philanthropic initiatives. Meaningful donations can be made only by the most affluent, since it is only those who enough can afford to give some of

[98] Lee, S. and B. Bozeman, 'The Impact of Research Collaboration on Scientific Productivity', *Social Studies of Science*, 35 (2005): 673–702.

[99] Debroy, 'Higher Education: Regulation and Control', in K. Basu and A. Maertens (eds), *The New Oxford Companion to Economics in India* (New Delhi: Oxford University Press, 2012), p. 336.

[100] Kapur, D. and P.B. Mehta, 'Higher Education', in K. Basu and A. Maertens (eds), *The New Oxford Companion to Economics in India* (New Delhi: Oxford University Press, 2012), p. 333.

it back, without the need to look for returns. But for this to happen, governments need to create suitable frameworks to design fertile grounds for breeding of money and intellectuals. In such structures, interdisciplinarity will bloom without external support.

Interdisciplinarity at an Early Age: Demand Side View

Lastly and perhaps most importantly, Indian policymakers in higher education need to recognize that integration of disciplines can, and needs to, happen within a single mind as well as among a team.[101] While team-led interdisciplinary approach can be cultivated in a relatively short term, integration in a single mind is a long-term process. To nurture minds that have a synthesizing ability, they need to be identified young. Hence, students should be taught multiple disciplines from an early age, and instructed not only about the diverse ways of thinking, but also about crucial methodologies involved. This way, a student gets sensitized towards problems, issues and concepts that would lie outside her specialized domain. This creates a rare individual able to appreciate complex issues at hand with greater ease and could also develop leadership potential. Multidisciplinary instruction should not be forced upon students. While some students will have a natural appreciation for disparate thoughts, others may want to drown into a single subject, and that diversity needs to be respected.

One such exercise is being effectuated in Delhi University, while this chapter is underway. Few months ago, Delhi University announced the four-year undergraduate programme—a pedagogical shift from the three-year programme which was in place since the British era.[102] With revolutionary flexibility to exit at certain points with differently nomenclatured degrees (and join later in time for enhanced degrees), the programme's curriculum in the first year covers eleven foundational courses like language, arts, commerce, science, mathematics, culture, and civilization, governance, and citizenship. In addition, there are four applied courses and 26 discipline courses. The weight of discipline courses increases as time progresses.

---

[101] C.S. Wagner, et al., 'Approaches to Understanding and Measuring Interdisciplinary Scientific Research (IDR): A Review of the Literature', *Journal of Informetrics*, 5, 1 (2011).

[102] See the approval note at http://www.du.ac.in/fileadmin/DU/DUCorner/pdf/09052013pr.pdf (accessed on 12 August 2013).

With dissenting reviews from several quarters,[103] the programme has been received favourable at large, evinced in the record receipt of admission forms this year,[104] quenching the fears that this may force the exodus of prospective students to other universities. If the rigorousness of the degrees is not diluted and extra cost of the fourth year does not militate against a student's desire not to opt out of the system, this proposal has immense potential for encouraging interdisciplinary thought.

IS IT A GOOD SIGHT TO BEHOLD?

The chapter does not in any way claim that disciplines are redundant. Understandably, Helmholtz claimed way back in 1896 (just as when disciplinary boundaries were being unknowingly cast in stone), that no one 'could oversee the whole of science and keep the threads in one hand and find orientation. The natural result is that each individual researcher is forced to choose an even smaller area as his workplace and can only maintain incomplete knowledge of neighbouring areas'.[105] What the chapter purports is to lend an alternative paradigm of understanding the way we teach ourselves, particularly when the workplace area has become too small (to the point of becoming inaccessible) to matter.

And there is no reason to believe that disciplinary experiences of education build better quality professionals. In an experiment conducted by Rhoten, et al. (2008), the authors compared graduate students participating in the IGERT (interdisciplinary programme of National Science Foundation, see note 13) with students with disciplinary training. They were placed in working groups (that controlled for gender, field and years of graduate training) and given a time-bound (two and half days) task for creating a proposal for charting next the generation of research on human-ecosystem

[103] http://articles.timesofindia.indiatimes.com/2013-05-24/delhi/39500932_1_proposed-four-year-undergraduate-programme-delhi-university-intellectuals (accessed on 12 August 2013).

[104] http://articles.economictimes.indiatimes.com/2013-06-19/news/40070020_1_four-year-undergraduate-programme-fyup-delhi-university (last accessed on 12 August 2013).

[105] Helmoltz, H. 'Über das Verhältnis der Naturwissenschaften zur Gesamtheit der Wissenschaften'. *Vorträge under Reden*, 4th edn, Vol. 1 (Braunschweig: Vieweg und Sohn, 1896), pp. 157–86; 162.

sustainability. They were monitored by trained observers and judged by a multidisciplinary panel of experts. It was found that IGERT groups with less training received highest score when assessed for 'whether and in what ways educational experiences change how young scientists work together and the quality of what they produce'.

India needs interdisciplinarly sensitive young minds. Investing in humanities is essential for survival of democracies.[106] Moving through obscene inequalities and crippling citizenship, India needs it more than ever. And the first thing that needs to be done is to have intellectuals speak with each other. Indian Statistical Institutes are one of the premier higher education units for learning, producing excellent research in economics and econometrics. Yet, most of its research is either too specific to add any value in policy design, or too incomprehensive (on account of mathematical models) to be applied.[107] And this is not just a case of Indian economists. Across the world, sustained disciplinary engagements produce scholars who speak only to fellow scholars. Real meaning of education is shoved out of the window, when it is draped with labels of disciplines.

To invoke Žižek, there is a parallax *view* glaringly apparent when we attempt to construct the locations of disciplines.[108] We realize that rise of disciplinarity is only part of the story. On the contrary, there is a need to view interdisciplinary mode of thinking as the dominant one, since it is exactly in this amorphous form that the world presents itself to us. Disciplines are merely artificial joints that we imagine nature can be divided at. Boundaries of disciplines were fashioned by varying social forces at the time. The borders of disciplines need to be not just porous but also sufficiently weak, so as to enable significant level of deterritorialization of disciplines. Any resistance to the process of amalgamation will convert disciplines into ideology (as we often see happening) left at the mercy of the hermeneutics of the discipline's own claims. While there are signs of Phoenix of interdisciplinary rising, it may require our help. And I believe it will be a good sight.

---

[106] Nussbaum, M.C. *Not for Profit: Why Democracy Needs the Humanities (New in Paper)* (Princeton University Press, 2012).

[107] Economists are notoriously insulated—evident from their relative low rate of citation of other social science research (Pieters R. and Baumgartner H. 2002. 'Who Talks to Whom? Intra- and Interdisciplinary Communication of Economics Journals'. *Journal of Economic Literature* 40: 483–509).

[108] Žižek, S. *The Parallax View* (Cambridge, MA: MIT Press, 2006).

15 The Role of Humanities in a University Education[1]

Alice Prochaska

I recently attended a talk in Oxford given by Montek Singh Ahluwalia.[2] It was an enlightening and inspirational vision of the challenges facing India now and in the future. Ahluwalia brought to bear a panoply of statistics on the growth of the Indian economy, the slow but steady progress on reducing the proportion of the population who live in poverty, and on key measures of national well-being including food security, productivity, and access to education. At dinner after the talk, a professor of philosophy posed the question: 'What are the values that underpin your planning?'

Values, as Ahluwalia agreed, provide the framework within which all planning ultimately must take place. They include integrity, an aspiration

---

[1] This chapter is based on a presentation made at the Conference on the Future of Indian Universities at O.P. Jindal Global University, 21–23 March 2013.

[2] This talk was delivered at an informal dinner hosted by the Blavatnik School of Government, Oxford (2013).

to excellence, respect for human rights, compassion and empathy, and the humility to understand other people's aspirations and priorities. Intellectual rigour and the ability to test all assumptions and conclusions are also critical.

Where do these values come from? How do we know when we are living up to them and when we are falling short? I would like to reflect here on just some of the ways in which an education in the humanities can provide a framework for both understanding and action. It will become apparent from some of my examples, that the humanities also provide a profound foundation for the sense of personal and national identity which in turn supports the international sensibilities that are vital to a true commonwealth of learning. My observations are based on my experiences as an administrator and a historian at the universities of Yale in the United States and Oxford and London in the United Kingdom; and also on work at the British Library where my role was to supervise the provision of the vast 'special collections' of scholarly resources there which are so heavily used by scholars from all around the world.

First, and here I will use the example of Yale, one of the ambitions that first led people to establish universities was the search for truth. Truth could be found in books, as the Protestant Christian ministers who founded Yale believed when they brought to the table gifts of books 'for establishing a college in this colony' in 1701. Their vision of truth may have been theologically narrow, but by the time their college had grown into a university aspiring to international standing in the mid-twentieth century, there was a more global view. Sterling Memorial Library, a huge cathedral of learning which opened its doors in 1930, celebrates the humanities in stone, wood carving, and engraved glass windows throughout the building. The front portico, with its celebration of world languages and the civilizations they represented, remind us that American universities teach as broadly and draw as boldly on the cultures of the world as those of any other nation. For all the dominance of US scholars in the sciences and social sciences, their contribution to humanities teaching provides equally enriching and diverse models.

The thread of cultural values leads me now to some examples from the incomparable collections of ancient religious manuscripts at the British Library. The Lindisfarne Gospels, the greatest example of early medieval, Anglo-Saxon graphic art, is also a textbook case of the importance of scholarly artefacts in the creation and understanding of identity.

The manuscript was almost certainly made in the north-east of England in the early eighth century of the Common Era. Created with deep reverence by a single devout monk, as were so many of the great religious manuscripts of the world, the Gospels manuscript was then augmented, two centuries later, by a scribe who wrote in between the lines, a vernacular translation from the Latin into Anglo-Saxon, the precursor language of modern English. This was highly significant in an era when all Christian ceremonial and reading was supposedly conducted in Latin, the preserve of a tiny educated elite.

It is also significant that the manuscript is illustrated in the richest of blues, golds and reds, using pigments that were not available in the far-flung, primitive outpost of northern Europe that was Anglo-Saxon England. Using modern spectroscopy it has been possible to establish whether the rich blue was actually lapis lazuli, which might have come from central or southern Asia, by trade routes which only recently became known to have existed. It certainly is the case that the illustrations display influences from Byzantium, and suggest that the artist-scribe had access at one time to works created several thousand miles away from his northern monastery. This rare surviving piece of evidence now invites the attention of humanities scholars in language study, history and art history; and chemical analysis by scientists, not least computer scientists responsible for high-level digital imaging, in a collaborative search for truths about patterns of human migration and influence. It also represents a highly contested piece of regional identity, for the people of north-eastern England can be as anti-metropolitan as people in other regions of the world; and they have made vigorous claims to take back the manuscript. Certainly it is a part of their regional identity, but so it is of the identity of Christian believers all over the world. To whom does it 'belong' and if it belongs to all of us, who should be its custodians? Values are seldom uncontested.

My life at the British Library was enlivened from time to time by other examples of contested regional and national identity, through encounters with the fierce, tribal loyalties that adhere to cultural artefacts, and bring them often into the realms of geo-politics. They ranged from the insistent demands of patriotic Rastafarians in Ethiopia to have their manuscripts returned, to the gracious and extremely moving expressions of gratitude by dignitaries of the newly re-established state of Armenia. For the Ethiopian Rastafarians, a pride in national identity combined with a reverence for their distinctive version of a Christian heritage to create an urgent sense of ownership. They did not bow to arguments that the manuscripts they prized almost certainly would not have survived the climatic and war-torn hazards of the twentieth century in their region. Nor did their claims acknowledge that during that century, scholars had worked on the cultural history of Ethiopia precisely because these treasures were available to them in a place of calm study; and thus had increased the international fame of the Ethiopian inheritance.

Armenian leaders, by contrast, speaking at an exhibition to celebrate seventeen centuries since the first Armenian state adopted Christianity, told us that in that time, their ancestors had treasured their manuscripts beyond all else, and carried them into war before their advancing armies. 'Now we are a state again' they said, 'we thank you for preserving our inheritance and placing it again on the international map'.

The people of north-eastern England, the Ethiopians claiming the restitution of their cultural treasures to their place of origin, and the Armenians who were proud to see their national identity celebrated in another part of the world, all convey messages about the foundations of humane learning. Without the work of scholars, curators, and conservators, and the transmission of their work through teaching, these vital artefacts of national identity would remain unknown. They provide the primary resources for an understanding about the interactions and the beliefs and value systems of people living in different parts of the world, which otherwise would not exist. Without these sources, and without the work of successive generations of humanities scholars who have decoded them and caused them to be respected and preserved for future generations, some critically important elements in our collective knowledge and understanding of humanity would be lacking.

I move now to a more recent and one of the most tragic episodes of cultural history in the modern world. A small band of US and British troops, commissioned into a joint unit known as the 'Monuments Men' in World War II, had the dangerous task of going ahead of the advancing Allied armies as they fought back against the Nazis, first in Italy and then in northern Europe. They were charged with identifying and protecting monuments, works of art, archives, and libraries from looting and destruction. It was an avowed policy of the Nazi regime to create an empire that would both bring together the most esteemed art of the West for the greater glory of the Germanic people, and deliberately destroy the national pride and sense of identity of the conquered peoples (the Slavic nations in particular) whose monuments and cultural treasures were seen as the locus of their pride.

The Monuments Men were responsible for rescuing tens of thousands of works of art and some priceless buildings and libraries; and before they were disbanded, for tracking down large quantities of loot and identifying its rightful owners. It was Dwight D. Eisenhower, who as Supreme Commander of the Allied Forces in Europe, authorized the setting up of the Monuments, Fine Art and Archives unit, and issued a directive to the armies, to respect the treasures of 'the civilisation that is ours' and on no account to allow mere military convenience to prevail over this priority. Eisenhower's directive was an extraordinary example (sadly, not always followed in recent times) of asserting humane values even in a time of global war. It is no accident that the 'Monuments Men' were recruited from among the leading art historians and historical scholars of their generation, nor that General, later President Eisenhower's own education had included a good element of what the Americans today call the 'liberal arts'. This experience in World War II has had a lot to do with shaping a subsequent body of international law, ethics and norms for practical action that now guide modern governmental and inter-governmental organizations, including amongst others, UNESCO.

* * *

After that plea for the international importance of an education in the humanities, let me illustrate the ways in which humanities inform the education offered by my own university, Oxford. Economic uncertainties and budgetary retrenchment have led to a sense of threat in British universities as in so many others. In Britain this is felt especially acutely because the university system is almost wholly subject to state funding and regulation (although in fact only about one-third of universities' finance actually comes directly from the state). The subvention given to teaching in the humanities has now almost vanished, and money for research is subject to a regime of assessment in which the 'impact' of scholarly research is measured through the Research Excellence Framework, or REF. These blunt instruments may be perceived as more threatening than they really are; but they are an influential part of the academic landscape.

At Oxford, the threat is felt as keenly as anywhere. The university has huge strength in the humanities nevertheless, and this is supported particularly by the college system which Oxford shares with Cambridge, uniquely in terms of the strength and autonomy of the colleges. Thirty-eight separate, free-standing colleges form part of the collegiate university, with a strong collaborative centre. Thirty of them teach both undergraduates and research students; the remainder being for graduate students only. Within each college, scholars deeply steeped in the humanities work side by side with scientists. Their research is informed on a daily basis by conversations that cross disciplinary boundaries. Students lead their lives in a collegiate environment without departmental boundaries.

A college community of scholars and students thus is especially well placed to foster interdisciplinary discussions, and in addition to that, the Oxford courses for both undergraduates and graduates are increasingly interdisciplinary. Not only do the sciences inform each other and share perspectives and methodologies at Oxford, but so do the humanities and social sciences.

Among undergraduate courses are the well-known philosophy, politics, and economics (PPE), a training ground for so many of Britain's politicians and some foreign ones as well, and joint degrees in history and economics, computer science with philosophy, modern languages with law and economics, and quite a few other examples. Postgraduate degrees increasingly require interdisciplinary agility from their students, as for example in one of the most recent additions, the master's in public policy which has been introduced at the new Blavatnik School of Government.

It is a notable feature of the collegiate structure at Oxford, that it fosters the establishment of small interdisciplinary centres, often collaborations between colleges, where new forms of scholarship can take place. More than forty such separate centres currently exist, and some that have been and gone, have left behind well-established permanent centres of excellence which in turn become part of the central university (The Blavatnik School of Government had its origin in one such centre, and another flourishing example is the School of Interdisciplinary and Area Studies.).

I will conclude by mentioning in this context the plans that my own college, Somerville, has for celebrating a proud part of our own identity: our long tradition of educating some of the most celebrated Indian women and now, since becoming a mixed college for women and men in 1994, some of the most promising of Indian's next generations. In 1937, the young Indira Nehru came to Somerville to study history in a long tradition of Indian women undergraduates at what was then still a college for women only. The

Figure 15.1 Architect's plans for the India building and Oxford India Centre for Sustainable Development at Somerville College, Oxford

Source: Picture Plane. Reprinted with permission.

college's first Indian student was Cornelia Sorabji, the first woman to read law at Oxford (she arrived in 1889) and later the first woman to practise law in India. We celebrate her both because she stands for the college's commitment to internationalism and diversity from our earliest days, and also because she is a role model for public service: having dedicated much of her life to helping women in purdah.

Now, building on great interdisciplinary strength in the sciences, Somerville is establishing an Oxford India Centre for Sustainable Development, with an Indira Gandhi programme in it. This will celebrate in particular, Mrs Gandhi's far-sighted and enduring concern for the natural environment, exemplified by her famous speech to the United Nations gathering in Stockholm in 1972 in which she said: 'The inherent conflict is not between conservation and development, but between environment and reckless exploitation of man and earth in the name of efficiency.' With support from the Government of India which I am most deeply proud and grateful to acknowledge, we are bringing fully funded postgraduate students from India to Oxford to work on a series of 'impact themes', starting with food security and all the scientific, social, and cultural questions that surround that huge problem. Subsequent themes will include the role of culture and philosophy in government, women's issues, and healthcare. We hope, by establishing this centre, to deepen and enrich the engagement of the University of Oxford with India, to contribute to the education of future Indian leaders, as Oxford is so proud to have done for many generations, and to enrich the experience of cultural exchange for all our students, giving them opportunities to learn from the Indian experience and to carry forward honoured traditions of public service in both countries.

Our aspiration for the new centre includes an archway leading out from Somerville College, to the University of Oxford's great new developments on the Radcliffe Observatory Quarter: adjacent on two sides to that temple of humane attainment, the headquarters of Oxford University Press, and on the right by the new Blavatnik School of Government. Values and aspirations give enduring shape to the future of scholarship and education, or so we hope, in bricks and mortar.

16 The Liberal Arts in the American Context

What India Can Learn from Western Liberal Education

Carol M. Bresnahan

The American writer and *New York Times* columnist Thomas Friedman said that, like many of his generation, he was ordered as a child to finish his dinner, because people in India were hungry. Now, years later, he tells his children to finish their homework, because people in India are hungry for his children's jobs.[1]

India has hundreds of universities, but most of them are less concerned with the liberal arts than they are with technical education. One need only consider the Indian Institutes of Technology, or IITs, created by the Institutes of Technology Act of 1961, to understand this point. The act

---

[1] Friedman, T. 'Doing our Homework', *New York Times* (accessed on 27 June 2013).

describes each IIT as 'an institution of national importance', a clear signal of the relevance of technology to Indian higher education.[2] The existence and prestige of the Indian Institutes of Management, or IIMs, further underscore this point. Early IIMs were based on American graduate business education, setting up the idea of using education in the United States as a model for India.[3]

If you talk to Indians today, whether in India or abroad, they will tell you of a distinct pecking order that exists when it comes to the areas that a higher-education student might choose to study. At the top of the pecking order are the highly technical fields of medicine and engineering. It is interesting that the IIT act specifically sets forth the teaching of technical fields as primary.[4] If a student cannot or will not study those areas, then commerce or business might be acceptable, but not as laudatory, even if necessary to the Indian and the world economies. Law might be permissible. But the liberal arts? They are well off the radar and absent from the pecking order, even though they are vital in the eyes of American employers, and should be for Indian employers (and educators) as well.

This lacuna is in clear contrast to American education, whose oldest institutions, like Harvard, were created in the liberal tradition, many of them in order to provide trained ministers. Often, these are also the best institutions. To be clear, outstanding technical education has a firm place in America—one need only consider the Massachusetts Institute of Technology or the California Institute of Technology, at the top of the reputational ladder, to see that this is so. Graduates of these institutions will continue to do well. This argument does not seek to disparage technical training. I am writing this piece on my laptop, and I certainly want my word processing application to work perfectly and seamlessly. When I go to the internet

---

[2] The act is available at http://www.iitb.ac.in/legal/IITsAct.pdf. The citation is from Chapter I. 2, of the act (accessed on 27 June 2013).

[3] The IIMs, while not offering degrees, are essentially postgraduate institutions. A very short general history of IIMs in India is available at http://www.iimb.ernet.in/about-iimb/history (accessed on 27 June 2013).

[4] The act calls on each IIT 'to provide for instruction and research in such branches of engineering and technology, sciences and arts, as the Institute may think fit....' Despite the mention of 'arts,' the IITs are—and their very name implies this—aimed at the teaching of technological fields. The citation is from the act, II. 6. a.

for the research on which articles like this one depend, I rely on highly trained and technically proficient programmers and designers to create the websites I need. An accountant may need to know tax law; when people drive over a bridge, they do not want to worry about whether the engineers who designed it were competent or not. However, the liberal arts impart invaluable skills that we take for granted, probably because they are less easily noticed in our culture or perhaps because they are wrongly considered skills that anyone, regardless of education, can attain.

Despite the lament that the liberal arts may be waning, surveys of employers reveal that the qualities that the liberal arts, at their best, impart in their graduates are among the top qualities employers seek in many of their new hires. In 2012, *Forbes* magazine pointed out that companies are looking for a 'cultural fit'. The traits of a successful job candidate include professionalism, high energy, confidence, and intellectual curiosity.[5] The *Wall Street Journal*, in the midst of a worldwide recession in 2011, noted that only 10 per cent of those working in highly technical fields in Silicon Valley, California, during its dramatic expansion in the 1990s held technology degrees. It added that, instead of seeking out technically trained employees, companies should train those they hire for the specifics of the job, and should, therefore, consider employing those who are adaptable to such training, 'even recent graduates who don't have much job experience.'[6] *U.S. News and World Report*, while praising technical abilities, says that a vital skill needed by a person who wants to be hired is facility in communication. The author of the piece points to the unfortunate prevalence among job applications of 'grammatically tragic cover letters', and advises that online or informal writing—that is, the incomplete sentences or unpunctuated phrases ('Hey bro'), emoticons (☺) and acronyms or abbreviations (LOL!) that are ubiquitous in tweeting and other forms of quick electronic communication—is not what she has in mind. One hiring

---

[5] Casserly, Meghan 'Top Five Personality Traits Employers Hire Most', http://www.forbes.com/sites/meghancasserly/2012/10/04/top-five-personality-traits-employers-hire-most/ (accessed on 27 June 2013).

[6] Cappelli, Peter 'Why Companies Aren't Getting the Employees They Need', http://online.wsj.com/article/SB10001424052970204422404576596630897409182.html (accessed on 27 June 2013). Cappelli wrote a similar article for *Time* at http://business.time.com/2012/06/04/the-skills-gap-myth-why-companies-cant-find-good-people/.

authority said her company requires its own writing test, and warns, 'That's one of the biggest ways people fail'.[7] Businesses seek graduates with the skills to communicate, work in teams and analyse. They want employees who understand that a single skill set or methodology is unlikely to address the complex problems that our world faces. The American Association of Colleges and Universities (AAC&U) adds that 69 per cent of the leaders in business see a liberal arts degree as 'very important'.[8]

Business Week, in 2008, presented the top qualities that characterize 'great hires'. In order, these were job understanding; communication skills; planning, coordination and execution; maintaining priorities and organization; fit; learning and growth; and commitment. It is interesting that the qualities did not include technical training.[9] The liberal arts have, at their core, the responsibility for imparting many of the key qualities employers are looking for and that are enumerated above. William Pannapacker, a frequent columnist for the *Chronicle of Higher Education* and writing in the *New York Times*, declared that 'the world is changing too quickly to make reliable predictions. Assume that you will have many careers, and that you will need to find ways to adapt your talents to the world's needs. I believe', he concluded, 'the best place to do that is a liberal arts college.'[10] The AAC&U cites a study that shows employers want, above all, employees who understand the importance of change and innovation. The report emphasizes the liberal arts as a clear path to this goal:

> *Employers recognize the importance of liberal education and the liberal arts.*
> The majority of employers agree that having both field-specific knowledge and skills and a broad range of skills and knowledge is most important for

[7] Graves, Jada A. '7 Key Skills You Need to Get Hired Right Now', http://money.usnews.com/money/careers/articles/2013/02/21/7-key-skills-you-need-to-get-hired-right-now (accessed on 27 June 2013).

[8] Cited in University of Denver, 'Liberal Arts in the News', http://www.du.edu/ahss/admissions/liberalartsadvantage/news.html, (accessed on 27 June 2013). The AACU statement about the importance of a liberal arts degree came in 2010.

[9] Kurtz, Rod 'The Qualities of a Great Hire', http://www.businessweek.com/smallbiz/tips/archives/2008/05/the_qualities_of_a_great_hire.html (accessed on 27 June 2013).

[10] Pannapacker, William 'A Liberal Arts Foundation', http://www.nytimes.com/roomfordebate/2013/03/24/for-the-college-bound-are-there-any-safe-bets/a-liberal-arts-foundation-for-any-career (accessed on 27 June 2013).

recent college graduates.... Few think that having field-specific knowledge and skills alone is what is most needed for individuals' career success. Eighty percent of employers agree that, regardless of their major, every college student should acquire broad knowledge in the liberal arts and sciences.[11]

What is it about the liberal arts that give such certitude? Pannapacker, along with others, believes that the liberal arts graduate can do anything. He points out that employers report, 'We love students with liberal-arts degrees. They are curious; they know how to ask good questions. They know how to conduct research. They are effective writers and speakers. And they learn quickly.'[12] The direct correlation between these qualities and those underscored by *Business Week* is strong.

The notion that, historically, the liberal arts were not aimed at preparing the student for making a living is as mistaken as it is widespread. But, perpetuating the error, *The New Catholic Encyclopaedia* states that the tradition liberal arts had as their goal 'to prepare the student not for gaining a livelihood' but for gaining knowledge.[13] But if one considers what the graduates of medieval and early modern study did with their educations, one sees that many entered the traditional professions, including law, medicine and the professoriate, and they did so to make a living. It is true that they pursued knowledge, but they also put their educations to practical use and sought education in order to make their way professionally. The humanists of the fifteenth century insisted on the connection between learning and moral philosophy—that is, doing the right thing, a very practical application of education. The fact that the sixteenth-century Jesuits required their members to complete a rigorous higher education, and that they opened numerous schools and colleges by the middle part of the century, is just one example of the continued application of the liberal arts to the 'real world'. The founder of the Jesuits, Ignatius of Loyola, placed emphasis on the 'relationship between learning and effective ministry', a 'traditional'

---

[11] Hart Research Associates, 'It Takes More Than a Major: Employer Priorities for College Learning and Student Success', http://www.aacu.org/liberaleducation/le-sp13/hartresearchassociates.cfm (accessed on 27 June 2013). The emphasis is in the original citation and is not added.

[12] Pannapacker, 'Liberal Arts Foundation.'

[13] *New Catholic Encyclopedia*, 'The Seven Liberal Arts', http://www.newadvent.org/cathen/01760a.htm (accessed on 27 June 2013).

belief.[14] Another example is the compilations, often the first of their kind, of grammars and dictionaries for native languages that had not previously been written down. Often created in order to educate native peoples in Catholic Christianity, these compendia became important for many other reasons as well. By the time of Ignatius of Loyola's death in 1556, the Society of Jesus had established well over thirty colleges in Europe.[15]

The report cited by the AAC&U noted the importance of both applied and liberal learning. American liberal arts colleges, while perhaps not the best place to gain strictly technical knowledge, nonetheless impart the values that are needed to sustain a thriving economy. Such education not only helps traditionally aged students, but also applies to non-traditionally aged students. At Rollins College, the Hamilton Holt School educates adult learners while remaining firmly grounded in the liberal arts. The Holt School recently won a grant of $ 140,000 for a Center for Lifelong Learning. It will put this funding toward the goal of offering 'innovative liberal arts programming for adults' over 50 years of age.[16] As Hamilton Holt, Rollins's eighth president and the man for whom the Holt School was named, would have agreed, it is never too late to learn or to apply one's learning. In fact, the point of liberal education is to create questioning, confident graduates who keep learning throughout their lives.

It is important to put to use what liberal education imparts. Rollins College has a history of 'pragmatic liberal education', a point made through its Explorations programme. This programme asserts 'that learning occurs when students reflect and make connections between theory and practice and by truly applying their liberal arts experience. The critical thinking skills [that] allow students to excel academically also yield students who are committed to lifelong learning and service'.[17] The application of liberal learning is vital to Rollins's vision of such learning.

[14] O'Malley, John W. *The First Jesuits* (Cambridge: Mass., 1993); see especially Chapter 6, 'The Schools'. The citation is found on p. 208.

[15] O'Malley, *First Jesuits*, 206–07.

[16] 'Rollins 360: Winter Park Foundation Grant Supports Holt's Center for Lifelong Learning,' http://360.rollins.edu/kudos/winter-park-heath-foundation-grant-supports-holts-center-for-lifelong-learn (accessed on 27 June 2013). The community response has, as of this writing, been very enthusiastic.

[17] 'Rollins Explorations: First-Year Programs,' http://r-net.rollins.edu/explorations/explorations.html (accessed on 27 June 2013).

In the *Hindustan Times* of Wednesday, 20 March 2013, Raj Kumar, Vice Chancellor of O.P. Jindal Global University, noting the number of Indian universities, feared that 'mediocrity has been institutionalized'. He added, 'We have a long way to go. The most important question that we need to ask is this—what future do Indian universities have?' Kumar's article spoke of India's failure to understand 'contemporary global realities of knowledge'. This statement suggests that we live in a world whose parts are connected—global, as Kumar put it—and implies that the failure to recognize this connectedness would lead to dire consequences. The first of several areas that the article highlighted is the lack of innovation. It is here, above all, that American liberal education can offer models.[18]

Prior to the conference on the liberal arts and the future of Indian universities at O.P. Jindal Global University in March 2013, a useful Concept Paper circulated, citing several ideals of the university. For instance, the chapter mentions the Kothari and the Radhakrishnan reports, which see institutions of higher education as focused on the ideals of 'scholarship and civilization',[19] two areas that have historically been among the aims of education, education's rapid changes notwithstanding. However, one might, in contrast, consider the work of Dr Nancy Cantor, the chancellor and president of Syracuse University in New York, USA. Cantor and her co-author, Dr Steve Schomberg, describe higher education as, in an ideal version, a safe haven that straddles the worlds of 'monastery and marketplace'.[20] In this view, the college or university serves as a centre for 'vibrant exchange'. It is like a monastery, because it protects those who inhabit it, offering a secure place for contemplation, learning, and research; it is also a marketplace, because it encourages the exciting clash among and exchange of ideas, discomfort, trial, failure, and success. Its goal is to balance insularity and too much order on one hand (the monastery), and chaos on the other (the marketplace). This balance represents liberal learning at its best.

[18] Kumar, R. 'Still Not in a Class of Their Own', *Hindustan Times* (20 March 2013), 10; or www.hindustantimes.com/StoryPage/Print/1028982.aspx (accessed on 27 June 2013).

[19] 'The Future of Indian Universities: Comparative Perspectives on Higher Education Reform: Concept Note', 1.

[20] Cantor, Nancy and Steve Schomberg, 'Poised between 2 Worlds: The University as Monastery and Marketplace', *Educause* (Mar-Apr 2003): 12–21. At this writing (June 2013), Dr Cantor has been announced as the incoming president of Rutgers University at Newark.

The Concept Paper asks several important questions, but one that bears emphasis is this: 'How does one sustain a liberal arts framework in an age of commodification of the university?'[21] This concern—sustaining a liberal arts framework—is shared by both public and private colleges and universities. American public institutions cannot continue to operate without thinking about their constituencies. These include the state legislators and governors who appropriate, or cut, funding for public and sometimes for private institutions. They include the parents of students, and the students themselves, who object to the ever-increasing percentage of the cost of education that they bear. One should not forget the general public, whose tax dollars are at stake and who look to technical training, and often not to liberal education, to jump start the economy. The ubiquitous talk about STEM education—that is, producing more graduates in science, technology, engineering, and mathematics—is ample proof of this concern. American President Barack Obama, who has degrees in the liberal arts (political science and law), recently announced that he is seeking an additional $ 12 billion for two-year colleges, which typically provide more technical, professional, or vocational training than do four-year institutions.[22]

American private colleges and universities agonize over how to contain runaway increases in the cost of tuition, room and board, which can quickly surpass $ 50,000 annually. By way of example, for the class entering in fall 2013, the sixteen private liberal arts institutions that comprise the Associated Colleges of the South (ACS), the consortium to which Rollins College belongs, plan increases over 2012–13 from zero per cent—which is the exception—to about 5 per cent, with the average closer to 4 per cent. Rollins College has announced, and its Board of Trustees has approved, an increase of 3.9 per cent for the academic year beginning in fall of 2013 to tuition, room, and board. For those who are arithmetically challenged, 4 per cent of $ 50,000 comes to $ 2,000. As a point of reference, my last year of undergraduate study at a selective private liberal arts college in the late 1970s came to over $ 5,500 for all expenses—and I (and my parents, who were generously paying for my education) recoiled at the significant

---

[21] 'Future of Indian Universities', 3.

[22] Lewin, Tamar 'A Boon to 2-Year Colleges, Affirming Their Value', http://www.nytimes.com/2009/07/15/education/15college.html?_r=0 (accessed on 27 June 2013).

costs involved. A first-year student at my undergraduate alma mater will pay, for the academic year 2013–14, a sticker price of $ 57,524 before any financial aid. Virtually all public institutions in the US charge a great deal more than $ 5,600 for tuition, let alone the cost of living, at present.

The emphasis on STEM education conveniently omits one uncomfortable fact. The cost of educating STEM graduates is much higher than the cost of educating, say, a major in English or history. The expense of faculty, labs, equipment, and the like is far greater for STEM graduates than for the humanities or social sciences. Speaking of the cost of education and the liberal arts, it is important to see that the liberal arts can pay for themselves. For example, the University of Michigan announced the receipt of a gift of $ 50 million in support of its programme in creative writing.[23] The Massachusetts Cultural Council showed through its well-named 'Cultural Investment Portfolio' that 'investment in non-profit arts, humanities, and science organizations' sends $ 1.2 billion into the local economy on an investment of only $ 3.4 million; over 27,000 full time, part time and contract jobs depended on this source of funding.[24]

The work of scholars and public intellectuals like Richard Florida proves that creativity has a growing role in society and that it leads in development of places enriched by a full cultural and intellectual life. Those who hold technical jobs, in other words, want to live in communities with flourishing theatres and museums, interesting films, excellent schools, and other amenities that the graduates of liberal arts majors often provide. The leaders of creativity are those who are liberally educated, who are at the centre of what Pannapacker called 'a life that's engaged with culture and thought'.[25]

Dr Stephen Briggs, former dean at Rollins College, former provost at The College of New Jersey, and now the president of Berry College in Georgia, noted that residential liberal education is expensive. But, as

---

[23] Gardner, Lee 'U of Michigan M.F.A. Program Receives a $50-Million Gift', *Chronicle of Higher Education* (7 March 2013), http://chronicle.com/blogs/bottomline/u-of-michigan-m-f-a-program-receives-a-50-mil (accessed on 27 June 2013).

[24] Massachusetts Cultural Council, 'Cultural Investment Portfolio', http://www.massculturalcouncil.org/programs/cultural_investment_portfolio.asp (accessed on 27 June 2013).

[25] See Florida, Richard. http://www.creativeclass.com/richard_florida, and Pannapacker, 'Liberal Arts Foundation' (accessed on 27 June 2013).

he put it, this model 'endeavours to do more than sell information'. He quotes a writer who says that 'people learn from the people they love'.[26] Technology-assisted education—that is, using technology to overcome distance or to enrich students' in-class learning—offers a great way to convey content, and, as Dr John Wood, Secretary General of the Association of Commonwealth Universities (ACU), London, indicated in his remarks at the March 2013 conference at O.P. Jindal Global University, it has a vital role in our future. However, we know that students want to talk about problems, argue, convince, be convinced, test evidence, apply solutions, derive rules, and a hundred other things that liberal education loves—and does well.

The word 'liberal' comes from a Latin word, *liber*, meaning 'free'. And freedom is exactly what a liberal education, at its best, conveys. Perhaps the American Association for the Advancement of Science has best identified what is important in liberal education when it emphasized the freedom that such an education brings: 'Ideally, a liberal education produces persons who are open-minded and free from provincialism, dogma, preconception, and ideology; conscious of their opinions and judgements; reflective of their actions; and aware of their place in the social and natural worlds.'[27]

Both public and private colleges and universities have reached the conclusion that the value of the liberal arts is no longer self-explanatory. When I began my career as a new assistant professor in the mid-1980s, I assumed that the importance of my field, history, was self-evident: a liberally educated person needed to know history. We used to wonder what impression a person ignorant of history would make at, say, a cocktail party, where that person's casual conversation companion might be a potential employer. If the person had never read Shakespeare's *Hamlet*, mistook the Ming Dynasty for the Qing Dynasty, did not know which side France fought on in World War I, or confused Martin Luther with Martin Luther King, he or she was showing appalling ignorance, and the assumption was that mastery of a certain canon of knowledge was the hallmark of liberal education.

---

[26] Briggs, Stephen R. 'The Purpose of Berry', *Berry Magazine* (Spring 2013): 10–11.

[27] Project on Liberal Education and the Sciences (1990). *The Liberal Art of Science: Agenda for Action* (Washington, DC: American Association for the Advancement of Science).

This may be true, but if we say that students who complete a liberal arts programme will think critically, operate effectively on teams, and understand that no single methodology is likely to solve the complex problems we face today, then we need to be able to prove to an increasingly sceptical public that our programmes provide students these skills. In addition, American regional accrediting agencies insist, and will continue to insist, on such assessment of the 'value-addedness' of our programmes.

It is important that all countries learn what we mean by liberal education and the values that are connected to it, for international institutions of higher education often seek liberal identities and talk a good game as they do so, but fail to support and display the values that underlie these identities. Khaled Fahmy, a professor in Egypt and chair of the Department of History at the American University in Cairo, described in the *Chronicle of Higher Education* why he did not attend a conference, in Dubai in the United Arab Emirates (UAE), at which he was invited to speak. He wrote,

> I had prepared a presentation on what I thought was the single most important factor threatening higher education in the Arab world, namely, the nearly complete absence of the very concept of liberal education.... I was going to argue that even when it comes to preparing students for the job market, Arab universities do not serve the students well by ignoring the principles of a liberal-arts education. I always tell my students who want to learn medicine and land a lucrative job as a physician that a good doctor is not only someone who knows his anatomy well; he must also understand hospital management, the history of his profession, the psychology of patients, how to deal with nurses.[28]

Fahmy went on to argue that a good architect is not a mere pourer of concrete, but that she must also know about art history, people, and aesthetics. He explained further, that he understood the challenges facing Arab universities, challenges that included a paucity of funding as well as censorship. He decried the Arab insistence on specialization in education that he sees as a legacy of the nineteenth century. Professor Fahmy planned to argue that the failure to understand or appreciate the value of liberal learning was a far greater threat to the advancement of the Arab world and

---

[28] Fahmy, Khaled, 'Why I Didn't Go to Dubai', *Chronicle of Higher Education* (3 July 2013), http://chronicle.com/blogs/worldwise/why-i-didnt-go-to-dubai/31935 (accessed on 27 June 2013).

Arab education than these problems, grave as they are. Deeply disturbed at the UAE's refusal to grant entry to an invitee over charges that the person denied entry had written critically of the monarchy of Bahrain, Fahmy decided not to attend. He expressed relief that the meeting itself was, ultimately, not held over complaints that academic freedom had been violated. In explaining his decision, he focused on the point that 'liberal education entails, indeed necessitates, training students to be civically engaged and politically aware,' which depends, in turn, on being free.

Michael Crow, President of Arizona State University, the largest university in the US with over 70,000 students *in toto*, and a person who might be expected to uphold the ideal of professional, non-liberal education, instead advocated for liberal learning. He wrote that 'the object of public universities should not be to produce predetermined numbers of particular types of majors but ... to focus on how to produce individuals who are capable of learning anything over the course of their lifetimes'. Besides being educated in sciences, Crow believed, 'every college student should acquire thorough literacy in ... the humanities and social sciences....'[29] This statement counters, fortunately, the words of Rick Scott, the governor of Florida, who derided public investment in liberal arts areas like anthropology, saying that taxpayers' money should go towards degrees that get the graduate a job, particularly a job in Florida. He said this despite the fact that his own daughter was found to be an anthropology major at the liberal-arts College of William and Mary, in great preparation for her own career and that it led to professional school for her.[30] Of course, Florida's governor may have had a political end in mind: one writer believes that '[the] liberal arts produce more culturally aware and progressive citizens, inclined to challenge ossified social conventions and injustices. Eliminate cultural and social sciences from public colleges and you'll ultimately produce fewer community organizers, poets, and critics....'[31] The same commentator noted that universities in

[29] Sal Gentile, 'Is a Liberal Arts Degree Worth It?' http://www.pbs.org/wnet/need-to-know/the-daily-need/is-a-liberal-arts-degree-worth-it/12107/ (accessed on 27 June 2013).

[30] See among other sources, Associated Press, Herald-Tribune, 'Rick Scott's Daughter Has Anthropology Degree', http://politics.heraldtribune.com/2011/10/12/rick-scotts-daughter-has-anthropology-degree/ (accessed on 27 June 2013).

[31] Stoller, Paul. 'The Limited Good of Rick Scott's Anthropology', http://www.huffingtonpost.com/paul-stoller/the-limited-good-of-rick-_b_1012356.html (accessed on 27 June 2013).

India are working to include the liberal arts in their curricula. O.P. Jindal Global University's commitment to opening a College of Liberal Arts and Humanities, discussed in more detail below, by 2014 is evidence. What does this liberal study do for those who follow it? As one person said, it imbues the student with curiosity. It gives him or her context. It provides an understanding of what motivates people. It makes one unafraid. As the president of North Shore Community College in Massachusetts said, 'A well-educated workforce … serves the long-term interests of democracy.'[32]

Liberal education in the US is closely associated with the AAC&U, which just released a new mission statement: 'To make liberal education and inclusive excellence the foundation for institutional purpose and educational practice in higher education.'[33] Harvard College states that it offers 'a liberal education—that is, an education conducted in a spirit of free inquiry undertaken without concern for topical relevance or vocational utility'. Regardless of which definition fits, it is clear, as Harvard puts it, that this kind of education prepares a student 'for the rest of life'.[34]

A news bureau in the US recently reported that 'liberal arts degrees get an unjustified bad rap'. The dean of the College of Liberal Arts and Sciences at the University of Florida stated that the evidence suggests that graduates will change careers—not just their jobs, but their careers—several times over the course of their working lives. 'A liberal arts degree is', he said, 'the ideal preparation for that kind of world….'[35] Why is this true? Surely, it is because of the ways of thinking rather than the content-specific skills that the liberal arts impart. Rollins College's president, Dr Lewis Duncan, has pointed out that education is like a 'T'. The top

---

[32] Burton, Wayne M. 'In long run, well-educated workforce is preferable to well-trained', in a letter to the editor of the *Boston Globe* on 14 June 2013, http://www.bostonglobe.com/opinion/letters/2013/06/13/long-run-well-educated-workforce-preferable-well-trained-one/UBA4s2DErptMqBbznRa9zL/story.html (accessed on 27 June 2013).

[33] American Association of Colleges and Universities, 'Big Questions, Urgent Challenges: Liberal Education and Americans' Global Future. Strategic Plan 2013–17', 2. The mission was adopted in November 2012.

[34] 'The Value of a Liberal Arts Education', http://www.admissions.college.harvard.edu/about/learning/liberal_arts.html, (accessed on 27 June 2013).

[35] Driscoll, Emily. 'What Is Liberal Arts Degree Worth These Days?' http://www.foxbusiness.com/personal-finance/2012/01/27/what-is-liberal-arts-degree-worth-these-days/ (accessed on 27 June 2013).

crossbar to the T is methodology or approach, it has breadth, and the minim (or up-down stroke) of the T is content or subject, which has depth, but is narrow. Much of the content a student learns will not be applicable within months or years as time and technology advance, but the methodology, the approach, the way of thinking that liberal education teaches will last, and will allow successful liberally educated individuals to negotiate different careers with nimbleness and to master the continued learning that doing so will require.

Is income the way in which we decide whether liberal art graduates do better than the graduates of other professional areas (for example, nursing or engineering)? One administrator notes, '... even though liberal arts graduates in an entry-level position tend to earn less than their counterparts who have very career-focused [degrees], within 10 to 20 years they tend to outpace their counterparts in terms of income.' Thus, the earning power of liberally educated graduates is not to be denied.

It is now time for a quiz. What do the following current or recent American chief executive officers, politicians, athletes, and others have in common?

Jeff Bezos, Amazon
Larry Ellison, Oracle
Mark Zuckerberg, Facebook Carly Fiorina, Hewlett-Packard Michael Eisner, Walt Disney
A.G. Lafley, Proctor and Gamble
Pierre Omidyar, eBay
George W. Bush, former US president
Hilary Clinton and Condoleeza Rice, former US secretaries of state
The late Sally Ride, US astronaut
Pro football quarterback Peyton Manning

These leaders share the study of the liberal arts, for among them are majors in history, philosophy, English, theatre, psychology, political science, French, and speech communication. It is true that they attended both smaller liberal arts institutions like Wellesley and Hamilton colleges, as well as larger institutions that provide both liberal arts and specialized education, like Princeton, Chicago, Harvard, Tufts, and Stanford. However, those larger institutions are adamant about the importance of liberal arts, and require all their undergraduate students to share a common grounding in them.

Liberal education faces several serious challenges. These include Massive Open Online Courses, or MOOCs. Harvard and MIT have committed

$ 60 million to EdX; Coursera, the largest provider of MOOCs, has recently doubled the number of universities with which it has agreements. As of spring 2013, the American Council on Education recommended credits for three math and two biology MOOCs. On a recent trip to India, British Prime Minister David Cameron spoke approvingly of courses available through the British MOOC provider Futurelearn, whose title suggests confidence in the future of MOOCs even if we can still debate the financial models that MOOCs and their operators are developing or debating. As Cameron said, MOOCs mean that 'Indian students can access some of the best teaching and learning online from their home in Mumbai or Delhi'.[36] Other challenges include the ones outlined here, most importantly the misperception that liberal education is not what the corporate world is looking for, when it is, in fact, exactly what the corporate world is looking for—and needs.

How, then, can liberal education best be 'imported' to India? There are undoubtedly many ways, but one way to do this is for Indian colleges and universities to understand the value of liberal learning and to partner with an American college that is equally committed to this idea. The creation of Jindal's undergraduate School of Liberal Arts and Humanities was announced in the presence of the prime minister of India in March 2013, and the school is noted as one of Jindal's five on its web page, http://www.jgu.edu.in/content/about-jgu. Officials of O.P. Jindal University are, at present, in serious discussions with their counterparts at Rollins to cement a partnership in which students would matriculate at the new liberal arts and humanities college at Jindal, where they will spend their first two years, and then move to Rollins College, where they would spend their last two years. The students could major in any subject, but would be best served by majors in areas in which Jindal has strength. Rollins faculty, who have high comfort levels with liberal learning and who have developed expertise in this area, could assist in the creation of the new Jindal curriculum. The collaborative development of this curriculum would ensure not only that Jindal students move seamlessly into Rollins's programmes, but that the curriculum at Jindal allows the students to learn what they must learn in their first two years so

---

[36] 'British MOOC Provider Expands; Prime Minister Promotes It in India,' http://www.insidehighered.com/quicktakes/2013/02/19/british-mooc-provider-expands-prime-minister-promotes-it-india#ixzz2LMdiCcd7 (accessed on 27 June 2013).

as to ensure their success in the US. Such students would, generally, return to their home countries, where they could either enter the workforce, flush with ways of thinking that will invigorate the companies who hire them, or seek additional education in, say, law or other areas. It is worth adding that American law generally permits graduates to remain in the US for a period after graduation in order to obtain further professional training.[37]

The institutions where I have so far spent my career include a large, complex public university; a smaller, but still complex, public undergraduate institution; and now a smaller, private liberal arts institution. Coming back to the last of these to me seemed like coming home. The encounters that were most formative in my own development were the things that my own undergraduate education at a liberal arts institution imbued. They included students who lived and learned together; undertaking what is now called faculty-student undergraduate research, which lit a fire in me to undertake more research in graduate school; and the priceless conversations that informed the development of my political and personal viewpoints. In my job, I use the skills that the liberal arts impart especially writing, appreciating complexity, and communicating, every day.

One may not know what should happen to the Indian university, nor how it should be 'remade,' even though 'Remaking the Indian University' was, formally, the topic under discussion at the March 2013 Jindal conference. What is clear is that there must be room in India for the liberal arts. Melding India's needs with a liberal arts education as practiced in western colleges and universities, particularly in American ones, and tying this melding to the conviction that a liberal education is invaluable, will help us to address these vital questions. We have, in this sense, returned full circle to the model that America offered to India when the latter was considering how to prepare for graduate business education through its IIMs.

* * *

Let's return, in conclusion, to Thomas Friedman's remark: that citizens of India are hungry for American jobs. If the world is flat, as Friedman

---

[37] Immigration reform may expand opportunities for international students who graduate with a degree from an American institution; see e.g., http://abcnews.go.com/ABC_Univision/News/immigration-reform-foreign-students-studying-us-stay/story?id=18922889#.UcxlKODA5UQ (accessed on 27 June 2013).

once said, they should be hungry. But if they want those jobs, they will have to partake in liberal education. Yes, the world needs and wants engineers—but it wants engineers who understand why it is important to build not just functional bridges, but beautiful bridges. As the president of Arizona State University put it, 'Inspired engineering ... could come as a consequence of familiarity with the development of counterpoint in Baroque music or cell biology.'[38] Can anyone doubt the value of liberal education in this view?

---

[38] Cited in Gentile, 'Is a Liberal Arts Degree Worth It?'

17   Public Policy as a Practice

Reflections Inspired by Alasdair MacIntyre's After Virtue[1]

R. Sudarshan

This chapter attempts to relate the pedagogy of public policy to the concept of practice articulated by Alasdair MacIntyre. It first discusses the challenges of establishing public policy as a discipline in India where it has been long assumed that only those employed in government need to acquire skills and knowledge essential for policy formulation, and also, by definition, all policies made by government must be in the public interest. This assumption is being challenged in recent times and opening up the possibility of fashioning a pedagogy for public policy that could make the subject meaningful to a variety of practitioners besides those serving

---

[1] This chapter draws extensively upon A.C. MacIntyre, *After Virtue: A Study in Moral Theory* (2nd edn) (Notre Dame, Indiana: University of Notre Dame Press. Cited hereafter as MacIntyre, 1984).

governments. In the quest for a philosophy of public policy as a practice an understanding of external and internal goods, the role of virtues, and limitations of economics, a dominant discipline in public policy schools, are examined. Finally, the importance of public policy practitioners and teachers connecting with the public whose interests and concerns provide the raison d'être for the discipline is underlined.

Teaching public policy in India has posed many challenges. In the first place, it is a new discipline in Indian universities.[2] Hitherto, public policy has been regarded as a discipline that is meant exclusively for government officials. Public policymaking has been assumed to be the exclusive concern of bureaucrats, not meant for those outside government. This attitude towards public policy as the sole preserve of officers serving the government is a legacy of the British Raj.

The Indian Civil Service (ICS) was established in 1858. Officers were recruited by competitive examination initially held in London but later also in India. These officers held all the key posts ranging from policymaking in the Viceroy's office to managing the business of government in the two hundred and fifty districts that comprised British India. Jawaharlal Nehru, later to be the first prime minister of India, declared in 1934, that he would have nothing to do with the ICS tradition. But when the constitution of India was drafted a successor service, Indian Administrative Service (IAS) was created, incorporating safeguards protecting tenure of service of its members. The last ICS officer inducted into the IAS retired in 1980 as the Cabinet Secretary.

On the advice of Paul Appleby (Dean, Maxwell School of Citizenship and Public Affairs, Syracuse University, and Ford Foundation consultant), the Indian Institute of Public Administration was established in 1954 with the Prime Minister as its founding President. Many other training centres for government officials that were subsequently established in all the states of India. The Centre for Public Policy (CPP) was established in 2000 in the Indian Institute of Management, Bangalore, through a partnership agreement between the Government of India and United Nations Development Programme, collaborating with the Kennedy School, Harvard, and the Maxwell School, Syracuse.

All these institutions focused on public administration, understood as involving an investigation of the different ways public services can be

---

[2] The first group in India with M.A. in Public Policy graduated only in August 2012.

delivered, and to a lesser extent on public policy, understood as the study of principles of public decision-making and formulation of programmes to solve policy problems. In practice, this is may be distinction without much difference.[3] All of them primarily cater to training needs of government officials and to a lesser extent, on executive education for managers from the corporate sector and civil society organizations. They generally award diplomas, not degrees recognized by India's University Grants Commission.[4]

Against this background, the M.A. in Public Policy degree offered at the O.P. Jindal University is a pioneering venture. But it faces the challenge of novelty. The degree in public policy equips students with skills and knowledge needed for a growing variety of employment, via lateral entry, into governments, in public-private partnership (PPP) ventures, in corporate social responsibility, in international development-focused institutions and in civil society organizations. Nevertheless, potential students continue to assume that public policy education is a requirement only for those who have already joined government. India's British Raj legacy is again responsible for want of familiarity with public policy education.

In the United States, at the policymaking level, there is no permanent civil service unlike countries that are members of the British Commonwealth. In the United States there has been steady movement of professionals from academia and corporate sector in and out of government. Many professionals, in anticipation of working within or with governments at the federal, state, and local level, value public policy education to a much greater extent than is the case in the Commonwealth till recently. One of the more recent consequences of globalization, and the influence of international actors and institutions on national public policymaking, has been to create a greater awareness of the usefulness of public policy education.

A second challenge for public policy education in India is the lack of fit between Indian realties, on the one hand, and availability of concepts and categories to grasp and adequately describe those realities. We live in times when the dominant form of political institutions is liberal democracy.

[3] Hur, Y. and M. Hackbart, 'MPA vs. MPP: A Distinction without a Difference?' *Journal of Public Affairs Education (JPAE)*, 15(4): 397–424.

[4] Master's courses in public administration (not public policy) in Indian universities began in the 1970s, mostly as electives in master's programmes in political science.

For liberal individualism a community is simply an arena in which individuals each pursue their own self-chosen conception of the good life, and political institutions exist to provide that degree of order which makes such self-determined activity possible. Government and law are, or ought to be, neutral between rival conceptions of the good life for people, and hence, although it is the task of government to promote the rule of law, it is, on the liberal view, no part of its legitimate function to inculcate any one moral outlook in people.

The dilemma posed by the lack of adequate concepts and categories to articulate and describe realities in non-Western countries, which do not share the same history and experience of liberal democracy, has been articulated in a 'manifesto' that was drawn up after a series of 'global conversations on democracy', organized by the Centre for the Study of Developing Societies, New Delhi.[5]

The manifesto states:

> Current definitions of democracy threaten to reduce it to an institutional checklist derived from idealized notions of the experience of a small part of the globe. The ideal of democracy is seen to be synonymous with the historical form of liberal democracy in advanced capitalist societies of Western Europe and North America. Often this is further reduced down to a few key institutional features. Yet, the historical experience of democracy in most of the world provides overwhelming evidence against this approach. More often than not, imported institutions do not produce the same consequences that they did in their home context. Similarity of form is no guarantee of democratic substance. In fact, a search for familiar form is an invitation to cynical and superficial copying for extraneous gains.
>
> On the one hand, experience of 'established democracies' shows that appearance of democratic form of government can be made compatible with rule of experts, dominance of corporates, control by private networks and decline of citizen participation. On the other hand, experience of democratic success outside the global North suggests that a departure from the mandated institutional form is often a pre-condition to the success.
>
> In particular, mass democracies of post-colonial societies tend to acquire depth through practices that may not have a legitimate institutional expression in the received wisdom on democracy. Institutions are no doubt crucial

[5] Mohapatra, Bishnu N. *The Democracy Manifesto: Re-Imagining Democracy*, Open Democracy, www.opendemocracy.net/bishnu-n-mohapatra/democracy-manifesto-re-imagining-democracy-in-our-time

to the formation and strengthening of democracies, but what institutions do depends on the context in which these are located.

We need to shift the focus from the form of an institution to its real life consequences in a given context. This is a challenge for public policy pedagogy because the West's intellectual hegemony determining terms of discourse used in different disciplines make it difficult to find more appropriate formulations to better grasp Indian and other non-Western realities.

A third challenge for public policy pedagogy is posed by the predominance of neoliberal prescriptions about what governments should do and not do. New Public Management (NPM), for instance, has inspired many government reforms all over the world. Market-oriented reform strategies have aimed to increase effectiveness, diminish bureaucracy, and reduce public spending. But the goals of greater efficiency and accountability, leaner and stronger governments have proved to be elusive.

CHALLENGES FOR PUBLIC POLICY TO EVOLVE INTO A PRACTICE

The hegemonic assumptions of public policy pedagogy are based on European Enlightenment ideas, especially positivism, developed and elaborated in the eighteenth and nineteenth centuries. 'The Enlightenment project' as Alasdair Macintyre called it, attempted to justify morality by universally accessible reason.[6] This project failed, according to MacIntyre, because Enlightenment started from the idea of 'man-as-he-happens-to-be'.[7]

In the Aristotelian tradition a good man is one who has developed his attitudes and abilities in the appropriate way, given his possibilities and capacities. A 'man living well is like a harpist playing well', a functional conception of man. Moral judgements are related to 'man-as-he- could-be-if- he-realized-his-essential-nature'. In developing and actually 'living' his virtues, such a man is oriented toward the *telos* of human life: the good life and, ultimately, happiness (*eudaimonia*). Modern individuals can claim their individual rights or proclaim utilitarian rules, but they cannot justify them in terms of the individual and collective ends they are supposed to help

[6] MacIntyre, *After Virtue.*
[7] MacIntyre, *After Virtue,* p. 54.

realizing. As modern politics is devoid of thinking about the good life and the good society, public policymaking, acting as the servant of democratic politics, can also be aimless, lacking a *telos*, focusing only in expediency of means to achieve ends that are chosen, not discovered or given.

MacIntyre uses the notion of characters to show that there is something fundamentally wrong with modern society and its culture. He does so by exposing flaws in the claims that are basic to these modern characters. The authority of managers' claims, in particular, rests on (a) 'the existence of a domain of morally neutral fact about which the manager is to be expert', and (b) the possibility of 'law-like generalizations and their application to particular cases derived from the study of this domain'. MacIntyre dismisses these two assumptions of moral neutrality and scientific expertise as false.

> There are strong grounds for rejecting the claim that effectiveness is a morally neutral value. For the whole concept of effectiveness is ... inseparable from a mode of human existence in which the contrivance of means is in central part the manipulation of human beings into compliant patterns of behaviour; and it is by appeal to his own effectiveness in this respect that the manager claims authority within the manipulative mode.[8]

Management, according to MacIntyre, is both an instrument and perpetrator of manipulation. Public managers contribute to the manipulative character of the modern state.

A practice, in his definition, is:

> Any coherent and complex form of socially established cooperative human activity through which goods internal to that form of activity are realized in the course of trying to achieve those standards of excellence which are appropriate to, and partially definitive of, that form of activity, with the result that human powers to achieve excellence, and human conceptions of the ends and goods involved, are systematically extended.[9]

What this means is that throwing a ball with some skill is not a practice, but soccer as a game is a practice. Brick-laying is not a practice, but architecture is a practice. Putting splashes of colour on canvas is not a practice, but painting as an art form is a practice. Being an argumentative Indian is

---

[8] MacIntyre, *After Virtue*, p. 74.
[9] MacIntyre, *After Virtue*, p. 187.

not a practice, but being a lawyer able to put arguments to use for the sake of delivering justice is a practice.

With respect to this definition of 'practice', MacIntyre makes some important distinctions. The first is between internal and external goods, or goods of excellence and goods of effectiveness.[10] With chess playing, or any other practice, one can usually gain money, honour, and the like. But these goods could also be obtained in other ways. They are in principle unrelated to the particular practice of chess. MacIntyre calls them external goods. However, there are also goods that cannot be achieved in any other way than by performing this particular practice, such as enjoyment and admiration of brilliance and beauty of certain moves on the chess board (even when they are made by the opponent in the game). These goods cannot be obtained in any other way than in being involved in the game of chess (even if in the audience). Such goods are called internal goods of the practice.

MacIntyre points out that institutions are indispensable for practices to exist, but they also often pose a threat to them. He says:

> Institutions are characteristically and necessarily concerned with what I have called external goods. They are involved in acquiring money and other material goods; they are structured in terms of power and status, and they distribute money, power, and status as rewards. Nor could they do otherwise if they are to sustain not only themselves, but also the practices of which they are the bearers. For no practice can survive for any length of time unsustained by institutions. Indeed so intimate is the relationship of practices to institutions—and consequently of the goods external to the goods internal to the practices in question—that institutions and practices characteristically form a single causal order in which the ideals and the creativity of the practice are always vulnerable to the acquisitiveness of the institution, in which the cooperative care for common goods of the practice is always vulnerable to the competitiveness of the institution.[11]

The point is that public policymaking and public managers have helped to build their institutions within the capitalistic-bureaucratic state which could obstruct aspirations for the realization of the good life and the good society.

---

[10] MacIntyre, *After Virtue*, pp. 188–91.
[11] MacIntyre, *After Virtue*, p. 194.

ROLE OF VIRTUES

To guarantee the well-functioning of practices, and to prevent damage to them by institutions, virtues are of the utmost importance: 'Without them, without justice, courage, and truthfulness, practices could not resist the corrupting power of institutions'.[12]

In MacIntyre's analysis virtues play a crucial role in practices and the achievement of internal goods: 'A virtue is an acquired human quality the possession and exercise of which tends to enable us to achieve those goods which are internal to practices and the lack of which effectively prevents us from achieving any such goods'.

Public policymaking and management cannot be readily regarded as a practice because they are predominantly concerned with realizing given ends and achieving external goods, often at the cost of sacrificing internal goods of the kind that proper practices, like healing, teaching, and playing games, all have. We teach students of public policy an amalgam of the social sciences to equip them to be effective, expecting that they will have the capacity to make law-like generalizations that would enable them to predict and control the social environment.

CHALLENGE OF HERMENEUTICS: PEOPLE ARE SELF-INTERPRETING AGENTS

The methods of the natural sciences are well suited to understanding the behaviour of Nature, the movements of the planets, or how a wheat plant will grow under certain conditions. But those methods are not well-suited to understanding human behaviour. The essence of freedom in human beings consists in the inherent degree of unpredictability. We are self-interpreting agents. The moment a theory is advanced by a well-known economist about how people will behave, the chances are that people will read that account and make it into a self-fulfilling prophecy or do exactly the opposite. The heavenly bodies, however, are always unmindful about theories scientists may advance about their movements.

One source of unpredictability in human behaviour is the possibility of external incidents that cannot be anticipated. Human unpredictability also flows from the human our ability to decide and makes choices. The

---

[12] MacIntyre, *After Virtue*, p. 194.

outcome of as yet unmade decisions cannot be predicted. A third level of uncertainty can arise because it is inherently impossible to predict the development of radical new concepts because one would need those concepts in the first place to formulate the prediction. As MacIntyre puts it, we can to an extent outsmart Fortuna, the 'bitch-Goddess' of unpredictability, but we cannot dethrone her.[13]

Economics attempts to imitate the methods of the natural sciences which are well-suited to understanding nature, but not so well suited to grasping human behaviour. Sir Peter Medawar once suggested that economics could be properly described as an 'unnatural science'!

We must not belittle the enormous understanding and advances in human knowledge that the discipline of economics has made possible. This is because a good deal (though not all) of human behaviour, with regularities, conditioned by habits, is for the great part predictable. Understanding these patterns of behaviour using analytical tools of economics, econometrics, and statistics, which are all disciplines with their own internal standards of excellence, can equip its practitioners to be the front ranks of public policymaking.

But we also need to appreciate what economists cannot do. They can explain market failure, but they not are able to explain our failure in upholding public values, or all of the ways in which public policy can be so corrupted that it is no longer a practice infused with ideals. The rise of professional policy analysis has in many ways contributed to the ascendance of the market failure model and the pervasiveness of microeconomics in public policy.

Policy analysis more easily speaks the language of economics than the language of the common good or, for that matter, politics. Policy-analysis-in-use typically involves the translation of decision alternatives into benefits, costs, discount rates, and transitive economic values, none of which accommodates the common good. The colossal failure of economists to anticipate the recent global financial crisis has not diminished the influence of 'ecocrats'. Ironically, the same set of 'experts' are in greater demand now to carry out post-mortems on the reasons for their failure! Economics masks certain kinds of conflicts over contestable concepts, imagining a world that is much more predictable and manageable than it really is. Bureaucracies legitimize their authority by using its methodology, and ironically, even

---

[13] MacIntyre, *After Virtue*, p. 93.

the unsuccessful employment of such social scientific knowledge results in more support for the same kind of knowledge.

MacIntyre's Aristotelianism provides an alternative for the Weberian conception of rational government. As a discipline, public policy should contribute in different ways to the prudence (*phronesis*) of policymakers. It should, for instance, assist and train policymakers and public administrators in developing moral and professional excellence.

WAY FORWARD FOR PUBLIC POLICY PEDAGOGY

Public policy pedagogy should aim at bringing out all possible corrupting instrumental tendencies in public institutions. It should help public policy practitioners in identifying important virtues which they should cultivate and to counter the corrosive influence of institutions on public policymaking conceived as a practice. As a practice, the primary duty of public policy ought to be sustaining the political community. The *telos* of politics and public policy as practices ought to be the common good which is different from the public interest or general good as it is often understood in modern discourses.

The public interest is often understood to be an aggregation of individual preferences. But the common good is concerned with the desirable (virtuous) development of individuals and not just their current preferences. The realization of common good entails public policies that enable and ensure the participation of the public because it is only by participating in the pursuit of the common good that one can develop the virtues and competencies required for that enterprise to be successful. The forms of public participation must not only give a voice to citizens to promote their particular interests but must also contribute to training people to cultivate the virtues for the purpose of realizing the common good.

For public policy to evolve into a proper practice the discipline must meet MacIntyre's criteria:

- Have coherence and complexity
- Adhere to socially established norms
- Require human cooperation
- Involve technical skills which are exercised within evolving traditions of values and principles
- Be organized to achieve certain standards of excellence
- Produce 'internal goods' in pursuit of excellence

- Increase human capability to achieve internal standards of excellence
- Systematically extend our conceptions of goods internal to the practice

'PUBLIC' IN PUBLIC POLICY

The institution most vital for public policy to become a practice, so that it does not remain a collective noun for technological fixes unrelated to the common good, is democracy. Democracy has intrinsic, as well as an instrumental, value. Although some values of democracy are means to non-political values, others grow out of democratic processes themselves.

Participation completes individuals, in part by enabling them to discover and develop their public dimensions in part by providing the kinds of interactions that develop capacities for autonomous judgements. The 'public' must be brought back into public policymaking. This is easier said than done. Ordinary people are, for the most part, rationally ignorant and cannot be expected to take an interest in all public policy debates. They also know that their vote in a democratic election, one in millions, can make little difference. But it does not mean they are unable to voice their views on matters related to public policy.

Public policy practitioners ought to uphold the right information. If there is an institutional design where those practitioners can become seriously engaged in weighing up competing arguments they could make informed and thoughtful judgements. The best way to pursue long-term democratic reform is to provide a context where the deliberative democracy of the people flourishes and can give voice to key concerns. Policy choices have to be made consonant with the informed preferences of the population. The public should be consulted about issues of collective political will, about the trade-offs they are willing to accept for the basic direction of policy. They should be consulted about the question of whether we should build nuclear power plants. They need not be consulted about the choice of nuclear reactors.

Public policy, if it is to evolve into a practice, with a teleological commitment to the common good, ought to draw the general public into dialogue and discussions. The purpose here need not be to hammer out a consensus. The purpose is simply deliberation and public understanding of policy issues. Public policy as a practice ought to cultivate the channels of public deliberation in order to change a flawed representative democracy into a deliberative democracy.

18 Global Studies in Indian Universities

Past Imperfect, Future Circumspect

Sreeram Chaulia

APATHY FOR THE DISTANT

The American humourist Ian Frazier once remarked, 'every once in a while, people need to be in the presence of things that are really far away'. It is inherent to human nature to seek to expand the horizon of the mind and explore further and beyond one's immediate environs. This is why the word 'far-sighted' has positive connotations in most contexts, as a marker of advanced mental faculties that can see, perceive, and explain matters which are not close either in space or time. Concepts like cosmopolitanism, universalism, and internationalism have emerged out of this innate human capacity to stare into the distances and to establish a connection with distant events, processes, and outcomes.

The poet laureate Rabindranath Tagore—a pioneer in developing global consciousness and breaking free of the tyranny of narrow, parochial visions—has aptly said, 'our mind has faculties which are universal, but its habits are insular'.[1] Sadly in Indian academia, this habit has turned into a malaise with no easy remedies on hand. Instead of developing what political scientist Sidney Tarrow terms as 'rooted cosmopolitanism', wherein individuals and activists remain attached to local issues, events, and spaces while 'moving cognitively and spatially outside their spatial origins',[2] Indian universities are peopled mostly with tunnel vision social scientists who are unable to connect with or develop expertise on distant regions, and diverse themes that operate in the wider world.

The progressive narrowing of intellectual lenses in Indian universities to confine themselves to the study of largely domestic or at best South Asian concerns, and the eschewing of the heritage of globalism and international-ism bequeathed from Tagore, Jawaharlal Nehru,[3] and Subhas Chandra Bose,[4] is a betrayal that has cost India as a nation, as it fumbles to find the scholastic fire-power to articulate its claim to major power status. If there is a 'reluctance that seems to define India's coming of age'[5] despite its gradual accumulation of material strength in the last two decades, the blame falls squarely on its universities and think tanks that have failed to generate the ideational basis for the nation to have a global foreign policy and global involvement.

If one were to take a compass from a geometry box and begin draw-ing concentric circles around India for how far the Indian strategist and academician should cast their eyes, where should the radius limit be set?

---

[1] Tagore, Rabindranath, *The English Writings of Rabindranath Tagore*, Vol. IV (New Delhi: Atlantic Publishers, 2007), p. 602.

[2] Tarrow, Sidney, *The New Transnational Activism* (New York: Cambridge University Press, 2005), p. 42.

[3] Cf. Chacko, Priya, 'The Internationalist Nationalist: Pursuing an Ethical Modernity with Jawaharlal Nehru', in Robbie Shilliam (ed.), *International Rela-tions and Non-Western Thought: Imperialism, Colonialism and Investigations of Global Modernity* (London: Routledge, 2010).

[4] Despite the popular notion that Bose was only a staunch Indian nationalist, he was an early advocate of studying world affairs rigorously. In his own words, 'we must have a correct appreciation of the world situation at every stage and should know how to take advantage of it'. Cf. Subhas Bose, *Words of Freedom. Ideas of a Nation* (New Delhi: Penguin, 2010), p. 57.

[5] Mattoo, Amitabh (ed.), *The Reluctant Superpower: Understanding India and its Aspirations* (Melbourne: Melbourne University Press, 2012).

This author has argued often that the entire known world should be the ambit for India's sight, attention, involvement, and action. The time for a maximalist globalized approach in India to understanding and plunging into the wider world rather than acting apologetically or in baby steps just within South Asia or East Asia is well upon us.

India's conservative career diplomatic corps often resist this expansionary vision, citing paucity of personnel and of investible budgets to become more globally proactive. Manjari Chatterjee Miller of Boston University has also documented how these foreign policy bureaucrats headquartered in New Delhi are insulated from outside influences and psychologically ill-prepared to assume international responsibilities and leadership owing to fears about 'raising expectations'.[6]

Outside the cautious and reactive Indian Ministry of External Affairs, does India have the intellectual means to push for and navigate a truly global journey from the Arctic to the Antarctic and from Vancouver to Vladivostok? In 2010, I argued that India's political leadership and news media had boxed themselves into a Pakistan- and China-obsessed community that has little interest or advanced knowledge of more distant regions of the world. So perverse is this myopia that any average discussion in the public realm about 'international' issues automatically implies something related to India's next-door neighbours only. A lengthy quote from my own problematization in 2010 better explicates this depressing scenario of a short supply of knowledge production on global issues and events:

> The narrow educational and experiential backgrounds of the current Indian political class and the obsessive media focus on just the country's immediate neighbours have reproduced a frog-in-the-well mentality that discourages knowledge accumulation and production beyond a certain geographical radius or comfort zone. There are, for example, countless Pakistan and Sri Lanka hands in and outside government in India but hardly anyone who has a masterly grasp of the politics and predilections of the Caribbean or Bolivarian America.[7]

Since 2014, Prime Minister Narendra Modi has delivered on much-needed global ambition and footprint in the way India approaches the world. Yet, a de-globalized mindset lingers in our universities. Until India does not

---

[6] Miller, Manjari 'India's Feeble Foreign Policy: A Would-Be Great Power Resists its Own Rise?' *Foreign Affairs* (2012): p. 14.

[7] Chaulia, Sreeram 'India in a Globalised World', *Geopolitics* (May 2010): p. 59.

build up a corpus of wide-ranging thematic and geographical area experts within its academia, it has no future as a prominent global player. Leaving the task of steering India's destiny in the international arena to the self-congratulatory and overcautious bureaucrats of its Ministry of External Affairs is no solution due to the mandarins' absence of initiative to think out-of-the-box and imaginatively.

Reforming India's foreign policy bureaucracy is not the mandate of this article,[8] but it suffices here to note that lacking a resurgence in world-class training and research in Indian universities, the fields of debate and critical stock-taking of success and failure of Indian diplomacy will remain underdeveloped or left to clever journalists who lack the systematic analytical lenses of academicians.

For India to heed Prime Minister Modi's call and overcome the reluctance to 'go global' and negate the stultifying apathy about distant lands and their problems, the onus is on its universities to come up with a new generation of independent-minded, globally cognizant and sharp thinkers from faculty members and graduate students who have excellent training in comparative perspectives and technical competence in specific issue areas.

How can Indian universities make versatile international affairs professionals, who can be useful to government as well as in the international non-profit and for-profit sectors? If change agents within universities ask such questions to start with, the answers are not very counter-intuitive or difficult to find.

REBOOTING GLOBAL AFFAIRS EDUCATION

None can gainsay the fact that excellence in universities comprises a most 'powerful, yet under-appreciated national resource.'[9] The examples of Japan and the Asian Tiger economies since World War II reveal how central school and university educational revamps were to trigger overall

---

[8] For a stinging critique of the Indian Foreign Service (IFS) officialdom and their refusal to innovate or evaluate their own flaws, see Shashi Tharoor, *Pax Indica: India and the World of the Twenty-First Century* (New Delhi: Penguin, 2012), Chapter Nine.

[9] Cf. Jonathan Cole, *The Great American University: Its Rise to Preeminence, its Indispensable National Role, Why It Must Be Protected* (New York: Public Affairs, 2010).

economic prosperity and rise of these societies as prominent actors in the international realm. The Pakistani economist Mahbub ul Haq has shown that there was an 'education miracle' behind the East Asian miracle from the 1960s, which drove up the human capital levels to unprecedented heights in the Asian context.[10]

If there is to be a South Asian miracle like the East Asian one, there is no escape from the imperative to build world-class universities and invest strategically in raising the quality of higher education, including the social sciences. The causal link between committing human and material resources to education and observing a marked economic and international rise in a nation should not be erroneously inverted. Countries like India cannot hope for improved educational standards after a certain level of increased living standards and GDP growth occur. Rather, the revolution in education must precede and accompany the ascent to major power status.

Nothing short of a radical re-education and retooling of India's social science stables and academic infrastructure on global studies can rectify the gaping holes which stunt the nation's aspirations to be great and good in the world at large. It will require a qualitative leap in the Indian university imagination to benchmark itself against peers internationally and develop a far more rigorous and intellectually engaging pedagogy and epistemology on foreign issues.

Since global studies are a sub-discipline of core social science disciplines like political science, economics, sociology, and history, the sorry fate that has befallen the social sciences in general in India is a generic cause for the low standards of research and teaching in foreign affairs. The same lack of funding, equipment, autonomy from government control, and freedom from politicization which bedevils all the social sciences in India[11] also afflict the study of global affairs.

If one were to just compare the library collections on international affairs in an average Indian university that has a department of political science or international relations with that of an average Chinese, Japanese, or South Korean university, it sends out a rough indicator of how behind India is in developing the software for its entry into the ranks of major

---

[10] Haq, Mahbub, *Human Development in South Asia* (Karachi: Oxford University Press, 1998), p. 31.

[11] Chaudhary, Shreesh 'Why Neglect Humanities and Social Sciences', *The Hindu* (12 July 2009).

world powers. But the rot goes a lot deeper than simply the absence of enough money and material. The rest of this chapter will identify how global studies in Indian universities has suffered from poor conceptual planning, badly structured incentives, non-achievement based organizational culture, parasitic relationships with the government and private sectors, and unproductive work ethics that hinder quality enhancement.

A MEDIOCRE GLOBAL STUDIES 'SYSTEM'

India's far and few between university departments dedicated to the study of foreign affairs have mostly missed the advent of the new phenomenon of global policy studies. The vast majority of them still offer graduate degree programmes in the obsolete 'International Relations' (IR) genre, which has been bypassed in the last two decades by spectacular shifts in the material distribution of power and wealth in the global economy. Cutting edge scholars like Stephanie Lawson of Macquarie University have posited that we have long since shifted into a 'post-international' world where non-state actors like gigantic multinational corporations (MNCs), transnational terrorist groups, borderless problems of the environment, health, conflict, and fluid movement of goods, capital, and services are rendering the very foundation of state-centric IR outdated.[12]

To be sure, the IR sub-discipline has been adjusting its stance towards non-state actors and there is widespread unease about the relevance of state-heavy theories within its fold.[13] But the fundamental rethinking of the field augured by economic globalization necessitates novel conceptualization and restructuring of the curriculums and pedagogy of global studies. I am not merely quibbling over nomenclature between IR and 'Global Policy Studies' or simply 'Global Studies'. We should not underestimate the importance of language and concept in shaping mind-sets and *Weltanschauung*.

What if the subject matter is defined as Global Studies instead of IR, which is a derivative of political science? It would immediately force an interdisciplinary turn in the academic approach to foreign affairs,

[12] Lawson, Stephanie, *International Relations* (Cambridge: Polity Press, 2012), p. 158.

[13] Legro, Jeffrey, and Andrew Moravcsik, 'Is Anybody Still a Realist?', *International Security*, vol. 24, no. 2 (1999).

particularly by introducing faculty members and students to the worth of understanding global business strategies. Right now, the IR departments across India are oblivious to the value of corporate strategy and corporate decision-making in determining outcomes.

Admittedly, there is a longstanding specialization of international political economy (IPE) within the IR sub-discipline, but IPE itself is not enough to cover all the facets of corporate power and tactics on an intercontinental scale. If one has to do justice to global studies, it will have to incorporate business studies, especially areas like strategic management, mergers and acquisitions, corporate competition, and the tremendous sway of markets over social and political life. The silo mentality which has been a bane in the social sciences divides IR scholars from working closely with business studies peers, but the twinning of the two is essential to get a better handle over the current state of the world.

Multidisciplinary social science is mostly an aspiration in India, as is evidenced by the fact that IR/Political Science departments rarely have International Business specialists within their faculty rosters. To reiterate, IPE is not a substitute for core Business Studies faculty members within a global studies department or at least within a larger university where students enrolled in degree programmes in IR can take a number of elective courses in business departments. Some prominent Indian universities are handicapped by ideological capture that prevents exposure of faculty members and students to Business strategies, thereby keeping them in the dark about what is arguably more important today than classic geostrategic analysis of statecraft.

How can Indian universities claim to train young minds in the field of 'strategy' without course work and detailed curricular integration between the old IR and Business Studies?

While the severe shock dealt by the global economic crisis since 2008 has pushed the discipline of Economics to re-evaluate its fundamental premises and assumptions,[14] IR scholars in India have not yet awoken to the value of understanding, say, the boardroom manoeuvres of a Goldman Sachs or JP Morgan and how it impacts on war, revolutions or inter-state tensions. Academicians in the West have, as always, taken the lead in pondering why 'the discipline of IR has inherently and structurally been

---

[14] Gardiner, Beth 'Back to School: Economists Rethink Theories in Light of Global Crisis', *The Wall Street Journal* (17 June 2010).

unable to engage with, and render intelligible, the latest financial crisis and its consequences'.[15]

Indian scholars who teach and conduct research within India are notably absent in theorizing about the way the world is transforming before we bat eyelids. There is a time gap between the global debates in the IR community and their transmission to Indian academia. Indian universities are mainly passive recipients of theoretical innovations that happen outside India and which seep in after a while.

Part of the blame for remaining trapped in a time warp, in theory, lies in the rigidity of the course curricula in global studies. In India's public universities, the syllabus for courses in IR and related themes is received down from centralized committees and expert groups that are glacially slow in staying updated with the fast-changing 'real world'. Although it is universally true that academia is one step behind actual developments in the fields it purports to study, Indian universities are aeons of steps behind. I was informed by a well-meaning academician in a leading public university that not even a few lines or lectures within a prescribed syllabus for a course can be altered or recalibrated without securing permissions from higher ups within the administrative hierarchy, who are least bothered about introducing new courses in keeping with the altering world situation.

Suppose I were a globally conscious teacher in an Indian university who wants to offer a course on maritime piracy or mass protest movements, given their upsurge in recent years, the hard truth is that I cannot do so until my proposal goes through various Byzantine layers of academic bureaucracy. By the time permission comes through, it is likely that global energies have moved on to some other pressing issue. Theoretical astuteness lies in assimilating new developments in the empirical world and testing whether these unexpected outcomes are accounted for in the existing paradigms or not. Indian universities are unable to attain such alacrity due to the overall slowness to adapt and innovate, a tendency that applies particularly to education in humanities and social sciences.

---

[15] Manokha, Ivan, and Mona Chalabi, 'The Latest Financial Crisis: IR Goes Bankrupt', *Paris: Sciences Po, Working Paper* (2011): p. 2; Robert Skidelsky, 'The Impact of the Global Economic Crisis on the Future of International Relations', *Einaudi Center's Foreign Policy Distinguished Speaker Series* (Ithaca: Cornell University, 2012).

Kanti Bajpai of the National University of Singapore has rightly pin-pointed the abject neglect of theory at large as an Achilles Heel of Indian academic endeavour in global studies. Lacking social scientific training at the graduate level to link theory with empirics and vice-versa, Indian IR scholars who are products of the Indian 'system' do a lot of 'descriptive studies which are rich in detail but fail to distinguish between more or less likely explanations'.[16] Long literature reviews and tedious narratives about facts, events, diplomatic summits, or wars do not make sense from a social scientific perspective, but this is what passes for IR scholarship in Indian universities.

Apart from theoretical inadequacies, Indian universities have not paid due attention to methodological and epistemological aspects of research. I find among Indian academics engaged in global studies a widespread distaste or plain bewilderment about making bold generalizations and abstract correlations that have universal applicability. So then, anyone versed in world-class social science methodology would ask, what is the 'external validity' of such research that is too contextual and localised in its findings? Obviously, young Indian IR scholars have not been trained by their doctoral dissertation supervisors to think comparatively and cross-contextually.

The practice of dividing IR departments into area specializing sub-units or centres, and the absence of critical thought along the lines of 'what is this particular case an instance of?', have made a mockery of postgraduate studies in Indian universities. Instead of asking the most probing questions that would promote a distinctive Indian voice in global studies, Indian universities are simply building databases of case studies about India's foreign relations with different regions of the world (here too, the favourite subjects remain India's immediate neighbours) without deeper introspection about how India exists within a bigger global system and what acts of omission and commission tell us about the behaviour of such emerging powers.

A typical doctoral dissertation in India's so-called top universities churning out IR academicians would read somewhat as follows: 'Investigation into Relations between India and Afghanistan during the Period 1990 and 1998'. There is no hint of systemic analysis in such works, with many doubts about even the originality of theses being submitted and passed for

[16] Bajpai, Kanti 'Obstacles to Good Work in Indian International Relations', *International Studies*, vol. 46, nos 1 and 2 (2009): p. 114.

award of advanced degrees. Needless to add, the conversion rate between doctoral theses on global studies being passed in Indian universities and their publication as books or journal articles in internationally peer reviewed and reputed outlets is abysmal.

Research is the cornerstone of quality in universities. The absence of sound social scientific bases for the conduct of research in global studies in India is the main reason why not a single Indian university figures in the top 100 in the field of Politics and International Studies under the QS World University Rankings. Jawaharlal Nehru University, which has an old and reputed School of International Studies, is rated as number 108 in this field, far behind fellow Asian institutions like University of Tokyo (number 9), Kyoto University (number 13), Peking University (number 22), Tsinghua University (number 23), Fudan University (number 25) and Korea University (number 47).[17]

Sadly, far from accepting the sinking standards in global studies as reflected in such neutral international rankings, Indian universities exist in a shell and cynically pooh pooh rankings as unreflective of their genuine contributions and greatness. A 'frog-in-the-well mentality', which I had cited earlier in this chapter, is not merely a function of personal or small group myopia but a system-level flaw in global studies administration within India.

What are the incentives that Indian universities provide to young scholars to publish their working internationally peer reviewed journals and books? Occasionally, through sheer individual brilliance and perseverance, one does see faculty members in Indian universities publishing globally and being cited for their original additions to the existing body of knowledge in global studies. But the average Indian IR scholar is uncompetitive vis-à-vis her counterparts in other emerging powers, not to mention those trained in advanced nations. As if the paucity of well-grounded theoretical and methodological skills were not already a deterrent, the way promotions and appraisals have been structured in Indian universities acts as a further disincentive to strive for excellence in research.

Ageism, a premium placed on seniority in terms of the number of years of service as opposed to the quality thereof, factionalism and groupism within faculty members, petty politicking for Deanships and

---

[17] QS, 'World University Rankings by Subject 2013—Politics & International Studies' (2013), URL: http://www.topuniversities.com/university-rankings/university-subject-rankings/2013/politics (last accessed on 29 July 2013).

Vice Chancellorships, favouritism and nepotism are some manifestations of the dark underbelly of global studies departments in Indian universities. An entry level Assistant Professor knows that she is better off placating and cultivating the right relations with administrative powers rather than indulging in laborious and intense research leading to internationally cited publications. This anti-meritocratic regime where personal discretion and arbitrariness triumph is a far cry from the tough tenure system that prevails in many top universities of the world, where an assistant professor could lose her job if she does not publish in noteworthy journals or books in a specified band of time.

One only has to attend academic conferences on global studies themes, where papers are presented by India-trained scholars, to realize the futility of the output being churned out by most average universities. I have chaired a number of seminars around India and found to my dismay that the panellists lack basic articulation or a broader view of the application of their narrow topics. They simply throw the kitchen sink at a research question that is sometimes unspecified and use a few fancy phrases and references to make the work sound impressive. What would be the level of motivation of students of such scholars in their classrooms?

Whenever I address students of global studies in India, there is a palpable sense of uninspired ennui and self-doubt. The confidence that one sees in masters or PhD students in top universities abroad, driven by outstanding training and belief in meaningful careers after completion of studies, is absolutely missing. I often urge the social science students in my audiences to overcome their inferiority complexes and hold their chins up, but the everyday grinding realities of their dysfunctional departments and their pettiness is not inspiring.

Global studies is anyway at the bottom of the pecking order in Indian societal and media priorities, which are overwhelmingly domestic. The spark to take up degree education in foreign affairs is thus artificially suppressed by the parochialism and localism I have broached earlier in this chapter. But adding to the woes is rank leadership failure in departments of Political Science/IR to ignite the fire of learning and creativity among young scholars.

Why would the brightest and most diligent students come to take up graduate education in global studies if their teachers are already resigned to the lack of lucrative careers awaiting their wards after they finish their education? The absence of career counselling and professional development services in IR departments, and the ensuing default outlook of graduate students that their only career hopes lie in academia or in government civil service, have diminished the utilitarian value of education in foreign affairs. Indian universities that are way behind their Asian and other international peers in rankings will need an infusion of fresh leadership that can generate realistic life chances for young entrants into the IR/global studies field.

Higher education must have an intrinsic and aesthetic value in terms of illuminating the mind,[18] but also a practical value that attracts the best applicants to take up studies. In India, global studies have drawn a blank on both these parameters because they are stuck in no man's land of being neither academically extraordinary nor vocationally efficient. What has not helped the cause of increasing the vocational attractiveness of foreign affairs education is the closed door of the Indian government to lateral entry by non-bureaucrats.

An air of derision, dismissiveness, and condescension prevails within India's Ministry of External Affairs towards academicians and foreign affairs commentators in the news media, who are belittled for their lack of 'inside knowledge' about 'what really happens' in diplomacy. The few academics who do get consulted or absorbed into India's national security and foreign policy apparatuses are handpicked not for contrariness or capacities to play Devil's Advocate but to be Yes Men who can provide intellectual justification or cover for the policies and strategies that have been decided in advance by the Foreign Service mandarins.

I have personally witnessed instances where senior Indian diplomats and their retired seniors have used credentialism to snub contrapuntals from outside government that dare to challenge the overall direction of India's foreign policy. Notwithstanding Prime Minister Modi's encouragement of new ideas, the Indian bureaucracy's non-receptive and tone deaf culture that is closed to learning is reinforced by obsequiousness among Indian academicians pursuing foreign affairs teaching and research to big names and influential figures in the foreign policy establishment. Whatever meagre research grants, overseas travel opportunities, and access to primary sources that Indian academics get is tied to the will of politicians and senior or retired diplomats, generating a patronage system that discredits merit and academic honesty or courage to call a spade a spade.

Bajpai has noted that, in India, 'Political Science/IR garnered less respect than the other social sciences and was dependent on state

---

[18] Gutting, Gary 'Why Do I Teach?' *The New York Times* (22 May 2013).

cooperation in a way that diminished its scholarly independence'.[19] It is also a fact that India's strategic and foreign affairs think tanks, where many university academicians are active, are plagued by a Yes Man culture when it comes to critiquing the government's foreign policy blunders or failures. Even where the Ministry of External Affairs might seek independent assessments and critiques on specific policy issues, the bulk of the commentaries pouring out of Indian think tanks try to rationalize and vindicate existing government viewpoints instead of issuing systematic critiques.

Amitabh Mattoo at the University of Melbourne has correctly identified government interference as a main impediment to uplifting the quality of Indian think tanks. Observing that the Indian government is 'still suspicious of independent think tanks', he adds that 'there are a larger number of instruments, some blunt others insidious, through which various agencies of the government like to exercise control over the work they produce.'[20] Privately funded think tanks also face their own struggles in being able to offer quality policy relevant research that might be seen as biting the hand that feeds them. Indian universities which often express themselves via these strategic elite think tank platforms are thus unable to assert their own voice and unique lines on global affairs. They remain disseminators of government and corporate interests rather than shapers of the same.

A GLOBAL STUDIES AGENDA FOR TWENTY-FIRST CENTURY INDIA

After pillorying the 'system' that afflicts global studies in Indian universities, it is incumbent upon us to offer realistic suggestions to reverse the declining quality and crisis that has befallen. The task of reform or renaissance is akin to cleaning up the Augean Stables and easier said than done. But some lessons stand out in sharp relief and can be implemented by visionaries who are pained to see the deteriorating quality in India's foreign affairs studies.

First, and this is unfortunately a copout from the angle of already existing institutions, India will need new universities that are drawn up from scratch with a different mission of generating world-class knowledge

---

[19] Bajpai, 'Obstacles to Good Work in Indian International Relations', p. 126.

[20] Mattoo, Amitabh 'Unthinking Think Tanks', *The New Indian Express* (5 February 2012).

in foreign affairs. Path dependency and inflexibility have corroded older universities so much that it is going to be a Sisyphean ordeal to get them to restructure any time soon. Meanwhile, India and its immersion into the world cannot wait for decades before world-class education in global affairs can emerge slowly from within the atrophied institutions.

The idea of global policy studies or just global studies, which was mooted in this chapter, can only be instituted where a new university or department is carved out with autonomy awarded to faculty members to brainstorm and sculpt something innovative and special. Given the limitations of locally trained social scientists, the faculty base itself has to draw from Indian scholars trained overseas as well as full-time foreign faculty members. It is not snootiness or elitism to contend that Indian universities badly need foreign staffers, but an acknowledgement of the realities of low quality research and non-original teaching that is ubiquitous in global affairs programmes across the country.

When the 'system' is clogged, it needs an inflow of fresh blood and human capital to act as vectors of change. The scholars who are freely critiquing the failures of the 'system' are either foreign-returned Indians or foreign scholars. Those who are diagnosing the malaise are the ones who can embark on treatment. Fears of Westernization of India's academic outlook on global affairs should not stand in the way of hiring qualified foreign faculty members on regular appointments. Drawing faculty from mainland China, Taiwan, South Korea, Singapore, Hong Kong, and Japan can help provide balanced non-Western transfusion into India's ossifying and navel gazing global affairs academic community.

The second big alteration at the level of hiring faculty must come in globalizing the expertise base in Indian universities to overcome the apathy for distance which this chapter has highlighted. Departmental heads in Political Science/IR schools must consciously groom world-class talent specializing in geographically distant and thematically rare issue areas. The lack of world renowned scholars on Africa, Latin America, and emerging issues like cyber warfare and trade and currency politics should alert Indian university administrators to launch a worldwide headhunting exercise.

The inability of the public university compensation structure to attract the gurus and would-be icons in such fields should not deter private universities with more autonomous pay models to look for the best and get them to come to India. This is what global universities with strong global studies faculties do, that is, become magnets for pooling talent that is mind-boggling by Indian standards. Indian universities, at least those which have the economic means, should aim to become hubs that house an ideologically diverse array of top notch academicians under one roof.

The third transformation which needs to happen at the faculty level is to push academicians specializing in their respective narrow fields to also grow as public intellectuals who publish and make appearances in the audio-visual media in India. At present, the visibility of Indian academics in public opinion formulation on global affairs is infinitesimal. The pundits commenting on foreign topics are mostly journalists or think tank wonks who may have flair with language and easy writing skills as opposed to academicians who are better informed but lack the abilities to write lighter articles that can educate the Indian public.

Editorial predilections to always look for an 'India peg', that is judge opinion articles or columns by whether or not their topics are directly connected to Indian interests, have caused a severe shortage in intelligent writing and commenting about distant regions and happenings. Academics with global consciousness can change this narrow definition of what constitutes 'world news' and increase awareness among lay readers of the Indian middle classes about matters far and wide. The pool of students wishing to take up graduate level studies in global affairs in Indian universities would go up automatically if academicians shape the public discourse and proffer more critical insights about international current events. To simply parrot the Government of India's line on some foreign problem as the best is to lull India's people into a false complacency.

The fourth change that Indian universities should undertake if they are to popularize global studies among the country's citizens is to move towards offering undergraduate level (Bachelor of Arts) degree programmes in global affairs. There is a discernible hunger among high school-leaving Indians to take up foreign studies as their concentration at the undergraduate level, but hardly any Indian university or affiliated college gives them this option. One might be able to do a BA in Political Science with one or two courses in IR embedded within them, but not a full-fledged BA in foreign affairs. This restricts the choice set and debilitates the pool of prospective candidates who can go on to do graduate school studies in global affairs, eventually leading to doctoral research.

As with any competitive sport, global affairs education can only compete and harvest the finest minds of a country if it catches them young. Indian high schools do have a social studies or global studies curriculum, and the exposure of India's teenagers to the wider world due to the Internet and telecommunications breakthroughs also attune them to thinking about their place within not just the national rubric but a far wider global canvas. All they need is a well-designed bachelors' level degree programme that taps into their energies and channelizes them.

If one visits any American university, the sight of hundreds of undergraduates doing their 'majors' (concentration) in world politics does not raise eyebrows and is taken for granted. The enrolment in 'IR 101' type of courses in US undergraduate colleges is phenomenal because American universities give such options and nurture the interest of youth in foreign affairs. Established Indian universities are buffeted by needless controversies every time even incremental changes are made to curriculums, degree programmes, or their structuring,[21] leaving little confidence among reformers to propose drastic changes. But the key to nourishing a future generation of global studies specialists and social scientists is in introducing it at the bachelor's level. Those who miss the continuum between undergraduate and terminal degree education can only be left lamenting that the quality of incoming students into Masters and PhD programmes in foreign affairs is unsatisfactory.

Fifth, there is a dire need for a cultural shift in pedagogical techniques in the classroom in Indian universities. Encouraging students to ask questions, deconstruct received wisdom, and counter ideas of big names and cult figures whose books and lectures they hear is something almost taken for granted in established universities abroad. But these good practices are not followed in most Indian universities, especially in the social sciences, due to regimented relationships between faculty members and students.[22]

For too long, in the name of inherited culture, Indian universities have not empowered students to challenge their own professors without fear of unfair consequences. Imposing ideological or favoured theoretical leanings on students is a form of soft brainwashing that is especially hurtful in political science sub-disciplines because of the implications of knowledge for power holders. India's social sciences are far more liberal and freer

---

[21] Saxena, Vishakha, 'Waiting for the Cut-Off Lists? DU Controversies You Need to Know', *Hindustan Times* (27 May 2013).

[22] Indiresan, P.V. and Valson Thampu, 'Does Indian Education System Encourage Questioning?', *Business Standard* (29 October 2008).

than that in authoritarian China, but as the QS rankings cited earlier in this chapter demonstrate, relative independence has not propelled Indian universities above those from mainland China in teaching or research excellence in global studies.

Faculty-student ratios and relationships are pivotal in any agenda to re-energize global studies in India. Many able researchers have abandoned the core connections with students so much that the latter are rudderless and dispirited. As stated before in this chapter, it is not uncommon to see graduate students pursuing foreign affairs in India to feel that they have no viable career awaiting them. Unless the pedagogical bond is democratized and made less hierarchical, this drift will continue to rob global studies in India of the most talented students.

Lastly, no global studies programme in India can be world class if it is not densely connected with partner universities abroad. The global part-nership element is often missing in Indian social science education due to lackadaisical approaches of department heads and faculty members who do not go out of their way to try and create more chances for students to go on semesters abroad, access long-distance learning through videocon-ferencing technology, or do double degree programmes involving tie-ups with foreign universities.

Given the budgetary limits to hiring foreign faculty members, web-based technological exchanges between universities are proving invalu-able to bring wider international expertise to Indian classrooms. Foreign affairs faculties in India need dedicated staff members to enhance global collaborations that can facilitate these wonders. Misplaced faith in one's own faculty's alleged all-round abilities as well as gratuitous nationalistic sentiments that abhor exposing one's students and junior faculty members to foreign perspectives have held back foreign studies in Indian universities from leaping into the twenty-first century. In some cases, Memoranda of Understanding (MoUs) do get signed on paper between Indian universities and foreign counterparts, but the jeremiad one often hears from the latter is that they remain pieces of paper that do not get easily activated due to lack of sustained interest on the Indian side or bureaucratically glacial pace of the average Indian university's response mechanisms.

I would like to conclude this chapter by recalling a couple of adages of Mahatma Gandhi.

'I do not want my house to be walled in on all sides and my windows to be stuffed. I want the cultures of all lands to be blown about my house as freely as possible.'[23] The dictatorship of parochialism and localism has eaten into the contours of India's foreign affairs education system. To emancipate it is nothing short of launching a new freedom movement in the country that begins with imbuing global consciousness from the high school and undergraduate levels to doing joint collaborative research with foreign universities at the PhD and post-doctoral levels. Protectionist and pseudo claims that foreign universities would deluge India, deny access to the poor, poach on Indian faculty members in existing universities, and pursue a 'hidden agenda' to take over the country[24] are oblivious about China's success in attracting foreign institutions while retaining the core nationalism and independence that motivates its global studies system.[25]

India needs more Gandhian self-confidence and less naysaying meant to protect turfs and fiefdoms that have arisen in departments where some individuals are anxious about losing their unaccountable and privileged sinecures with the advent of world class competition.

The second Gandhian adage which should guide the agenda for a Global Studies revolution in India is the famous 'talisman' of the Mahatma about recalling the face of the poorest person and asking whether the step one must take 'is going to be of any use to him [her]'.[26] Indian university administrators and departmental heads who have some room for innovation and fresh endeavours within their might should recall the faces of the youth of the country who are literally starving for high quality education in foreign affairs that is not only intellectually stimulating but also rewarding as a worthwhile career choice.

If those who have the means and the authority to strive for serious reforms do not abdicate their responsibilities to the coming generations and work strategically to convert India from an educational laggard to a superpower, the future of global studies in the country will look a lot less circumspect.

[23] Mohandas Karmachand Gandhi, 'No Culture Isolation for Me', *Young India* (1 June 1921).

[24] Kumar, Anoop and R. Ganesan, 'Foreign Universities in India-Ethical Issues in New Scenario', *IOSR Journal of Business and Management*, vol. 8, no. 3 (2013).

[25] For China as a model of internationalization of higher education collaboration, see Mike Willis, 'How Chinese Universities and Foreign Universities Cooperate in an International Education Market: The Development and Application of a Four-Tiered Sino Foreign Higher Education Cooperation Model', *Griffith University ANZMAC 2000 Conference Paper* (2000).

[26] Cited in Panter-Brick, Simone. *Gandhi and Nationalism: The Path to Indian Independence* (London: I.B. Tauris, 2012), p. 25.

19 Clinical Legal Education and Democracy in India

Sital Kalantry

Formal clinical legal education programmes with instructors teaching clinics in a classroom and practice setting are not common in Indian universities. There are, however, programmes in which law students provide legal services on a voluntary basis to poor communities. Jindal Global Law School is one of the few institutions where there is a formal clinical legal education curriculum. There are many reasons law schools and universities in India should institute clinical legal education programmes—through these classes, students learn practical lawyering skills and at the same time, students provide assistance to people who could not otherwise afford legal services. One less explored rationale for clinical legal education is the relationship between clinical legal education and the promotion of democracy. I teach an International Human Rights Clinic at a law school in the United States where I work both on international issues and on domestic human rights problems in the United States. Through my experience in co-teaching a clinic at the Jindal Global Law School,[1] I develop the connection between democracy in India and clinical legal education.

UNIVERSITIES AND COMMUNITIES

At the outset it is important to point out a premise on which this chapter rests. Many of the quality higher education institutions in India are not representative of the economic, social, and geographic diversity of the country as a whole. To enter the best higher education institutions in India (many of which are public/government-supported), students must take competitive exams. Performance in these exams depends on the level of preparation for the exams themselves and the quality of primary and secondary education that a student receives.

Despite great efforts by the government to improve the education system as noted by the adoption of the Right to Education Act in 2009, many government schools lack the quality of education that trains their students to achieve admission to the most competitive schools. The wealthy classes in India send their children to private schools, which tend to have superior teachers, materials, and infrastructure. Thus, students from rich families are typically better prepared to gain admittance into elite institutions of higher education.

The situation is similar (albeit less acute) in the United States. Unlike in India, middle-class Americans send their children to public schools. Indeed, 90 per cent of all American children attend public schools. But the quality of public schools across the United States is uneven. Schools are largely funded by property taxes. As a result, schools in poor communities have less funding to pay teachers, maintain infrastructure, and other expenses needed to provide high quality education.

Some have noted that there is an 'achievement gap' between white people and minorities in the United States. Because of this and other reasons, the population of students who enter the top universities in the United States is not representative of population as a whole in the United States.

---

[1] 'Promoting Clinical Legal Education in India', *A Joint Report by Cornell Law School and Jindal Global Law School* (July 2012), available at http://papers.ssrn.com/sol3/papers.cfm?abstract_id=2112429.

Consisting of a disproportionate number of wealthy students from privileged communities, universities by and large have not engaged with the communities around them. Instead, they have often erected physical barriers that separate the communities from the university (such as gates or fences around the university). Where there aren't physical barriers, there can be private security forces to protect people within a university campus. To break these barriers that further deepen the divide between universities and their communities, it is imperative for Indian law schools and universities to develop curriculum that requires students to engage with the communities around them.

Universities in the United States are increasingly engaging with the communities around them. 'Civic engagement' departments and initiatives are emerging in many universities. There are a number of ways in which this engagement is taking place. For example, universities are engaging faculty to conduct research in issues that impact the community. Universities are also investing resources to economically develop their local communities. For example, University of Pennsylvania invested $ 150 million in retail development in areas around it. Another way of community engagement, which I focus on here, is to encourage students to interact with the communities surrounding the schools. At the undergraduate level, these initiatives are being described as 'service-learning'. Although not exactly the same, law school clinical education programmes can be seen as a form of inherent community engagement.

CLINICAL LEGAL EDUCATION IN INDIA AND THE UNITED STATES

In the United States, 'clinics' are small law school classes taught by full-time faculty where students learn lawyering skills by undertaking legal services, typically on behalf of poor or marginalized people and communities. Clinical programmes in American law schools burgeoned in the 1960s alongside the civil rights movement and the national focus on eliminating poverty. Most clinics at the time engaged students in providing routine legal services to local community members who could not otherwise afford them. Today most law schools in the United States offer clinics as part of their curricular offerings, in many different subject areas of law.

Although clinics vary a great deal, there are a few key features of clinics in the United States. First, there are typically low student/teacher ratios. To ensure that students are closely supervised in the legal work they perform and to provide them with appropriate feedback, clinic classes are typically limited to eight students per instructor. Second, most law schools have dedicated clinical faculty with extensive practice experience. In some schools, these professors are on the same tenure track as non-clinical professors, but in many other schools they work on long-term contracts. Third, virtually all clinics are offered to students for law school credit. This allows students to participate in clinics while simultaneously working toward their credit requirements.

Even though most Indian law schools do not offer clinics defined in this way, many have 'legal aid cells' where students, largely without faculty supervision, perform legal services for poor communities. In India, there have been waves of national-level reform efforts concentrating on the development of a skills-based curriculum.[2]

The Bar Council of India issued a directive in 1997 that requires law schools to include certain classes focused on practical training.[3] Where schools have introduced these classes, it is common for more than 80 students to be enrolled in one class. This makes it virtually impossible for instructors to provide supervision to students in undertaking legal work. In a 2002 report, the Law Commission of India suggested that clinical legal education should be mandatory.[4] Today there are a number of 'legal aid cells' in Indian law schools where students, largely without faculty guidance or supervision, provide direct legal services to individuals.[5]

Despite these national calls for reform, most law schools in India lack robust clinical education programmes where faculty directly supervises

[2] For an excellent review of policy reform efforts in Clinical Legal Education in India, see Frank Bloch and M.R.K. Prasad, 'Institutionalizing a Social Justice Mission for Clinical Legal Education: Cross-National Currents from India and the United States', *Clinical Law Review*, vol. 13 (2006): p. 165.

[3] Bar Council of India, Circular No. 4/1997; see United Nations Development Programme India, A Study of Law School Based Legal Service Clinics 2 (2011), available at http://www.in.undp.org/content/dam/india/docs/a_study_of_law_school_based_legal_services_clinics.pdf (covering seven major states: Bihar, Chhattisgarh, Jharkhand, Madhya Pradesh, Orissa (now Odisha), Rajasthan, and Uttar Pradesh) [hereinafter UNDP Study].

[4] Law Commission of India, 184th Report (2002) available at http://lawcommissionofindia.nic.in/reports/184threport-PartI.pdf.

[5] For some examples of law school based legal services clinics in India, see UNDP Study.

students in experiential learning. A recent UNDP report surveying 39 law schools with legal aid cells found that although 82 per cent of those schools had faculty designated to supervise legal aid cells, 63 per cent of those schools gave no academic credit to students.[6] Where law schools do undertake legal aid activities, most involve legal literacy camps.[7] According to this UNDP study, the key problems in developing clinical legal education in India are that: (1) no credit is given to students who undertake these activities, which is a disincentive to students to conduct them and discourages them to follow through on their commitments; (2) there is no workload reduction given to faculty who are designated to supervise legal aid cells; (3) communities are not aware that the law schools provide free legal services; and (4) under the Advocates Act, full-time law teachers and students are not allowed to represent clients before courts.[8]

TRADITIONAL JUSTIFICATIONS FOR CLINICAL LEGAL EDUCATION

Clinical Legal education emerged in the United States from a desire to give greater access to poor and marginalized communities to legal services. Law students, working under the supervision of lawyers, could provide basic services, such as drafting wills or leases or assisting with landlord-tenant disputes and divorces. Typically, only those who fall below a certain income level can qualify for these services and such individuals would likely not have access to the legal services were it not for law school clinics.

In addition to the public service that law clinics provide, another reason that is increasingly cited to justify clinical legal education is that it trains students in skills that will prepare them to practice law. In contrast to the casebook method that prevails in law school (where students read legal opinions), clinics require law students to actually work on cases or projects that involve representing clients or advocating for certain policy changes.

In today's increasingly challenging legal market for law graduates in the United States, some law schools have renewed their focus on clinical

---

[6] UNDP Study, pp. 16, 20.

[7] UNDP Study, p. 45.

[8] UNDP Study, pp. 33–44.

legal education. To give their law graduates better tools to succeed in practice, law schools require students to participate in clinics. The New York Bar association recently mandated that anyone who wishes to gain admission to the New York Bar must have performed at least 50 hours of pro bono services.[9] Through working on cases, students learn interviewing, client representation, fact-finding/investigation, report-writing and documentation, empathetic lawyering, and formulating and advocating policy reforms.

DEMOCRACY AND CLINICAL LEGAL EDUCATION

To supplement the other justifications for clinical legal education, all of which are valid and applicable in India and other contexts, I would like to offer another theory for why it is crucial for universities in India to incorporate clinical legal education: it will promote the proper functioning of democracy in India.

John Dewey, who was a philosopher at the University of Chicago, is known as an important proponent of education to advance democracy. Dewey emphasized the need for democratic citizens to understand and consider the welfare of the society as a whole. In order to balance their personal needs with the needs of others, citizens must gain an understanding of the lives and experiences of other citizens.

Dewey also theorized in favour of experiential learning. Dewey maintained that mere memorization of facts was not education; instead 'genuine education would be derived from life experience that was accompanied by opportunities for discussion and reflection. In the absence of reflection, experience by itself has the potential for 'mis-education' or a faulty interpretation of experience'.[10]

This theory was further developed by Martha Nussbaum in her book *Not for Profit: Why Democracy Needs the Humanities*.[11] She is concerned

---

[9] Pro Bono Admission Requirement, see http://www.nycourts.gov/attorneys/probono/baradmissionreqs.shtml.

[10] Kenny, Maureen E. et al. (eds), *Learning to Serve: Promoting Civil Society Through Service Learning* (Kluwer Academic Publishers, 2002), p. 18.

[11] Nussbaum, Martha, C. *Not for Profit: Why Democracy Needs the Humanities* (Princeton University Press, 2010).

that globally education policies are focusing on teaching students technical skills or other skills needed to enhance economic growth and development at the cost of instilling critical thinking and other ways of thinking that are needed to enhance democratic participation.[12] She is particularly worried about the lack of emphasis and funding for the humanities and arts. In contrast with recent trends in education policy, she points out that the goals of education should include the promotion of 'a humane, people-sensitive democracy dedicated to promoting opportunities of "life, liberty, and the pursuit of happiness" to each and every person.'[13] She gives a concrete list of abilities to achieve this goal. I include those that are relevant to this chapter below:

1. The ability to think about political issues affecting the nation, which gives the ability to think about the good of the nation as a whole, not just that of one's own local group.
2. The ability to recognize fellow citizens as people with equal rights, even though they may be of different race, religion, gender, and sexuality.
3. The ability to have concern for the lives of others, to grasp what policies of many types mean for the opportunities and experiences of one's fellow citizens.
4. The ability to see one's nation as a part of a complicated world order in which issues of many kinds require intelligent transnational deliberation for their resolution.

To further education for democracy, she favours a model of active learning, rather than desk-learning where students memorize information.[14]

Clinical legal education in India (as well as other countries) can accomplish many of the goals of promoting the functioning of a democracy that values equality and enhances opportunities for all citizens rather than just a select few. In clinics at many law schools in the United States, students enter into a relationship with a person (client) who is typically from different and often disenfranchised community where the student serves as an advocate for the individual. Sometimes the representation may involve

[12] Nussbaum, *Not for Profit: Why Democracy Needs the Humanities*, pp. 1–3.
[13] Nussbaum, *Not for Profit: Why Democracy Needs the Humanities*, p. 25.
[14] Nussbaum, *Not for Profit: Why Democracy Needs the Humanities*, p. 18 and chapter 4.

more than one individual, but a community, or in other cases, the student must advocate in favour of certain issues. During the course of his or her work, the law student often interviews/meets with his or her client, which may require him/her to go into neighbourhoods or places that he/she does not normally travel to.

For example, during the course of our work on investigating whether police were illegally entering into homes to find out if there were undocumented people living there, we travelled to a home only one hour away from our university in the United States to interview dairy farm workers. Students would not be able to understand the conditions that many people live in without seeing them. There were ten unrelated individuals with a few children living in a run-down house without adequate furniture. The workers worked in shifts, some of which were overnight. They risked their lives travelling from Guatemala to engage in low-paid labour not far from Cornell University.

Although much of the conversation between the student and client will involve gathering facts and developing legal strategy, discussions often move beyond that. During the 'ice-breaking' or introductory stage, students will establish a relationship or common ground with the client to facilitate open discussion and trust. This relationship can mature and deepen over the course of time and multiple meetings. Through these interactions, the student often develops a personal relationship with the client. The student may learn of the difficulties some people encounter who do not have a stable place to live or who may not have regular phone access or Internet. They also learn that they may have a lot in common with their clients who have similar desires, views, or goals for their families as the students do.

As students develop relationships with clients and understand the similarities and differences between themselves and their clients, their perspectives often change. One student was afraid to even meet a client who was in jail because he had illegally entered the United States and was also charged with drug possession and dealing. She did not personally meet with him, but communicated with him by phone. She learned that he accepted only $ 50 for driving a car that contained marijuana. He said he needed the money to pay his rent. In writing an appeal brief on his behalf, she learned how his family was killed by a gang in another country. She dedicated herself to obtaining justice for him. From a 'criminal' he became a person to her. Serving in a client-attorney relationship, can be very humbling as well as eye-opening for students.

Humanizing people from different walks of life can have a lasting impact on a student. Many of our students become legislators, judges, prosecutors; they will draw upon these experiences in their work to come up with fairer laws and better decisions. Clinical work can impact the career choices they make. Through their experience of working in a clinic, some students may decide to devote their lives to fixing inequalities and others may undertake pro bono services for free.

AN EXAMPLE OF DEMOCRACY AND CLINICAL LEGAL EDUCATION

With the support of the Fulbright-Nehru fellowship, I had the opportunity to live in New Delhi for the Fall semester in 2012. During this time, I co-taught a clinic with Professors Elizabeth Brundige (Cornell), Priya S. Gupta (who was a professor at Jindal Global Law School at the time), and Ajay Pandey (Jindal Global Law School).

The Cross-National Human Rights and Rural Governance Clinic ('Cross-National Clinic') was a unique collaboration between the Good Rural Governance and Citizen Participation Clinic ('Citizen Participation Clinic') at Jindal Global Law School and the Cornell International Human Rights Clinic ('Human Rights Clinic') at Cornell Law School. The Citizen Participation Clinic aims to address the disconnect between the Indian Constitution's promise for a dignified life for every citizen and the reality of undignified human existence for the majority of the population, particularly in rural India. The Human Rights Clinic works with organizations and individuals around the world to promote human rights through a multi-faceted approach, including through litigation, human rights education, and law reform.

The Cross-National Clinic was taught by videoconference to students both based at Cornell Law School and Jindal Global Law School. Students from Jindal Global Law School and Cornell Law School participated in class discussions and exercises, which involved intensive interaction among students on both sides of the videoconference screen. Students gained substantive exposure to the principles of clinical legal education, international human rights law and its implementation, and the theory and practice of good rural governance and citizen participation. Through simulation activities, students developed skills in investigation and interviewing, explored strategies for the enforcement of human rights, and reflected critically on difficult questions of ethics and professional responsibility in human rights lawyering. Other sessions offered students an opportunity to present, discuss, and receive feedback on their clinical project work.

In addition to the seminar component of the course, the students worked on clinical projects that aimed to promote good governance and citizen participation in India. At Jindal, students furthered the Citizen Participation Clinic's mission by supporting the effective participation of rural communities in bringing good governance to their villages. They consulted with community members about their concerns, advised them on potential avenues for redress, and assisted them in filing complaints and petitions under the Right to Information Act, and writing letters to relevant government authorities. During the course of the semester, the Jindal students attended weekly *sabha*s (meetings) with community members and shared their work and experiences with the Cornell students through the videoconference format. The Cornell students conducted legal and factual desk research on the Citizen Participation Clinic's model of clinical legal education and its contributions to the advancement of human rights. They also prepared sample interview questions to guide their subsequent field research.

In March 2012, the Cornell students travelled to Sonipat, India, to engage in person with the Jindal students, to learn first-hand about the implementation of India's human rights obligations, and to gain an understanding of the mechanics of the Citizen Participation Clinic. Jindal and Cornell students interviewed community members, teachers, employees of non-governmental organizations, and policymakers. They conducted site visits of government-run day care centres (*aganwadi*), ration distribution centres, and government schools in two villages in the state of Haryana.

The Citizen Participation Clinic is a community-based clinical programme that relies on a continuous dialogue with communities in order to learn from them and to secure their effective participation in the political processes. In addition to formulating their own goals and articulating their needs, participants take action on their own behalf to the furthest extent possible. In this way, community members gain skills they can use in the future, gain the knowledge to teach those skills to other villagers, and develop confidence and self-sufficiency. To the extent community members need their assistance, students assist them in writing letters and other petitions.

THE PROMOTION OF DEMOCRACY

An old lady gave a hand written letter to me, which stated all her grievances with regard to the management of the village, expressing her hope and faith that I, as a law student, should on her behalf make her letter reach the appropriate authorities who will take the required steps to address her grievances. This was very touching, and I felt that I owe an obligation to the society members and should put my legal knowledge or resources to fruitful use and betterment of fellow citizens, especially those who cannot voice their opinions before the government, policymakers, and other stakeholders. It is my duty to become the bridge between these two ends with the State on one end and the marginalized on the other.

—a student from Jindal Global Law School who participated in the Cross-National Clinic.

During the course of teaching the Cross-National Clinic, I observed the many ways that the goals of education for democracy promotion proposed by Professor Nussbaum were achieved. For many students, it was the first time that they interacted directly with people from poor villages. They went to visit the villagers in their own communities and observed their daily living conditions. Some of these villagers might be the same people who are working as domestic workers in the homes of the students. The roles were reversed, however, as the students were providing services to the villagers rather than vice versa.

By meeting and interacting with villagers on a weekly basis, students formed relationships with them and came to know of the serious problems they face and difficulties they have in achieving their solutions. One student observed the importance of the weekly meetings in creating an equality among people: 'The villagers, law students, law professors, and NGO workers all sat together as equals on a mat and discussed issues of concern to them in their communities'. Students worked on a project that required them to investigate the conditions of government child-care centres and primary schools. They witnessed first-hand the low quality care and education provided.

The clinic students demonstrated sensitivity to the plight of the poor and expressed a desire to use their privileged position as lawyers to improve the lives of disadvantaged populations. One second-year student said that the clinic has provided him with a 'very good grounding for social responsibility'. When asked what his primary goal was in participating in the course, he responded, 'We are trying to get equality before the law'.

Another second-year student reflected upon the problems of inequality in India, saying, 'The rich people are getting richer day by day. We have to change that on behalf of the citizens and the law.'

These experiences impacted the career goals of some students. One student mentioned that he would like to pursue a career in public interest law and assist in the implementation of government schemes for the poor. Other clinic students, who do not plan to work with poor communities after graduation, nevertheless see the value of the clinical programme to their future careers. Another student who wants to enter the judiciary after graduation, says that the clinical programme has benefited her because she now understands how the law intersects with reality and how the government works.

In whatever career path students pursue, they will benefit from a clinical programme that has given them invaluable insight into the lives of the rural poor and a better understanding of the human rights problems that plague much of India's population. When lawyers spend their entire careers in luxurious offices and ivory towers, it is easy for them to forget that an important objective of the legal profession is to promote social justice.

Through the course of the semester students met with, developed relationships with, undertook work and advocated on behalf of, and witnessed the daily lives of poor villagers in rural communities outside their law school. They learned the concerns and issues that villagers in India face, including lack of access to educational opportunities, poverty, and violence in their communities. They learned to humanize individuals and appreciated the shared humanity in their experiences. While one of the goals of the Citizen Participation Clinic is to empower Indian citizens to use the accountability tools available to them and to become more effective participants in the government, the education received by the students has also promoted democracy in another way. When working as policymakers, lawyers, and even as voters in a nation, students who have engaged in this type of education, will work towards the promotion of a democracy that values and considers the perspectives of all citizens.

To train the future lawyers as political and business leaders, there is an urgent need to develop clinical legal education in India to support the values of equality on which the Indian democracy was founded.

Appendix 1: SONIPAT DECLARATION on
World-Class Universities in BRICS and Emerging Economies

We, the representatives of higher educational institutions from around the globe, meeting at the invitation of the *Times Higher Education (THE)*, O.P. Jindal Global University (JGU), and the International Institute for Higher Education Research and Capacity Building (IIHEd), on the occasion of the **THE BRICS and Emerging Economies Universities Summit** on the theme: **"Why Emerging Economies need World Class Universities"** held in Sonipat (Haryana), National Capital Region of Delhi, India, from 2–4 December 2015, declare the following principles to guide the creation and development of world-class universities within our countries.

Principle 1. *The mission of world-class universities is the pursuit of knowledge and promotion of innovation*

1.1. A world-class university is one that considers access to higher education to be a human right and a public good. It recognizes that the pursuit of knowledge for knowledge's sake is itself part of the academic enterprise and should always be valued. The objective of a world-class university is not only to produce a skilled workforce but also to prepare citizens to serve society and to understand and share human values. It is therefore incumbent on such universities to provide a liberal education, including the social sciences and humanities, so that students acquire, beyond professional preparation, the ability to think critically and to understand and appreciate their civilizational heritage and their role in a complex world.

1.2. Universities in the BRICS and Emerging Economies should encourage creative thought and value the diverse backgrounds of the different university stakeholders. Universities should be free, open, and liberal spaces where the heritage of the past is transmitted to new generations, where critical thinking is stimulated, and where innovation is promoted.

Principle 2. *The highest qualities of students, faculty, and staff must be promoted*

2.1. Recruitment, selection, retention, and promotion of students, staff, and faculty should reflect a balanced commitment to both excellence and equity and not be distorted by ideological, political, or financial pressures.

2.2. Gender equality within the university environment should be a priority goal at the student, staff, and faculty levels.

2.3. Special efforts should be made to ensure the highest quality of teaching, based on how students learn, and, for that purpose, teaching staff should be motivated and trained to achieve excellence in teaching.

Principle 3. *Research should adhere to the highest standards*

3.1. World-class universities in the BRICS and Emerging Economies have a special challenge to promote and produce the highest quality research at the undergraduate, graduate and professional school levels.

3.2. It is essential that all who engage in such research adhere to the highest standards of academic honesty and integrity and, in particular, that they ensure that all ideas, data, findings, reasoning, conclusions, and recommendations that are not original be properly attributed by faculty and researchers in their scholarship and by students in all the work they submit.

3.3. Governments should not interfere with the autonomy and academic freedom of higher education institutions. Research excellence should be a priority of universities in the BRICS and Emerging Economies in their pursuit of world-class status.

Principle 4. *Universities must be provided appropriate resources to achieve greatness*

4.1. Universities in the BRICS and Emerging Economies cannot achieve greatness unless they have sufficient financial and human resources, which may be from public or private funding. Governments have a particular responsibility to provide adequate resources to higher education and to facilitate private support for universities while ensuring that private support does not interfere with the other principles in this Declaration.

4.2. The role of philanthropy has been crucial historically in creating world-class universities and is beginning to provide the resources for quality education in the BRICS and Emerging Economies. This trend should be encouraged in ways that maintain the independence of the institution while encouraging private contributions to the funding of higher education.

4.3. Access to higher education should be affordable. While it is also sometimes necessary for students to pay tuition and fees for higher education, the burden on students and their families should be limited and adequate financial support should be provided to qualified students with limited financial means through scholarships and loans.

4.4. Funding from industry may be a valuable source for research but must be administered so as to avoid any conflict of interest and interference with academic integrity and freedom. A conflict-of-interest policy should be made explicit and transparent by the university, which should require a conflict of interest statement by the researcher receiving such support.

4.5. Excellent facilities and technology constitute an essential element of the resources needed to achieve world-class status for universities in the BRICS and Emerging Economies. Investments by governments and philanthropic entities in physical infrastructure should be strongly encouraged.

Principle 5. *Governance of universities must provide an environment for free enquiry and career development*

5.1. As part of their effort to achieve world-class status, universities in the BRICS and Emerging Economies must adhere to the highest standards of academic freedom, honesty, and integrity. Academic freedom requires that students, faculty, and other researchers have freedom to teach and disseminate ideas and information, however inconvenient to university or state authorities, without fear of reprisals from university or state officials, including providing legal safeguards where appropriate.

5.2. While maintaining the above standards, universities may have a valuable role to play in informing government policy at the local and national levels to help governments address issues affecting public welfare.

5.3. Universities should adhere to the best global policies and practices in ensuring the well-being of its faculty members and students, both in terms of infrastructure as well as social support systems.

Principle 6. *Universities can enhance the quality of teaching and research through local and global connections*

6.1. Part of building world-class universities is fostering local and international collaborations. Engagement with local communities through such activities as participatory action research and community outreach enhances the role and relevance of the university with local realities and in cultivating local knowledge and indigenous traditions.

6.2. In addition, universities should cultivate collaborations with institutions across the globe through joint teaching, faculty and student exchanges, joint research, seminars, training programs and conferences, and joint publications.

* * * * * * * * * *

The above principles are designed to guide universities in the BRICS and Emerging Economies to advance towards world-class status. Ranking of universities may be a useful stimulus for improvement and in future should reflect achievements in relation to these principles.

Appendix 2: Speech Delivered by the President of India, Shri Pranab Mukherjee at the Conference on 'The Future of Indian Universities: Comparative Perspectives on Higher Education Reforms for a Knowledge Society' (O.P. Jindal Global University, Sonipat, Haryana 21.03.2013)

It is indeed a privilege for me to be present on the inauguration of the conference on 'The Future of Indian Universities: Comparative Perspectives on Higher Education Reforms for a Knowledge Society' being hosted by O.P. Jindal Global University. I am thankful to O.P. Jindal Global University for organizing this conference. This Conference, I believe, could not have been organized at a more appropriate time.

The need to make critical reforms in our educational system is more compelling now, in many ways, than at any time before. There is an urgent need to raise the quality of teaching, faculty and research in our universities.

There could be no second opinion on the critical role that education plays in the development of a nation. It is the most powerful tool that can spawn societal changes and transform the economic fortunes of a country. In the words of Benjamin Franklin, 'an investment in knowledge pays the best interest'. I compliment O.P. Jindal Global University for choosing a subject of such topical relevance and importance for the country for this conference that is being held today. I take this opportunity also of paying homage to Late Shri O.P. Jindal, a leading industrialist of this country in whose fond memory this university is established.

There are several important reasons why we need to focus our attention on the educational sector. I hardly need to emphasize that we have a young population and the demographic profile of our country can be a boon. It would be a boon if we are able to harness their potential. But our failure to do so and channelize their productive energies may visit us with terrible negative consequences.

These challenges can be daunting. By the year 2020, the average age of an Indian will be 29 years, which will be much lower than the average age of 40 years in the US, 46 years in Japan and 47 years in Europe. Over two-third Indians will be of working age by 2025.

These statistics make it imperative for us to focus on the educational needs of our young population. We must recognize that the demographic dividend can only be reaped if the young population is provided higher education and training in vocational skills.

At the end of the Eleventh Five Year Plan period, India had 659 degree awarding institutions and 33,023 colleges. These numbers are indeed impressive but many more would have to be established. They are required to meet the growing demands for higher education, especially in the rural areas in the country.

There are several areas in the country far removed from any college or university. This has led to the low rate of enrolment in higher education. Only around 7 per cent of those aged between 18–24 years join higher education in India, while it is 21 per cent in Germany and 34 per cent in the US.

Increased access would not only help expand the base of the educational pyramid, but also promote inclusiveness. It can also be promoted by making education affordable to the marginalized sections of the society. Student aid programmes like scholarships, education loans and self-help schemes should therefore be liberalized for deserving students.

We lack universities that can provide quality education that meet global benchmarks. It is a matter of concern that there is not a single Indian university in the top 200 universities in the world as per an international survey of universities. This position is not at all acceptable. This calls for serious introspection. With educational standards that fall short of international benchmarks, India would be grievously handicapped in this competitive world.

The National Knowledge Commission in its Report in 2006 described the falling standards of higher education in the country as a 'quiet crisis that runs deep'. We cannot wait any longer before we take remedial action. We do not have the luxury of time.

We must promote a culture of excellence in our educational system. I can suggest a concrete step in this direction which would be to identify one department in every university and transform it into a Centre of Excellence. To achieve this, the Ministry of Human Resource Development, the University Grants Commission and the Universities would have to work together in close collaboration.

Amongst the academic challenges that we face, is the large number of vacancies in the Universities. In Central Universities alone, the vacancy of teachers is around an unacceptable level of 38 per cent. This has to change. We cannot expect to impart quality education without qualified teachers who are most equipped to provide guidance to students and encourage research.

There are several steps that we may need to take to achieve qualitative improvement in our educational system, to make it as good as the best in the world. For this, the Ministry of Human Resource Development, the University Grants Commission and Universities and all stakeholders should work out a common approach. The focus should be on quality, affordability and accessibility, the three cornerstones of higher education. The private sector should be encouraged to play a larger role in our educational system. Some of the top universities of the world have been built on the initiative of the private sector. In India, the private sector has left its mark in several key sectors like health, transport and financial services. I see no reason why the Indian private sector cannot replicate its efforts in the higher education sector as well. But, care should be taken to ensure that there is no dilution in educational standards. Here again I take this opportunity of congratulating the O.P. Jindal Global University to take the lead.

Affiliated colleges enroll about 87 per cent of all students and are at the core of our higher education system. The affiliating universities should, however, exercise due diligence to ensure that adequate curricula and evaluation systems are adopted by such colleges.

We should also be able to harness the power of technology to promote education. Classroom teaching in one university could be transmitted for the benefit of a wider student population in other universities using modern technology. For instance, lectures of eminent professors could be transmitted to educational institutions situated away from the main towns and cities using the facilities offered by the National Mission on Education through Information and Communication Technology.

The National Knowledge Network, which aims at the connection of knowledge generating institutions through high speed broadband network, has made substantial progress. We have been able to link 955 out of the 1,500 institutions to this Network. The balance one-third institutions should be connected on priority basis to bring its benefits to remote areas.

Our universities would also benefit immensely by fully utilizing the services of 'inspired teachers'. About 10 to 20 such teachers who can spark the student minds to seek knowledge beyond the text book could be identified. When such teachers interact with their peers and with students, it will result in the qualitative improvement in the capacity to impart and absorb knowledge.

The progress of nations will be determined in large measure by their capacity to innovate. India's performance indicators in this segment are discouraging in comparison to her major competitors. Though Indians represent about 17 per cent of the global population, only 2 per cent of the patent applications in the world in 2011 were filed in India. In the same year, the number of patent applications filed in India was around 42,000. In comparison, 5 lakh plus patent applications were each filed in China and the US.

Universities and Research Centres should become fertile grounds for innovation. Setting up industry incubation parks, enhancing the coverage of research students by fellowships, promoting inter-disciplinary research through inter-university and intra-university collaboration, and empowering our centres of excellence would be important steps in this direction.

We should erect innovative structures to encourage and retain intellectual resources in our academic and research centres. Indian scholars working overseas in important research and teaching positions should also be encouraged to take up short-term assignments in Indian Universities. This would facilitate dissemination of knowledge and cross-fertilization of ideas.

In our country, there are many innovations that take place at the grass-root levels. But for the nation to derive benefit from them, we need to make them commercially marketable. Our universities should be equipped to encourage grass-root innovators and play the role of a mentor.

With a view to evolving a time-bound action plan and make innovative changes in the higher education sector, a conference of the Vice Chancellors of the Central Universities was organized in the Rashtrapati Bhavan in February of this year. The Conference identified certain immediate, short-term and medium-term measures that would need to be taken to reform the education system. The changes are being worked upon by the Ministry of Human Resource Development. I hope to see substantial progress in the implementation of the measures by the time we hold the next conference in February 2014.

I had stated in my Address to the Nation on the eve of the last Republic Day that it is high time for us, for the nation as a whole, to reset its moral compass. Our universities and other institutes of higher learning should aid in this process. A beginning may be made by introducing value education that would supplement the academic curricula, thereby preparing students to face the test of career and life with equanimity.

I once again congratulate the O.P. Jindal Global University for taking the initiative and providing a platform to facilitate a greater understanding of the challenges of the higher education sector by all stakeholders. I am confident that this Conference would throw up new ideas and thoughts.

I wish the organizers every success in the conduct of this Conference.

References

Abbott, A. 2001. *Chaos of Disciplines*. New Jersey: The University of Chicago Press.

Agarwal, Pawan. 2009. *Indian Higher Education: Envisioning the Future*. New Delhi: Sage Publications.

———. 2006. 'Higher Education in India: The Need for Change'. ICRIER Working Paper no. 180. New Delhi, India: Indian Council for Research on International Economic Relations.

Altbach, Philip. 2012. 'India's Higher Education Challenges', in Pawan Agarwal (ed.), *Fifty Years of Higher Education*. New Delhi: Sage Publications.

Altbach, Philip and Pawan Agarwal. 2013. 'Scoring Higher on Education'. *The Hindu*, New Delhi, 12 February.

Ashby, Eric and Anderson Mary. 1966. *Universities: British, Indian, African: A Study in the Ecology of Higher Education*. Cambridge: Harvard University Press.

Ayyar, R.V. Vaidyanatha. 2009. *Public Policy Making in India*. New Delhi: Pearson.

Bachelard, G. 1994. *The Poetics of Space*. New York: Beacon Press.

Bajpai, Kanti. 2014. 'Three Big Things We Need to Do for Indian Higher Education—Or Else', in Nalini Menon (ed.), *Educating India*. New Delhi: Pearson.

———. 2009. 'Obstacles to Good Work in Indian International Relations', *International Studies* 46(1&2): 114.

Bajpai, Kanti, Scott A. Fritzen, and Kishore Mahbubani. 2013. 'Global Public Policy as a Field of Study: A View from Asia', in Kanti Bajpai, Scott A. Fritzen, Kishore Mahbubani, and Kenneth P. Tan (eds), *Lee Kuan Yew School of Public Policy:*

Building a Global Policy School in Asia. Singapore: Lee Kuan Yew School of Public Policy and World Scientific.

———. 2012. 'Global Public Policy as a Field of Study: A View from Asia', *Jindal School of Public Policy Journal* 1(1): 8–25.

Banerjee, A. and Esther Duflo. 2011. *Poor Economics: A Radical Rethinking of the Way to Fight Global Poverty*. USA: Public Affairs.

Barker, Derek. 2004. 'The Scholarship of Engagement: A Taxonomy of Five Emerging Practices', *Journal of Higher Education Outreach and Engagement* 9(2): 123–37.

Bashir, Sajitha. 2007. 'Trends in International Trade in Higher Education: Implications and Options for Developing Countries', The World Bank (March), Washington, D.C.

Basu, A. 2002. 'Indian Higher Education: Colonialism and Beyond', in P.G. Altbach and V. Selvaratnam (eds), *From Dependence to Autonomy: The Development of Asian Universities*. Chestnut Hill, MA: Center for International Higher Education, Boston College.

———. 1982. *Essays in the History of Indian Education*. New Delhi: Concept.

———. 1974. *The Growth of Education and Political Development in India*. New Delhi: Oxford University Press.

Beck, Ulrich. 1992. *The Risk Society: Towards a New Modernity*. New York: Sage Publications.

Ben-David, J. and R. Collins. 1966. 'Social Factors in the Origin of a New Science!' *American Sociological Review* 31: 451–65.

Bhargava, A. 2008. 'Randomized Controlled Experiments in Health and Social Sciences: Some Conceptual Issues', *Economics and Human Biology* (6): 293–8.

Bloch, Frank and M.R.K. Prasad. 2006. 'Institutionalizing a Social Justice Mission for Clinical Legal Education: Cross-National Currents from India and the United States', *Clinical Law Review* 13: 165.

———. 2005. *Our Underachieving Colleges: A Candid Look at How Much Students Learn and Why They Should Be Learning More*. Princeton: Princeton University Press.

Bok, Derek. 2001. 'Universities and the Decline of Civic Responsibility', *Journal of College and Character* 2(9).

Bose, Subhas. 2010. *Words of Freedom. Ideas of a Nation*. New Delhi: Penguin.

Bourke, Alan. 2013. 'Universities, Civil Society and the Global Agenda of Community-engaged Research', *Globalisation, Societies and Education* 11(4): 498–519.

Braeman, J. 1996. 'The German Influence on American Education: A Review Essay', *Journal of Higher Education* 37(2): 101–03.

Braun, T. and A. Schubert. 2003. 'A Quantitative View on the Coming of Age of Interdisciplinarity in the Sciences 1980–1999', *Scientometrics* 58(1): 183–9.

Bremmer Ian. 2012. *Every Nation for Itself: Winners and Losers in a G-Zero World*. New York: Portfolio/Penguin.

Bridgstock, M., et al. 1998. *Science, Technology and Society: An Introduction.* Cambridge: Cambridge University Press.

Briggs, Stephen R. 2013. 'The Purpose of Berry', *Berry Magazine* (Spring): 10–11.

Brint, S. 2005. 'Creating the Future: "New Directions" in American Research Universities', *Minerva* 43: 23–50.

Brockington, John. 2003. 'The Sanskrit Epics', in Gavin Flood (ed.), *Blackwell Companion to Hinduism*, pp. 116–28. Oxford: Blackwell Publishing.

Brockman, John. 1995. *The Third Culture: Beyond the Scientific Revolution.* New York: Simon and Schuster.

Brown, M. Christopher and James Earl Davis. 2001. 'The Historically Black College as Social Contract, Social Capital, and Social Equalizer', *Peabody Journal of Education* 76(1): 31–49.

Burgess, J., et al. 2007. 'Deliberative Mapping: A Novel Analytic-deliberative Methodology to Support Contested Science-policy Decisions', *Public Understanding of Science* 16: 299–322.

Burton, Wayne M. 2013. 'In Long Run, Well-Educated Workforce Is Preferable to Well-Trained,' *Boston Globe* (a letter to the editor), 14 June.

Butterfield, H. 1965. *The Whig Interpretation of History.* New York: W.W. Norton.

Calhoun, C. 2001. 'Foreword', in K. Worcestor, *History of the Social Science Research Council.* New York: SSRC.

Calhoun, C. and D. Rhoten. 2010. 'Integrating the Social Sciences: Theoretical Knowledge, Methodological Tools, and Practical Applications', in R. Frodeman, J.T. Klein, and C. Mitcham (eds), *The Oxford Handbook of Interdisciplinarity*, pp. 103–18. New York: Oxford University Press.

Cantor, Nancy and Steve Schomberg. 2003. 'Poised between 2 Worlds: The University as Monastery and Marketplace', *Educause* March–April: 12–21.

Carnoy, M., P. Loyalka, M. Dobryakova, R. Dossani, I. Froumin, K. Kuhns, J. Tilak, and R. Wang. 2013. *University Expansion in a Changing Global Economy: Triumph of the BRICs?* Stanford, CA: Stanford University Press.

Carr, Nicholas. 2013. 'Lovers of Ink and Paper, Take Heart. Reports of the Death of the Printed Book May Be Exaggerated', Don't Burn Your Books—Print Is Here to Stay,' *Wall Street Journal*, Updated 5 January.

———. 2010. *The Shallows: What the Internet Is Doing to Our Brains.* New York: WW Norton.

Chacko, Priya. 2010. 'The Internationalist Nationalist: Pursuing an Ethical Modernity with Jawaharlal Nehru', in Shilliam, Robbie (ed.), *International Relations and Non-Western Thought: Imperialism, Colonialism and Investigations of Global Modernity.* London: Routledge.

Chaudhary, Shreesh. 2009. 'Why Neglect Humanities and Social Sciences', *The Hindu*, 12 July.

Chaulia, Sreeram. 2010. 'India in a Globalised World', *Geopolitics*, May, p. 59.

Chen, Shu-Hsiang (Ava), Jaitip Nasongkhla, J. Ana Donaldson. 2015. 'University Social Responsibility (USR): Identifying an Ethical Foundation within Higher Education Institutions', *The Turkish Online Journal of Educational Technology* 14(4).

Cole, Jonathan. 2010. *The Great American University: Its Rise to Preeminence, Its Indispensable National Role, Why It Must Be Protected.* New York: Public Affairs.

Collini, S. 2013. 'Sold Out', *London Review of Books.*

———. 2012. *What Are Universities For?* London: Penguin Books Ltd.

———. 2011. 'From Robbins to McKinsey', *London Review of Books* 33(16): 9–14.

Corbridge, Stuart, John Harriss, and Craig Jeffrey. 2013. *India Today: Economy, Politics, and Society.* Cambridge: Polity.

Dahl, Robert. 1989. *Democracy and Its Critics.* New Haven: Yale University Press.

Damodharan, Dipin. 2014. 'Five-Point Agenda for Education Minister', *Education Insider*, 27 June.

de Jong, T. and Ferguson-Hessler, MGM. 1997. 'Types and Qualities of Knowledge', *Educational Psychologist* 31(2): 105.

Debroy, B. 2012. 'Higher Education: Regulation and Control', in K. Basu and A. Maertens (eds), *The New Oxford companion to Economics in India.* New Delhi: Oxford University Press.

Dickson, David. 1984. *The New Politics of Science.* Chicago: The University of Chicago Press.

DiMaggio, P. and W.W. Powell. 1983. 'The Iron Cage Revisited: Institutional Isomorphism and Collective Rationality in Organizational Fields', *American Sociology Review* 48(2): 147–60.

Dudman, J. 2012. *Guardian Professional*, Tuesday, 6 March.

Dye, T. 1995. *Understanding Public Policy.* New Jersey: Prentice-Hall.

Ellingson, S. 1995. 'The Emergence and Institutionalization of the Major-Minor Curriculum, 1870–1910'. Unpublished paper, Department of Sociology, University of Chicago (referred to in Abbott 2001).

Eyler, Janet, Dwight E. Giles Jr, Christine M. Stenson, and Charlene J. Gray. 2001. *At a Glance: What We Know about the Effects of Service-Learning on College Students, Faculty, Institutions and Communities, 1993–2000*, Third Edition, Vanderbilt University.

Fang, Ferric C., R. Grant Steen, and Arturo Casadevall. 2012. *Proceedings of the National Academy of Sciences of the United States of America* 109(42): 17028–33.

Farrington, D. and D. Palfreyman. 2007. 'The Law of Higher Education', in W.A. Kaplan and B.A. Lee (ed.), *The Law of Higher Education*, Student Version, Fourth edn., John Wiley & Sons, Inc., p. 123.

Foster, John Bellamy, et al. 2010. *The Ecological Rift—Capitalism's War on the Earth.* New York: Monthly Review Press.

Frank, J.D. and J. Gabler. 2006. *Reconstructing the University: Worldwide Shifts in Academia in the 20th Century*. Stanford, CA: Stanford University Press.

Frank, Newman, Laura Couturier, and Jamie Scurry. 2004. *The Future of Higher Education: Rhetoric, Reality, and the Risks of the Market*. New York: Jossey-Bass.

Frenk, Julio. 2009. *Globalization and Health: The Role of Knowledge in an Interdependent World*. Bethesda, Maryland, 15 December.

Frenk, Julio, Lincoln Chen, Zulfiqar A. Bhutta, Jordan Cohen, Nigel Crisp, Timothy Evans, Harvey Fineberg, et al., 2010. 'Health Professionals for a New Century: Transforming Education to Strengthen Health Systems in an Interdependent World', *The Lancet* 376(9756): 1923–58, 10.

Friedman, T. 2004. 'Doing Our Homework', *New York Times*, 24 June.

Frodeman, R., J.T. Klein, and C. Mitcham (eds). 2010. 'Introduction' in *The Oxford Handbook of Interdisciplinarity*, pp. i–xxxix. New York: Oxford University Press.

Fuller, S. 2010. 'Deviant Interdisciplinarity', in R. Frodeman, J.T. Klein, and C. Mitcham (eds), *The Oxford Handbook of Interdisciplinarity*, pp. 50–64. New York: Oxford University Press.

———. 2003a. *Interdisciplinarity: The Loss of the Heroic Vision in the Marketplace of Ideas*. Prepared for Rethinking Interdisciplinarity, Interdisciplines, Paris, 1 October. Available at http://www.interdisciplines.org/medias/confs/archives/archive_3.pdf, last accessed on 11 August 2013.

———. 2003b. *Kuhn vs. Popper: The Struggle for the Soul of Science*. Cambridge: Icon Books.

Funtowicz, S. and J. Ravetz. 1993. 'Science for the Post-Normal Age', 25(7): 739–55.

Gandhi, Mohandas. 1921. 'No Culture Isolation for Me', *Young India*, 1 June.

Gardiner, Beth. 2010. 'Back to School: Economists Rethink Theories in Light of Global Crisis', *The Wall Street Journal*, 17 June.

Gardner, Howard. 1999. *Intelligence Reframed. Multiple Intelligences for the 21st Century*. New York: Basic Books.

Gardner, Lee. 2013. 'U of Michigan M.F.A. Program Receives a $50-Million Gift', *Chronicle of Higher Education*, 7 March.

Gibbons, M., et al. 1994. *The New Production of Knowledge*. London: Sage Publications.

Gingerich, Jonathan and Aditya Singh. 2010. 'Writing Requirements, Student Assessment and Plagiarism in Indian Law Schools', *India Law News*, Fall: 12.

Goswami, A. 2012. *Higher Education Law and Privately-Funded University Education in India, Towards a Vision?* Indian Infrastructure Report, Chapter 17, p. 185.

Goswami, Ranjit. 2013. 'India's Population in 2050: Extreme Projections Demand Extreme Actions', *East Asia Forum*, 5 April.

Government of India, Ministry of Human Resource Development. 2012. 'All India Survey for Higher Education, Provisional Figures'. Government of India.

———. 2011. 'Report of the Working Group on Higher Education for the XII Five Year Plan'. Ministry of Human Resource Development, Higher Education Department, Government of India (September).

———. 2006. 'National Knowledge Commission Report to the Nation', p. 43, Government of India (January 2007).

———. 1966. *Report of the Education Commission 1964–1966*. Delhi: Government of India Press.

Green, V.H.H. 1974. *A History of Oxford University*. London: Basford.

Guha, Ramachandra. 2008. *India after Gandhi: The History of the World's Largest Democracy*. New York: Harper Perennial.

Gupta, Akhil. 2012. *Red Tape: Bureaucracy, Structural Violence, and Poverty in India*. London: Duke University.

Gupta, Amita. 2007. *Going to School in South Asia*. Westport: Greenwood Publishing Group.

Gutting, Gary. 2013. 'Why Do I Teach?', *The New York Times*, 22 May.

Haq, Mahbub. 1998. *Human Development in South Asia*. Karachi: Oxford University Press.

Haraway, Donna J. 1991. *Simians Cyborgs and Women: The Reinvention of Nature*. London: Routledge.

Harrison, John Fletcher Clews. 2013. *Learning and Living 1790–1960: A Study in the History of the English Adult Education Movement*. New York: Routledge.

Harriss-White, B., et al. 2011. 'Revisiting Technology and under Development: Climate Change, Politics and the "D" of Solar Energy Technology in Contemporary India', in V. Fitzgerald, J. Heyer, and R. Thorp (eds), *Overcoming the Persistence of Inequality and Poverty*, pp. 92–127. New York: Palgrave-Macmillan.

Hearn, W. Mark, James L. Thomas, and Richard Cobb. 2012. 'University Outreach Programs: Service to the Surrounding Communities while Developing Faculty', *Research in Higher Education Journal* 16(1).

Ho, Karen Z. 2009. *Liquidated: An Ethnography of Wall Street*. Durham: Duke University Press.

Hodgson, G. 2001. *Why Economics Forgot History*. London: Routledge.

Hur, Y. and M. Hackbart. 2009. *MPA vs. MPP: A Distinction without a Difference? Journal of Public Affairs Education (JPAE)* 15(4): 397–424.

Indiresan, P.V. and Valson Thampu. 2008. 'Does Indian Education System Encourage Questioning?', *Business Standard*, 29 October.

Irwin, Alan. 1995. *Citizen Science: A Study of People, Expertise and Sustainable Development*. London: Routledge.

Jacobs, J.A. and S. Frickel. 2009. 'Interdisciplinarity: A Critical Assessment', *Annual Review of Sociology* 35: 43–65.

Jayaram, N. 2004. 'Higher Education in India: Massification and Change', in P.G. Altbach and T. Umakoshi (eds), *Asian Universities: Historical Perspectives and Contemporary Challenges*. Baltimore: Johns Hopkins University Press.

———. 1990. *Sociology of Education in India*. Jaipur: Rawat.

Jones, Susan R. and Kathleen E. Hill. 2003. 'Understanding Patterns of Commitment: Student Motivation for Community Service Involvement', *The Journal of Higher Education* 74(5): 516–39.

Kak, Kapil (ed.). 2010. *Comprehensive Security for Emerging India*. Delhi: KW Publishers and the Centre for Air Power Studies.

Kaplan, W.A. and B.A. Lee. 2007. *The Law of Higher Education*, Student Version, 4th edn., John Wiley & Sons, Inc., p. 34.

Kapur, D. and P.B. Mehta. 2012. 'Higher Education', in K. Basu and A. Maertens (eds), *The New Oxford Companion to Economics in India*. New Delhi: Oxford University Press.

———. 2008. 'Mortgaging the Future: Indian Higher Education', in S. Bery, B. Bosworth, and A. Panagariya (eds), *Brookings-NCAER India Policy Forum* (Vol. 4). New Delhi: Sage Publications.

Karlan, D., N. Goldberg, and J. Copestake. 2009. 'Randomized Control Trials are the Best Way to Measure Impact of Microfinance Programs and Improve Microfinance Product Designs', *Enterprise Development and Microfinance*. Practical Action Publishing. 20(3): 167–76.

Kenny, Maureen E., et al. (eds). 2002. *Learning to Serve: Promoting Civil Society Through Service Learning*. New York: Kluwer Academic Publishers.

Khandwalla, Pradip N. 1996. 'Management Education in India', *International Encyclopaedia of Business and Management* 3: p. 2805. London: Routledge.

Khilnani, S., Rajiv Kumar, Pratap Bhanu Mehta, Prakash Menon, Nandan Nilekani, Srinath Raghvan, Shyam Saran, and Siddharth Vardarajan. 2012. *Non-Alignment 2.0: A Foreign and Strategic Policy for India in the Twenty First Century*. New Delhi: Centre for Policy Research.

Klein, J.T. 2010. 'A Taxonomy of Interdisciplinarity', in R. Frodeman, J.T. Klein, and C. Mitcham (eds), *The Oxford Handbook of Interdisciplinarity*, pp. 15–30. New York: Oxford University Press.

———. 2005. *Humanities, Culture and Interdisciplinarity*. New York: State University of New York Press, Albany.

———. 1996. *Crossing Boundaries: Knowledge, Disciplinarities, and Interdisciplinarities*. Charlottesville: University Press.

———. 1990. *Interdisciplinarity: History, Theory and Practice*. Detroit: Wayne State University.

Kuhn, T.S. 1970. *The Structure of Scientific Revolutions*, 2nd edn. Chicago: The University of Chicago Press.

Kumar, Anoop and R. Ganesan. 2013. 'Foreign Universities in India—Ethical Issues in New Scenario', *IOSR Journal of Business and Management* 8(3).

Kumar, Brajesh. 2014. 'Govt. Directs over 40 Varsities to Fill Faculty Posts', *Hindustan Times*, 26 October.

Kumar, C. Raj. 2016. 'India's Tryst with World Class Universities', *Deccan Herald*, 8 August.

———. 2015. 'Need for SEZs in Higher Edu', *Deccan Herald*, 28 November.

———. 2014a. 'Take a Qualitative Leap', *The Week*, 1 June.

———. 2014b. 'A New Imagination for Indian Universities', *The Hindu*, 20 December.

———. 2014c. 'Fresh Ideas, Not More Institutions', *The Hindu*, 16 June.

———. 2004. 'Building World-Class Universities in India', 653 Seminar 98.

———. Kumar, R. 2013. 'Still Not in a Class of Their Own', *Hindustan Times*, 20 March. *Education* (New York: Public Affairs, 2006).

———. 2014. 'Take a Qualitative Leap', *The Week Magazine*, 1 June.

Kumar, Rajiv and Santosh Kumar. 2010. *In the National Interest: A Strategic Foreign Policy for India*. New Delhi: BS Books (an imprint of Business Standard Limited).

Lawson, Stephanie. 2012. *International Relations*. Cambridge: Polity Press.

Lee, S. and Bozeman, B. 2005. 'The Impact of Research Collaboration on Scientific Productivity', *Social Studies of Science* 35: 673–702.

Lefebvre, H. 1992. *The Production of Space*. London: Wiley-Blackwell.

Legro, Jeffrey and Andrew Moravcsik. 1999. 'Is Anybody Still a Realist?', *International Security* 24(2).

Leys, C. 2001. *Market-driven Politics: Neoliberal Democracy and the Public Interest*. London: Verso.

———. 2005. 'The Cynical State', in L. Panitch and C. Leys (eds), *Telling the Truth*, pp. 1–27. New York: Merlin Press.

———. 2007. *Total Capitalism*. London: Merlin Press.

MacIntyre, A.C. 1984. *After Virtue: A Study in Moral Theory* (2nd edn). Notre Dame, Indiana: University of Notre Dame Press.

Mackenzie, Norman. 2007. 'Starting A New University', *Higher Education Quarterly* 15(2).

Mahbubani, Kishore. 2013. *The Great Convergence: Asia, the West, and the Logic of One World*. New York: Public Affairs.

Majumdar, R.C., H.C. Raychaudhuri, and Kalikinkar Datta. 1946. *An Advanced History of India*. London: Macmillan.

Manokha, Ivan and Mona Chalabi. 2011. 'The Latest Financial Crisis: IR Goes Bankrupt', Paris: Sciences Po, Working Paper, p. 2.

Marcus, Jon. 2013. 'All Hail MOOCs! Just Don't Ask if They Actually Work', *The Hechinger Report*, 12 September.

Marginson, Simon and Marijk Van der Wende. 2009. 'The New Global Landscape of Nations and Institutions', *Higher Education* 2030(2): 17–57.

Mathur, Kuldeep. 2013. *Public Policy and Politics in India: How Institutions Matter.* New Delhi: Oxford University Press.

Mattoo, Amitabh (ed.). 2012a. *The Reluctant Superpower: Understanding India and its Aspirations.* Melbourne: Melbourne University Press.

———. 2012b. 'Unthinking Think Tanks', *The New Indian Express*, 5 February.

McClelland, C. 1980. *State, Society, and University* in *Germany, 1700–1914.* Cambridge: Cambridge University Press.

McGann, James G. 2012. *Global Go to Think Tanks Report and Policy Advice.* Thank Tanks and Civil Societies Programme, International Relations Programme, University of Pennsylvania, Philadelphia.

McGettigan, A. 2012. 'New Universities: Will the Public Good Yield to Private Profit?' *The Guardian.*

Menon, Raja and Rajiv Kumar. 2010. *The Long View From Delhi: To Define the Indian Grand Strategy for Foreign Policy.* New Delhi: Indian Council for Research on International Economic Relations and Academic Publishing.

Miller, C.A. 2010. 'Policy Challenges and University Reform', in R. Frodeman, J.T. Klein, and C. Mitcham (eds), *The Oxford Handbook of Interdisciplinarity*, pp. 333–44. New York: Oxford University Press.

Miller, Manjari. 2012. 'India's Feeble Foreign Policy: A Would-Be Great Power Resists its Own Rise?', *Foreign Affairs*, p. 14.

Mohapatra, Bishnu N. 2011. 'The Democracy Manifesto: Re-imagining Democracy', *Open Democracy*, 11 May.

Mookerji, R.K. 1951. *Ancient Indian Education: Brahmanical and Buddhist.* 2nd edn. Delhi: Motilal Banarsidass.

Mudur, G.S. 2012. 'In plagiarism too, China Beats India', Calcutta, India: *The Telegraph*, 2 October.

Nandy, Ashis. 1989. 'Shamans, Savages and the Wilderness: On the Audibility of Dissent and the Future of Civilizations', *Alternatives* 14(3) (July): 267.

Nanthikesan, S. 2001. 2001 Human Development Report: *Trends in Digital Divide.* New York: UNDP.

National Academy of Sciences. 2004. *Facilitating Interdisciplinary Research.* Washington, DC: Natl. Acad. Press.

National Knowledge Commission. 2008. 'Towards a Knowledge Society: Three Years of Knowledge Commission'. Government of India: New Delhi (October).

Newell, W. and J.T. Klein. 1996. 'Interdisciplinary Studies into the 21st Century', *Journal of General Education* 45(2): 152–69.

Newman, Frank. 1985. *Higher Education and the American Resurgence: A Carnegie Foundation Special Report.* New Jersey: Princeton University Press.

Newman, John Henry Cardinal. 1999. *The Idea of a University: Defined and Illustrated*. Massachusetts: Regnery Publishing.

Ni, C., and C.R. Sugimoto. 2012. 'Using Doctoral Dissertations for a New Understanding of Disciplinarity and Interdisciplinarity', *Proceedings of the American Society for Information Science and Technology* 49(1): 1–4.

Nussbaum, M.C. 2012. *Not for Profit: Why Democracy Needs the Humanities* (New in Paper). New Jersey: Princeton University Press.

———. 2010. *Not for Profit: Why Democracy Needs the Humanities*. Princeton: Princeton University Press.

O'Malley, John W. 1993. *The First Jesuits*. Cambridge, Mass: Harvard University Press.

Oleson, A. and J. Voss (eds). 1979. *The Organization of Knowledge in Modern America*. Baltimore: Johns Hopkins University Press.

Panter-Brick, Simone. 2012. *Gandhi and Nationalism: The Path to Indian Independence*. London: I.B. Tauris.

Parikh, Indira J. 2012. 'Celebrating Learning', 2012–'Management perspectives' published in the souvenir specially designed for the golden Jubilee of Air India Staff College.

———. 1988. 'Transience and Transitions in Organizations', in Vipin K. Garg and Pulin K. Garg (eds), *Proceedings of the International Conference*. Ahmedabad: ISISD Publication.

Pfirman, S. and P. Martin. 2010. 'Fostering Interdisciplinary Scholars', in R. Frodeman, J.T. Klein, and C. Mitcham (eds), *The Oxford Handbook of Interdisciplinarity*, pp. 387–403. New York: Oxford University Press.

Pieters, R. and H. Baumgartner. 2002. 'Who Talks to Whom? Intra- and Interdisciplinary Communication of Economics Journals', *Journal of Economic Literature* 40: 483–509.

Planning Commission. 2012. *Twelfth Five Year Plan (2012–2017)*, Volume III, pp. 89–123, New Delhi.

Player, S. and C. Leys. 2011. *The Plot against the NHS*. London: Merlin Press.

Polanyi, K. 1957. *The Great Transformation*. Boston: Beacon Press.

Popper, K.R. 1963. *Conjectures and Refutations: The Growth of Scientific Knowledge*. New York: Routledge and Kegan Paul.

Project on Liberal Education and the Sciences. 1990. *The Liberal Art of Science: Agenda for Action*. Washington, DC: American Association for the Advancement of Science.

Rajan, R. 2014. 'Environment and Development in India', in D. Davin and B. Harriss-White (eds), *China-India: Pathways of Economic and Social Development*. London: OUP for the British Academy.

Rajan, S. Ravi. 2002. 'Disaster, Development and Governance: Reflections on the "Lessons" of Bhopal', *Environmental Values* 11(3): 369–94.

Raman, Papri Sri and T.V. Padma. 2011. 'Indian Scientists Call for Checks on Plagiarism', *One World South Asia,* 21 July.

Reddy, Sanjay G. 2012. 'Randomise This! On Poor Economics', *Review of Agrarian Studies* 2(2).

Ross, D. 1991. *The Origins of American Social Science.* Cambridge: Cambridge University Press.

S. Bawa, Kamaljit. 2012. 'India's Path to Knowledge', *Science* 335(6076): 1573, 30 March.

Sa, C. 2008. 'Interdisciplinary Strategies in U.S. Research Universities', *High. Educ.* 55: 537–52.

Saxena, Vishakha. 2013. 'Waiting for the Cut-Off Lists? DU Controversies You Need to Know', *Hindustan Times,* 27 May.

Searle, John R. 2010. *Making the Social World: The Structure of Human Civilization.* New York: Oxford University Press.

Sen, A. 1999. *Development as Freedom.* Oxford: Clarendon Press.

Seth, S. 2007. *Subject Lessons: The Western Education of Colonial India.* Durham: Duke University Press.

Sharma, S. 2002. *History and Development of Higher Education in India* (Vol. 5). New Delhi: Sarup & Sons.

Sharp, H. (ed.). 1920. *Selections from Educational Records, Pt I: 1731–1839.* Calcutta: Bureau of Education.

Shinagel, Michael, *'The Gates Unbarred': A History of University Extension at Harvard, 1910–2009.* Cambridge, MA: Harvard University Press.

Sikiri, Rajiv. 2009. *Challenge and Strategy: Rethinking India's Foreign Policy.* New Delhi: Sage Publications.

Skidelsky, Robert. 2012. 'The Impact of the Global Economic Crisis on the Future of International Relations', Einaudi Center's Foreign Policy Distinguished Speaker Series, Ithaca: Cornell University.

Skocpol, T. 1992. *Protecting Soldiers and Mothers: The Political Origins of Social Policy in the United States.* Cambridge, MA: Belknap Press of Harvard University Press.

Srinivasan, A. 2009. *Donald Michie on Machine Intelligence, Biology and More.* New York: Oxford University Press.

Stewart, F. 1975. 'A Note on Social Cost-Benefit Analysis and Class Conflict in LDCs', *World Development* 3(1): 31–40.

Stone, Richard. 'Science in India', India Rising. *Science* 335(6071): 904–10, 24 February.

Stichweh, R. 1984. *Zur Entstehung des Modernen Systems Wissenschaftlicher Disziplinen: Physik in Deutschland 1740–1890.* Frankfurt am Main: Suhrkamp.

Stukas, Arthur A., Mark Snyder, and E. Gil Clary. 1999. 'The Effects of "Mandatory Volunteerism" on Intentions to Volunteer', *Psychological Science* 10(1): 59–64.

Tagore, Rabindranath. 2007. *The English Writings of Rabindranath Tagore*. New Delhi: Atlantic Publishers, Volume IV.

Talbot-Smith, A., et al. 2004. 'Questioning the Claims from Kaiser', *British Journal of General Practice* (54): 415–21.

Tandon, R. and Wafa Singh. 2015. 'Transforming Higher Education through Community Engagement', *University World News* (20 February, Issue no. 335).

Tao, L., M. Berci, and W. He, 'The Commercialization of Education', *The New York Times*, http://www.nytimes.com/ref/college/coll-china-education-005.html.

Tarrow, Sidney. 2005. *The New Transnational Activism*. New York: Cambridge University Press.

Teichler, Ulrich and Henry Wasser (eds). 1992. *German and American Universities: Mutual Influences—Past and Present*. Kassel: Centre for Research on Higher Education and Work, Comprehensive University of Kassel in cooperation with Center for European Studies, Graduate School and University Center, City University of New York.

Tharoor, Shashi. 2012. *Pax Indica: India and the World of the Twenty-First Century*. New Delhi: Penguin.

Tickoo, C. 1980. *Indian Universities: A Historical, Comparative Perspective*. Bombay: Orient Longman.

Trow, Martin. 2010. 'Academic Standards and Mass Higher Education', in Michael Barrage (ed.), *Twentieth Century Higher Education—Elite to Mass to Universal*. Baltimore: The Johns Hopkins Press.

———. 2000. 'From Mass Higher Education to Universal Access: The American Advantage', *Minerva* 37(Spring): 1–26.

U. Salam. 2014. 'Commodification, Capitalism and Crisis', in J. Heyer and B. Harriss-White (eds), *Indian Capitalism in Development*. Routledge.

UN MDG Gap Task Force. 2012. 'Millennium Development Goal 8. The Global Partnership for Development: Making Rhetoric a Reality'. New York: United Nations.

UNESCO World Heritage list. 1980, Taxila: Brief Description. 2007. 'History of Education', in *Encyclopaedia Britannica*.

Vasilescu, Ruxandra, Cristina Barna, Manuela Epure, and Claudia Baicu. 2010. 'Developing University Social Responsibility: A Model for the Challenges of the New Civil Society', *Procedia-Social and Behavioral Sciences* 2(2): 4177–82, 4178.

Venkatshamy, Krishnappa and Princy George. 2012. *Grand Strategy for India 2020 and Beyond*. New Delhi: Institute for Defence Studies and Analyses and Pentagon Security International.

Veysey, L.R. 1970. *The Emergence of the American University* (Vol. 596). New York: The University of Chicago Press.

Von Helmoltz, H. 1896. 'Über das Verhältnis der Naturwissenschaften zur Gesamtheit der Wissenschaften'. *Vorträge under Reden,* 4th edn, Vol. 1, pp. 157–86. Braunschweig: Vieweg und Sohn.

Wagner, C.S., et al. 2011. 'Approaches to Understanding and Measuring Interdisciplinary Scientific Research (IDR): A Review of the Literature', *Journal of Informetrics* 5(1): 14–26.

Waldrop, M.M. 1993. *Complexity: The Emerging Science at the Edge of Order and Chaos.* New York: Simon and Schuster.

Watts, Phil and Lord Holme. 1999. *Corporate Social Responsibility: Meeting Changing Expectations.* Geneva: World Business Council for Sustainable Development.

Weiler, Hans N. 2009. 'Whose Knowledge Matters? Development and the Politics of Knowledge', in Theodor Hanf, Hans N. Weiler, and Helga Dickow (eds), *Festschrift for Peter Molt.* Entwicklung als Beruf, pp. 485–96. Baden-Baden: Nomos.

Weingart, P. 2010. 'A Short History of Knowledge Formations', in R. Frodeman, J.T. Klein, and C. Mitcham (eds), *The Oxford Handbook of Interdisciplinarity,* pp. 4–14. New York: Oxford University Press.

———. 2003. 'Growth, Differentiation, Expansion and Change of Identity: The Future of Science', in B. Jörges and H. Nowotny (eds), *Social Studies of Science and Technology: Looking Back Ahead,* (Sociology of the Sciences Yearbook, Vol. 23), pp. 183–200. Dordrecht: Kluwer Academic Publishers.

Weiss, Brennan. 2016. *The Rise of Social Responsibility in Higher Education,* University World News (12 August 2016, Issue No: 423).

Weisz, G. 1983. *The Emergence of Modern Universities in France.* Princeton: Princeton University Press.

Welch, Edwin. 1973. *The Peripatetic University: Cambridge Local Lectures, 1873–1973.* Cambridge, UK: Cambridge University Press.

Whitehead, Alfred North. 1925. *Science and the Modern World.* New York: The Macmillan Company [edition of 1960].

Whitley, R. 1984. *The Intellectual and Social Organization of the Sciences.* Oxford: Clarendon.

Willetts, S. 2002. 'Weapons at the Turn of the Millennium', in Barbara Hariss-White (ed.), *Globalisation and Insecurity.* New York: Palgrave-Macmillan.

Willis, Mike. 2000. 'How Chinese Universities and Foreign Universities Cooperate in an International Education Market: The Development and Application of a Four-Tiered Sino Foreign Higher Education Cooperation Model', Griffith University ANZMAC 2000 Conference Paper.

Wilson, Edward O. 1998. *Consilience. The Unity of Knowledge.* New York: Vintage Books.

World Bank. 'Investing in the Youth Bulge in South Asia: Summary of Findings and Recommendations from World Development Report 2007—Development and the Next Generation', World Bank Working Paper, Report No. 70368, 22 June 2012.

Wu, Xun, M. Ramesh, Michael Howlett, and Scott A. Fritzen. 2010. *The Public Policy Primer: Managing the Policy Process.* London: Routledge.

Zakaria, Fareed. 2009. *The Post American World.* New York: W.W. Norton.

Žižek, S. 2002. 'Welcome to the Desert of the Real!', *South Atlantic Quarterly*, Spring, 101(2): 385–9.

Žižek, S. 2006. *The Parallax View.* Cambridge, MA: MIT Press.

Editor and Contributors

Pawan Agarwal is a civil servant from the Indian Administrative Services and is currently Chief Executive Officer, Food Safety and Standards Authority of India (FSSAI), Government of India. He was the Director in the Ministry of HRD, handling the higher education and technical education and later Financial Advisor and Coordinator of new initiatives in the University Grants Commission. During the year 2005–06, he was a Fulbright New Century Scholar on higher education from India. He was visiting scholar under the Science and Engineering Workforce Program at the Harvard University and at the India-China-America Institute at Emory University, Atlanta (United States). His book *Indian Higher Education: Envisioning the Future* has been published by SAGE in 2009.

Kanti Bajpai is Wilmar Professor on Asian Studies at the Lee Kuan Yew School of Public Policy, National University of Singapore. His areas of interest include international security, Indian foreign policy, and national security. Before joining the LKY School, he was Professor of International Politics, Jawaharlal Nehru University, and Professor in the Politics and International Relations of South Asia, University of Oxford. From 2003 to 2009, he was Headmaster, The Doon School, India. He taught at the Maharajah Sayajirao University of Baroda, and has held visiting appointments at Wesleyan University, Columbia University, and the University of Illinois, Urbana-Champaign. He has also held visiting appointments at the Rajiv Gandhi Foundation, Joan B. Kroc Institute for Peace, Notre Dame University, the Brookings Institution, and the Australian Defence Force Academy. Most recently, he was Distinguished Fellow, Institute for Defence Studies and Analyses, New Delhi. Bajpai writes a regular column for the *Times of India* (New Delhi).

Carol M. Bresnahan is former Provost and Vice President for academic affairs at Rollins College. Bresnahan completed her PhD in history from Brown University in 1986. Before starting work at Rollins College in 2011, where she is also a tenured professor of history, Bresnahan was Provost and Executive Vice President at the College of New Jersey and also worked as vice provost for academic programs and policies at the University of Toledo.

Sreeram Chaulia is Professor and Dean of the Jindal School of International Affairs. He was a Radhakrishnan British Chevening Scholar at the University of Oxford, UK, where he obtained a Bachelor of Arts (B.A.) in Modern History. He also has a Bachelor of Arts Honours (B.A. Hons.) from St. Stephen's College, University of Delhi, India. Professor Chaulia's areas of specialization include diplomacy, foreign policy, comparative politics, international political economy, international organizations, armed conflict, humanitarian practices, and contemporary world history. He has over 380 publications to his credit and has published widely in journals in the USA, UK, Australia, Canada, and India. His op-eds have also appeared in leading newspapers of Asia.

Yugank Goyal is Associate Professor and Assistant Dean (Research), Jindal School of Liberal Arts & Humanities, Deputy Director, International Institute for Higher Education Research & Capacity Building (IIHEd) and Honorary Research Fellow, Jindal Global Law School at O.P. Jindal Global University. He holds a Ph.D. (Hamburg, Rotterdam and Bologna – Erasmus Mundus Fellow), LL.M. (Manchester), and B.Tech. (Surat, India). His research interests include Regulation, Legal Institutions, Law and Development, Institutional Economics, Higher Education, Intellectual Property Rights.

Barbara Harriss-White is Emeritus Professor of Development Studies at the University of Oxford and Emeritus Fellow of Wolfson College, Oxford.

Professor Harriss-White is Senior Research Fellow, Area Studies and Co-ordinator, South Asian Research Cluster at the University of Oxford. She was the Founder-Director of University of Oxford's Contemporary South Asian Studies Programme in the School of Area Studies and organizer of the world's first MSc in Contemporary India. She has written, edited or co-edited 40 books, over 200 scholarly papers, and 60 working papers. Her book *Rural Commercial Capital* won the Edgar Graham prize.

A. Francis Julian is Senior Advocate in the Supreme Court of India and is a member of the Supreme Court Bar Association in New Delhi. He has 35 years of professional experience at the Bar. His doctoral degree is in the area of international financial law and he has published articles relating to international finance, constitutional law, human rights, right to information law, disaster management law, money laundering, maritime law and international commercial arbitration. He has presented papers in several national and international conferences on the above topics. He is a member of the Governing Body and Board of Management of O.P. Jindal Global University.

Sital Kalantry is Clinical Professor of Law at Cornell Law School where she founded the International Human Rights: Policy Advocacy Clinic and co-founded the Avon Global Center for Women & Justice. Prior to joining the clinical faculty at the Cornell Law School, she was the founder and director of the International Human Rights Policy Advocacy Clinic at the University of Chicago Law School. Her scholarly work focuses on using quantitative approaches to understand and promote the enforcement of international human rights law. She received a Fulbright-Nehru Senior Research Scholar grant to conduct research in India. Her works have been published in, among other places, the *Human Rights Quarterly*, the *National Law Journal*, and the *Stanford Journal of International Law*.

N.R. Madhava Menon is Chancellor, National University of Educational Planning and Administration, New Delhi. He served National Law School of India University (NLSIU) as Founding Vice-Chancellor for 12 years. From 1998 to 2003, he served as the Founder Vice-Chancellor of the National University of Juridical Sciences from where the Supreme Court sought his services to set up the National Judicial Academy at Bhopal. Professor Menon was the Founder Director of NJA till 2006 after which he took retirement from active employment. Professor Menon is the author of over a dozen books on legal education, legal profession, legal aid, judicial training and administration of justice. *Turning Point*, published by Universal Law Publishers, Delhi (2010), is on the life and works of Professor Menon. There is an annual Best Law Teacher Award of a lakh of rupees and a plaque instituted in Professor Menon's name by the Society of Indian Law Firms to commemorate his services to the legal profession and legal education for more than half a century.

Indira J. Parikh was a faculty at IIM-A for over 30 years and Deans from 2002 to 2005. She has also taught at INSEAD, Fontainebleau (France) and Texas A&M University. She has specialized in organization development and design, and institution-building. Professor Parikh has been honoured with three lifetime achievement awards: Lifetime Achievement Award for Best Teacher in Management on 18 January 2001 in World HRD Congress held at Mumbai, Lifetime Achievement Award for the contribution on HR on 3 October 2003 in the second Regional HR Conference held at Pune organized by Indira Group of Institute, Pune, and Life Time Achievement Award by PGP Students Indian Institute of Management, Ahmedabad (2003–05 batch).

Alice Prochaska is Pro Vice Chancellor, University of Oxford & Principal, Somerville College, Oxford. She was elected Principal of Somerville in June 2009, and took up the position in September 2010. She started her career as a museum curator and subsequently as an archivist at the Public Record Office (now the National Archives). From 1984 to 1992, she was the administrator and deputy to the director of the University of London's Institute of Historical Research. From 1992 to 2001, she served as Director of Special Collections at the British Library, with responsibility for Maps, Manuscripts, Music, the National Sound Archive, the Oriental and India Office Collections, and Philatelic Collections. In August 2001, Dr Prochaska took up the position of University Librarian at Yale University in Connecticut, where she remained until August 2010, heading one of the great research libraries of the world.

C. Raj Kumar was appointed as the Founding Vice-Chancellor of O.P. Jindal Global University in India at the age of 34. Professor Kumar has academic qualifications from the University of Oxford, Harvard

University, University of Hong Kong, University of Delhi, and Loyola College. He was a Rhodes Scholar at the University of Oxford, UK, where he obtained his Bachelor of Civil Law (B.C.L.) degree; a Landon Gammon Fellow at the Harvard Law School, USA, where he obtained his Master of Laws (LL.M.) degree and a James Souverine Gallo Memorial Scholar at the Harvard University. He was awarded the Doctor of Legal Science (S.J.D.) by the University of Hong Kong. He also obtained a Bachelor of Laws (LL.B.) degree from the University of Delhi, India; and a Bachelor of Commerce (B.Com.) degree from the Loyola College of the University of Madras, India. Professor Kumar's areas of specialization include human rights and development, terrorism and national security, corruption and governance, law and disaster management, comparative constitutional law and legal education. He has over 150 publications to his credit including seven books and has published widely in journals and law reviews in Australia, Hong Kong, India, Japan, and USA.

Pramath Raj Sinha is Founding Trustee, Ashoka University, Sonipat, a Senior Advisor of Albright Stonebridge Group, India and the Founder and Managing Director of 9.9 Mediaworx Private Limited. Prior to founding 9.9 Media, he worked with McKinsey & Company and led the ABP Group, one of India's leading and most diversified media conglomerates. Pramath helped set up and served as the Founding Dean of the Indian School of Business (ISB). He holds a bachelor's degree from IIT Kanpur and an MSE and PhD from the University of Pennsylvania.

Shailendra Raj Mehta is the President and Director, MICA, Ahmedabad and Distinguished Professor for Innovation and Entrepreneurship at MICA. Before joining MICA, he was the Chairman of the Board of Management at Auro University where he served as Acting Vice Chancellor and Distinguished Professor of Strategy and Provost/Vice Chancellor of Ahmedabad University. He has done extensive research in the areas of entrepreneurship, industrial organization, information economics, and experimental economics. Over the years, Dr Mehta has consulted with and taught senior executives worldwide including executives from North America, Europe, Africa and Asia (including senior executives in Pakistan). The companies that he has worked with include Bharat Petroleum, Black Management Forum of South Africa, Eli Lilly, Genpact, Honeywell, IBM, Infosys, Lockheed Martin, Medtronic, Microsoft, P&G, PriceWaterhouse Coopers, State Bank of India, and the Tata Group, among others. He has conducted long-range scenario planning, envisioning and simulation exercises with a wide variety of executives in government and in industry.

Stephen P. Marks is the François-Xavier Bagnoud Professor of Health and Human Rights, Director of the Program on Human Rights in Development at the Harvard School of Public Health and Senior Fellow at Harvard's University Committee on Human Rights Studies. He is also Distinguished Visiting Professor and Special Advisor to the Vice-Chancellor, O.P. Jindal Global University. The emphasis of Stephen Marks's work is on the interface of health and human rights, drawing on the disciplines of international law, international politics, international organizations, and international economics. He has published books, articles, and chapters in each of these areas. His publications include a co-edited book on *Development as a Human Right: Legal, Political and Economic Dimensions* and a reader on *Perspectives on Health and Human Rights,* as well as the edited *Health and Human Rights: Basic International Documents.*

Y.S.R. Murthy is Professor and Registrar, Executive Director, Centre for Human Rights Studies, and Senior Fellow, International Institute for Higher Education Research & Capacity Building at O.P. Jindal Global University. In his previous stint as a civil servant in the Government of India, he held a number of responsible positions, among others, in the National Human Rights Commission, Ministry of Finance, Prime Minister's Office, President's Secretariat and Cabinet Secretariat.

Anamika Srivastava is Assistant Professor of economics and education at Jindal Global Law School and a Fellow at International Institute for Higher Education Research and Capacity Building (IIHEd) at OP Jindal Global University (JGU), India. She has been the lead author of the *State Higher Education Plan for Haryana,* developed under Rashtriya Ucchatar Shiksha Abhiyan (RUSA), a Government of Haryana project at IIHEd. She is currently assisting an international project on Federalism and Higher Education, funded by the British Council, India.

R. Sudarshan is Professor and founding Dean of the Jindal School of Government and Public Policy in the O.P. Jindal Global University. He is an alumni of Bangalore (B.A. Hons), Delhi (M.A. Economics), Oxford

(M.Phil. Politics, Rhodes Scholar) and Cambridge (research scholar) universities. He served the UNDP for 22 years as senior economist, policy advisor for governance and justice and at the Ford Foundation in New Delhi for seven years as program officer for human rights and social justice.

Shiv Visvanathan is Professor, Vice Dean and Executive Director, Centre for the Study of Knowledge Systems, Jindal Global Law School, O.P. Jindal Global University. He is a social anthropologist with a Ph.D. from the University of Delhi. He has taught at several universities across the world and was Senior Fellow, Centre for the Study of Developing Societies, Delhi. His books include *Carnival for Science: Essays on Science, Technology and Development* (1997) and *Theatres of Democracy: Between the Epic and the Everyday* (2016).

Index